The Muvipix.com Guide to

Adobe Premiere Elements 15

Steve Grisetti

The tools, and how to use them, to make movies on your personal computer using Adobe's best-selling video editing software program.

About Muvipix.com

Muvipix.com was created to offer support and community to amateur and semi-professional videomakers. Registration is free, and that gets you access to the world's friendliest, most helpful forum and lots of ad-free space for displaying your work. On the products page, you'll find dozens of free tips, tutorials, motion backgrounds, DVD templates, sound effects, royalty-free music and stock video clips. For a small annual subscription fee that we use to keep the site running, you'll have unlimited downloads from the ever-growing library of support materials and media.

We invite you to drop by and visit our thriving community. It costs absolutely nothing – and we'd love to have you join the neighborhood!

http://Muvipix.com

About the author

Steve Grisetti holds a master's degree in Telecommunications from Ohio University and spent several years working in the motion picture and television industry in Los Angeles. A veteran user of several video editing programs and systems, Steve is the co-founder of Muvipix.com, a help and support site for amateur and semi-professional videomakers. A professional graphic designer and video freelancer, he has taught classes in Photoshop, lectured on design and even created classes for lynda.com. He lives in suburban Milwaukee.

Other books by Steve Grisetti

Adobe Premiere Elements 2.0 In a Snap (with Chuck Engels)
The Muvipix.com Guides to Adobe Premiere Elements 7, 8, 9, 10, 11, 12, 13 and 14
The Muvipix.com Guides to Photoshop Elements & Premiere Elements 7, 8, 9, 10, 11, 12, 13, 14 and 15
Cool Tricks & Hot Tips for Adobe Premiere Elements
The Muvipix.com Guide to DVD Architect Studio 5
The Muvipix.com Guides to Vegas Movie Studio HD 10 and 11
The Muvipix.com Guides to Sony Movie Studio 12 and 13
The Muvipix.com Guides to CyberLink PowerDirector 12, 13 and 14

An Introduction

Adobe continues to improve Premiere Elements in its version 15, adding a couple of very nice features, including a couple of cool enhancements under the hood.

Among the new, high-profile tools is the Video Collage creator, an easy-to-use tool for creating a split-screen effect that includes up to seven videos on screen at the same time. This is definitely my favorite of the new features in version 15, and it includes options for adding music and animation as well as options for uploading your collage directly to a social media site.

Another cool new feature is the Music Remixer, a tool for creating custom-length music tracks from virtually any music source. Add a song to your timeline, trim it to the length you need and the Music Remix tool will remix and blend it into a smooth beginning, middle and end – usually so naturally your audience won't even know you've shortened the song!

Inspired by a similar tool in Photoshop Elements, the program now includes a Haze Reduction tool, for removing fog and haze from a video. Increasing the contrast and sharpening the picture, the tool can save a shot that's become lost in the mist.

And, in addition to automatically adding Auto Tags, based on the content of your video and pictures, the Auto Analyzer/Media Analyzer now recognizes faces in your media, incorporating that information into the Smart Trim, Video Story and Pan & Zoom tool. In fact, the Pan & Zoom tool will even self-generate a motion path from face to face in your photos.

You'll also find improvements in Elements Organizer's media file management system, with a completely revamped search and filter workspace that can locate your files using Boolean logic.

In all, Adobe has once again taken this great little program and made it even better. It handles virtually all camcorder formats (including 4k video and video from Go Pro cams), and it offers a growing bundle of production tools. We hope you enjoy getting to know version 15 as much as we have!

Muvipix.com was created in 2006 as a community and a learning center for videomakers at a variety of experience and skill levels. Our community includes everyone from amateurs and hobbyists to semi-pros, professionals and even people with broadcast experience. You won't find more knowledgeable, helpful people anywhere else on the Web. I very much encourage you to drop by our forums and say hello. At the very least, you'll make some new friends. And it's rare that there's a question posted there that isn't quickly, and enthusiastically, answered.

Our learning center consists of video tutorials, tips and, of course, books. We also offer a wealth of support in the form of custom-created DVD and BluRay disc menus, motion background videos, licensed music and even stock footage. Much of it is absolutely free – and there's even more available for those who purchase one of our affordable site subscriptions.

Our goal has always been to help people get up to speed making great videos and, once they're there, provide them with the inspiration and means to get better and better at doing so.

Why? Because we know making movies is a heck of a lot of fun – and we want to share that fun with everyone!

Our books, then, are a manifestation of that goal. And my hope for you is that this book helps *you* get up to speed. I think you'll find, once you get over the surprisingly small learning curve, making movies on your home computer is a lot easier and more fun than you ever imagined! And you may even amaze *yourself* with the results.

Thanks for supporting Muvipix.com, and happy moviemaking!

Steve
http://Muvipix.com

The Muvipix.com Guide to Adobe Premiere Elements 15

Part IV: The Elements Organizer

Chapter 21

Export & Share Your Video Projects.............. 255

Outputting from Premiere Elements 15

A Premiere Elements Appendix...................... 273

More things worth knowing

Get to Know the Premiere Elements Workspaces

Basic Video Editing Moves

What's New in Version 15?

Chapter 1

Get to Know Premiere Elements 15

What's what and what it does

The interface for Premiere Elements has been designed by Adobe to be as simple and as intuitive as possible. It is also remarkably customizable, with a wealth of powerful tools in obvious and, once in a while, not so obvious places.

There have been major changes to the interface in the last few versions of the program. But you'll quickly find that, for the most part, it makes for an improved editing experience all around – for the newbie as well as for the veteran.

Elements Live

The first time you launch any of the Elements programs, the interface will default to **eLive**, a link directly from the programs to an exclusive website full of exciting ideas, tutorials (including a number created by yours truly!) and other content especially for Elements users.

eLive (Elements Live) can be accessed from any computer with a live internet connection by clicking the **eLive** link at the top center of the program's interface.

Panels, pop-ups and the Toolbar

The Premiere Elements interface has been designed with efficiency and readability in mind.

The interface is bright and clean with big, easy-to-find buttons and text throughout.

Its tools are tucked out-of-the-way – but easily retrievable with just a click or two.

Many of the tools are hidden away in pop-up panels that snap open with just a click on a tab or button.

The bulk of the tools can be accessed through buttons on the **Toolbar**, which runs along the right side of the Premiere Elements interface.

When it comes to the actual editing, the program offers two separate (though connected) workspaces – **Quick** View and **Expert** View – workspaces that allow you to go as deeply into the process as you'd like. (More on them on page 4.)

Additionally, the program includes a **Guided Edits** library, available in both Quick and Expert View. **Guided Edits** take you step-by-step through a number of key editing tasks – like having your own personal teacher built right into the program! (For more information on **Guided Edits**, see **Chapter 3**.)

If you right-click on the Monitor panel, you'll find options for setting the Magnification and Playback Quality.

The Monitor panel

The **Monitor** is the panel on which you'll preview your movie as your work. It usually rests in the top center of the interface – though it can change position to accommodate the **Adjustments** and **Applied Effects** panels when necessary.

The Timeline

Both Quick View and Expert View (discussed on the following page) share a similar workspace for assembling your video: The **Timeline**.

Your timeline is really where the bits and pieces become a movie.

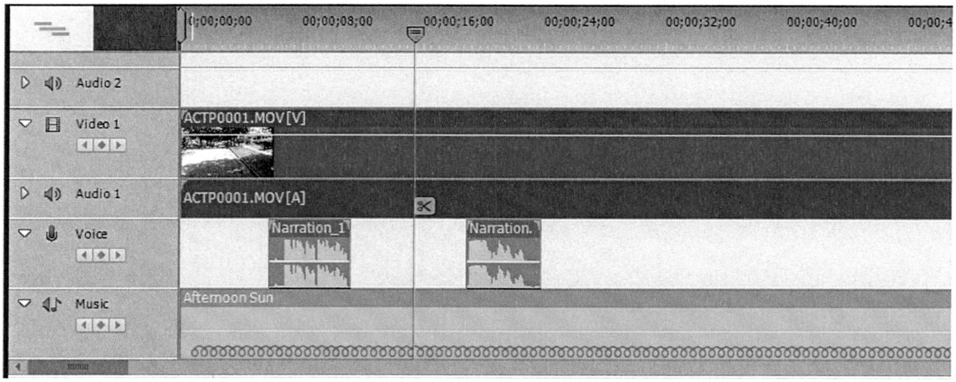

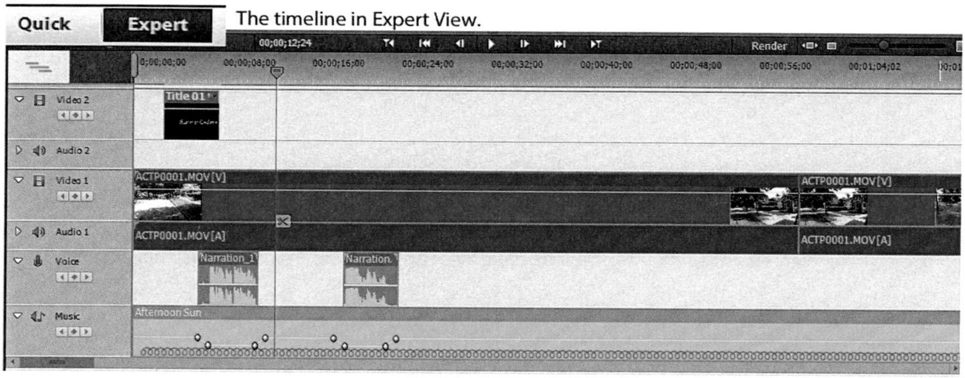

The timeline in Expert View.

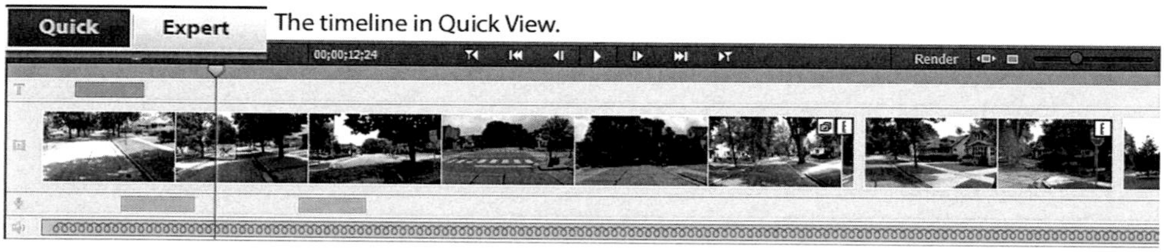

The timeline in Quick View.

Quick View and Expert View

Premiere Elements offers you two somewhat different workspaces in which to edit your video project: Quick View and Expert View. In both views, you edit on a timeline. However, the timeline, and its features, vary a bit from view to view.

Quick View and Expert View aren't so much totally different interfaces as they are two different ways to approach the same project. In fact, you can switch between them as you work on your project, taking advantage of the best aspects of each.

Quick View	Expert View
Media clips are added directly to the timeline from your computer, camcorder or recording device.	Media clips are gathered into the **Project Assets** panel before they are added to your timeline.
The timeline consists of four tracks: Titles, Video, Narration and Audio.	The timeline can include up to 99 video and 99 audio tracks.
Only the Video track can include video. Only titles and text can be added to the Title track.	Multiple tracks of video can be combined to create effects, including Videomerge, Chroma Key and Picture-in-Picture
Audio levels can be set using tools available in Smart Mix, on the Audio Mixer and on the Adjustments panel.	Audio levels can be controlled at specific points using keyframes created right on the timeline.
A limited number of effects and titles are readily available in Quick View.	The complete set of effects is available.

Customize your workspace

The sizes and the arrangements of the various panels in the interface are easily customizable. Panels can be resized by dragging on the seams between them.

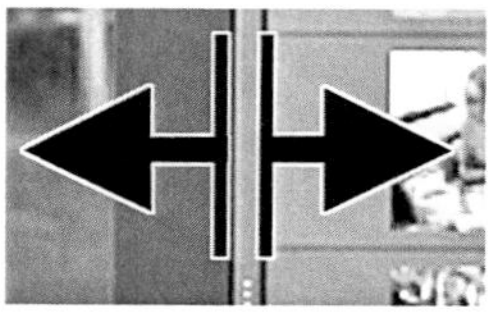

To resize your panels, hover your mouse over the seams between the panels until you see the double arrows – then click and drag.

Feel free to experiment and resize the panels by dragging on the borders between them.

Many of the pop-up panels also allow you to stretch them longer so that you can see more of the assets, effects, templates, etc., at once.

And, if you ever find the program misbehaving or if you just feel like you've lost control of your workspace, you can easily get back to the default look by simply going to the **Window** drop-down menu and selecting **Restore Workspace**.

Minimum screen resolution

Because of the size of the panels and the number of tools that Adobe fits into some rather tight spaces, **we recommend that this program not be used on a computer with a monitor with less than 1280x1024 resolution.**

There's simply no room for it all to fit otherwise! And, on a smaller screen, you'll spend a lot of time scrolling and resizing panels, trying to get to all the tools.

What's a CTI?

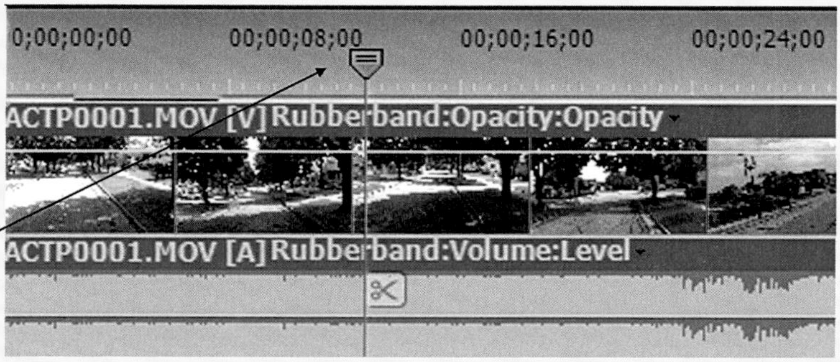

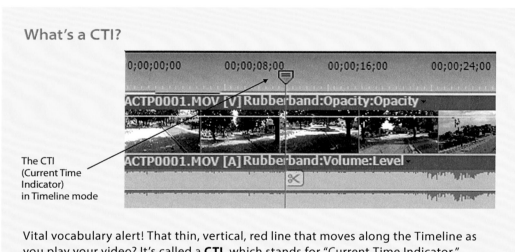

The CTI (Current Time Indicator) in Timeline mode

Vital vocabulary alert! That thin, vertical, red line that moves along the Timeline as you play your video? It's called a **CTI**, which stands for "Current Time Indicator."

That's an all-important vocabulary term that you'll definitely want to know as we continue to work.

Trust us on this. Especially since there's no other word that comes close to describing this thing – and we're going to use the term often throughout this book.

Basic editing moves

No matter what you plan to do with your video and no matter how creatively you plan to do it, the video editing process itself will still fit the same basic structure.

Here's a brief walkthrough of the steps you'll take for creating any video project in Premiere Elements.

1 Gather your media

The assets, or media, you gather to create your movie can come from a variety of sources. It can be video, audio, music, photos or graphics. If you are working in Quick View, any media you gather will go directly to your timeline. If you are working in Expert View, it will go into your **Project Assets** panel.

To import your media into your project, click on the **Add Media** tab on the upper left of the interface.

There are basically three ways to get your media into your project, all accessed by one of the six buttons on the **Add Media** panel (illustrated below). We show you how and when to use each in **Chapter 5, Add Media to Your Project**.

- **Download your video from a hard drive camcorder, flash based camcorder or other video recording device.**

  Video clips from hard drive and flash drive recording devices, including high-definition AVCHD and Go Pro camcorders as well as smart phones, are *downloaded* into your Premiere Elements project when you select the **Videos from Cameras & Devices** option. Media can also be downloaded from other sources, including DVDs, using the **DVD Camcorder or PC DVD Drive** option. Photos can be added from cameras and other devices by selecting the **Digital Still Cameras & Phones** option.

Add Media options

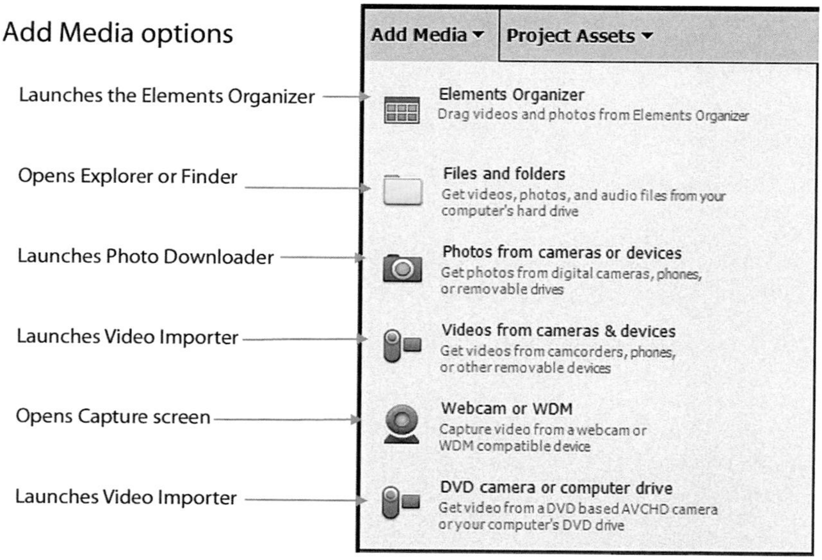

Video **streamed** from your webcam is captured live through the Premiere Elements Capture workspace.

Video from non-tape-based sources – including hard drive and AVCHD camcorders, DVDs and smartphones – is **downloaded** into your Premiere Elements project by the Video Importer, while still photos are downloaded from your digital camera or phone by the Photo Downloader.

When you select the option to Add Media from the Organizer, you can locate the photos, video and audio files already on your computer using the Organizer's management tools and **import** it into your project.

- **Stream, or capture, your video into your project.**

  If you've got a Webcam or other WDM (Windows Device Model) video or audio device attached to your computer, you can use Premiere Elements to *capture* the live video directly into your Premiere Elements video project.

  Premiere Elements 15 does not include tools for capturing tape-based video, including video from HDV and miniDV camcorders. However, video from digital tape camcorders *can* be captured as Premiere Elements-compatible video data using various third-party software and then added to your Premiere Elements project. We show you how to capture this type of video in our **Premiere Elements Appendix**, on page 275.

- **Browse to gather and import media files that are located on your computer's hard drive(s).**

  When you click the **PC Files and Folders** button under **Add Media**, Windows Explorer or the Mac OSX Finder will open, allowing you to *import* video, stills, graphics or music files already on your computer's hard drive. The **Elements Organizer** is a companion file management program that can be used to manage and search media files on your computer. (We explore the Organizer in detail in **Section IV** of this book.)

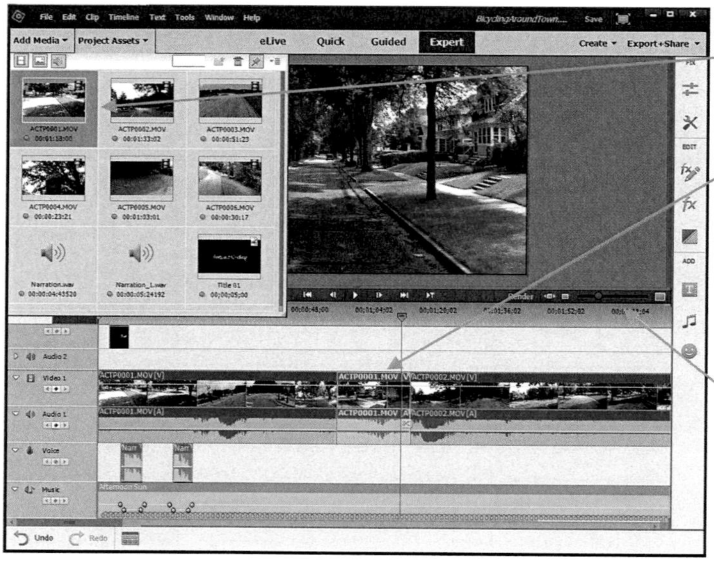

To add a clip to your timeline in Expert View, simply drag it from the Project Assets panel.

As you add clips tp the middle of a project, the other clips will "ripple", or move to the right.

To override the ripple effect (as when you're adding music or a video clip to a parallel track) hold down the Ctrl key as you add the clip (or the Command key on a Mac).

Zoom in or out on the timeline by pressing + or - or using the Zoom slider.

2 Assemble the clips on your timeline

Once you've imported your media clips into a project, you can begin the process of assembling your movie. If you are working in Quick View, any media you add to your project will be loaded directly to your timeline. If you are working in Expert View, the clips will be added to your **Project Assets** panel. Editing this video is as simple as dragging these clips from this panel to your timeline.

Once you add your files to your timeline, you'll have a number of options:

- **Trim your clips.** Trimming means removing footage from either the beginning or the end of a clip. To trim a clip, click to select the clip on your timeline and then drag in from either its beginning or end, as in the illustration on the following page.
- **Split your clips.** Splitting means slicing through your clips so that you can remove footage from the middle or delete a sliced-off segment completely. To split a clip, position the **CTI** (playhead) over your clip at the point at which you'd like the slice to occur and then click on the scissors icon on **CTI**.
- **Place your clip on an upper video or audio track**. An important feature of editing in Expert View is the ability to place your video or audio on tracks other than **Video 1** and **Audio 1**.

  The use of multiple tracks of video is, in fact, key to the creation of many of the more advanced video effects, including **Chroma Key** and **Videomerge.**

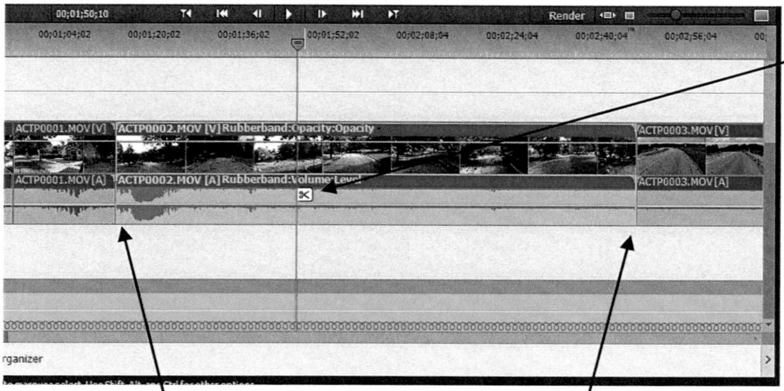

To slice a clip in two, click the scissors icon on the CTI playhead.

If a clip is selected on the timeline, only that clip will be split at the position of the CTI; If no clips are selected, all clips on every track on the timeline will be split at the position of the CTI.

Trim from Beginning of clip

Trim from End of clip

To trim a clip on the timeline, hover your mouse over the beginning or end of a clip until the Trim from Beginning or Trim from End icon appears, then click and drag in or out.

We discuss how to assemble your movie in both Quick View and Expert View in **Chapter 2** and **Chapter 7** respectively. We also show you how to use multi-track editing in order to create a variety of effects and take advantage of several key storytelling techniques.

We'll also show you how to use both automatic and manual tools to work with your audio clips.

3 Add and adjust effects

Premiere Elements comes loaded with dozens of video and audio effects as well as hundreds of preset effects for working magic on your movie.

Adding an effect in Premiere Elements is very easy, as we show you in **Chapter 13, Add Video and Audio Effects**.

1 As illustrated on the next page, click the **Effects** button on the **Toolbar** along the right side of the program.

This will open the **Effects** panel.

2 Locate an effect.

Go to any category of video or audio effects by clicking the title bar (The bar along the top of the panel) and selecting from the list that appears.

You can also quickly locate any effect by clicking the **Quick Search** magnifying glass button at the top right of the panel and typing in the effect's name.

We'll discuss **Effects** in detail in **Chapter 13.**

3 Apply the effect.

To apply an effect, drag it from the **Effects** panel onto a clip on your timeline.

4 Adjust the effect's settings.

Once you've applied your effect, you may or may not see an immediate change in your video clip. To intensify or fine tune your effect, ensure the clip is selected on your timeline, then open the **Applied Effects** panel by clicking its button on the **Toolbar**.

The **Applied Effects** panel is a tremendously powerful workspace. Not only can you use it to change the settings for individual effects but also as the main workspace for creating and adjusting **keyframes**, Premiere Elements' tool for creating animations, motion paths and effects that change over the course of the clip's playback.

On the **Applied Effects** panel, locate your effect's listing, then click on it to open the effect's settings.

In **Chapter 14**, we'll show you how to customize and fine tune your effects in the **Applied Effects** panel.

Then, in **Chapter 15**, we'll show you how to use keyframes to animate effects and motion paths.

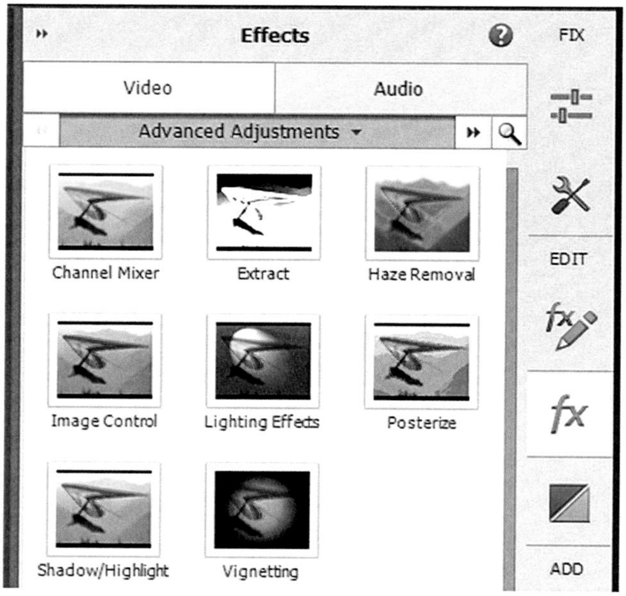

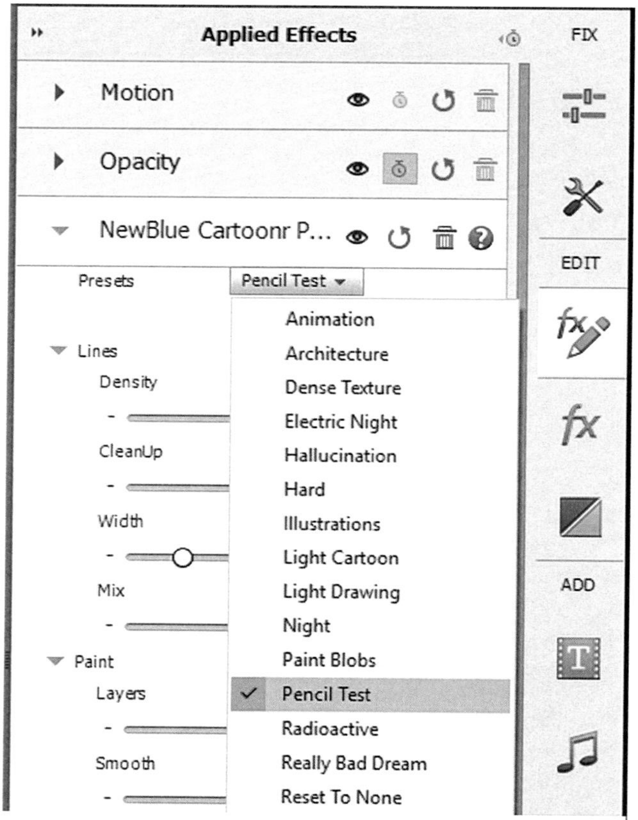

Effects that have been added to a clip appear in that clip's Applied Effects panel, where they can be adjusted and customized.

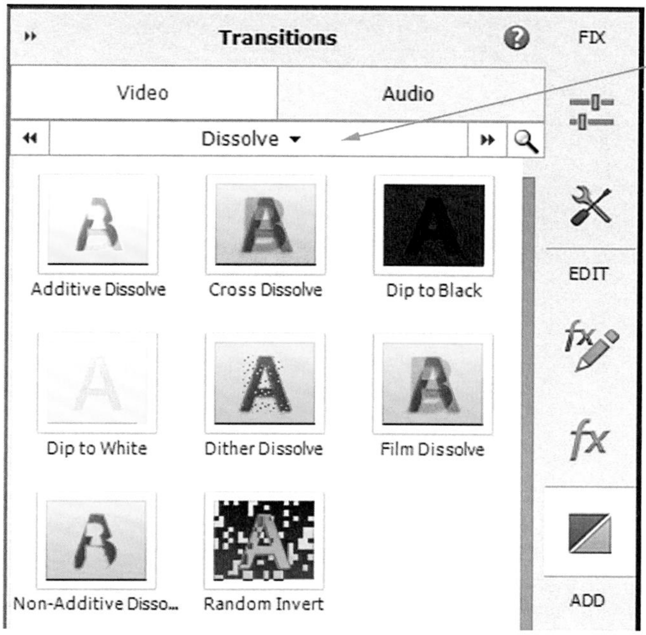

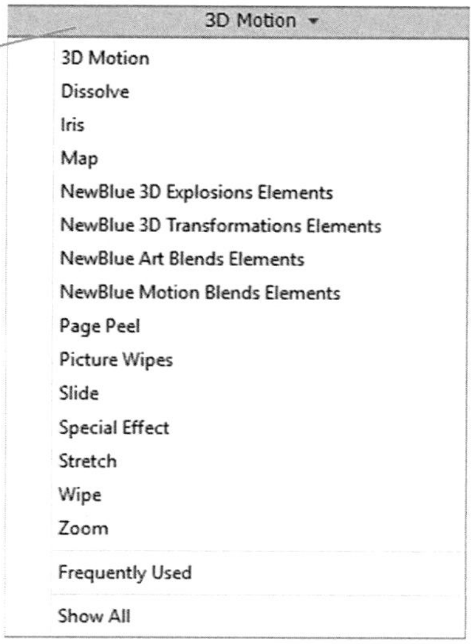

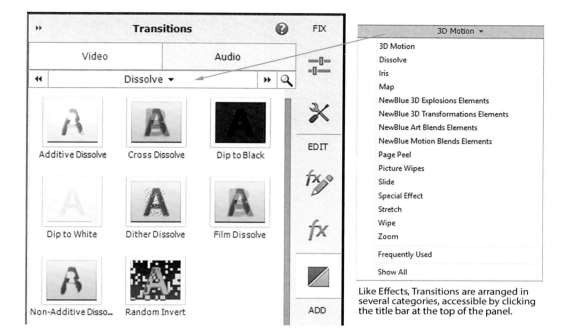

Like Effects, Transitions are arranged in several categories, accessible by clicking the title bar at the top of the panel.

4 Add and adjust transitions

Transitions are the effects or animations that take your movie from one clip to another. Some are gentle and nearly invisible – others are showy and draw attention to themselves. Most transitions are added to your timeline and adjusted similarly to effects:

1 Click on the **Transitions** button on the **Toolbar**.

The **Transitions** panel will open.

2 Locate a transition.

Select any category of video or audio effects by clicking the title bar (The bar along the top of the panel) and selecting from the pop-up list that appears.

You can also quickly locate any effect by clicking the **Quick Search** magnifying glass button at the top right of the panel and typing in the transition's name.

3 Apply the transition.

Apply a transition by dragging it from the **Transitions** panel onto the intersection of two clips on your timeline.

4 Customize your transition.

Nearly all transitions include a number of properties that can be customized, depending on the nature of the transition.

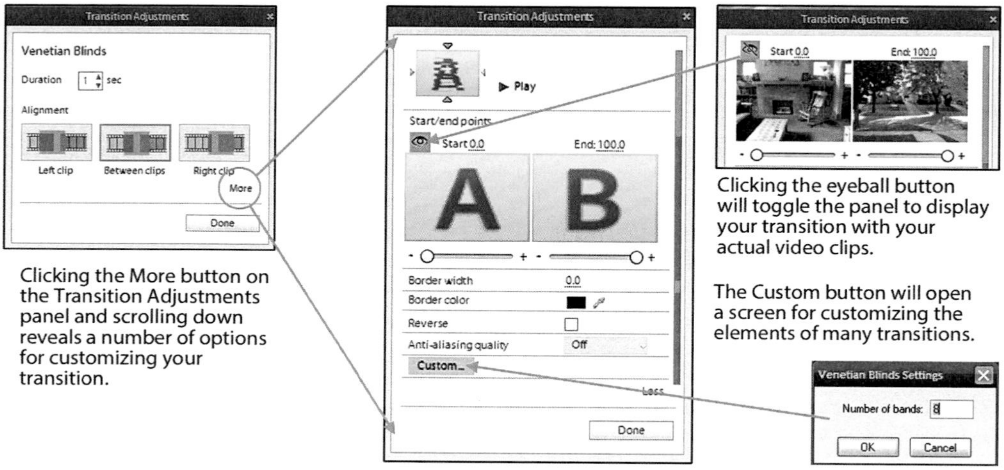

Clicking the More button on the Transition Adjustments panel and scrolling down reveals a number of options for customizing your transition.

Clicking the eyeball button will toggle the panel to display your transition with your actual video clips.

The Custom button will open a screen for customizing the elements of many transitions.

Virtually all transitions include options for designating where the transition centers and the duration of the transition as well as an option for setting the transition to reverse its movement (i.e., wiping from right to left rather than left to right).

We'll show you just about everything there is to know about adding and customizing transitions – including why they sometimes seem to behave in very strange ways – in **Chapter 11**. And, as a bonus, we'll even show you how to use the **Gradient Wipe**, a tool for creating your own custom transition effects!

5 Add titles

Titles are text, and sometimes graphics, placed over your clips to provide additional visual information for your video story. Once you've selected a title template, you'll create and customize your titles in Premiere Elements' **Title Adjustments** workspace.

To add a title or text to your movie:

1 Click the **Titles & Text** button on the **Toolbar**.

The **Titles & Text** panel will open.

As with **Effects** and **Transitions**, the panel has several categories of title templates. Among these are text-only stationary titles, titles with graphics and rolling and animated titles

In addition to standard title templates, the library includes a collection of **Motion Titles**, animated tiles with several customizable elements.

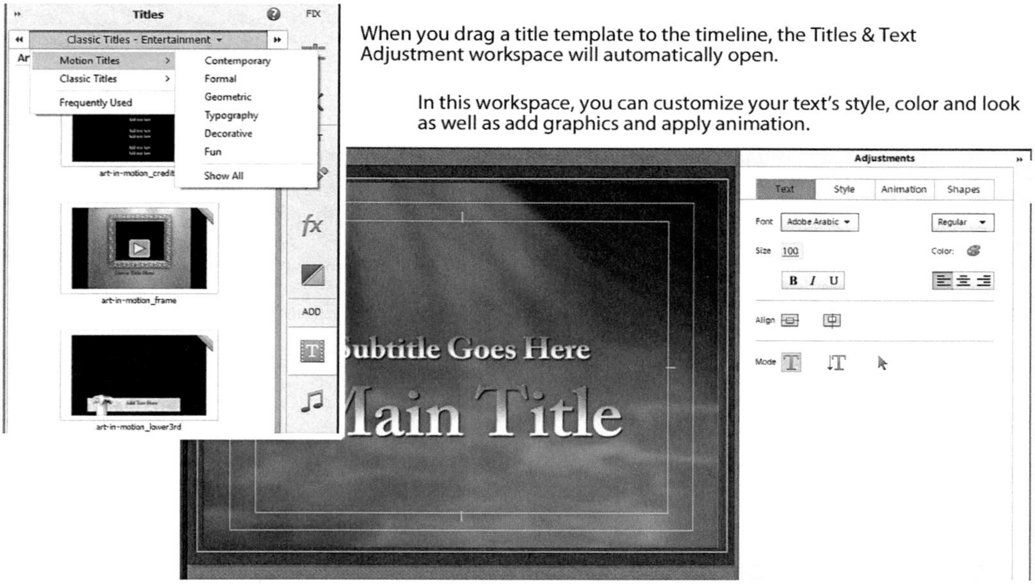

When you drag a title template to the timeline, the Titles & Text Adjustment workspace will automatically open.

In this workspace, you can customize your text's style, color and look as well as add graphics and apply animation.

2 Add the title to your timeline.

Drag the title from the **Titles & Templates** panel to your timeline. The **Title Adjustments** workspace will automatically open.

3 Customize your title's text.

Type your custom text over the placeholder text.

With your text block selected, you can customize the text's attributes – including the font, size, style and alignment. You can also apply a style to your selected text by clicking on one of the **Text Styles** listed on the panel.

4 Customize your title's look and animation.

The **Title Adjustments** workspace has tools for customizing the look and style of your text, adding and placing graphics and adding very cool text animations. You can also create rolling and crawling titles.

When you want to return to the regular editing workspace, click on the timeline.

We'll show you pretty much everything you could want to know about using Premiere Elements' tools for creating and customizing your titles and text in **Chapter 12**.

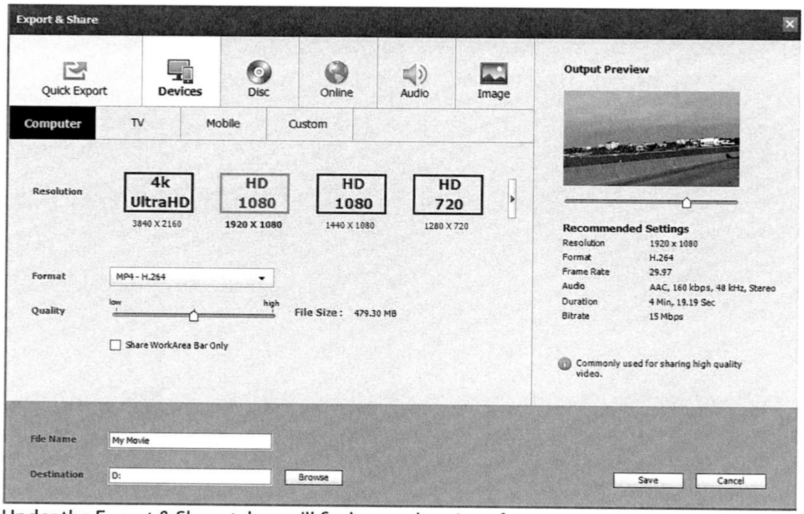

Under the Export & Share tab, you'll find several options for outputting your movie.

6 Export & Share your movie

When you're happy with the movie you've created, you'll find a number of options for publishing and sharing it, as we discuss in **Chapter 21**. We'll show you how to output your movie to:

- **Devices.** The program will save your finished project as an AVI file, MPEG, QuickTime (MOV) file, AVCHD video, Windows Media (WMV) file or an audio file on your computer's hard drive. Once the output is complete, you can then use these files any number of ways, including posting them online or using them as segments in a larger video project.
- **Disc.** Built into Premiere Elements are tools for creating menus and scene markers so that you can produce great-looking DVDs and BluRay discs.
- **Online.** The program comes complete with tools for loading your finished video to a social media site like YouTube, Vimeo or Facebook.
- **Audio** or **Image.** Premiere Elements also includes tools for outputting an audio file or a still photo from your movie.

And that's basically it!

You gather your assets; you assemble them on your timeline; you add effects, transitions and titles; then you share your masterpiece with the world.

But between the lines of this simplicity are the countless variations that can elevate your movie project from the realm of a basic structure to something truly amazing!

And that, of course, is what this book is all about.

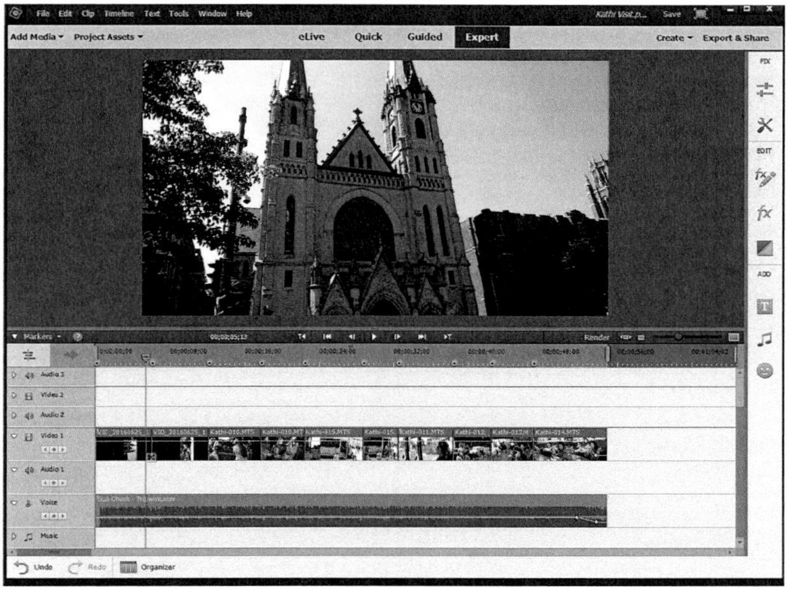

What's new in version 15?

Adobe has added a number of interesting new features in its latest version Premiere Elements. It's also done some fine-tuning of the interface to make it easier to locate effects and to focus on the audio aspects of your videos.

The Toolbar

The most noticeable change in Premiere Elements 15 is that the interface has been greatly simplified. All of the program's effects and tools can now be accessed by clicking a button on the **Toolbar** that runs along the right side of the program, as illustrated above.

On this **Toolbar**, you'll find one-click access to **Adjustments, Tools, Effects and Effects Adjustments, Transitions, Titles & Text, Music Scores** and **Graphics**.

Video Collage creator

A new tool that makes a fairly complicated effect very easy to produce, the **Video Collage** creator offers a library of grid patterns for creating a split screen effect of up to seven clips at once. Clips are added to the grid with a simple drag-and-drop, and the program even adds an introductory animation to each clip.

We show you how to use this very cool tool on page 90 of **Chapter 8, Create an InstantMovie, Video Story or Video Collage**.

Haze Removal effect

A cool new effect for removing haze and fog from your videos has been added to its library of **Video Effects**.

Haze Removal has both automatic and manual settings. We discuss it in more detail on page 156 of **Chapter 13, Add Audio and Video Effects**.

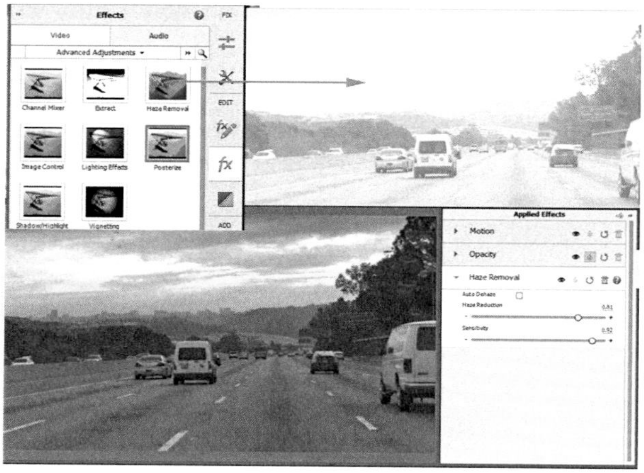

Music Remix tool

A sophisticated new addition to version 15 is the **Music Remix** tool, a tool for creating musical clips at custom lengths from virtually any existing music.

The tool works automatically. All you need to do is trim your music clip to a custom length and the program will automatically remix it so that it has a natural beginning, middle and end. We show you how to use this cool tool on page 193 of **Chapter 16, Mix Your Audio and Add Music**.

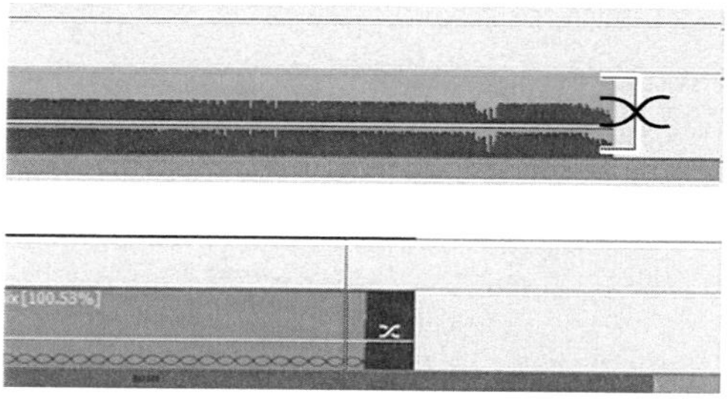

Face Recognition

Sophisticated **Face Recognition** tools have also been added to the program.

Smart Trim identifies segments of your videos that include faces as part of its **Auto Analysis**.

And, as we show you on page 102, the **Pan & Zoom** tool will even automatically create motion paths that pan from face to face.

Organizer improvements

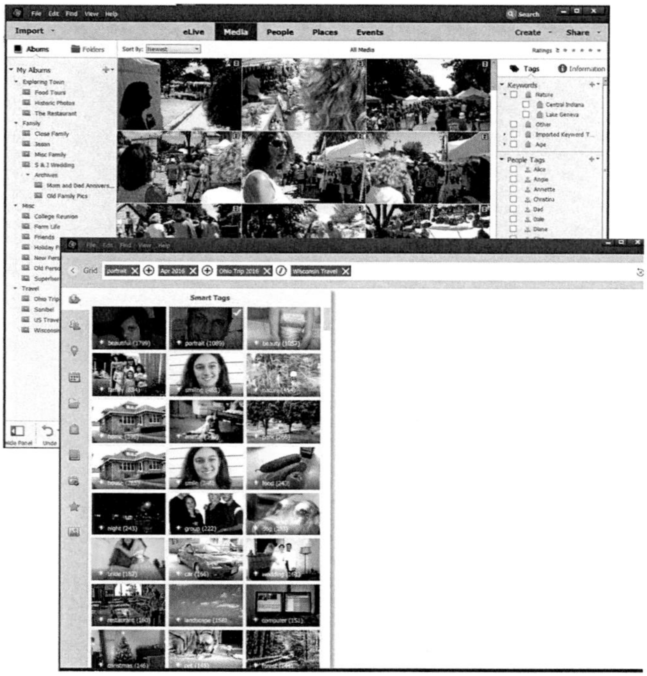

Adobe also continues to improve the file management and search tools in the Elements Organizer. Improvements in the **Auto Analyzer** mean that the program not only identifies and recognizes faces in your photos, but it also creates very intuitive **Auto Tags** based on the content and subject matter of your pictures!

Its upgraded **Search** feature gives you the ability to filter your media searches based on a variety of data. And the program includes even more integration with social media and cloud-based storage sites like OneDrive and Google Photos.

We explore all the amazing tools in this powerful little program in **Chapters 17, 18** and **19** of this book.

Part I

Editing in Quick View and Guided Edits

Adding Media to Your Quick View Timeline

Trimming and Slicing Your Video

Adding Transitions

Adding and Adjusting Audio

Adding Titles

Chapter 2

Assemble Your Video in Quick View

The drag-and-drop editing space

Quick View is Premiere Elements' workspace for quickly pulling together a video and applying effects to it.

It combines the simplicity of sceneline editing with the power of a full-fledged Premiere Elements timeline.

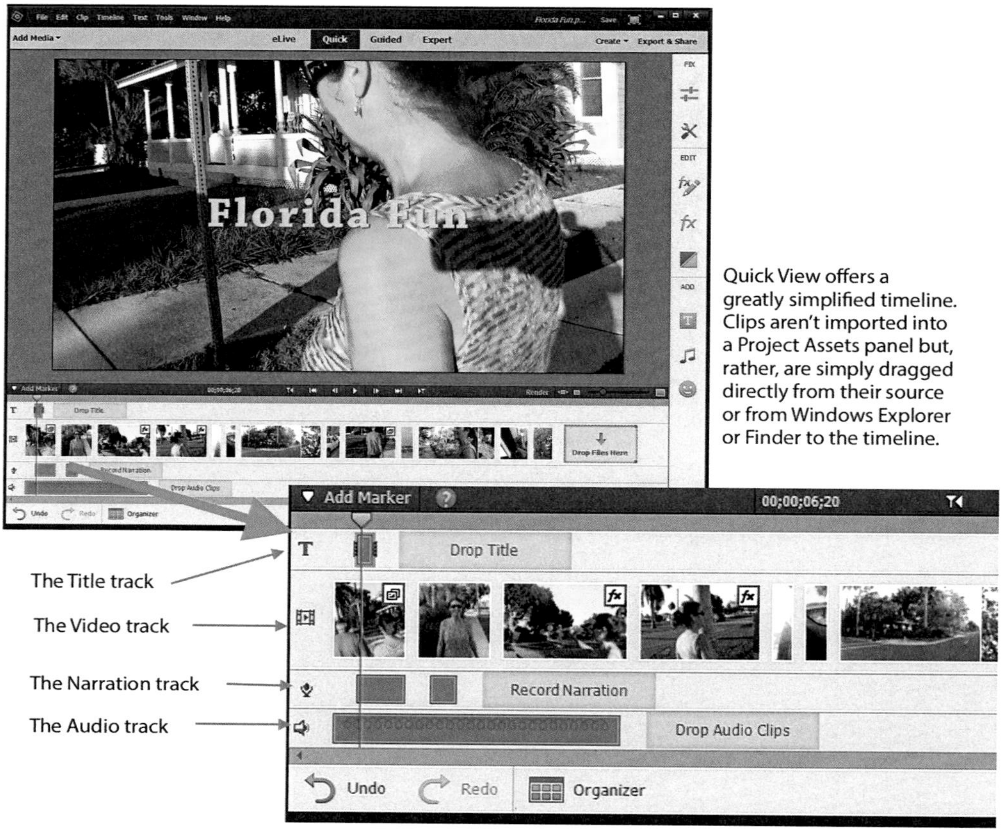

Quick View offers a greatly simplified timeline. Clips aren't imported into a Project Assets panel but, rather, are simply dragged directly from their source or from Windows Explorer or Finder to the timeline.

Premiere Elements' Quick View timeline makes assembling your movie as fast and easy as possible. It combines the simplicity of the old Sceneline mode with the power of a full-fledged Timeline.

The Quick View timeline includes four tracks in which you can assemble your movie. They are, from top to bottom:

The Title Track. This is where text or titles that will overlay your video is placed. (If you'd prefer your titles with a black background or no background at all, you can also place your titles directly on the **Video Track**. However, only text and titles can be placed to the **Title Track**.) For more information on adding titles to your movie, see **Chapter 12, Add Titles & Text**.

The Video Track. This is the track on which your movie will be assembled. It will also include your video's accompanying audio.

The Narration Track. Although any audio may be added to this track, this is the track that any recorded narration (see page 97) will appear on by default.

The Audio/Music Track. Music or any other peripheral audio may be added here. For information on adding music to your movie, see **Chapter 16**.

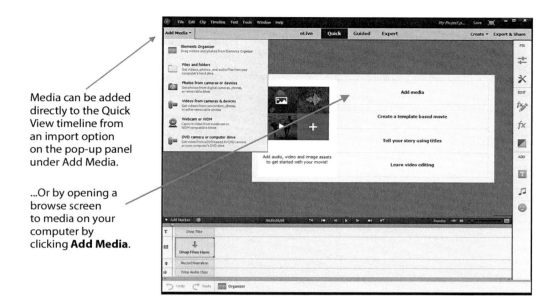

Media can be added directly to the Quick View timeline from an import option on the pop-up panel under Add Media.

...Or by opening a browse screen to media on your computer by clicking **Add Media**.

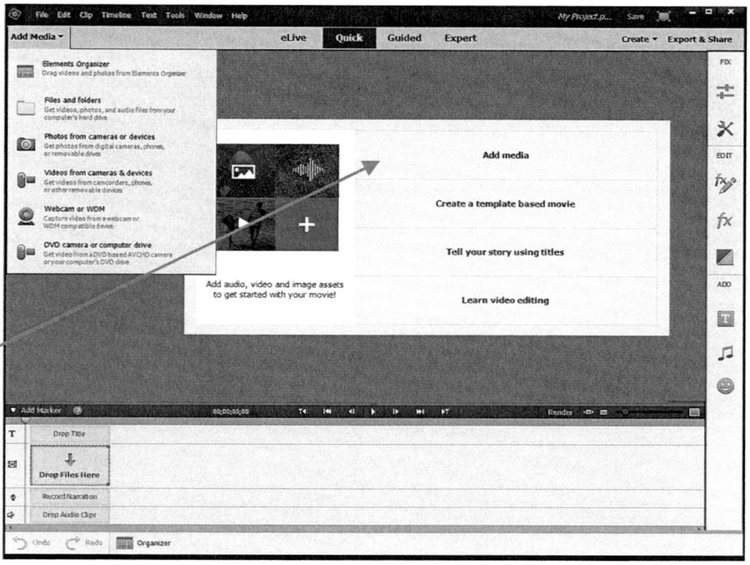

Add media to your Quick View timeline

In Quick View, the video clips and other media you add to your project are added directly to your timeline. There is no **Project Assets** panel in which you gather and prep your clips. You simply add your media to your timeline and start editing! The program will automatically set up your project by matching its settings to the specs of the first video clip you add.

You can add your media to your project in a number of ways:

- Video and other media from Flip, AVCHDs, cameras, phones or removable drive devices are imported to your timeline over a USB connection (as discussed in **Chapter 5**, pages 52-55).
- Live video can be captured from your webcam directly to your timeline (as discussed on page 53).
- Media that's already on your computer can be browsed to by selecting the **Files and Folders** option or located through the **Elements Organizer**.

The tools for importing your media are accessed through the pop-up menu under the **Add Media** button in the upper left of the program's interface. (For more information on **Add Media**, see **Chapter 5**.) Or, when you first start your project, you can simply click the **Add Media** button in the center of the interface, as illustrated above. (Note that the +**Add Media** button will be replaced by the **Monitor** panel once you begin to assemble clips on your timeline.)

Your media can also be added directly from your computer's Windows Explorer or Mac Finder screens. Simply drag your audio and video clips directly to your Quick View timeline!

Your view of your timeline can be set using the Zoom Slider or by using the Zoom In/Out buttons.

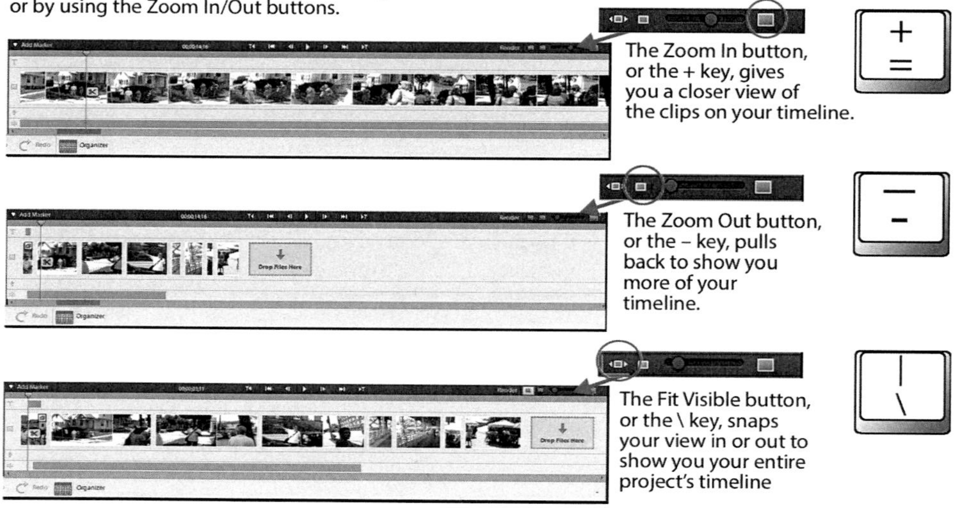

The Zoom In button, or the + key, gives you a closer view of the clips on your timeline.
The Zoom Out button, or the – key, pulls back to show you more of your timeline.
The Fit Visible button, or the \ key, snaps your view in or out to show you your entire project's timeline

Zoom in or out of your timeline

Once you've added media to your timeline, you may want to zoom out to see the entire movie at once, or zoom in to a single moment or frame to make some fine adjustments.

Along the upper right of the Quick View timeline are controls for zooming in and out of your movie. (These controls have the same function on the Expert View timeline.) There are also keyboard shortcuts for settings these views:

The **Zoom In** button incrementally zooms in on your timeline. You can also zoom in by pressing your keyboard's **+** key.

The **Zoom Out** button incrementally zooms out from your timeline. You can also zoom out by pressing your keyboard's **–** key.

The **Fit Visible Timeline** button sets the zoom level so that your entire movie project is visible. You also set this level by pressing the **** key on your keyboard (above the **Enter/Return** key).

The **Slider** can be used to set your zoom level precisely.

Add transitions

A library of transitions can be browsed by clicking on the **Transitions** button on the **Toolbar** along the right side of the interface.

In Quick View, you only have access to a handful of transitions. If you'd like to access the full transitions library, switch over to Expert View, where you can access over 100 video transitions in 15 categories plus 2 audio transitions. To learn more about working with transitions in Expert View, see **Chapter 11, Add and Customize Transitions**.

To apply a transition, simply drag it from the Transitions pop-up panel on the Toolbar to the intersection between two clips (indicated in green).

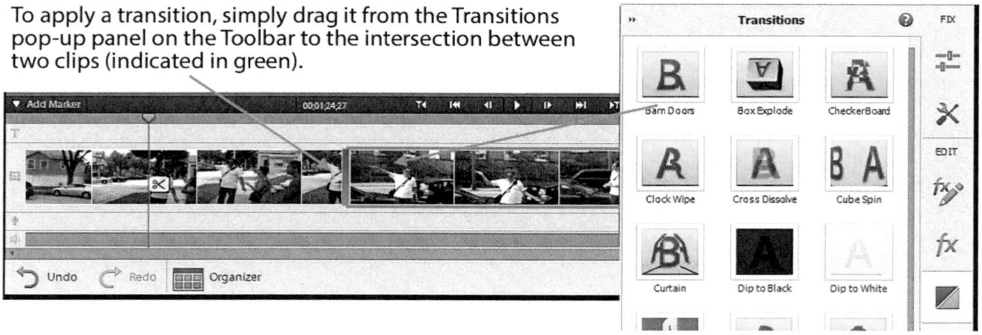

To apply a transition, drag it from the **Transitions** panel to your timeline, as illustrated above. A green highlight will indicate where the transition will be applied.

When you apply a transition, a pop-up menu (illustrated on the right) will prompt you to choose where you'd like the transition applied in relation to the clips. In most cases, you'll choose **Between Clips**.

This menu also allows you to set the **Duration** of the transition, in seconds. This number can be set by clicking on the up and down arrows or by clicking directly on the number and typing in a custom duration. Increments of seconds (such as .5) can be used.

To re-access this panel and revise these properties at any time, **double-click** on the transition on your timeline.

Most transitions also allow for much deeper customization. For more information on customizing your transitions, see page 132.

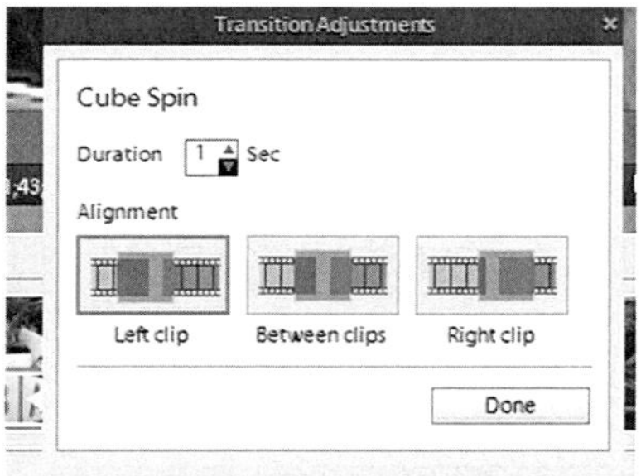

When you apply your transition (or when you double-click on an existing transition), a pop-up menu will appear offering options for how the transition's duration and how the transition rests between your clips.

To replace one transition with another, simply drag the new transition from the **Transitions** panel onto the existing.

To remove a transition, click to select it on the timeline and press **Delete** on your keyboard.

How your transitions behave can be affected by the amount of "head" and "tail" material available on your clips. For more information on this, see **How Transitions Work** on page 136.

Trim or split your video

Video clips, audio clips and even titles can be **Split** or **Trimmed**. To indicate which clips you want to **Split** or **Trim**, click to select the audio or video clip on your timeline so that it is surrounded by a blue highlight, as illustrated on the following page.

Splitting your video means cutting a larger clip on your timeline into smaller clips.

To Split your video:

1. Position the **CTI** playhead so that the frame that displays in you **Monitor** indicates the exact spot you want to slice your video.
2. Click on the scissors icon on the **CTI**.

Splitting means dividing a clip into smaller clips at the point of the CTI playhead.

Split clips are indicated with ticker markers.

Ticker markers indicate that there is "hidden" video beyond the clip's end points.

Trimming means shortening (or lengthening) a clip on your timeline by adjusting the clip's start and end points.

To trim a clip:

1. Hover your mouse over the beginning or end of a clip on your timeline until the **Trim** indicator appears, as illustrated above.
2. Click and drag to the left or right.

Trimming cuts (or extends) video from the beginning or end of a clip. To trim, hover your mouse over an end of a clip until the trim indicator appears, then click and drag.

A trimmed clip is indicated with a ticker marker.

A clip that has been split or trimmed is indicated with the icon.

Once a clip has been split, it becomes two smaller clips. Each of these clips can also be trimmed.

Add audio to your Quick View timeline

As you add your camcorder video to your **Video Track**, the accompanying audio will be added automatically, as part of an unseen audio track.

The Quick View timeline offers two additional tracks in which you can add audio: The **Narration Track** and the **Audio Track**.

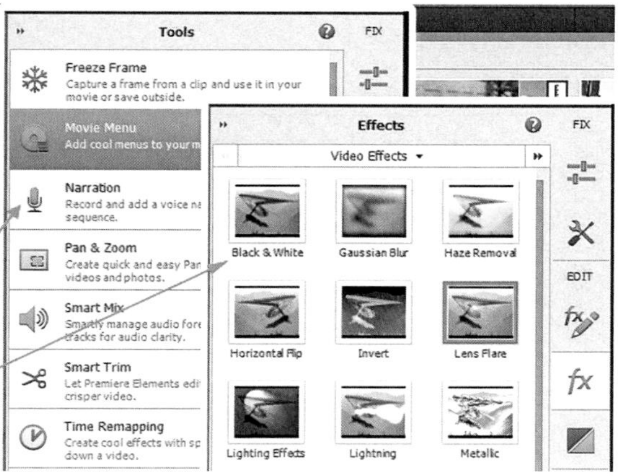

Music or other audio can be added to either the Narration track or the Audio Clip track.

The Toolbar includes tools for adding Effects and creating custom Music tracks.

Although technically you can add audio or music to your movie project on either track, you need to be careful where you place your audio or music if you plan to record narration. Narration gets priority on the **Narration Track**. This means that narration will overwrite any existing audio or music on this track!

You can place any audio or music clips on the **Audio Track**.

As with your video clips, your audio clips can be **Split** and **Trimmed**, as described on the facing page.

The limitations of Quick View

Although most of the program's features are available in both Quick View and Expert View, a number of features function to a lesser degree or not at all in Quick View. They include:

Multi-track editing. Because the Quick View timeline is limited to one video track, J-Cuts, L-Cuts, split screen and picture-in-picture effects can not be easily created in Quick View.

Chroma Key and Videomerge. Because **keying** effects, including **Videomerge**, require at least two tracks of video in order to create their composite effects, these effects can not be effectively created on the Quick View timeline.

Audio Keyframing. Audio cannot easily be to specific levels at specific points in a clip on the Quick View timeline using keyframes. Audio levels can only be set using the **Smart Mix, Adjustments** and **Audio Mixer** tools.

Fortunately, you can easily switch between Quick View and Expert View as you work on your project so that you can take advantage of the features on each timeline. (However, video and audio added to upper tracks in Expert View will not be visible when you switch to Quick View.)

Adjust your audio levels and mix your audio

The Quick View timeline has a limited number of ways for you to adjust the audio levels or to mix your audio so that one or more audio tracks' levels are lower so that another can dominate.

Smart Mix (discussed on page 104) will automatically mix and adjust your audio levels based on parameters you define.

The Audio Mixer (discussed on page 99) will set audio keyframes on the fly for you as you raise and lower levels as your video plays.

However, each of these methods has its own challenges and limitations. The single best way to precisely control your levels and mix your audio is with audio keyframes (described on page 189), a feature most easily applied on the Expert View timeline.

Add titles

A library of title templates can be browsed by clicking on the **Titles & Text** button on the **Toolbar** along the right side of the interface.

The titles library is arranged in categories, and you can browse through the categories of transitions by clicking the backward and forward arrows at the top of the pop-up panel, as illustrated on page 140.

The title templates range from basic text to rolling titles and templates.

Once you've selected a title, drag it to either the **Titles Track** on the Quick View timeline (if you'd like to overlay your video) or to an area on the **Video Track** (if you'd like it to appear with a black or no background).

Once you've placed a title, the **Title Adjustments** workspace will open. In this workspace you'll find options for changing your text's color, style, font or size. You can also add animations and/or graphics to your text.

For more information on working with titles and text, see **Chapter 12, Add Titles & Text.**

Like audio and video clips, titles can be **Split** and **Trimmed**. If your text has animation or a roll or crawl applied to it, the longer you stretch the title on the timeline, the slower the animation and vice versa.

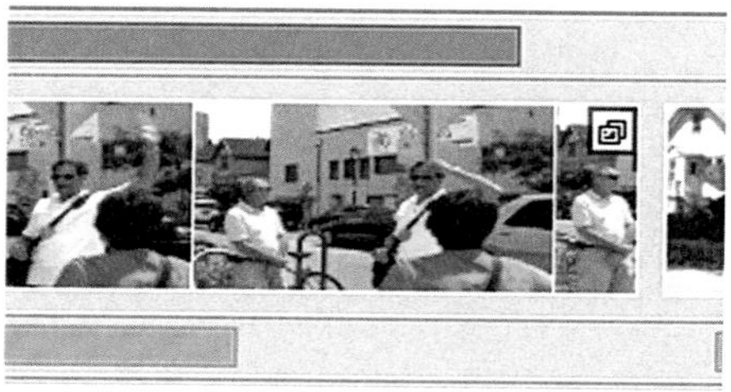

The presence of a title or other video clip on an upper video track is indicated on the Quick Edit timeline with an overlay marker in the upper right corner of the effected clip.

Guided Startup with Premiere Elements

Adding Transitions

Adding Scores

Adjusting Contrast, Brightness and Color

Adding Titles

Recording Narration

Creating Video Effects

Color Pop

Slow Motion

Adjustment Layers

Chapter 3

Use Guided Edits

Simple, step-by-step editing

If you're new to video editing or to Premiere Elements, you might appreciate the program's helpful Guided Edit feature.

Guided Edits walk you through a number of basic editing moves, step by step, explaining how each tool and adjustment works along the way.

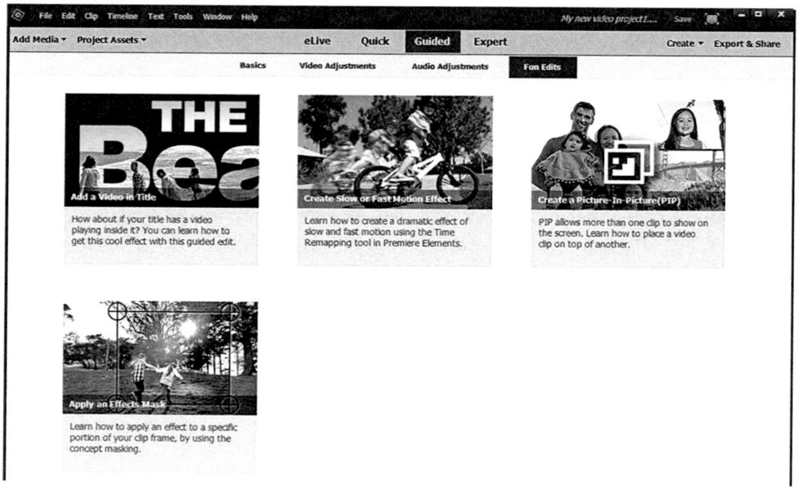

Guided Edits – launched by clicking the tab at the top of the program in either Quick or Expert view – is a library of walk-throughs designed to take you step-by-step through a number of processes and effects in the program, showing you which panels to open and how to use each tool. It's like having your own personal instructor built right into the program!

With version 15, Adobe has completely redesigned the Guided Edits library space. (It's now very similar to the library space in Photoshop Elements.) **Guided Edits** are arranged under four category tabs:

Basic Guided Edits

Get Started shows you how to start a project, gather your media and assemble your media files on your timeline.

Trim & Split Clips demonstrates the basics of trimming and splitting the video clips on your timeline.

Add Transitions Between Clips shows you how to add transitional video effects between the clips on your timeline.

Add a Title to Your Movie shows you how to select, add and modify a title template.

Video Adjustments

Fix Brightness, Color & Contrast shows you how to improve or enhance the color, lighting or contrast in your movie.

Color Pop walks you through the process of stripping all but one color from your movie.

Animate Graphics walks you through the process of overlaying a graphic onto your movie and then controlling its movement across your video frame.

Add an Adjustment Layer walks you through the process of adding effects to entire sequences in your movie rather than individual clips.

Audio Adjustments

Add Narration walks you through the process of recording narration into your movie project as your movie is playing.

Add a Music Score shows you how to add and customize music tracks.

Fun Edits

Add Video in a Title walks you through the process of using the Track Matte to create an effect in which your video is seen through your text rather than around it.

Create Slow or Fast Motion shows you how to time shift the playback speed of your movie using the **Time Remapping** tool.

Create a Picture-In-Picture (PIP) walks you through the process of adding a video clip to your movie as a picture-in-picture inset.

Apply an Effects Mask shows you how to use a mask so that an effect is confined to a designated area of your video.

In each case, the program will explain to you which tool to use, then it will highlight on the program's interface the button to click to access or apply the tool or effect.

Guided Edits can be accessed in both the **Quick** and **Expert** view workspaces, though some of these **Edits** will require you to switch over to **Expert** view.

You'll likely outgrow the need for **Guided Edits** fairly quickly, once you learn a few basic moves. However, if you've opened the program for the first time and don't have a clue where to start, **Guided Edits** can help you find your way!

Get Started

This **Guided Edit** will walk you step-by-step through the process of setting up, editing and outputting your movie, including:

Add Media to Your Project by either browsing to video files, still photos or audio on your computer or capturing or downloading video from your camcorder.

Open the Project Assets Bin and showing you how to add your media files from this bin to the timeline.

Control Timeline Zoom and the **CTI**.

Trim and Split the clips on your timeline.

Add Transitions between the clips on your timeline and customizing how the transition positions itself between your clips.

Export & Share your finished movie.

Trim & Split Clips

This **Guided Edit** will walk you step-by-step through the process of trimming and splitting your movie clips, including:

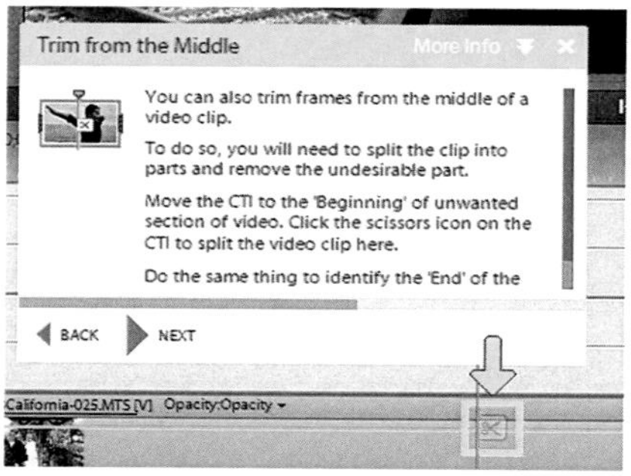

Trim from the Beginning of a clip on your timeline.

Trim from the End of a clip on your timeline.

Trim from the Middle by splitting a clip in your movie.

Add Transitions Between Clips

This **Guided Edit** is specific to the process of adding and customizing transitions to your movie. It's steps include:

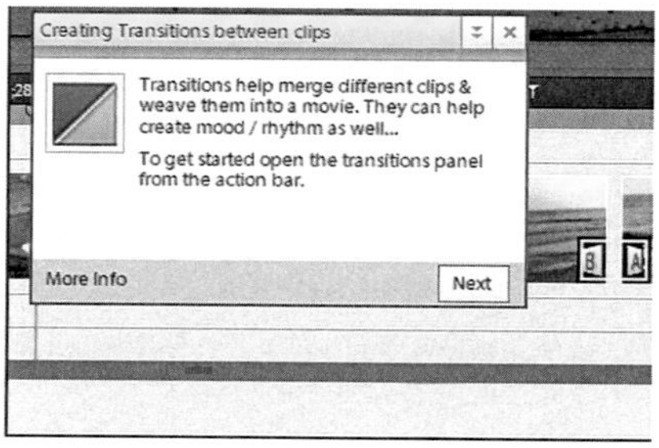

Locate a Transition and add it to your movie.

Customize the Transition's position between your clips.

For more detailed information on using some of the deeper customization tools for creating transitions, see **Chapter 11, Add and Customize Transitions**.

Add a Title to Your Movie

This **Guided Edit** will walk you step-by-step through the process of adding and customizing a title, including:

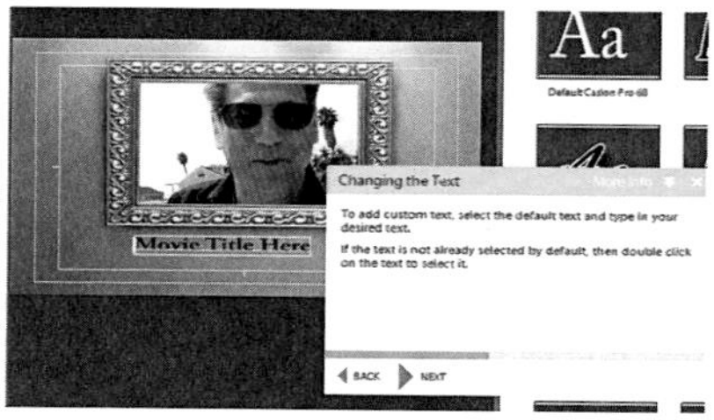

Work with the Titles Panel and selecting a title template.

Change the Text in the **Title Adjustments** workspace.

Apply Styles to Your Text to change its look and other characteristics.

Adjust Text Properties, including font, color and alignment.

Apply Animation to Your Text using the Titles Animation templates.

For more detailed information on creating and customizing titles and text in your movies, see **Chapter 12, Add Titles & Text**.

Fix Brightness, Color & Contrast

This **Guided Edit**, as you might expect, will walk you through the process of adjusting and enhancing the brightness, contrast and color in a selected video clip. Its step-by-step instructions include:

Select a video clip on your timeline and opening the **Adjustments** panel.

Use the Lighting Quick Fix Preview tool to set the video clip's brightness and contrast.

Use the Color Quick Fix Preview tool to set the video clip's hue, lightness, saturation and brightness.

For more detailed information on using the tools in this panel to correct and enhance your video's color and lighting – as well as the tools for varying these settings using keyframes – see **Chapter 10, Make Adjustments to Your Video and Audio**.

Color Pop

This **Guided Edit** shows you how to use the **Red Noir Hollywood Look** to strip away all but one color in your video:

Select and Apply the Red Noir Hollywood Look, which desaturates most of the colors in your video clip.

Reduce Saturation by designating which color or colors will remain visible and which will be desaturated to black & white.

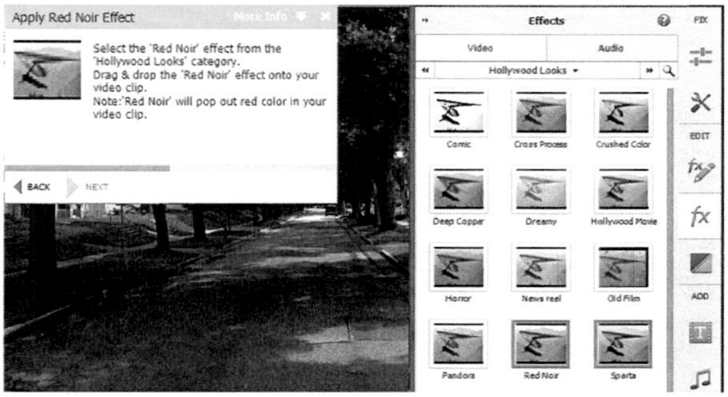

For more information on using **Hollywood Looks** to add cool effects to your movies, see page 158 of **Chapter 13, Audio and Video Effects**.

Animate Graphics

This **Guided Edit** will walk you through the process of adding and creating motion paths for a Premiere Elements graphic, including:

Add a Graphic from the **Graphics** panel.

Use Animation and **Keyframe Controls** on the **Applied Effects** panel.

Enable Animation Parameters and **Add Keyframes** to create a motion path for your graphic.

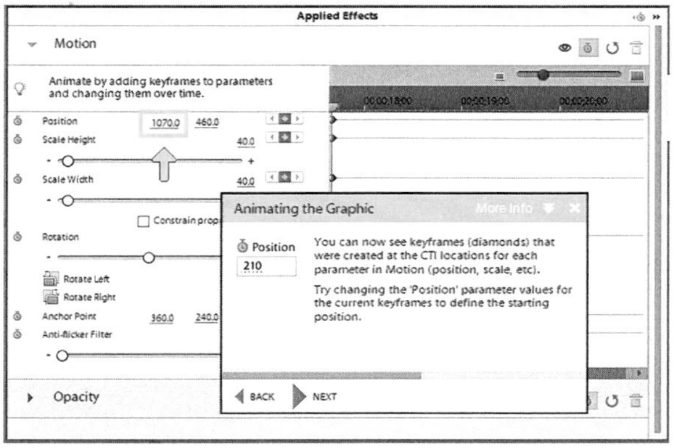

For more detailed information on creating your own custom animations with Premiere Elements, see **Chapter 15, Keyframing**.

Add an Adjustment Layer

This **Guided Edit** will walk you through the process of adding and creating motion paths for a Premiere Elements graphic, including:

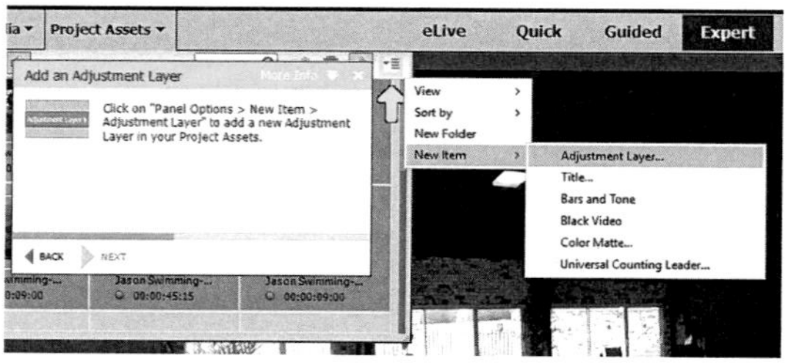

Add an Adjustment Layer by selecting the **New Item** option on the **Project Assets** panel and adding it to your timeline.

Extend the Adjustment Layer to cover your clips to be affected.

Open the Adjustments panel and adjust the **Temperature & Tint** of the clips under the **Adjustment Layer**.

For more detailed information on making adjustments and using **Adjustment Layers** with Premiere Elements, see page 126 of **Chapter 10, Make Adjustments to Your Video and Audio**.

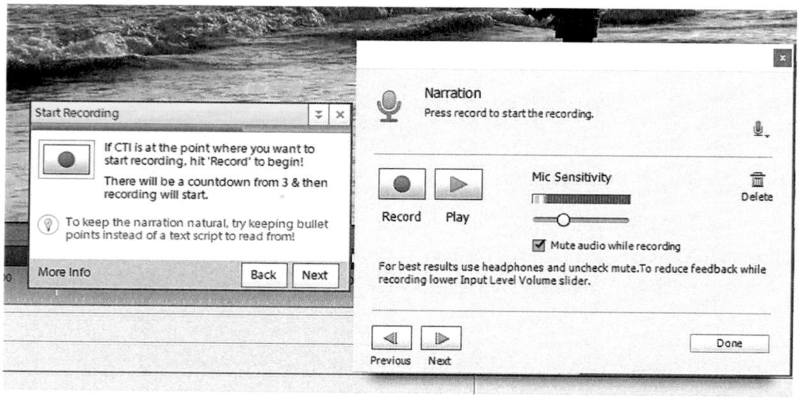

Add Narration

This **Guided Edit** will walk you step-by-step through the process of recording narration to your movie's timeline. It's steps include:

Attach Your Microphone and making sure it's properly configured in the program's ASIO Settings.

Launch the Narration Tool and starting your recording.

Stop your recording and reviewing the results.

For more detailed information on configuring your microphone and using the **Narration** tool, see **Add Narration** on page 101 of **Chapter 9, Use the Premiere Elements Toolkit**.

Add a Music Score

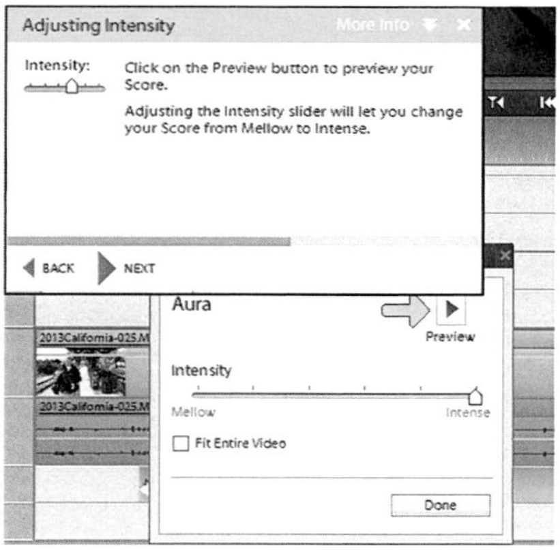

This **Guided Edit** will walk you step-by-step through the process of adding and customizing Premiere Elements music tracks, including how to:

Work with the Audio Panel and select a **Scores** track.

Adjust Intensity of the **Scores** track.

Select the Fit Entire Video option.

For more detailed information on using **Scores** to create custom music tracks in your movie, see page 191 of **Chapter 16, Mix Your Audio and Add Music.**

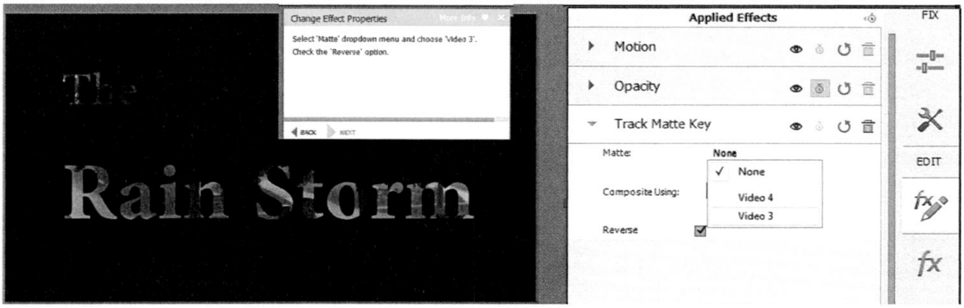

Add Video in a Title

This **Guided Edit** shows you how to use the **Track Matte** in such a way that your text becomes a sort of a cookie cutter. The result will be a black video frame with your video visible through your title's text. The **Guided Edit** shows you how to:

Create a Black Video clip using the **New Item** feature on the **Project Assets** panel and adding it to the track above your video.

Add a Title to the video track above your black video.

Add and Apply the Track Matte Key to create the cookie cutter effect, based on your title, through the black video.

Create Slow or Fast Motion Effect

This **Guided Edit** shows you how to use the **Time Remapping** tool to control your playback speed at specific points in your video. The **Guided Edit** will show you how to:

Open the Time Remapping Tool, a workspace for controlling the playback speed of your video clip.

Position the CTI Playhead to where in your clip you'd like your slow motion effect to begin.

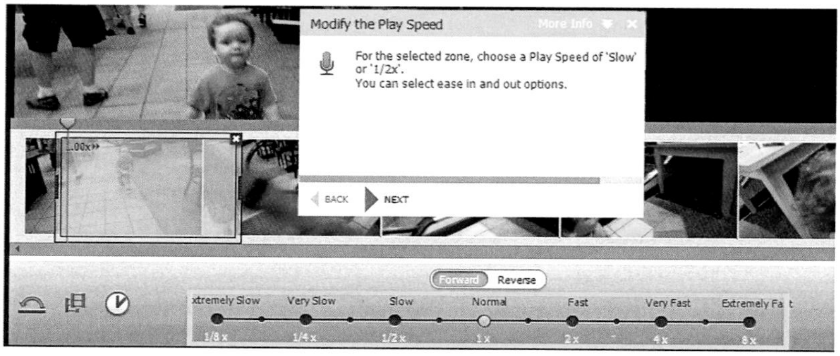

Create a Time Zone to indicate the area of your clip you'd like the slow motion effect applied to.

Set the playback speed by adjusting the **Time Remapping** slider.

For more detailed information on this tool, see **Create cool Time Remapping effects** on page 107 of **Chapter 9, Use the Premiere Elements Toolkit**.

Create a Picture-in-Picture (PIP)

This **Guided Edit** will walk you step-by-step through the process of adding a picture-in-picture inset to your movie, including how to:

Add Your PiP Video by first selecting where you'd like it to appear.

Get the Foreground Video for use as your PiP.

Set the End Point for the Overlay by trimming your PiP clip.

Adjust the Position of the Overlay over the main video clip.

Apply an Effects Mask to your video

This **Guided Edit** shows you how to use the **Effects Mask** to limit the area of your video frame that is affected by a video effect. The **Guided Edit** will show you how to:

Create an Effects Masking, which duplicates your video clip and places the duplicate on the video track directly above the original.

Adjust and Position the Mask Area to designate the area that will be affected by your effect.

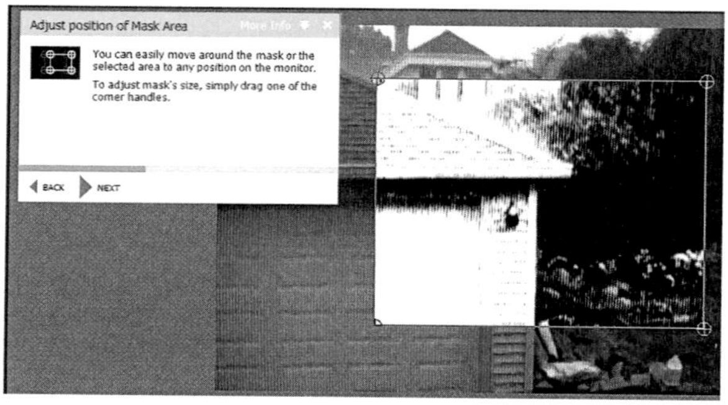

Select and apply an effect. The effect will only be applied to the area of your video within the **Effects Mask**.

For more detailed information on creating an **Effects Mask**, see **Isolate an effect area with the Effects Mask** on page 160 of **Chapter 13, Audio and Video Effects**.

Part II

Editing in Expert View

Starting a New Project

Selecting Project Settings

Opening an Existing Project

Chapter 4

Start a Premiere Elements Project

Creating and opening your video projects

In early versions of Premiere Elements, setting up your project was a vital, and sometimes challenging, part of the process of making your movie.

Much more happens automatically in Premiere Elements 15 – though there is still much to be said for making sure your project gets off to a good start.

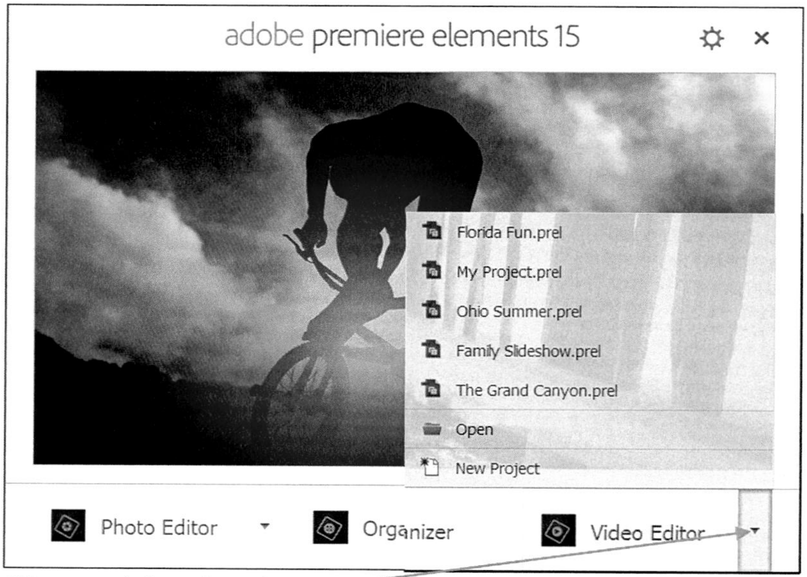

When you click on the Video Editor button, you will see the options to start a new project or open an existing one.

The Welcome Screen

When you first start up Premiere Elements, you'll be greeted by the **Welcome Screen**. Very similar to the **Welcome Screen** in Photoshop Elements, it is a launching point for the workspaces of the program.

From this **Welcome Screen** you can start a new Premiere Elements project, open an old one or launch the Elements Organizer. If you have Photoshop Elements installed on your computer, you'll also be able to launch it from this screen.

Bypass the Welcome Screen

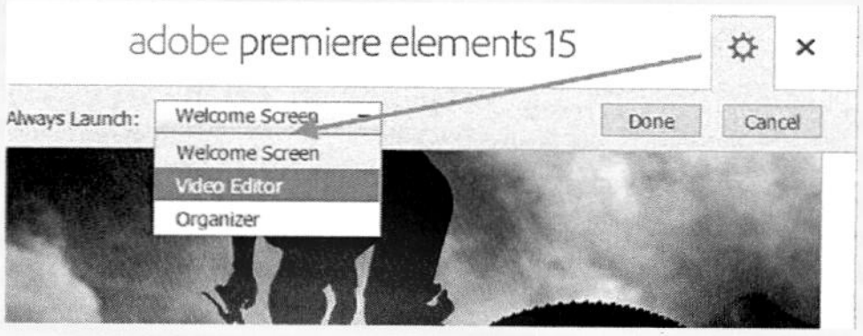

If you'd prefer not to be greeted by the **Welcome Screen**, you'll find options for setting how the program launches by clicking on the cog icon at the top right of this screen.

Your selection determines if the program opens to the **Welcome Screen**, the Elements Organizer or directly into the Premiere Elements editor.

The Elements Organizer

The Elements Organizer is a powerful media file management program that interfaces with both Premiere Elements and Photoshop Elements.

The Organizer allows you to catalog and search your media files based on a wide variety of criteria. Additionally, the Organizer includes a number of tools for creating and sharing your video and photo projects.

The Organizer reads the EXIF data from your digital photos, adds **Keyword Tags** (both manually and automatically) to your media clips, gives you the ability to sort your files into **Albums** and serves as a launching point for a number of Photoshop Elements and Premiere Elements functions.

We discuss its features and functions in more detail in **Part IV** of this book.

Start a new project

Selecting the **New Project** option from the **Welcome Screen** takes you to the Quick View or Expert View workspace of Premiere Elements. If you open in the Quick View workspace, you can go to work **Adding Media** and assembling it on your timeline (as described in **Chapter 5**).

By clicking on the Expert button at the top of the interface, you can switch the program to Expert View, with its much more powerful timeline and multi-track capabilities. In Expert View, you gather your media into the **Project Assets** panel before assembling it on the timeline.

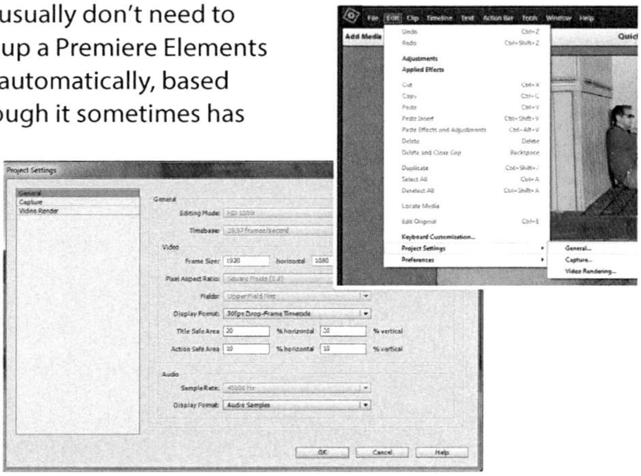

Unlike in earlier versions of the program, you usually don't need to worry about selecting settings when starting up a Premiere Elements project. The program will set up your project automatically, based on the ***first clip you add to your timelin***e. (Though it sometimes has trouble matching settings to still photos and many forms of QuickTime/MOV files – in which case we recommend you **Manually choose your Project Settings** when you start your project, as discussed on the bottom of page 42.)

Meantime, to see which settings your project is currently using, just go to the **Edit** menu and select **Project Settings**.

Starting a new Premiere Elements project

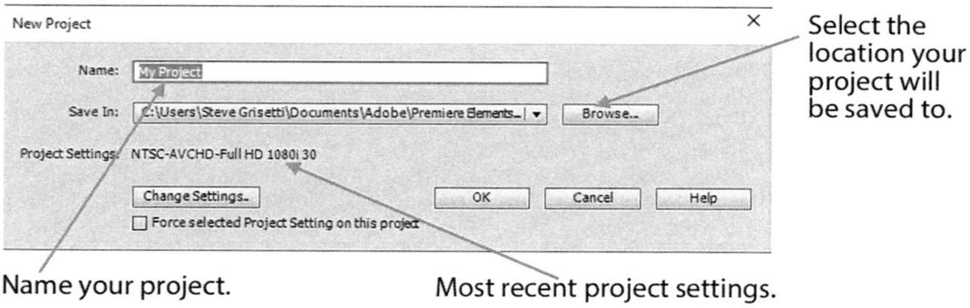

To start a new Premiere Elements project:

1 Click the **File** menu at the top of the interface and select **New** then, from the submenu, **Project**.

The **New Project** option screen will appear, as illustrated above.

Type the title for your new project in the box displayed at **Name**.

2 Click the **Browse** button to choose a location to save your new project file.

We at Muvipix recommend always selecting the **Browse** option and, wherever you choose to save your file, *creating a new folder* for every new project file.

This little bit of housekeeping keeps all of your new project's files in one neat, little folder. And, when your project is done and you want to clear it from your computer, you can then remove not only the project file but all of the temp, render and scratch disk files Premiere Elements has created for that project simply by deleting that single folder!

This makes post-project cleanup a much easier and neater process.

Manually choose your Project Settings

In most cases, it's not necessary to manually select your project's settings. Whether you're working in Quick View or Expert View the program will automatically set up your project's settings based on the specs of the first video clip you add to your timeline.

And in most cases, that's good enough.

But there are times when you'll want to impose settings on your project. You may want to set up your project for a specific purpose – creating a project for a DVD, for instance – or if you're mixing different formats of video and you don't want the program to automatically switch project settings on you. Also, at times (particularly when you're editing MOV or MP4 files), the program may have trouble recognizing your video file's specs and matching your project settings to it.

In those cases, you can opt to **Force Selected Settings** on your new project.

3 Click the **Change Settings** button at the bottom of the **New Project** panel.

This will open the **Project Settings** panel, as illustrated on the facing page.

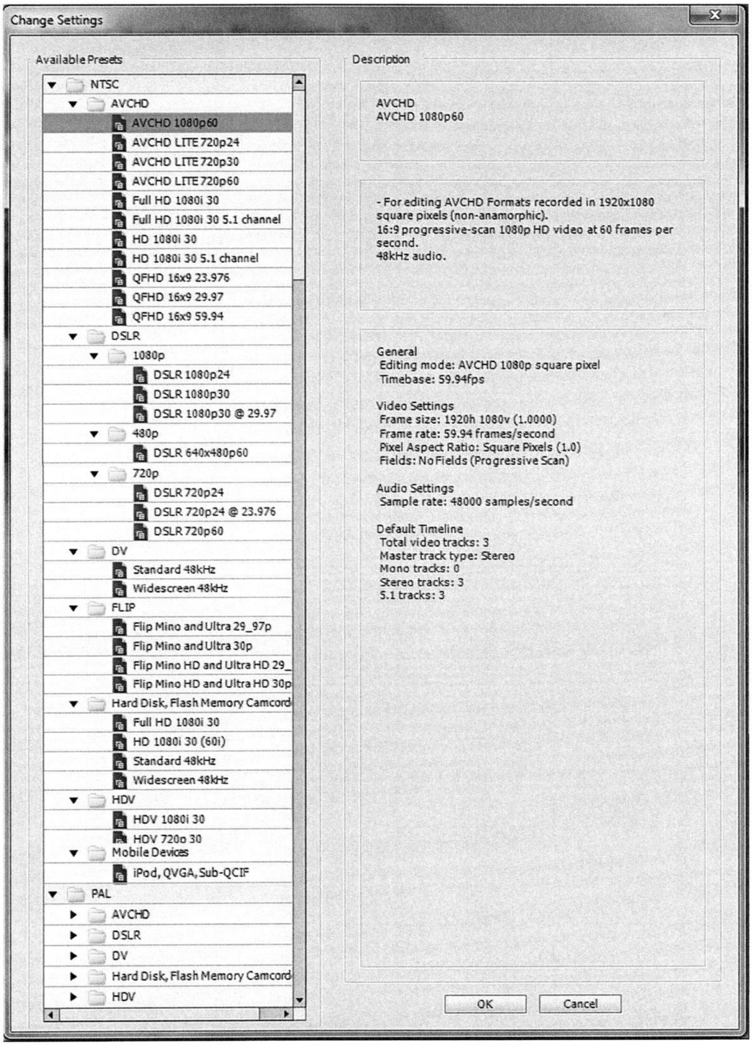

4 Select your project settings (based on the chart on the following pages).

Then click **OK**.

5 Back at the **New Project** panel, check the box **Force Selected Project Setting on This Project**, as illustrated at right.

Your project's settings will not automatically reset when you add a new clip to your timeline.

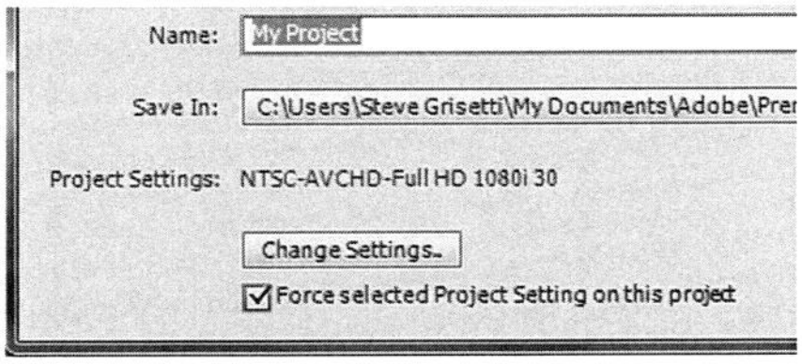

Premiere Elements 15 project preset options

Premiere Elements includes a wealth of project setting options for editing your video.

In most cases – whenever Premiere Elements recognizes the format of the video – the program will automatically select the appropriate project setting, based on the first video clip you load into your project (though it sometimes has trouble identifying MOV file specs).

AVCHD	AVCHD 1080p60	Full 1920x1080 AVCHD video shooting 60 progressive fps.
	AVCHD Lite 720p24	AVCHD video (1280x720) shooting at 23.976 progressive fps.
	AVCHD Lite 720p30	AVCHD video (1280x720) shooting at 29.97 progressive fps.
	AVCHD Lite 720p60	AVCHD video (1280x720) shooting at progressive 59.94 fps.
	Full HD 1080i 30	AVCHD video (1920x1080 60i/30 fps square pixel, hard drive, high definition) from camcorders that shoot in stereo audio.
	Full HD 1080i 30 5.1 Channel	AVCHD video (1920x1080 60i/30 fps square pixel, hard drive, high-definition) from camcorders that shoot in 5.1 channel audio. *This is the most common format for most newer hard drive, high-definition camcorders.*
	HD 1080 30	AVCHD video (1440x1080 60i/30 fps non-square pixel, hard drive, high definition) from camcorders that shoot in stereo audio.
	HD 1080 30 5.1 Channel	AVCHD video (1440x1080 60i/30 fps non-square pixel, hard drive, high-definition) from camcorders that shoot in 5.1 channel audio. This is the most common format for older hard drive, high-definition camcorders. *Note that, although this format uses less horizontal pixels, it produces the same high-quality, 16:9 image as 1920x1080 video. The pixels are just non-square, or wider than they are tall – as in the traditional television standard.*
	QFHD 16x9 23.976	4K files at 3840x2160 pixel resolution, 23.976 fps.
	QFHD 16x9 29.97	4K files at 3840x2160 pixel resolution, 29.97 fps.
	QFHD 16x9 59.94	4K files at 3840x2160 pixel resolution, 59.94 fps.
DSLR Presets – Use these presets for working with high-quality video from digital still cameras (such as the Canon EOS Movie Full HD series).		
1080p	DSLR 1080p24	1920x1080 16:9 video shooting at 23.976 progressive fps.
	DSLR 1080p30	1920x1080 16:9 video shooting at 30 progressive fps.
	DSLR 1080p30 @29.97	1920x1080 16:9 video shooting at 29.97 progressive fps.
480p	DSLR 640x480p60	640x480 16:9 video shooting at 59.94 progressive fps.
720p	DSLR 720p24	1280x720 16:9 video shooting at 24 progressive fps.
	DSLR 720p24 @23.976	1280x720 16:9 video shooting at 23.976 progressive fps.
	DSLR 720p60	1280x720 16:9 video shooting at 59.94 progressive fps.

continued on facing page

More Premiere Elements project presets

DV	Standard 48 khz	720x480 4:3 video from miniDV tape-based camcorders.
	Widescreen 48 khz	720x480 16:9 video from miniDV tape-based camcorders.
Flip	Flip Mino or Ultra Flip 29.97	Flip standard definition (640x480) video camcorders shooting at 29.97 fps.
	Flip Mino or Ultra Flip 30	Flip standard definition (640x480) video camcorders shooting at 30 fps.
	Flip Mino HD or Ultra HD 29.97	Flip high definition (1280x720) video camcorders shooting at 29.97 fps.
	Flip Mino HD or Ultra HD 30	Flip high definition (1280x720) video camcorders shooting at 30 fps.
Hard Disk, Flash Memory Camcorder	HD 1080i 30	High-definition video (1920x1080) from non-AVCHD hard drive or flash memory camcorders (such as the JVC GZ-HD7).
	HD 1080i 30 (60i)	High-definition video from (1440x1080) from non-AVCHD hard drive or flash memory camcorders that record in 60i format. (The PAL equivalent is, of course, 50i.)
	Standard 48kHz	Standard-definition (720x480) 4:3 video from hard drive camcorders as well as video from DVDs. *It is very important to use this or the following preset with standard-definition MPEG or VOB sources because it will automatically reverse the field dominance in your video, correcting an interlacing issue that can otherwise cause stuttering in your output videos.*
	Widescreen 48 kHz	Video from standard-definition (720x480) 16:9 hard drive camcorders and video from DVDs.
HDV Presets	HDV 1080i 30	Video from tape-based, high-definition HDV camcorders that shoot full HDV at 1440x1080 pixels.
	HDV 720p 30	Video from tape-based, high-definition HDV camcorders that shoot full HDV at 1280x720 pixels (progressive scan at 30 fps).
Mobile Devices	iPods, QVGA, Sub-QCIF	Video from iPods or other mobile devices shooting 640x480 (progressive scan 15 fps). Video shot at 1280x720p using iPads, smartphones or other devices will use the Flip HD 30 fps project settings.

PAL presets

The PAL and NTSC options are identical except that the frame rates for PAL presets are 25 fps rather than 30. Additionally, video listed on this chart as shooting at 60i or 60p would appear as 50i and 50p in the PAL system.

There are no Flip presets for PAL. All project presets for Flip cameras are located under NTSC.

The PAL standard definition video frame (the DV and Hard Disk presets for standard and widescreen) would appear as 720x576 rather than 720x480.

Open an old project from the Welcome Screen

Clicking the **Existing Project** button on the **Welcome Screen** will get you access to any work-in-progress or old Premiere Elements projects.

Your most recent projects will appear in the drop-down menu, as illustrated on page 40. Additional Premiere Elements projects on your computer can be accessed by selecting the **Existing Project** option.

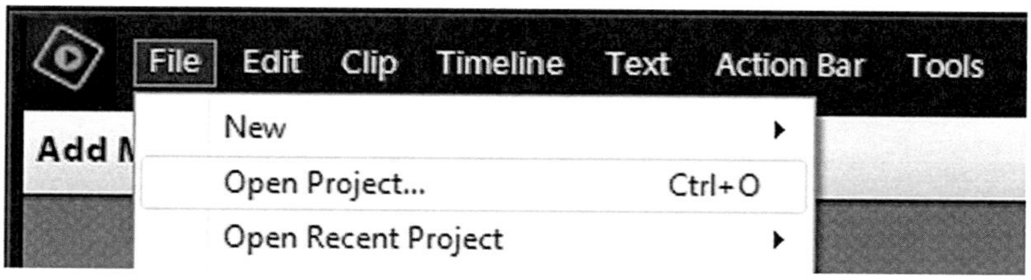

Open a project from within the program

Naturally, you don't have to go all the way out to the **Welcome Screen** to create a new project or to re-open an old one.

Both options are available from the **File** drop-down menu on the top left of the program's interface.

Selecting Ne**w Project** from this menu gives you access to the same **New Project** settings available from the **Welcome Screen**.

Open a project created by a previous version of the program?

Our advice: Don't do it.

It should work. And sometimes it does work. But, for the most part, Premiere Elements goes through such an overhaul from generation to generation, that it usually just leads to trouble. Open only version 15 projects with version 15, version 13 projects with version 13, etc.

Doing otherwise often leads to buggy behavior – audio tracks that mysteriously disappear, clips that behave really strangely, a **Project Assets** panel that seems to have lost its mind. And sometime the project file is even corrupted and made unusable.

Your smartest workflow is to finish your Premiere Elements project in the same version of the program you began it in. Trust us on this.

Once it's far enough along that you consider it (or the segment you're working on) to be finished, you can export it from your current project and then import the finished video into a new version 15 project, as described in **Output video for use in another project** on page 259.

But we very much recommend against opening, say, a version 10 project in version 15.

Getting Video from Your Camcorder

Importing Media Already on Your Computer

Working with Photos

Working with Music

Chapter 5

Add Media to Your Project

Capturing video and importing video, audio and photos into your project

Whether you're working in Expert View or Quick View, before you can edit your video, you need to get it (along with your other source media) into your Premiere Elements project.

This is a relatively simple process, but unfortunately one that can occasionally present some challenges.

Before you can begin editing your Premiere Elements movie, you need to gather your video, still photos, music and audio clips into your project.

The tools for gathering this media can be accessed by clicking on the **Add Media** tab at the top left of the interface or by using one of the other options listed in the sidebar at the bottom of this page.

The options that appear on this **Add Media** pop-up panel launch any of a number of built-in utilities for gathering your media clips.

Because Premiere Elements does not include capture software for interfacing with miniDV and HDV camcorders, we've included information on getting video from both digital and analog tape-based camcorders using third-party software in our Appendix, starting on page 275.

As the chart on the facing page indicates, there are really only three basic ways to get your media files into a Premier Elements project:

Download your media from a camcorder or other device over a USB connection or rip it from your computer's DVD/CD drive;

Capture live video from your webcam or WDM device; or

Import media that is already on your computer into your project from your hard drive folders or through the Elements Organizer.

Once you've streamed, downloaded or imported your media into your Premiere Elements project, you can either add it directly to your project's timeline (in Quick View) or gather it into your **Project Assets** panel (in Expert View) in preparation for assembling it into a movie on your timeline (as we discuss in **Chapter 6**).

In this chapter, we'll look at each of the major media devices and media file sources and show you how to best gather your media from each.

We'll also show you how to work with photos, music and other media.

Four ways to the Add Media option menu

1. Click on the **Add Media** tab; or
2. **Right-click** on a blank area in the **Project Assets** panel and select the **Get Media From** option; or
3. Select **Add Media From** from the **File** drop-down menu; or
4. Drag media to your project directly from the Elements Organizer's **Media Browser** (see **Chapter 17**).

Methods for adding media

There are three basic ways to get media into your Premiere Elements project:

- **Download** your video or other media from a hard drive or SD card-based memory camcorder, camera or other device over a USB connection;
- **Capture** live video from your Webcam or WDM device; or
- **Import** media into your project from your computer's hard drive.

The chart below lists the methods of getting media from a number of sources.

MiniDV tape-based camcorders	Capture video over a FireWire connection using a third-party program like WinDV (see page 275 of the **Appendix**) and then **import** it into your project using **Add Media/Files and Folders**.
HDV tape-based hi-def camcorders	Capture video over a FireWire connection using a third-party program like HDV Split (see page 275 of the **Appendix**) and then **import** it into your project using **Add Media/Files and Folders**.
Webcams	**Capture** live video using the Premiere Elements capture interface as discussed on page 53.
AVCHD and other hard drive hi-def camcorders	**Download** video from your camcorder to your computer using the Premiere Elements **Video Importer** over a USB connection as discussed on page 52.
GoPro or other sport camcorders or portable devices, like smartphones and iPads	**Download** video from your camcorder or device to your computer using the Premiere Elements **Video Importer** over a USB connection as discussed on page 53.
Flash-based or memory card camcorders, such as the JVC-GZ series	**Download** video from your camcorder to your computer using the Premiere Elements **Video Importer** over a USB connection as discussed on page 52.
DVD camcorders or DVDs	With the finalized disc in your computer's DVD drive, rip and **download** the video files to your computer using the **Video Importer** as discussed on page 54.
Analog video	Capture through a DV bridge or pass-through set-up then **import** it into your project, as discussed on page 276.
Digital still cameras and other portable devices, such as iPads, iPods and phones.	**Download** stills from the camera using the Premiere Elements **Photo Downloader** or video using the **Video Importer** over a USB connection as discussed on page 54.
Music or audio from CDs	Rip the music to your hard drive from the CD and then **import** it into the file(s) using the **Add Media** option **PC Files or Folders** as discussed on page 54.
Video, music or still photos already on your computer's hard drive	**Import** media into your project by browsing to it using the **Add Media** option **PC Files or Folders** as discussed on page 54 or by locating it through the Elements Organizer's **Media Browser** as discussed on page 51.

Add Media options

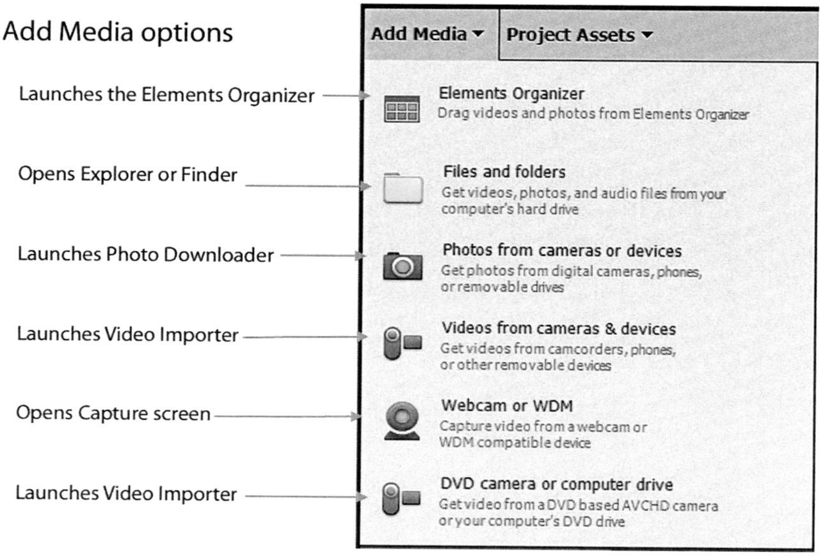

Premiere Elements' Add Media tools

The tools for bringing your media into your project are most simply launched from the **Add Media** pop-up panel, opened by clicking the tab at the top left of the interface.

On this panel, Premiere Elements offers six options for bringing your media into your project (as illustrated above).

- The **Elements Organizer** option will launch the Organizer's **Media Browser** within the **Add Media** panel, as illustrated on the facing page. As we discuss in **Chapter 17**, the **Elements Organizer** is a companion file management program that can be used to manage and search media files on your computer.
- The **Files and Folders** option will open Windows Explorer or the OSX Finder so that you can import media already on your computer (as discussed on page 55).
- The **Photos from Cameras or Devices** option will launch the Adobe **Photo Downloader** (as discussed on page 54), an interface for selecting and downloading still images from a camera or other portable device.
- The **Videos from Cameras & Devices** option will launch the **Video Importer** (see pages 52-54), an interface for selecting and downloading video from a camcorder or other video recording device.
- The **Webcam or WDM** option will launch the program's video capture workspace (see page 53), an interface through which you capture your live Webcam video.
- The **DVD Camera or Computer Drive** option will launch the **Video Importer** (see page 54), which can be used to select and rip video from a DVD disc.

The Organizer media browser

Media files on your computer can be accessed through the Elements Organizer's Media Browser.

Media in the Organizer can be searched by clicking the search button in the upper right corner of the panel, media can be filtered by selecting a media type, or media can be located by selecting an Album or or sub-Album.

Add media from the Organizer

The Elements Organizer is a file management program that comes bundled with Premiere Elements and Photoshop Elements.

When you select the **Elements Organizer** option under the **Add Media** tab, the Organizer's **Media Browser** will open within the panel. From this panel, you can access any video, photos or audio files in your Organizer catalog. (For information on creating a catalog and using the Organizer's file management tools, see **Chapter 17**.)

To search your media files, click on the magnifying class at the top right of the panel and type in a search term, as illustrated above.

To filter your media files by type, turn on or off the photo, video and audio filter buttons on the top right of the panel.

To see only media files you've assigned to a particular Album, select an **Album** from the listing along the left side of the panel.

Once you've selected the media files you'd like to add to your project, click the **Add Files** button along the lower right of the panel.

Your video or photo files will be added to your **Project Media** as well as added to the **Video 1/Audio 1** tracks on your timeline.

If the **CTI** is positioned within rather than at the end of your movie, the new clips will be *inserted* into your movie and all clips to the right on the timeline will ripple further right. For more information on inserting clips into your movies, see **Controlling your timeline's ripple function** on page 71.

Click **Done** to return to the Premiere Elements editing workspace.

The Video Importer

Select the camcorder or device you're connecting to from the drop-down list (such as your computer's DVD drive, if you are "ripping" files from a disk to your computer).

Check the boxes next to the clips you'd like to download to your computer.

Any video clip can be previewed before being selected for download.

Add video from AVCHD, Hard Drive, Flash Drive or SD Card camcorders

As with other hard drive camcorders, the video from AVCHD camcorders is downloaded into Premiere Elements.

1. Connect your AVCHD camcorder (in VTR mode) to your computer's USB port.
2. Select the **Videos from Cameras & Devices** option from the **Add Media** panel.

   This will launch the **Video Importer**, illustrated above.
3. Select your camcorder from the **Source** drop-down menu at the top of the **Video Importer**. The clips on the camcorder will be displayed as thumbnails, which can be selected and previewed.
4. Set the **Save In** menu to indicate where on your computer you'd like to save your downloaded files.
5. By default, your video clips will be copied to your hard drive maintaining the random name assigned to them by your camcorder.

   To give your video clips a custom name, set the **Presets** drop-down menu to **Custom Name-Number**. The clips will then be renamed as they are copied to your hard drive in the form CustomName-001, CustomName-002, etc.
6. Use the **checkboxes** to select which clips you'd like copied to your hard drive.

   You may also select the option to **Delete the Clips After Copying** from your camcorder, **Add the Clips to the Timeline** and/or send the clips directly to an **InstantMovie** (see page 84)
7. Click **Get Media** to download your selected clips to your hard drive and add them to your Premiere Elements project.

Add video from Go Pro, Flip camcorders, iPads, iPods, smartphones and other portable devices

While some devices plug right into your computer, most devices are attached via USB cable. As with hard drive camcorders, the video from Flip camcorders is *downloaded* rather than streamed or captured into Premiere Elements.

1. Connect your sport camcorder, iPad, smartphone or other video device to your computer's USB port.
2. Select the **Videos from Cameras & Devices** option from the **Add Media** panel.

   This will launch the **Video Importer**, as illustrated on page 52.
3. Select your media recording device (Flip, smartphone, iPod, etc.) from the **Source** drop-down menu at the top of the **Video Importer**, then browse and select the video clips you'd like to add to your project.
4. Set the **Save In** menu to indicate where on your computer you'd like to save your downloaded files.
5. Click **Get Media** to download your selected clips to your hard drive and add them to your Premiere Elements project.

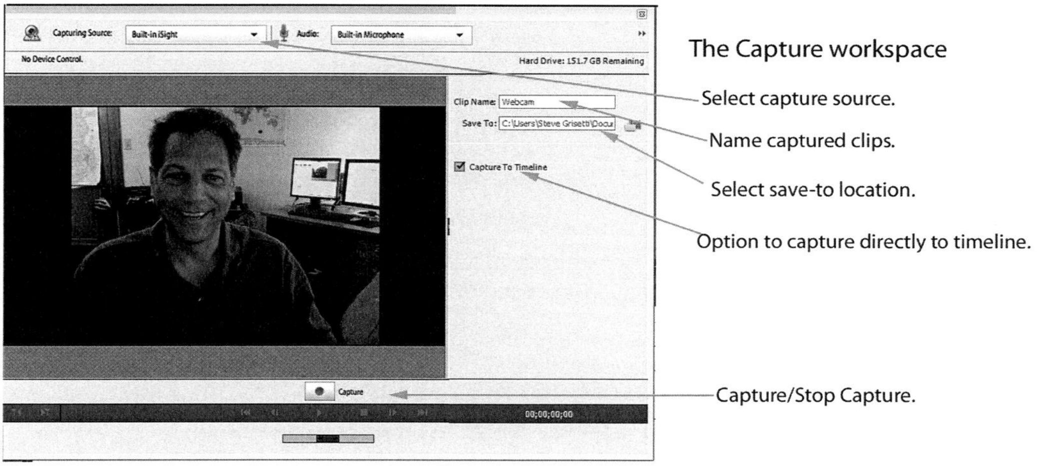

The Capture workspace

Capture video from Webcams or WDM Devices

The **Capture** workspace in Premiere Elements is capable of capturing live video from most Webcams and other Windows Driver Model devices.

To capture webcam video:

1. Select the **Webcam or WDM** option from the **Add Media** panel.

   This will launch the **Capture** workspace, as illustrated above.
2. When you are ready to capture your live video, click the red dot **Capture** button.

   When want to stop your capture, click the **Stop Capture** button.

Add video from DVDs and DVD Camcorders

Video from DVDs or DVD camcorders is downloaded into Premiere Elements using Adobe's **Video Importer** software, as illustrated on page 52.

To get video from a DVD or DVD camcorder:

1. Place the DVD into your computer's DVD drive

   Note that discs from DVD camcorders must be *finalized* before Premiere Elements can rip the video from them.

2. Select the **DVD Camera or Computer Drive** option from the **Add Media** panel.

   This will launch the **Video Importer**, as illustrated on page 52.

3. Select your computer's DVD drive from the **Source** drop-down menu at the top of the **Video Importer**, then browse and select the video clips you'd like to rip to your project.

4. Click the **Save In** button to indicate where on your computer you'd like to save the DVD's files, then click the **Get Media** button at the bottom of the panel to rip the selected video clips to your hard drive.

Add video from DSLR still cameras and other devices

As with hard drive camcorders, the video from digital cameras and smartphones is *downloaded* rather than streamed or captured into Premiere Elements.

1. Connect your device to your computer's USB port.

2. Select the **Videos from Cameras & Devices** option from the **Add Media** panel.

   This will launch the **Video Importer,** illustrated on page 52.

3. Select your USB-connected device from the **Source** drop-down menu at the top of the **Video Importer**, then browse and select the video clips you'd like to add to your project.

4. Click the **Save In** button to indicate where on your computer you'd like to save your selected clips, then click the **Get Media** button at the bottom of the panel to download your video.

Add still photos from digital cameras and cell phones

1. Connect your still camera to your computer's USB port.

2. Select the **Photos from Cameras or Devices** option from the **Add Media** panel.

   This will launch the **Photo Downloader** as illustrated at the top of page 55.

3. From the **Add Media From** drop-down menu at the top of the **Photo Downloader**, select your camera or other device – then browse and select the photos you'd like to add to your project.

4. Click the **Browse** button to indicate where on your computer you'd like to save the captured files, then click the **Get Media** button at the bottom of the panel to download your video or photos.

As we indicate in **Use photos in your Premiere Elements project** on page 56, for best results your still photos should be resized to an optimal, video resolution size.

The Photo Downloader

Select your camera or other photo device from the drop-down list at Get Photos From.

Import photos, video, music and other audio files that are already on your computer's hard drive into your project

To load video, audio or stills already on your computer into your Premiere Elements project:

1. Select the **Files and Folders** option on the **Add Media** panel (or select the **Elements Organizer** option to launch the Elements Organizer program, as described on page 51).
2. Browse to the file(s) you'd like to import on your hard drive.

   Select the file or files you'd like to add and click **Open**.

You can also quickly open a browse screen from which to import your media files by **double-clicking** on a blank space (beyond the media listings) in the **Project Assets** panel.

Music and other audio clips

We've learned from experience that you'll get the best performance from Premiere Elements if you only use music and other audio files in your projects that are in the **WAV** format – even if you're using the Mac version of the program. (Most audio formats can be converted to WAVs using the free PC-based software **Audacity**, as we discuss on page 275 of our **Appendix**.)

Also, note that many musical clips (***particularly those downloaded from iTunes***) include **digital rights management**, copy protection software that will prohibit their use in Premiere Elements. Adding protected music to your project will often trigger an error message.

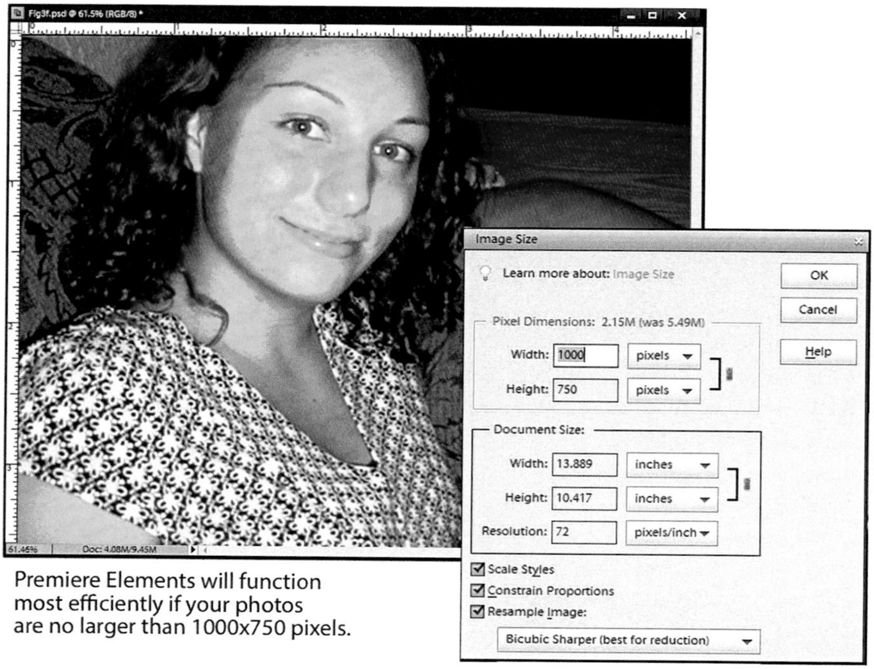

Premiere Elements will function most efficiently if your photos are no larger than 1000x750 pixels.

Use photos in Premiere Elements

Premiere Elements can work with virtually any of the major photo or graphics formats, including JPEGs, GIFs, TIFs and PSDs (native Photoshop and Photoshop Elements files).

The exceptions are images using the CMYK color mode or RGB photo files using other than standard 8-bit color. But, if you are creating your graphics or using photos from a consumer graphics program (such as Photoshop Elements) or from a digital camera, scanner or other device, then you don't need to worry about these exceptions. Virtually all photo and graphics files from these sources are compatible with the program.

Premiere Elements will also support transparency (alpha channels) so that file formats like GIF, PNG and PSD files with transparent areas will display, when used in a video project, with these areas transparent.

This is particularly useful if you're using one of these graphics file types on an upper video track with a video layer behind it (see **Use L-cuts, J-cuts and multiple tracks** on page 78 of **Chapter 7, Edit Your Video in Expert View**) or as a graphic added to a title (see **Add a graphic to your title** on page 147 of **Chapter 12, Add Titles & Text**).

Photos make great source files for a Premiere Elements project, but you'll find the highest quality results and the best performance from the program if the sizes of your photos are properly optimized before you bring them into your project.

We urge you to make sure that any photo you use (especially if you use several in a slideshow) has been resized to no larger than 1000x750 pixels for a standard DV or DVD project or 2500x1875 pixels for a high-definition video project before you bring it into your Premiere Elements project. This will ensure the best quality and optimal program performance. (Photos taken directly from digital cameras can be 10 to 25 times that size!)

At first this may seem to go contrary to common wisdom.

Traditionally, the higher the resolution of your photo, the better the quality of the output. But remember that Premiere Elements is a *video* editing program, and video is a relatively low resolution medium (essentially the equivalent of 640x480 pixels). And, to a point, reducing the resolution of a photo or graphic to be used in a video actually *improves* the quality of the video output. (1000x750 pixels and 2500x1875 pixels seem to be that sweet spot for standard definition and high-def video, respectively.)

The reason for this has to do with a process called downsampling, the system a video program uses to bring high-resolution photos down to video resolution. Premiere Elements does a fair job of this – but, as any pro knows, nothing that happens automatically will be as clean or as efficient as what you do manually. "Down-rezzing" is definitely one of those things.

But there's also a more pressing reason for downsampling your photos yourself. The process of "down-rezzing," like the process of assimilating non-DV-AVI files into a video project, is a very intensive process. So intensive, in fact, that it is *the single biggest reason Premiere Elements crashes*, particularly during the rendering or disc burning process.

It also takes a lot longer for the program to down-rez, for instance, a 4000x3000 pixel photo than it does a 1000x750 pixel photo.

Much, much longer. And would you rather wait a half an hour or so for the program to create your DVD or 10 hours for a process that might end up with the program choking and dying anyway?

Graphics and photo formats for Premiere Elements projects

For photos, the most size-efficient file format is the JPEG. As an alternative, PSD files and TIFs use less compression and, though larger, also produce excellent results.

However, because JPEGs are highly compressed, they do not make the best format for graphics that include clean, distinct edges, such as logos or graphics that include text.

For photos or image files that include text or other fine-edged graphics, PSDs, TIFs and even PNGs produce the crispest lines.

Trust us on this. Optimize your photo sizes to 1000x750 pixels for standard definition video or DVDs and 2500x1875 pixels for a high-definition video project before you import them into Premiere Elements. It can save you hours of anguish and misery in the end.

Photoshop Elements, by the way, has a very nice batch resizing feature that can resize a whole folder full of photos in just a few clicks. This feature is called **Process Multiple Files**, and it is located under the Photoshop Elements **File** menu.

Also, *before* you do bring those photos into your video project, go to Premiere Elements' **Preferences/General** (under the **Edit** menu on a PC) and uncheck **Default Scale to Frame Size**.

Left checked, **Scale to Frame Size** automatically squeezes down your photo to fill your video frame, giving a false representation of your photo's size – in addition to negatively impacting resolution when you're trying to add motion paths to your photos.

In the event this option was checked when you imported your photos into your project, you can also turn it off for each photos individually by **right-clicking** on each photo on the timeline and unchecking the **Scale to Frame Size** option on its pop-up menu.

For information on applying flicker removal to the photos and still graphics in your Premiere Elements project, see **Add still photos to your project** on page 76 of **Chapter 7, Edit Your Project in Expert View**.

The Project Assets Panel

Color Bars and Countdown Leaders

The Clip Monitor

The Create Slideshow Tool

Chapter 6

Explore the Project Assets Panel

The parts that will form your movie

In Expert view, Project Assets is the panel into which you will gather the video, still photos, music and audio that you will use to create your movie.

In the Project Assets panel, you can arrange and categorize your project's media files and then pre-trim them prior to adding them to your timeline.

Only available in Expert view, the **Project Assets** panel is the area where you gather the media you've captured, downloaded or imported into your project.

The **Project Assets** panel is opened by clicking on the **Project Assets** button on the upper left of the program's interface.

But in addition to serving as a holding area for your video project's media, this panel includes a number of great tools for managing, ordering and preparing your clips for your movie's timeline.

Where are my Project Assets in Quick view?

Quick View does not include a **Project Assets** panel.

In Quick View, any media files you add to your project are added directly to your timeline.

However, Expert and Quick View are actually just two views of the same project. Media files added directly to your timeline in Quick View are added to the Project Assets panel automatically.

So, if you switch from Quick view to Expert view while working on your project, you will find that any media you've added to your Quick View timeline has automatically been added to that project's Expert View **Project Assets** also.

Project Asset views

By default, the media clips in your **Project Assets** panel are displayed in **Grid View** – video and stills displaying as thumbnails and music and other audio displaying as speaker icons. Below the title for each clip is an indicator of the clip's duration (measured in hours, minutes, seconds and frames). Clips used in your movie project are indicated with a little green dot.

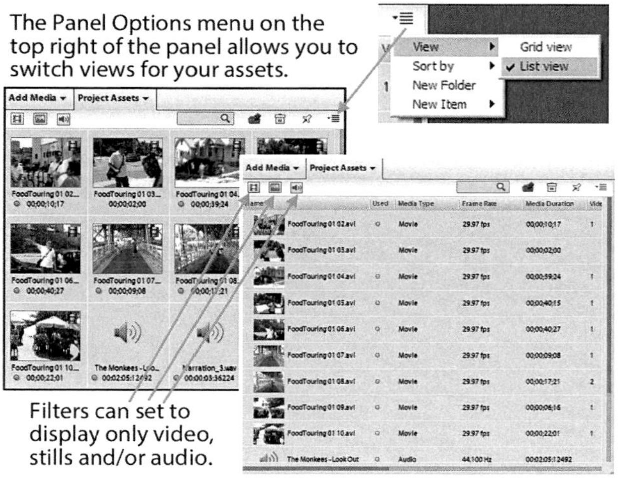
The Panel Options menu on the top right of the panel allows you to switch views for your assets.
View
Sort by
New Folder
New Item
Grid view
List view
Add Media
Project Assets
Filters can set to display only video, stills and/or audio.

To switch your **Project Assets** to **List View**, click on the **Panel Options** button in the upper right of the panel and select **View**, as illustrated to the right.

In **List View**, your media clips appear in a list with columns listing their **Media Type, Frame Rate** and **Duration**. In the **Used** column, a little blue dot indicates that your clip is in use on your timeline and the **Video Usage** column indicates how many times your clip appears in your movie.

The clip listing can be re-ordered by clicking on the column header for any column. For instance, clicking on the **Media Duration** column header will list your clips according to the length of each clip. Clicking on a column header a second time will reverse the order for that column's listing.

Along the top left of the panel are three buttons for toggling on and off which media are displayed in the panel. If you toggle on the **Video** button, for instance, and you toggle off the **Still Image** and **Audio** buttons, you will filter the panel to display *only* the video in your project and hide the other two types of media files.

Organize your media files with folders

View
Sort by
New Folder
New Item

This is one of my favorite Premiere Elements features, extremely valuable when you're trying to sort through a large number of media files.

Folders allow you to sort the clips in your **Project Assets** panel into little bundles, like directory folders on your computer, making it easier to keep all the clips you'll need for a given segment of your project in one neat little place.

To create a folder, select the **New Folder** option under the **Panel Options** menu at the upper right of the panel. (You can also select the option from a context menu when you **right-click** on an empty area of the **Project Asset** panel.)

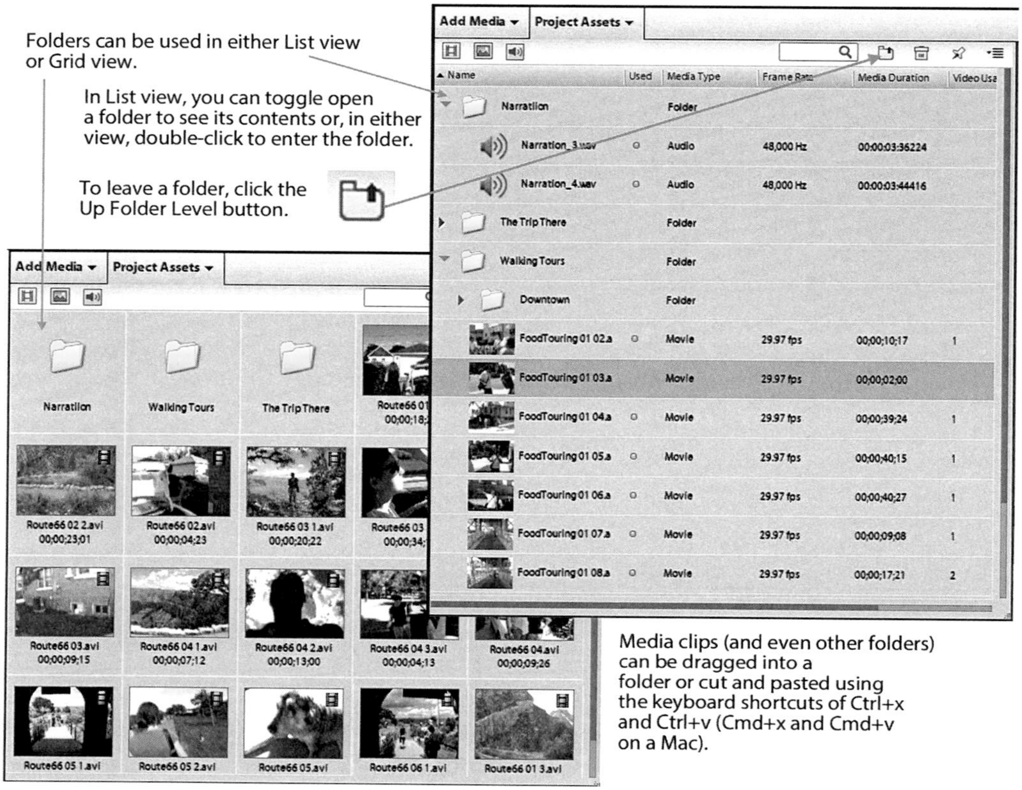

Folders can be used in either List view or Grid view.
In List view, you can toggle open a folder to see its contents or, in either view, double-click to enter the folder.
To leave a folder, click the Up Folder Level button.
Media clips (and even other folders) can be dragged into a folder or cut and pasted using the keyboard shortcuts of Ctrl+x and Ctrl+v (Cmd+x and Cmd+v on a Mac).

Once you have a folder created, you can drag your media files into it – sorting your clips so that all of your files for a particular sequence of your project are in the same folder, for instance.

You can even create sub-folders within your folders – and even sub-sub-folders! – so that it becomes very easy to manage and locate the files you need without having to scroll through a long list of clips.

Even as you're editing, you can drag your media clips around, and in and out, of folders to get them out of your way without affecting their positions or function on your timeline.

Delete clips from your Project Assets panel

There are two ways to remove a clip from your project:

Right-click on the clip in **Project Assets** and select **Clear**; or

Select a clip in **Project Assets** and press your keyboard's **Delete** key.

Either way, the media clip will be removed from your project – though it will *not* be deleted from your computer's hard drive.

Create color mattes, bars and tone and countdown leaders

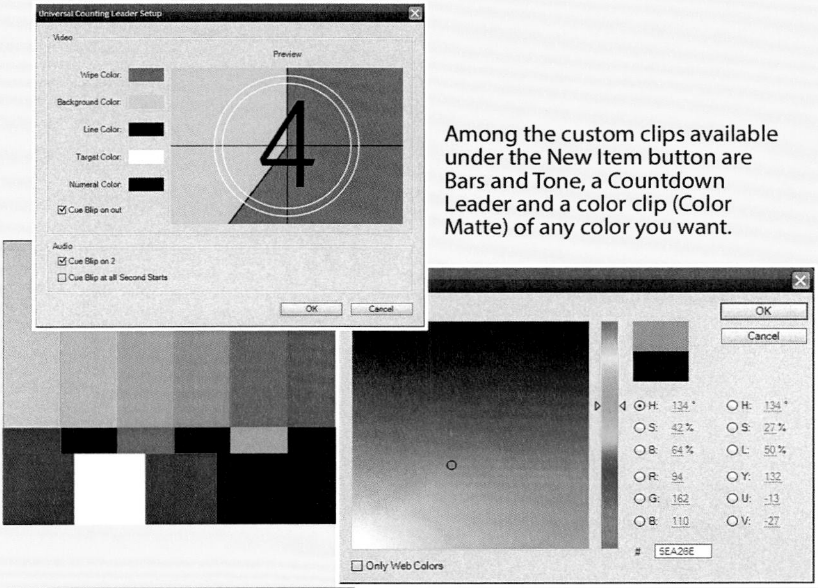

Among the custom clips available under the New Item button are Bars and Tone, a Countdown Leader and a color clip (Color Matte) of any color you want.

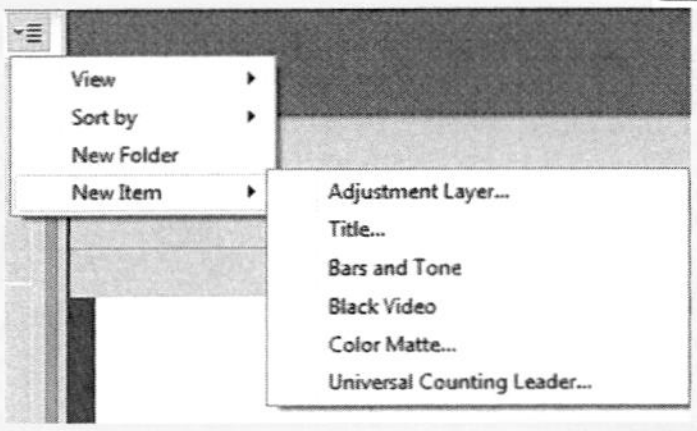

A host of very cool tools for creating special clips are available under the **New Item** sub-menu on the **Panel Options** menu on the upper right of the panel.

These special clips include:

Adjustment Layer creates a layer from which you can make non-permanent adjustments to your video. We discuss this feature in more detail on page 126.

Title launches the Premiere Elements **Titles & Text** workspace. We explore this tool in much greater detail in **Chapter 12, Add Titles & Text.**

Bars and Tone creates a clip of color bars and audio tone, which broadcasters often require at the beginning of a video in order to calibrate their equipment to your movie's sound levels and color profile.

Black Video and **Color Matte** create blank clips of whatever color you designate. These clips can then be used behind titles or as blank spaces in your video.

Universal Countdown Leader (not available on the Mac version) creates a customizable countdown sequence (including an audio "blip" at two seconds) that can be placed at the beginning of your video – another feature broadcasters often require so that they can cue up the beginning of your movie.

Pre-trim your clips in the Clip Monitor

The **Clip Monitor** is a pop-up screen for previewing playback of a clip. It's also a work area in which you can pre-trim a clip prior to adding it to your project's timeline by setting **In** and/or **Out** markers.

The **Clip Monitor** can be used to trim clips in the **Project Assets** panel or clips that have already been added to your timeline.

A clip's **Clip Monitor** is launched either by **right-clicking** on the clip and selecting the **Open in Clip Monitor** option – or by simply **double-clicking** on the clip.

Running along the bottom of the **Clip Monitor** is a little timeline representing the duration of the clip.

As illustrated on the facing page, when you set **In** or **Out** markers in your **Clip Monitor**, only the segment of the clip between those markers will be displayed during the clip's playback in your movie.

In other words, if you have a 5-minute clip, you can set the **In** and **Out** markers so that only a 30-second segment of the clip is actually displayed in your movie – rendering the clip essentially a 30-second clip.

In the **Clip Monitor,** the "live" segment of the clip is indicated with a lighter, blue segment area on the **Clip Monitor's** mini-timeline. You can adjust this live area's length by either dragging the end points in or out, or by playing the clip using the playback controls at the bottom of the **Clip Monitor** and pressing the "i" on your keyboard to set an in point or the "o" to set an out point..

The **In** and **Out** markers in the **Clip Monitor** can be used to isolate segments in audio clips as well as video.

Take a shortcut to "Add Media"

If you want to import additional media from your computer into your Premiere Elements project, or if you want to launch a video capture without leaving the **Project Assets** panel, there is a shortcut to the **Add Media** option menu built right into the panel.

As illustrated at the top of page 66, if you **right-click** on a *blank* area of the **Project Assets** panel, beyond your media listings, you will have access to the same **Add Media** options as are available on the **Add Media** panel.

Additionally, you can quickly open a browse screen so that you can import media already on your computer by simply **double-clicking** on a blank area after your **Project Assets** panel's listings.

The Clip Monitor launches when you double-click on any clip on the timeline or in the Project Assets panel.

Clips can be trimmed in the Clip Monitor either by dragging the in and out points on the mini-timeline or by playing the clip and pressing the i ("in") and o ("out) keys on your keyboard.

Although the original clip remains its original length, only the "trimmed" segment (the blue highlighted segment in Premiere Elements) will display when the clip is placed on the timeline.

You can not set **In** and **Out** markers on titles and still images, however, because they are stationary elements.

Once the **Clip Monitor** has been launched, it will stay open as long as you keep your project open or until you manually close it.

Because this panel tends to pop up in the middle of the workspace whenever it launches, I usually launch it as soon as I open a project. Then I position it off to the side, out of the way, and leave it open. That way, if I later need to open a clip in this panel for previewing or trimming, the **Clip Monitor** will play this clip where I've positioned it instead of in the middle of my work.

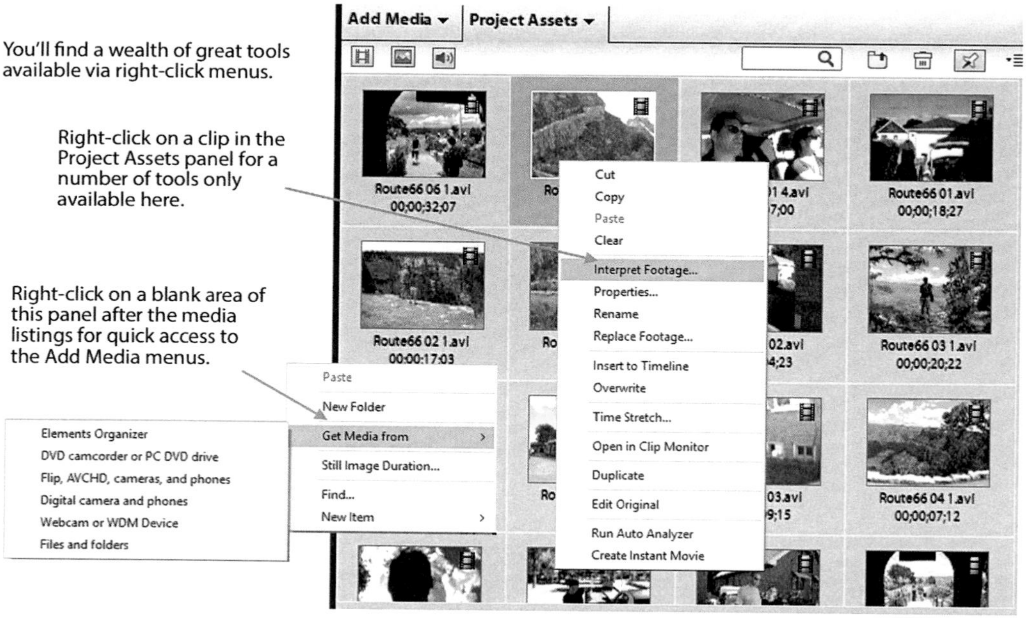

Valuable Project Assets panel right-click tools

There are a number of great tools available throughout Premiere Elements that can be (and sometimes can *only* be) accessed by **right-clicking** on clips or in panels.

Here are a some of my favorite right-click tools available in the **Project Assets** panel.

Interpret Footage – Believe it or not, 4:3 standard definition video and widescreen 16:9 standard definition video use exactly the same number of pixels (720x480 or 720x576 PAL) to create a video frame. The difference is that the pixels (the tiny squares of color that combine to create every frame of video) are shaped differently. Widescreen 16:9 pixels are much wider than standard 4:3 video pixels.

Right-clicking on a clip and selecting **Interpret Footage** gives you access to options for conforming a widescreen clip to fit in a standard video or vice versa.

This tool is invaluable if, for some reason, you find yourself with a clip that looks strangely squished, stretched or distorted (as when you add a 16:9 video to a 4:3 project).

Duplicate – This selection makes a duplicate of the clip you've right-clicked on. This is very helpful, for instance, if you've created a title slide with a style you'd like to re-use. You merely **duplicate** it and then revise the duplicate as needed. (Also see **Duplicate a title** on page 152.)

Rename – You can rename a clip by selecting this **right-click** option or by simply double-clicking slowly on the name of the file in the **Project Assets** panel listing so that the name becomes highlighted. Renaming a clip doesn't change the name of the file on your hard drive, by the way. Nor does it affect the clip's position or function on the timeline. But it can make it easier for you to identify the file later.

Create a slideshow in the Project Assets panel

One of my favorite "hidden" features in the Premiere Elements **Project Assets** panel is the **Create Slideshow** tool.

To access this great little tool, select a number of clips or stills from the **Project Assets** panel (by holding down the **Shift,** the **Ctrl** or the Mac's ⌘ key as you select) and then **right-click** on the selected clips and select **Create Slideshow.**

As you can see below, in the illustration of the **Create Slideshow** option screen, you can set the **Ordering** of your slides in a couple of ways.

Sort Order. In **Sort Order**, the **Slideshow Creator** places your slides in the same order as they appear listed in the **Project Assets** panel.

Selection Order. In **Selection Order**, the **Slideshow Creator** places your slides according to the order you click-selected them in the **Project Assets** panel.

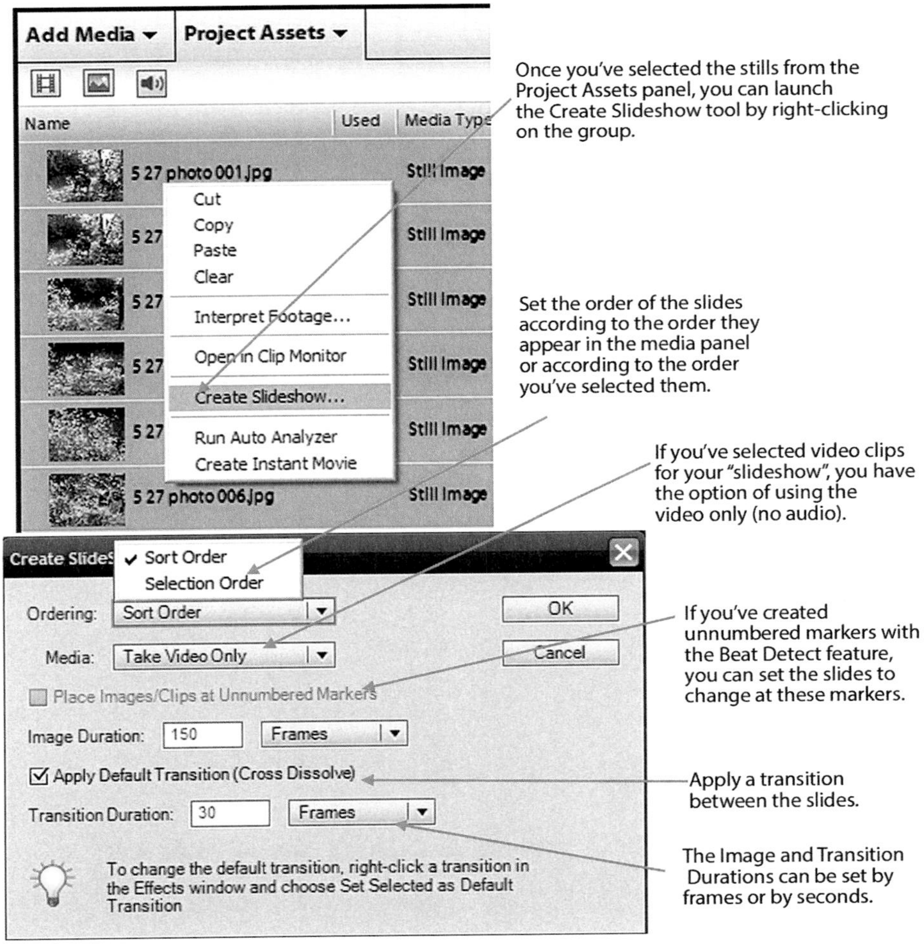
Add Media
Project Assets
Name
Used
Media Type
5 27 photo 001.jpg
Still Image
Cut
Copy
Paste
Clear
Interpret Footage...
Open in Clip Monitor
Create Slideshow...
Run Auto Analyzer
Create Instant Movie
5 27 photo 006.jpg
Sort Order
Selection Order
Ordering:
Media:
Take Video Only
OK
Cancel
Place Images/Clips at Unnumbered Markers
Image Duration:
150
Frames
Apply Default Transition (Cross Dissolve)
Transition Duration:
30
To change the default transition, right-click a transition in the Effects window and choose Set Selected as Default Transition
Once you've selected the stills from the Project Assets panel, you can launch the Create Slideshow tool by right-clicking on the group.
Set the order of the slides according to the order they appear in the media panel or according to the order you've selected them.
If you've selected video clips for your "slideshow", you have the option of using the video only (no audio).
If you've created unnumbered markers with the Beat Detect feature, you can set the slides to change at these markers.
Apply a transition between the slides.
The Image and Transition Durations can be set by frames or by seconds.

On the **Create Slideshow** option screen, you also have a number of ways to set the duration of your slides:

Image Duration. You can set your slides to change after a designated interval of time.

Unnumbered Markers. You can set them to change at **Unnumbered Markers** on the **Timeline** (For more information on **Unnumbered Markers**, see **Detect beats in your music** on page 189 of **Chapter 16, Mix Your Audio and Add Music**).

You can use either video or still clips in your slideshow – although only stills can be set to change at a given duration or at the unnumbered markers created by the **Detect Beats** tool.

If you use video clips in your slideshow, the **Create Slideshow** panel includes the option to remove the audio from the clips, as illustrated on the previous page.

You can also select the option to apply a **Default Transition** between your slides. (For information on designating the **Default Transition**, see page 134 of **Chapter 11, Add and Customize Transitions**.)

For information on how to optimize your stills for a slideshow, see **Use photos in Premiere Elements** on page 56 of **Chapter 5, Add Media to Your Project**.

There are actually a number of different ways to create a slideshow in Premiere Elements, including a **Slide Show Creator** tool built into the Elements Organizer (see page 231) and **InstantMovie** slideshow themes. (For more information on creating **InstantMovies**, see **Chapter 8**.)

Adding Clips to Your Timeline

Auto Enhancing Your Clips

Splitting and Trimming Your Clips

Working with Multiple Tracks of Video

Rendering Your Timeline

Chapter 7

Edit Your Video in Expert View

Where your movie comes together

The Expert View timeline is where your clips are gathered, ordered, trimmed, split, rearranged, and where effects are applied. It's where your movie finally comes together – just as in Quick View.

But Expert View gives you a much more powerful timeline, greater access to your clips and more professional-level tools for working with them.

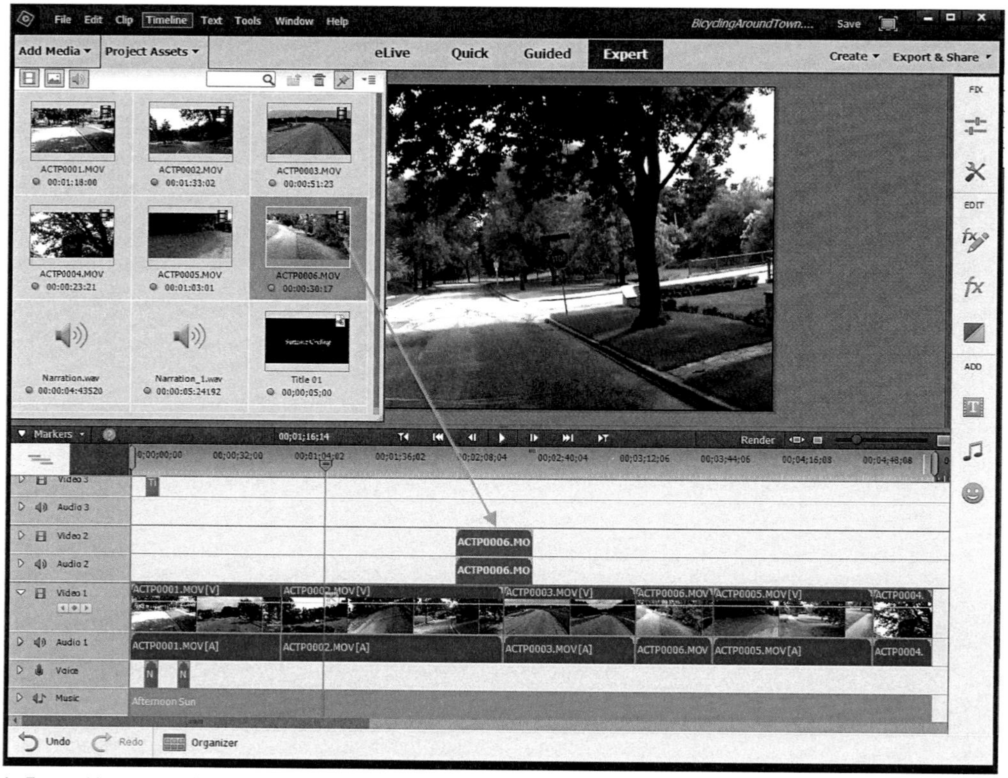

In Expert View, your clips are dragged from the Project Assets panel to any of up to 99 audio and/or video tracks. Transitions are added to points at which clips meet.

Expert View in Premiere Elements is the more professional-style workspace.

There are three main differences between the Quick View and the Expert View timelines:

In Expert View, media is added to the **Project Assets** panel before it is brought to the timeline. In the **Project Assets** panel, your media can be more easily managed and even pre-trimmed before it is added to the timeline. (For more information on the **Project Assets** panel, see **Chapter 6**.)

While Quick View is limited to four tracks, the Expert View timeline includes the option for up to 99 tracks of video and up to 99 tracks of audio. Multi-track editing allows for some effects that are virtually impossible in Quick View.

In Expert View, video and audio clips can be manipulated at specific points using keyframing right on the timeline, allowing you to create and control fade ins or outs and, more importantly, allowing you to control and mix audio levels at specific points using keyframing (see page 189).

Nonetheless, Quick View and Expert View are still just two faces of the same project. In other words, you can switch between the two views as needed as you develop your timeline, taking advantage of the benefits of each view as you work.

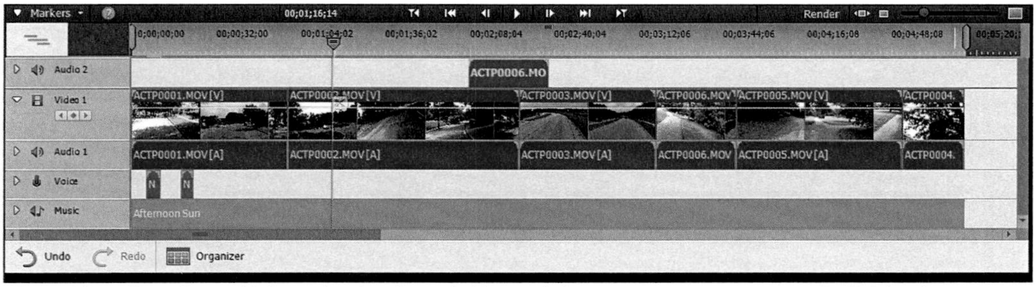

Expert View allows for multiple tracks of audio and video and gives you greater access to each clip's levels.

Controlling the timeline's "ripple" function

Video 1 and Audio 1 on your timeline in Premiere Elements are set, by default, to "**ripple**" as you add, remove and trim clips on the timeline.

In other words, by default:

When you Insert a clip into an assemblage of clips, the clips on all tracks on the timeline will **split** and/or *ripple* to the right to accommodate the new clip.

When you trim or extend a clip on Video 1 or Audio 1, the rest of the clips on the timeline will ripple, or move right or left, to accommodate this change.

When you add audio to your Narration or Soundtrack, the timeline will *not* ripple.

When you Delete a clip from Video 1/Audio 1 on your timeline, the clips on all tracks will ripple to the left to fill in the gap –unless there is a clip filling this gap on a parallel audio or video track.

When you Delete a clip from a track *other than Video 1 or Audio 1*, the timeline will not ripple. To ripple the timeline left to fill this gap, **double-click** to select the gap and press the **Delete** key on your keyboard or **right-click** and select **Delete and Close Gap.**

In most cases, rippling will work to your advantage. If you've got an assemblage of audio and video clips in your movie and you decide to reorder them or add a clip to the middle of your project, you'll want the rest of the clips in your movie to stay in relative position, moving as a group to allow for the inserted or removed clip.

But there may also be times when you'll want to override this ripple function. To override the ripple function:

Hold down the Ctrl key on a PC or the ⌘ key on a Mac as you add your new clip(s) to your timeline. When you override the ripple function, the rest of your clips will remain locked in their positions on your timeline as you add or remove a clip, and you'll be able to place your music on an audio track – or any clip on any other audio or video track – without disturbing the rest of your movie.

Hold down the Alt/Option key as you insert a clip to your timeline to limit the timeline's rippling to the track you're adding your clip to. The rest of your movie's video and audio clips will remain in place.

Smart Fix your clips

When your clips have been Auto-Analyzed and Smart Tagged, the program will offer to apply a Smart Fix Auto Enhance when you place the clip on your timeline – correcting the contrast and brightness and, if necessary, stabilizing the camera movement.

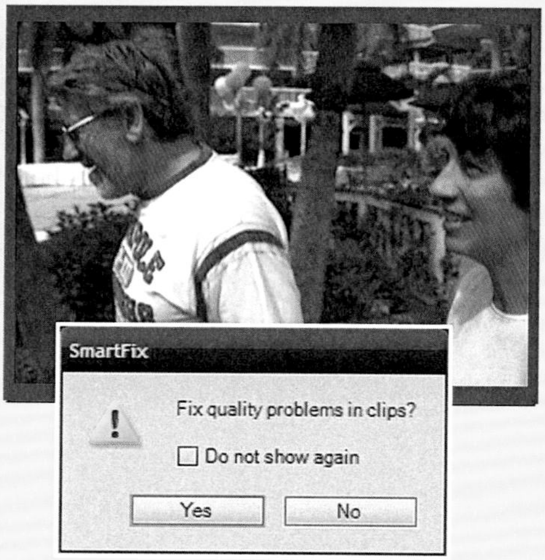

Premiere Elements includes the option to have the program automatically apply a **Smart Fix** to your clips as you add them to your timeline or sceneline.

When this tool is enabled in the program's **Preferences** (under the **Edit** menu on a PC, as discussed below), an option panel will appear each time you add a new clip to your timeline or your sceneline, asking if you would like the program to "**Fix quality problems in your clips?**" (This option panel will only appear if your clips have been **Smart Tagged** prior to your adding them to your project, as discussed on the facing page.)

If you select **Yes**, Premiere Elements will automatically apply the necessary contrast levels to the clip and, if it judges the clip as too shaky, will apply automatic image stabilization!

If the clip is very long and has inconsistent quality issues, the program will even keyframe variations of contrast! (There is no way to set this feature to correct only contrast *or* only stabilization, by the way. Your options are only to have both applied or neither.)

In our experience, the results are usually very good (even if the applied effects mean that the program must then render the clips before they play back smoothly).

This feature can be turned off at any time by checking the **Do Not Show Again** box in the **Smart Fix** pop-up panel, as illustrated above.

To re-activate this feature later, go to the **Edit** drop-down on the Menu Bar and select **Preferences.** On the preferences **General** page, check the box that says **Show All Do Not Show Again Messages.**

Smart Fix can also be applied manually to clips that are already on your timeline using the **Smart Fix** tool located on the **Adjustments** panel, as discussed on page 119).

As discussed in the sidebar on the facing page, the automatic **Smart Fix** tool will only be available for clips that have been previously **Auto-Analyzed.**

Timeline views

Premiere Elements includes a number of features for viewing your timeline, depending on how closely you want to look at your movie.

Using the zoom tool, for instance, you can zoom out to view your entire movie at once – or you can zoom in close enough to see your video's individual frames.

To zoom in or out on your timeline, drag the slider (on the upper right of the **Timeline** panel) left or right – or use the following keyboard shortcuts:

- Pressing the **–** key on your keyboard zooms out.
- Pressing the **+** key zooms in.
- Pressing the **** key (above the **Enter/Return** key) automatically zooms out to display your entire movie.

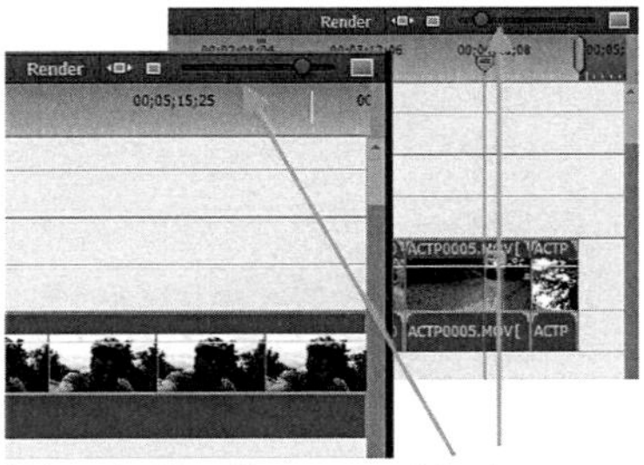

Using the Timeline zoom slider (or your +, – and \ keys) you can zoom out to see your whole project or zoom in close enough to see individual frames.

Open or closed video and audio tracks

In Premiere Elements, you can also toggle the views of the individual tracks on your timeline to display as either open – which allows you to view your video clips as thumbnails and your audio clips as waveforms – or closed, reducing the amount of vertical space the **Timeline** panel requires when you are using multiple tracks of video and audio, as illustrated on the right.

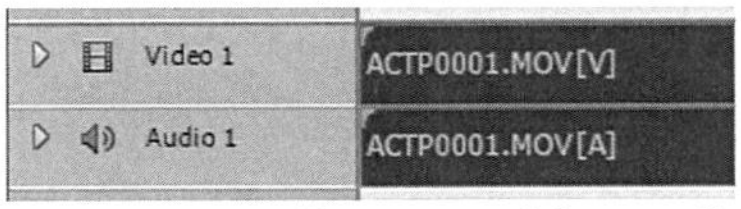

To make more efficient use of the panel's vertical space, individual tracks on the Timeline can be toggled between a compressed and an open view.

Clips must be Auto Analyzed in order to be Smart Fixed

The **Smart Fix** option panel, discussed on the facing page, will appear as you add your clips to your timeline if these clips have been previously **Auto Analyzed**. This is because the **Smart Fix** tool takes its cue from information gathered by the **Media Analyzer/Auto-Analyzer,** an Elements Organizer feature that automatically analyzes and records metadata to your clips based on content and quality issues. (For more information, see page 208.) This feature works quietly in the background when your computer is idle.

You may, as an alternative to this automatic function, manually prep your clips for **Smart Fix** (or the other Premiere Elements tools that require **Auto Analyzing)** by selecting clips in the Elements Organizer **Media Browser** or the Premiere Elements **Project Assets** panel, either one at a time or several at once, **right-clicking** and selecting the option to **Run Auto Analyzer** from the context menu.

To add a clip to your timeline, simply drag it from the Project Assets panel.

As you add new clips, the other clips will "ripple", moving aside if you add the clip in the middle of a project.

To override the ripple effect (as when you're adding music or a video clip to a parallel track) hold down the Ctrl key (or the Cmd key on a Mac) as you add the clip to your timeline.

Zoom in or out on the timeline by pressing + or - or using the Zoom slider.

Add clips to your timeline

Adding clips to your project's timeline in Expert View is about as intuitive as it can possibly be. You simply drag the clips from the **Project Assets** panel to a video or audio track.

You can reorder the clips on the timeline by dragging them around. Placing a clip to the left of another clip will cause it to slide it aside ("ripple" it) to accommodate the move. (See page 71 for information on overriding the ripple feature on your timeline.)

To delete a clip from your timeline, click to select it and press the **Delete** button on your keyboard or **right-click** on it and select **Delete and Close Gap**. Unless there are clips on parallel video or audio tracks, the timeline will ripple to fill in the gap.

To remove a clip *without* causing the other clips to ripple or fill in the gap, **right-click** on the clip and select **Delete** instead.

Once your clips are assembled, you can apply transitions between them. More information on transitions can be found in **Chapter 11, Add and Customize Transitions**.

Trim or split your clips

Once a clip is on your timeline, you can edit it to remove unwanted portions by **trimming** and/or **splitting** it.

Trimming removes footage from the beginning or end of a clip.

Splitting divides your clip into smaller segments, which you can then remove or rearrange.

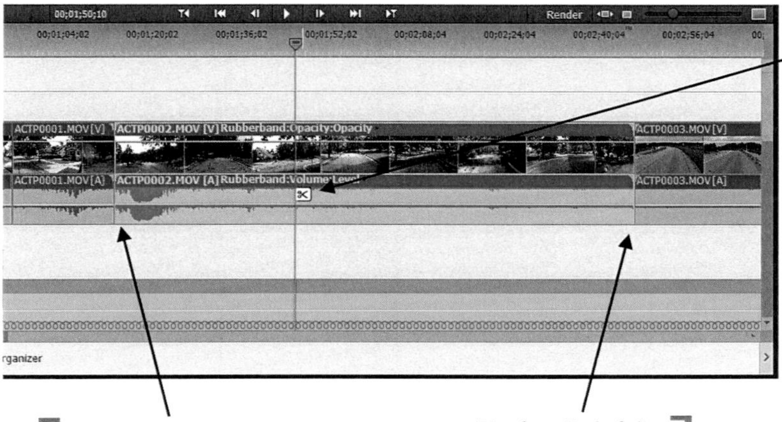

To slice a clip in two, click the scissors icon on the CTI playhead.

If a clip is selected on the timeline, only that clip will be split at the position of the CTI; If no clips are selected, all clips on every track on the timeline will be split at the position of the CTI.

Trim from Beginning of clip

Trim from End of clip

To trim a clip on the timeline, hover your mouse over the beginning or end of a clip until the Trim from Beginning or Trim from End icon appears, then click and drag in or out.

Trim a clip on your timeline

To **trim a clip**, click to select the clip on your timeline and hover your mouse over the clip's beginning or end.

As you hover your mouse over either end of a clip, it will switch to trim mode (becoming a or a cursor). Click and drag the end of the clip to trim it – removing footage from or adding footage to the clip's beginning or end.

The **Monitor** will preview the new in or out point as you drag. (For information on pre-trimming your clip before you drag it to the timeline, see **Pre-trim your clips in the Clip Monitor** on page 64 of **Chapter 6, Explore the Project Assets Panel**.)

If you find, after removing a segment, that you've removed too much of a clip – or not enough – you can simply re-drag the end of the clip to replace or remove the extra frames. (In non-linear editing, nothing is ever permanently removed from a clip.)

Split a clip on your timeline

To **split a clip** – either to remove a portion of it or to isolate a segment so that you can move, or add an effect to, it – position the **CTI** (Current Time Indicator) at the point on your timeline you'd like to slice and then click the **Split Clip** (scissors icon) button on the **CTI**, as illustrated above.

If you have a clip *selected* on your timeline, this tool will slice only that clip; if you have no clips selected, this tool will slice through *all* of the clips on all tracks at the **CTI's** current position except the **Narration** and **Soundtrack** tracks.

If you then want to delete the segment you've sliced (or sliced on either side of), click to select the segment, **right-click** and choose **Delete** or **Delete and Close Gap**, depending on whether or not you'd like the timeline to ripple to fill the gap.

Remove audio or video from your clip

As you can see on page 81, **right-clicking** on a clip on your timeline gives you access to a number of helpful features, tools and options.

To make a clip on your timeline video only, **right-click** on the clip and select **Delete Audio**.

To make a clip on your timeline audio only, **right-click** on the clip and select **Delete Video**.

Fade in and out of your clip

The simplest way to fade into or out of a clip on your timeline is to **right-click** on it and, from the **Fade** sub-menu, select **Fade In**, **Fade Out** or **Fade In and Out.** (In Expert view, separate options are offered for fading in or out of your video, your audio or both, if your clip includes both, as illustrated on page 81.)

By default, your fades will last one second. You can, however, adjust the keyframe positions to lengthen or shorten that time.

To do this, look for the white dots that Premiere Elements has placed to create the fade on the thin, horizontal, yellow **Rubber Bands** (representing the video's **Opacity** or the audio's **Volume**) that run through your clips.

Add still photos to your project

By default, when a still photo is added to your Premiere Elements project timeline, its duration is **five seconds.**

(This default can be changed under **Edit/Preferences** – although changing it will only affect photos brought into the program *after* the preference has been changed.)

You can increase or decrease how long a photo displays on the timeline by dragging to trim or extend it, just as you would to trim or extend a video clip, as described in **Trimming and Splitting** on page 75.

As explained in **Use Photos in Premiere Elements** (page 56) in **Chapter 5, Add Media to Your Project**, you'll get the best performance from stills in a standard video project if they are sized to no larger than 1000x750 pixels (or 2500x1875 pixels for a high-def project).

Additionally, once you've placed a photo on your timeline, you can eliminate an occasional problem (related to interlacing) by **right-clicking** on the still on the timeline and selecting **Field Options** and then selecting the **Flicker Removal** option.

Applying this setting will preempt a fluttering problem that sometimes manifests itself in video outputs when highly detailed or high contrast photos are used in Premiere Elements projects.

These dots are called **keyframes**, and we discuss them in much greater detail in **Chapter 15, Keyframing**.

By default, this yellow **Rubber Band** on a video clip represents its **Opacity** (or transparency). On an audio clip, the **Rubber Band**, by default, represents its **Volume** level.

See how the line slants down before or after that keyframe? That's your fade in or fade out of the clip's **Opacity** or **Volume** levels.

Adjusting those dots' positions relative to the end of the clip, by clicking on them and dragging them to new positions, extends or shortens the duration of your fade in or fade out.

To find out more about adjusting your audio's volume and how to control it at specific points in your movie, see **Adjust audio levels at specific points on your timeline** on page 189.

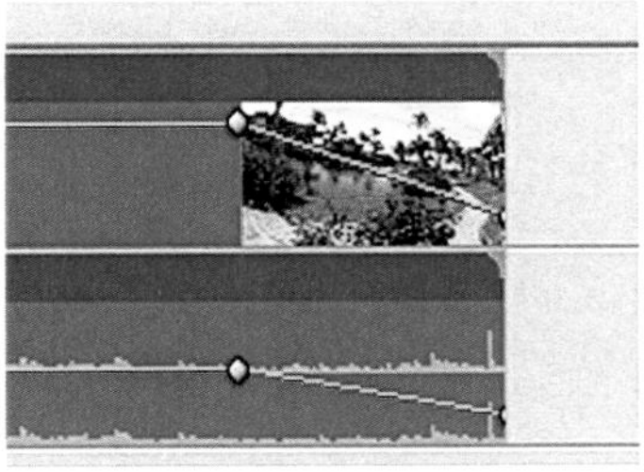
Fade ins and fade outs are really just keyframed Opacity and Volume properties. You can change the length of the fade by changing the positions of the keyframe points on the timeline.

Output a segment of your video using the Work Area Bar

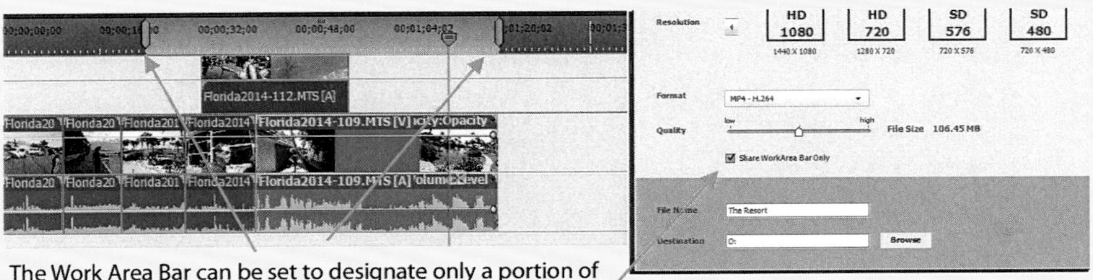

The Work Area Bar can be set to designate only a portion of your video project. Most Export + Share options allow you to output the Work Area Bar segment only.

The **Work Area Bar** is the lighter gray area that runs along the ticker at the top of the timeline, defined by a silver marker on either end. By default, this bar covers your entire video project and grows and shrinks automatically with your project as you edit.

But, by dragging its beginning and end handles, you can manually set the **Work Area Bar** to cover only a portion of your video editing project, as illustrated above. In this way, you can designate only a portion of your project for output.

Nearly all of the output options under the **Export & Share** tab include a checkbox option for **Export Work Area Bar Only**, as in the illustration above. Checking this option directs the program to output *only* the segment of your project you've defined with the **Work Area Bar**. For more information on this function, see the discussions under each output option in **Chapter 21, Export & Share Your Video Projects**.

To reset the **Work Area Bar** to cover your entire project, **double-click** on its top edge.

Use L-cuts, J-cuts and multiple tracks

The ability to compose your video using several video tracks greatly expands your ability to use interesting and professional-style editing techniques in your video projects.

Think of multiple tracks of video as a stack, like a stack of photos. In most cases, only the uppermost photo or video in the stack will be visible.

However, if you change the size and position of the video on the top of the stack, you can reveal all or part of the video underneath. One such effect the can be achieved using multiple video tracks is the **Picture-in-Picture** or **PiP** effect. (**PiPs** can be created using **Presets**, as we discuss on page 166, or by manually changing the **Size** and **Position** properties of the upper video, as we discuss on page 173.)

You can also reveal portions of clips on lower tracks by using effects such as **Chroma Key** (as discussed on page 162 of **Chapter 13, Add Video and Audio Effects**), any of the **Matte** effects or even the **Crop** effect to make areas of some clips transparent.

By keyframing the effects in the **Applied Effects** panel, you can also make these positions, sizings or other settings change over the duration of the clip, creating an animated effect. (For more information, see **Chapter 15, Keyframing**.)

Using multiple tracks of video and then scaling and positioning your clips on each, you can have any number of video images in your video frame at the same time. (Think of the grid of faces in the opening credits of *The Brady Bunch* – or see my multiple-panel illustration below.) The products page at Muvipix.com offers a wealth of tutorials describing techniques for achieving these effects using a number of video tracks and effects. (A split screen effect can also be achieved using the very cool, new **Video Collage** tool, as discussed on page 90.)

Two popular professional techniques that use multiple tracks of video are the **L-cut** and the **J-cut** – so named because, back in the days of cut-and-paste film editing, when a segment of film had to be removed and the audio left in place to allow for the placement of alternate visuals, the cut film and audio clip resembled an "L" or a "J" (depending on which segment was removed).

Imagine a TV news report that features video of a reporter standing in front of a burned-out building, describing the fire that destroyed it.

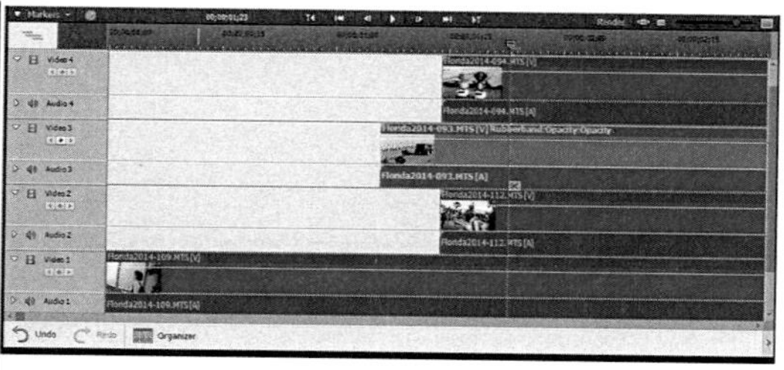

Using Scaling and Position settings combined with the Crop tool on multiple tracks of video allows for Picture-in-Picture effects as well as the opportunity to do split screens, showing several video clips on screen at once

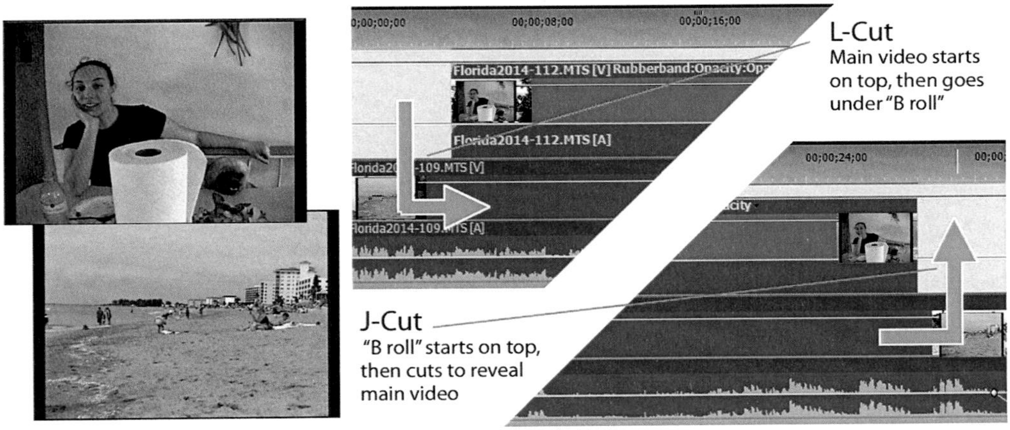

As audio from main clip continues, video cuts to or from "B roll" footage.

As he continues speaking, the video cuts away to footage shot earlier of the fire itself. That's an **L-cut**. (A **J-cut**, on the other hand, begins with the cut-away video and the reporter's voice, then cuts to the video of the reporter finishing his report.)

Creating an **L-cut** is easy with multi-track editing.

1. Put the main video, the clip of the reporter speaking to the camera (we'll call it **Clip A**), on Video track 1.
2. Holding the **Ctrl** key (or the ⌘ key on a Mac) to override the timeline's ripple function, place the second video – the footage of the fire (**Clip B**) – on Video track 2.
3. Overlap the latter part of **Clip A** with **Clip B**, as seen in the illustration on the previous page.
4. **Right-click** on **Clip B** and select **Delete Audio**, if you need to remove its audio track.

Voila! Tweak **Clip B**'s position for maximum effect and you're done! We begin with the reporter speaking to the camera and, as he continues to speak, we cut away to the footage of the fire.

L-cuts and **J-cuts** are very effective for news-style reports as well as for interviews, in which you cut away from the person speaking to separately shot footage of what he or she is describing. It's a great way to reinforce, with images, what's being presented verbally.

By the way, here's some professional vocabulary to impress your friends with. That secondary footage that plays as the main video's audio continues? It's commonly called "**B-roll footage**", a relic from the days when this kind of editing actually did involve pasting in footage from a separate roll of film or video.

Render your timeline

When you are working in Expert View, as you add effects and transitions or other video sources to your project (including photos), you will see yellow-orange lines appear above the clips, as illustrated on the right.

These orange lines are indications that these segments of your timeline need to be rendered – converted to the workflow video format. As more and more of your project requires rendering, your computer will begin to operate more sluggishly and the program may even notify you that your system is running low on memory. Your preview video will also suffer a reduction in quality.

An orange line just below the ticker along the top of the timeline indicates a segment that requires rendering.

You can render your timeline by pressing Enter or clicking the Render button.

Once the sequence is rendered, the orange line will turn green.

This is because, until you manually render these segments, the program is continually creating "soft renders" of them –"on the fly" previews of your unrendered files. And that puts a lot of strain on your system.

In Quick View, there is no orange line on the timeline to indicate the need to render. The only indication will be little pop-ups suggesting that it might be a good idea to render to improve your performance.

To **Render** your video projects' timeline, click the **Render** button on the top right of the timeline.

Alternatively, you can just press the **Enter/Return** key on your keyboard – or select **Render Work Area** from the **Timeline** drop-down at the top of the interface. (Note that only the area of your timeline covered by the **Work Area Bar** – see the sidebar on page 77 – will be rendered.)

Manually rendering your project will create temporary video segments that the program can use to create a clean, clear preview playback of your project – while greatly reducing the strain on your system's resources.

Once your clip has been rendered, the orange lines above the clip will turn green and your playback will be much cleaner and smoother.

You can render your clips continually as you're working. Or you can wait until your playback performance starts to lag. It's up to you.

But do be aware that, if you're having playback problems and your timeline has a lot of yellow-orange lines running across the top, a few seconds of rendering can usually do a lot to improve the program's performance.

Setting your Timeline Render quality

The quality of your **Timeline Rendering** has nothing to do with how your final video output will look. **Timeline Rendering** is purely for your own personal preview as you edit.

In the program's **Preferences/General** (under the **Edit** menu on a PC), you have the option of selecting either **High Quality Timeline Render** (which is slower but prettier) or **Draft Quality** (which is faster but uglier). Choose whichever best fits your priorities.

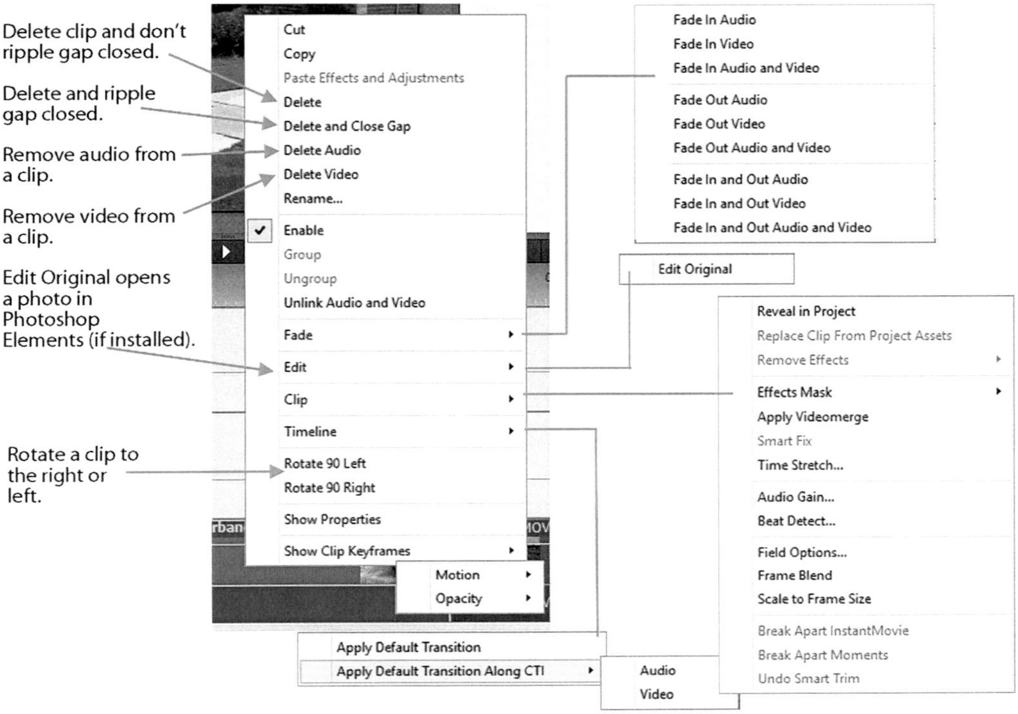

Valuable right-click tools on the timeline

Right-clicking on a clip on your timeline gives you access to a number of valuable tools. To simplify navigation, Adobe has placed many of these right-click options in sub-categories.

To delete a clip without changing the position of any other clip on your timeline, select **Delete**.

To delete a clip and "ripple" the timeline to fill in the gap, select **Delete and Close Gap**. (The gap will only close, however, if there are no clips on parallel video or audio tracks preventing it from being a true gap!)

To remove the audio or video portion of a clip, select **Delete Audio** or **Delete Video**, as discussed on page 76.

To remove all effects and adjustments applied to a clip, select **Clip/ Remove Effects**.

To break apart the audio and video tracks of a clip so that each can be positioned separately, select **Unlink Audio and Video**.

To **Fade In** or **Fade Out** the audio, video or both, select a **Fade** option, as discussed on page 76.

To change the gain level of an audio clip, select **Clip/Audio Gain**, as discussed on page 190.

Selecting an InstantMovie Theme

Customizing Your Theme's Elements

Creating a Video Story

Chapter 8

Create an InstantMovie, Video Story or a Video Collage

Quick and easy ways to create movies

InstantMovies, as the name implies, are easy, automatic ways to assemble movies from your video clips – complete with titles, special effects and music.

Video Stories give your more control in the process. You select and arrange the clips, and the Video Story tool will provide the magic!

Additional content

You may notice a little blue flag over the upper right corner of a number of InstantMovie themes and Movie Menu templates.

This blue flag indicates that the template or theme is available but has not yet been installed on your computer. When you select this template or theme, the program will automatically download it for you from the Adobe site – a process that should only take a moment or two.

If you'd like to download all of these themes or templates at once, right-click on any one and select the Download All option.

Make an InstantMovie

InstantMovie Themes are packaged templates containing effects, transitions and music which can be applied to your raw footage to create an exciting movie pretty much automatically. To create an **InstantMovie**, you merely provide the raw footage and select a **Theme**, and Premiere Elements does the rest!

To create an **InstantMovie:**

1 Gather your clips on the timeline.

InstantMovies can be created in either Quick View or Expert View.

In Quick View, use **Add Media** to bring your video or still photos to your project's timeline. In Expert View, gather your video or stills from your **Project Assets** panel and drag them to your timeline.

Ideally, you'll want at least 2-3 minutes of footage. Place the clips on the timeline in the order you'd like them to appear in your **InstantMovie**.

InstantMovie will use – *and then replace* – all of the footage on this video track.

2 Click the **Create** button in the upper right of the interface and select **InstantMovie**.

The pop-up panel will display a library of movie **Themes**, as illustrated above.

The title bar at the top of the panel is set to **Show All** by default. To filter your view of these **Themes**, click on this title bar and select from the **InstantMovie** categories.

You can see an animated preview of any **Theme** by selecting its thumbnail and then clicking on the play button that appears.

3 Once you've selected a **Theme** for your **InstantMovie**, click the **Next** button in the lower right of the panel.

4 The panel will display a list of the optional elements that make up your **Theme's** template, as illustrated on the right.

Type the titles you'd like included in the boxes provided, then select or deselect the elements you'd like applied to your movie.

You can even swap out music by selecting the **My Music** option and browsing to a music file on your computer.

(You may need to scroll down to see the entire list of optional elements, then click on the little triangles to the left of the listed categories of options to see the entire options list.)

Once you've selected and customized the elements you'd like included, click the **Apply** button in the lower-right corner of the panel.

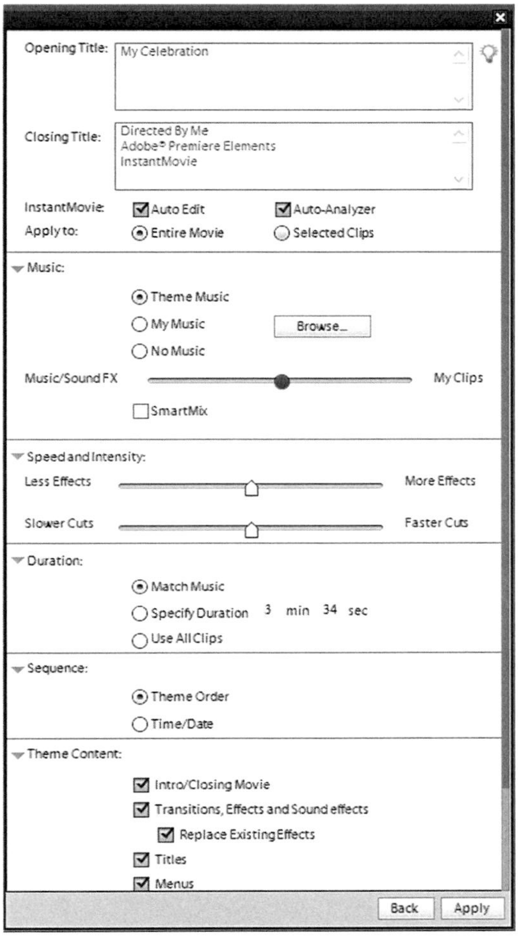

Once you've selected a Theme, you can customize it by including your own text and selecting which elements will be applied.

Premiere Elements will **Auto-Analyze** the clips on your timeline (see page 208), process all of the options and then apply the **Theme** elements you've selected.

After your automatically-generated movie appears on your timeline, the program will offer to render it for you.

It's a good idea to accept this offer, as your movie will likely need to be rendered before it will play at full quality. The rendered video will provide you with a much cleaner representation of what your final video output will look like.

For more information on the rendering process, see **Render your timeline** on page 80 of **Chapter 7, Edit Your Video in Expert View**.

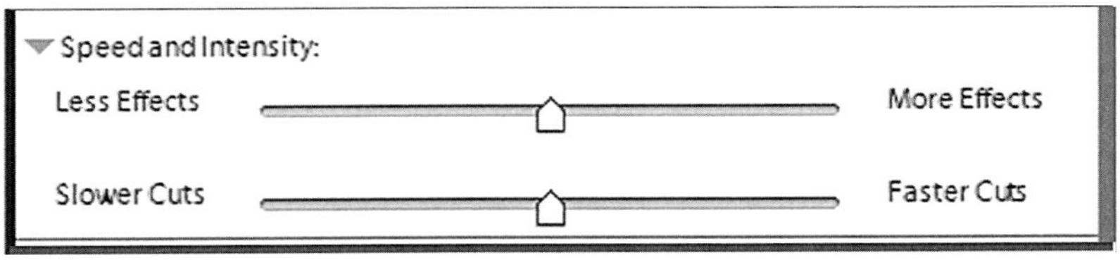

Instant Movie Themes include sliders for setting the speed of the cuts and the intensity of the effects.

Once you've created your **InstantMovie**, you have the option of using **Export & Share** to output it as is – or you can break it apart in Premiere Elements and continue to edit and customize it.

To break apart an **InstantMovie**, select and right-click the InstantMovie clip on your timeline and select the option to **Break Apart InstantMovie**.

The **InstantMovie** will be broken into its individual video and audio clips, titles and effects.

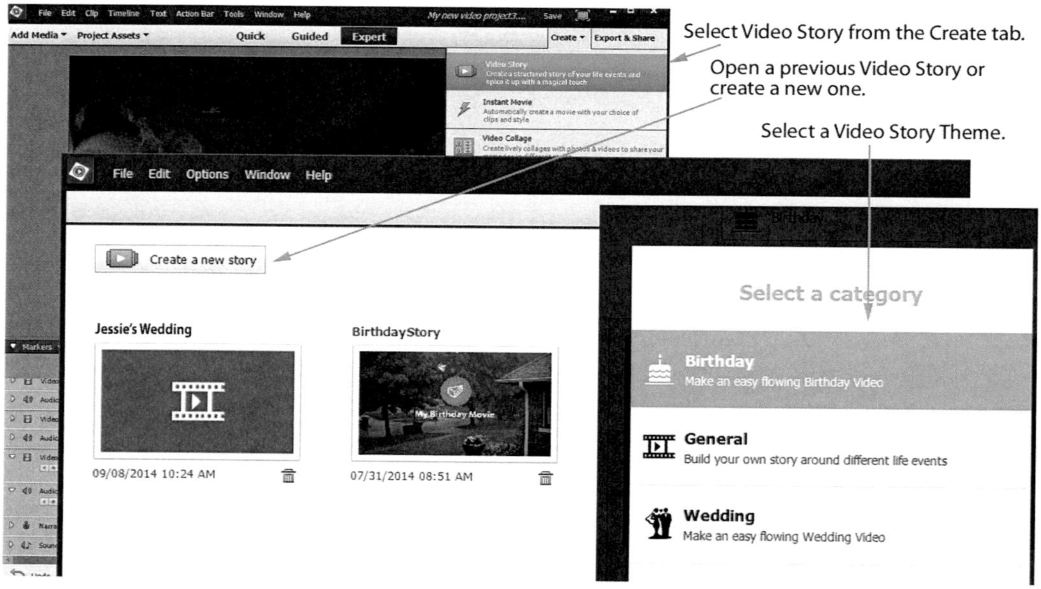

Create a Video Story

Video Story is a wizard-like tool for building stories out of your raw video footage.

A little more hands-on than **InstantMoviemaking**, **Video Story** walks you through the process, step by step, providing simple drop-in templates along the way and yet still leaving plenty of room for customization.

1 Click the **Create** button in the upper right of the interface and select **Video Story**.

A panel will open which displays your previously created **Video Stories**. To start a new story, click the **Create a New Story** button as illustrated above.

A **Video Story** introduction screen may display. You can view it or select the **Skip** option to go directly to the **Video Story Theme** panel in the future.

2 Select a **Video Story Theme**.

Click to select a theme or category for your **Video Story**.

A preview panel will open. On this preview panel, you can see a sample of what your **Video Story** theme in action.

If you want to return to the **Video Story Theme** panel, click the name of your theme at the top of the panel. Otherwise, click **Get Started**.

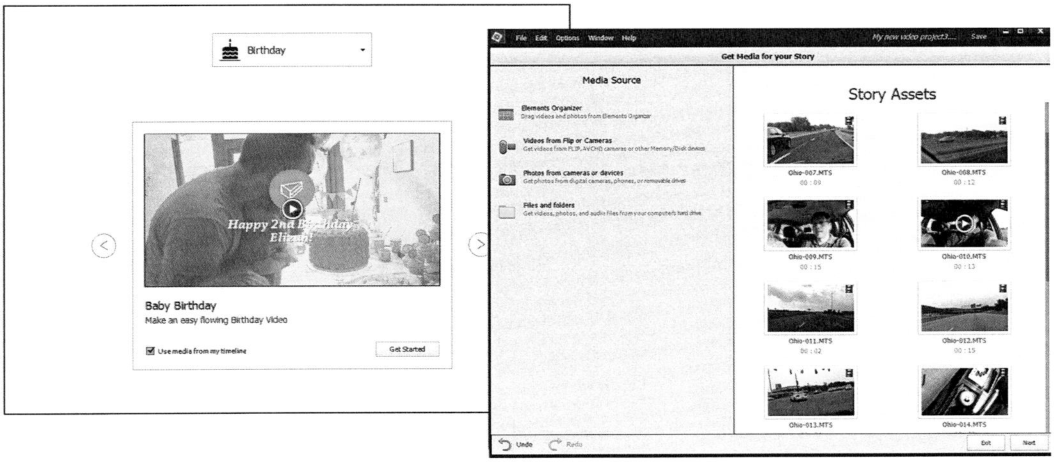

If the video that you want to use in your **Video Story** is already on your timeline, check the **Use Media From My Timeline** box.

3 Add media to your project.

On the **Get Media for Your Story** screen (illustrated above), select a video source from the left panel. You can add your video by browsing the Elements Organizer, get video from your camcorder or portable device (see pages 52-53), get photos from your still camera (see page 55) or import video or photos from your computer's **Files and Folders** (see page 55).

Drag your media from the **Add Media** panel onto the **Story Assets** panel or, if you are browsing files and folders on your computer, select the files you'd like to add and click the **Open** button.

Your video or photos will be added to your **Story Assets**.

Click **Next**.

4 Add media to your project's chapters.

Drag your media clips from the **Story Assets** panel, on the left, to the placeholder boxes in the **Story Overview** panel. These placeholder boxes represent the chapters in your **Video Story**, so you can add several clips to a single placeholder. (**Title** placeholders can include only one clip each).

To remove a chapter from your movie, click the trashcan icon at the bottom of a placeholder box.

To gather additional media for your project, click the **Add Media** button in the upper right of the **Story Assets** panel.

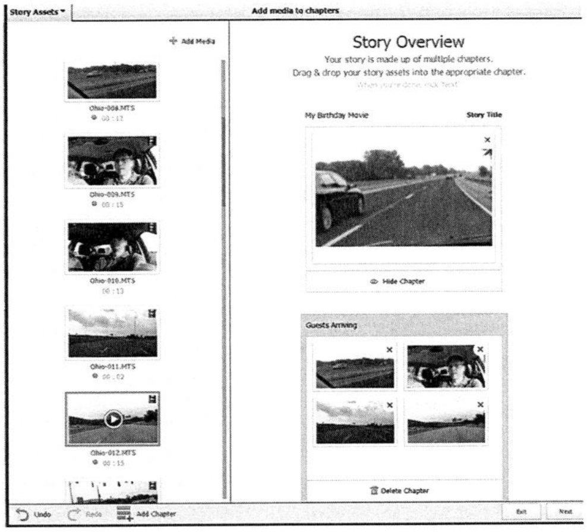

You'll be returned to the **Get Media** panel, as in **Step 3.**

Click **Next**. The tool will **Auto Analyze** your media clips and assemble your movie into a thumbnail preview.

5 Arrange and customize your **Video Story**.

The panel along the left side of the **Detail View** window lists your **Video Story's** chapters, as illustrated below. Select a chapter to customize and edit its elements.

When a chapter is selected, you have the options of dragging the clips in that chapter into a new order and customizing the chapter's title.

- To change the name of a chapter, click on the chapter's name in the box at the top left of the panel and overwrite it.
- To set the overall mood of your **Video Story**, select from the **Chapter Mood** drop-down menu at the top right of the **Detail View** panel.
- To do more in-depth customization, click the **cog** to the right of the **Chapter Mood** drop-down, as illustrated below. This will open a settings panel in which you can select your own custom music track, apply or remove a video filter to your clips and/or change your movie's pace (**Edit Speed**).
- To **Add a Chapter** or to **Add a Caption** or **Add Narration** to the current chapter, click a button along the bottom of the workspace panel.

To see your entire **Video Story** displayed, click the **Overview** button at the top of the **Detail View** panel. All of your **Video Story's** chapters and

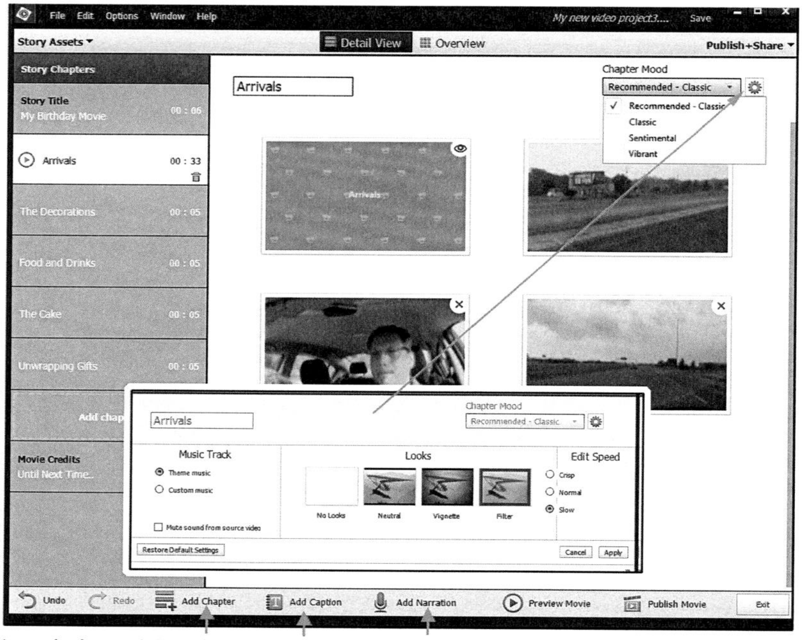

In each chapter's Detail View, you can add or rename a chapter, select a mood, add your own music, add a chapter, add a caption or record narration.

media clips will be displayed at once. In this view, you can arrange or customize the individual elements and even drag the chapters themselves into a new order.

Hover and click on the star to open the clip in the Favorite Moments workspace.

6 Edit the individual clips.

To edit an individual clip in any chapter, ensure you are in **Detail View** and hover your mouse over the clip. Click the white star that appears, as in the illustration above. Your clip will open in the **Favorite Moments** workspace (see page 110). In the **Favorite Moments** workspace, you can designate the segment(s) from the clip you'd like included in your final movie.

7 Publish your movie.

Click **Preview Story** in the lower right of the panel to play a preview of your **Video Story**.

Click **Save to Timeline** to return to the editing workspace.

Click **Export & Share** to output your finished movie. (**Export & Share** options are discussed in **Chapter 21**.)

Click **Exit** to cancel the project.

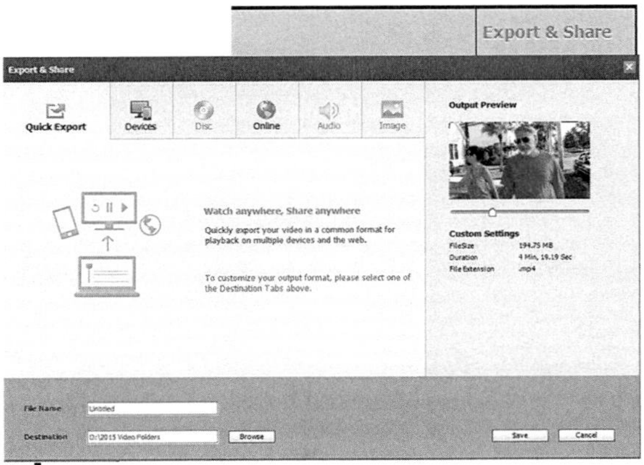

Build a Video Collage

A cool new feature in version 15, the **Video Collage** creator makes a composite of several video clips, shown split-screen in your video frame.

Traditionally, creating a Video **Collage** involves working with several tracks of video and combining **Position** and **Crop** settings to arrange them in your video frame. But with the new Premiere Elements **Video Collage** tool, building a video a collage is as simple as dropping clips into a template.

To build a **Video Collage**:

1. Click the **Create** button in the upper right of the interface and select **Video Collage**.

   The **Video Collage** workspace will open.

   The center of the workspace will display the template into which you will drop your clips.

   The right side of the workspace will display a library of **Video Collage** grid templates. In this library you'll find templates for three, four, five, six or seven clips.

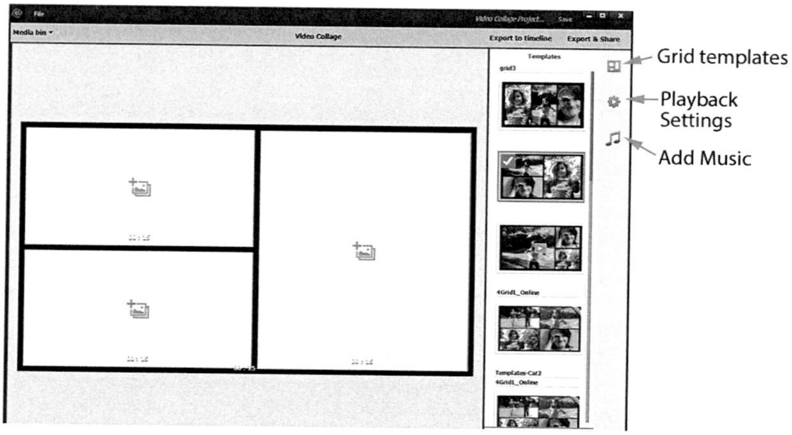

These templates include animations. To preview a template's animation, hover your mouse over the template, then click on the play button that appears.

2 Select a template.

Double-click to select a template. You may get a warning that any previous edits to your **Video Collage** will be lost – which you can disregard (or select the option not to see again).

3 Add media.

Click the **Media Bin** button in the upper left of the program. Select the video clips or photos you'll add to your collage either by browsing the **Albums** in your Organizer catalog (see page 51) or by selecting **Files and Folders** and browsing your hard drive.

4 Add the media to your template.

Drag a photo or clip into each of the placeholders on your template.

5 Position your clips.

As you hover your mouse over each clip in the grid, a blue hand will appear. Click and drag on this hand to adjust the positioning of each clip in the grid.

Use the **Zoom** slider that appears to zoom into or out of the clip.

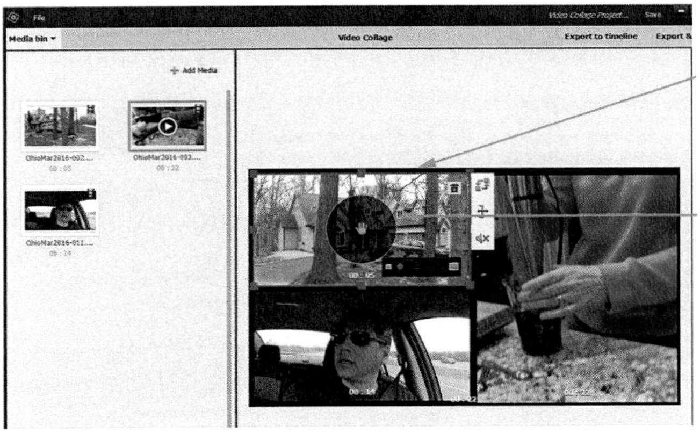

Drag media from the Media Bin into the grid.

Drag over the "hand" to position the clip in the grid or use the zoom slider to zoom in or out on the clip.

6 Change **Playback Settings**.

Your collage can be set up play all of your clips simultaneously or to play through one clip at a time.

To change these settings, click the **Playback Settings** button in the upper right of the workspace.

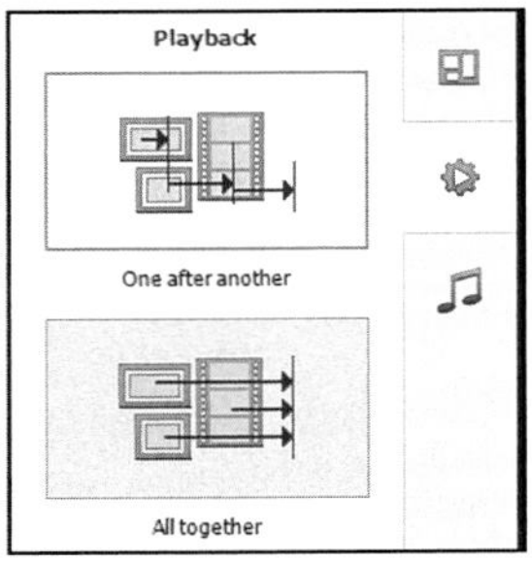

To trim the duration of each clip, click the Trim option and then shorten the length of the clip's "live area" in the Clip Monitor.

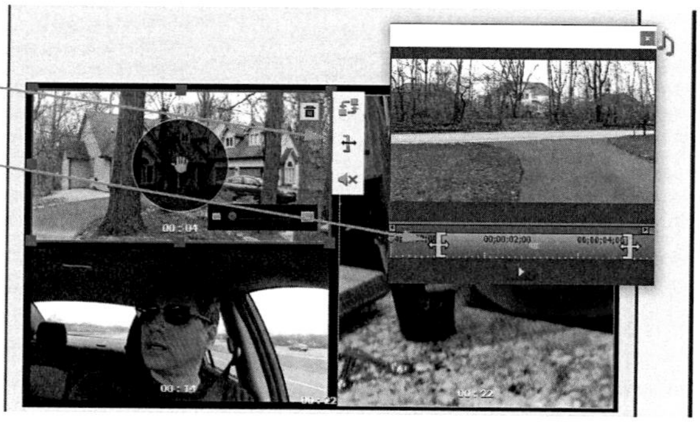

If you've selected the option for all your collage's clips to be playing simultaneously, you may face a challenge in that your clips will most likely not be of the same duration.

Since the total duration of your collage will be based on the running time of the longest clip, only the longest clip will play throughout the entire collage. The shorter clips will play until they run out of footage and then freeze – which is probably not the effect you want.

In other words, if you set your **Playback Settings** to play all of your clips at once, you may want to trim the clips so that they are all the same duration.

7 Trim your clips.

The duration of each clip will be displayed as a timecode along the bottom the clip in the grid. Click to select the clip you want to trim.

In the menu that appears on the upper right or upper left, select the **Trim** option. Your clip will open in a **Clip Monitor** (see page 64).

Trim the clip by dragging the in and out points at either end of the clip. The new duration of the clip will be displayed on the lower right of the **Clip Monitor** window.

When you're finished trimming, close the **Clip Monitor**.

8 Swap media.

To swap the videos in two grid squares, click the **Swap** button on the pop-up menu that appears on the upper right or upper left of a selected square. Drag the video from this square to another.

9 Keep or mute audio.

To mute the audio for a video clip in your collage, select a clip and click the **Mute** button on the pop-up menu that appears on the upper right or upper left of the selected square, illustrated above.

10 Select music.

To add music to your **Video Collage**, click the **Add Music** button on the right side of the workspace (as illustrated on page 90).

This will open the **Scores** library, from which you can select royalty-free music from a variety of style categories.

For more information on adding music using **Scores**, see page 191.

11 Output your **Video Collage**.

Test drive your **Video Collage** at any time by clicking the **Preview** button along the bottom of the workspace. When you're happy with your collage, you can either output it as a video file, upload it to YouTube, Vimeo or Facebook or save it to your timeline.

To output your **Video Collage** as a video file or upload it to a social media site, click the **Export & Share** button in the upper right of the workspace. For more information on the options available under **Export & Share**, see **Chapter 21, Export & Share Your Video Projects**.

To save your **Video Collage** to the timeline of your current project, click the **Save to Timeline** button in the upper right of the workspace.

You will be prompted to save the **Video Collage** (as a .vc file). Once you save the **Video Collage**, it will be added as a clip to the end of your current project's timeline.

To re-edit a **Video Collage** (.vc file), go to the Premiere Elements **File** menu and select **Open**. Locate and select the .vc file. The file will re-open in the **Video Collage** workspace.

When you are finished re-editing your **Video Collage**, it will be saved as a new media clip and .vc file.

Your finished Video Collage can be output as a movie, uploaded to a social media site or added to your project's timeline.

Part III

The Premiere Elements Toolbar

Mixing Your Audio

Grabbing a Freeze Frame

Recording Narration

Creating Pans & Zooms

Smart Mixing and Smart Trimming

Time Remapping and Time Stretching

Selecting Favorite Moments

Motion Tracking an Object in Your Video

Adding Graphics

Chapter 9

Access the Premiere Elements Toolkit

Powerful tools on the Toolbar

The Toolbar that runs along the right side of the Premiere Elements interface offers quick access to a whole array of features, effects and media.

Clicking the Tools button on this Toolbar will give you access to tools for editing your "favorite moments" from a video, creating pans and zooms over your photos, controlling playback speed, adding narration and creating menus for your DVDs and BluRay discs.

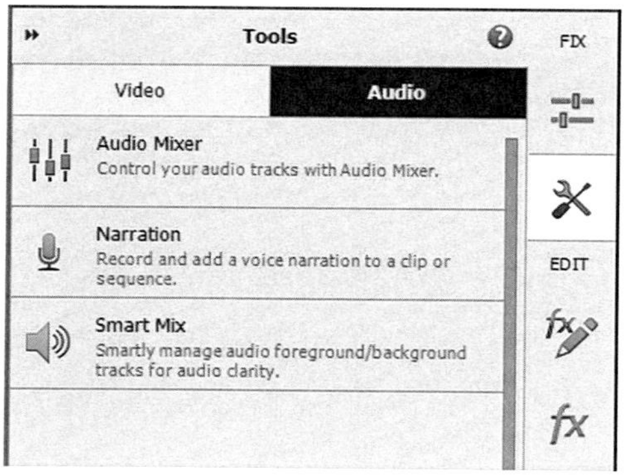

The Premiere Elements Toolkit is divided by tabs into Audio and Video Tools.

The Audio Mixer is only available in Expert View.

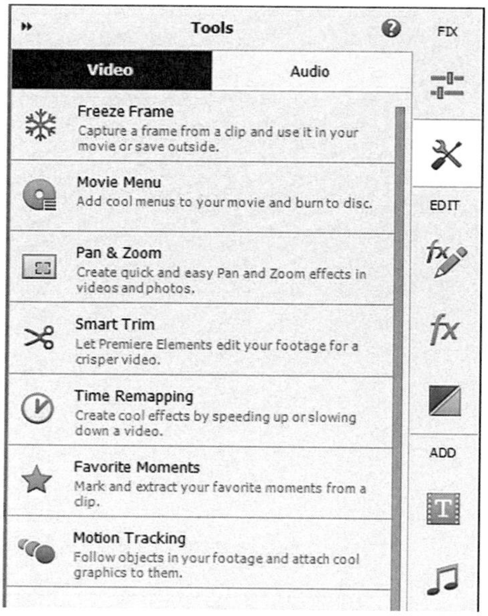

Running along the right side of the program's interface is the **Toolbar**. This **Toolbar** gives you easy access to dozens of tools, effects, transitions and graphics.

Clicking the **Tools** button on the **Toolbar** launches a pop-up menu with several very cool tools, listed under a **or** and an **Audio** tab in Expert View.

Video tools include:

Freeze Frame, a tool for saving a still photo of a frame of your movie.

Movie Menu, which opens a workspace for building a menu system for your DVDs, AVCHD or BluRay discs. (We discuss this feature in detail in **Chapter 20**.)

Pan & Zoom, which opens a very intuitive workspace for creating pan and zoom motion paths for your slideshows.

Smart Trim, a tool for automatically removing poor quality video from your project.

Time Remapping, an amazing new workspace for creating fast-motion and slow-motion segments in your movie.

Favorite Moments, a tool for selecting the best segments of a video clip and compiling a new sequence from them.

Motion Tracking, a cool tool that allows you to link a graphic to an object or person in a clip so that it will automatically follow this object or person around your video frame.

Audio tools include:

Audio Mixer (available only in Expert View), a tool for monitoring and setting the volume levels of your movie's audio.

Narration, a tool for recording a live narration track as your movie plays.

Smart Mix, a tool which automatically mixes the audio levels for your movie, based on criteria you define.

Mix and monitor your audio levels

The **Audio Mixer** can be used to monitor as well as adjust the audio levels on specific tracks.

To open this tool, select **Tools/Audio** on the **Toolbar** and click on the **Audio Mixer**. (Note that this tool is available in Expert View only.)

The **Audio Mixer** displays the audio levels for each of your active audio tracks and offers controls for raising and lowering these audio volume levels.

The Audio Mixer will display separate controls for each audio track.

If adjustments are made while playback is stopped, adjustments will affect the entire clip. If made during playback, audio keyframes will be created.

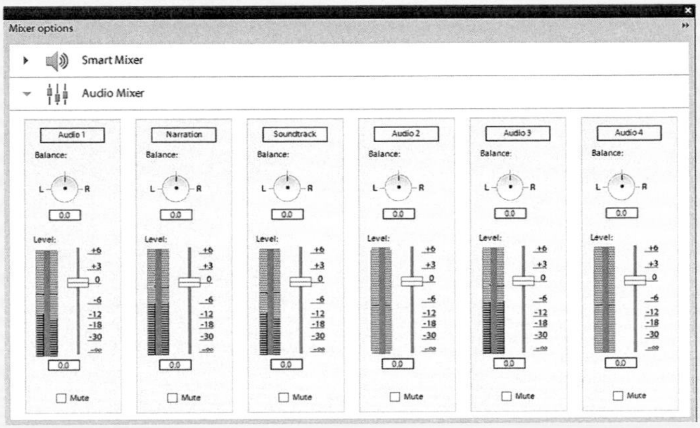

The **Audio Mixer** is a great panel to keep open as much as possible while you work so that you can monitor your movie's audio levels, particularly as you begin the final phases of editing your movie. For best results, never let your audio levels peak in the red. Overmodulated audio can sound distorted and fuzzy.

The **Audio Mixer** can also be used to adjust the levels for your individual audio clips:

- When you're not playing your video project, click to select a clip on the timeline at the position of the **CTI** (Current Time Indicator). Raising or lowering the **Audio Mixer** slider for that track will raise and lower the volume level for that entire clip.
- If you adjust the sliders as your video is playing, on the other hand, keyframe points will be added to your clips so that the audio is raised or lowered in real time at the points at which you adjusted the sliders.

As you play your project, watch the meters for each track, adjusting the sound levels as necessary to keep these levels as much as possible in the green, with the bulk of the audio peaking at zero.

In our opinion, this tool serves much more effectively as an audio meter than an audio level adjustment tool.

If used to adjust volume levels while the video is playing, it simply places too many hard-to-adjust audio keyframes on the timeline. You'll get much neater and much more effective results if you use the technique we describe in **Adjust audio levels at specific points in your video** on page 189.

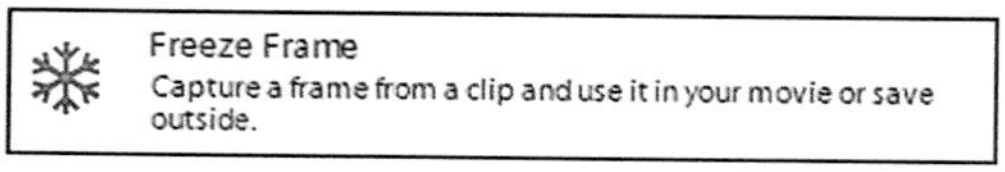

Freeze Frame
Capture a frame from a clip and use it in your movie or save outside.

Freeze Frame options

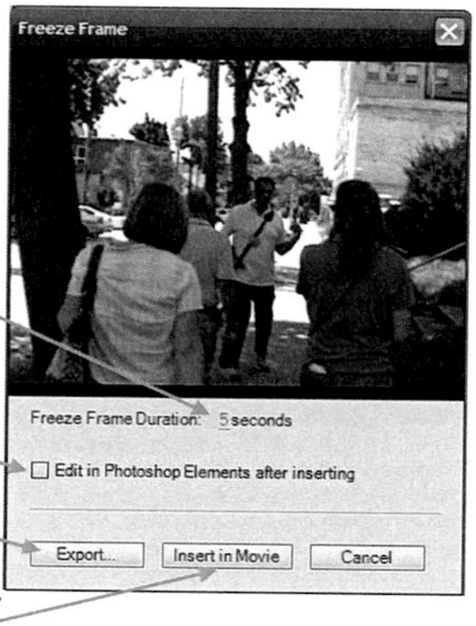

Duration of still if added directly to timeline.

Option to launch in Photoshop Elements editor.

Option to export as a BMP picture file.

Option to insert still directly to movie's timeline.

Grab a Freeze Frame

Freeze Frame might more accurately be called a "frame grab" tool, since it doesn't so much *freeze* a frame of your movie as much as it *grabs* a frame from it and saves it as a photo file.

Selecting this tool from **Tools/Video** on the **Toolbar** brings up an option screen which displays the grabbed frame from your video (based on the position of the **CTI** on your timeline) as well as a number of options for saving it, as illustrated above.

- You can choose to simply **insert** the still in your movie. The inserted still will display in your video project at whatever duration you've indicated in **Freeze Frame Duration**.
- Selecting the option to **Edit In Photoshop Elements After Inserting** loads the still into your movie and simultaneously launches it in the edit space of Photoshop Elements.

  Once you've made any adjustments to the photo in Photoshop Elements and saved the file, the updates will automatically appear in the photo in Premiere Elements.
- Whether or not you choose to insert the still into your movie, your **Freeze Frame** will be saved to your hard drive as a Bitmap (BMP) file and will appear in your current **Project Assets** panel.

One thing to note is that many video formats (DV-AVIs, for instance) store picture data in non-square pixels. So, if your video is, for instance, 720x480 anamorphic pixels in size, your **Freeze Frame** may look a bit squished or stretched when you print it or open it in Photoshop Elements.

If you'd prefer to save a **Freeze Frame** of your movie as a JPEG or TIF for use in either another video, Web or print project, you may prefer to use the **Still Image Share** output option that we discuss on page 268 of **Chapter 21, Export & Share Your Video Projects.**

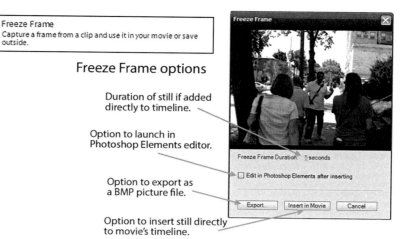

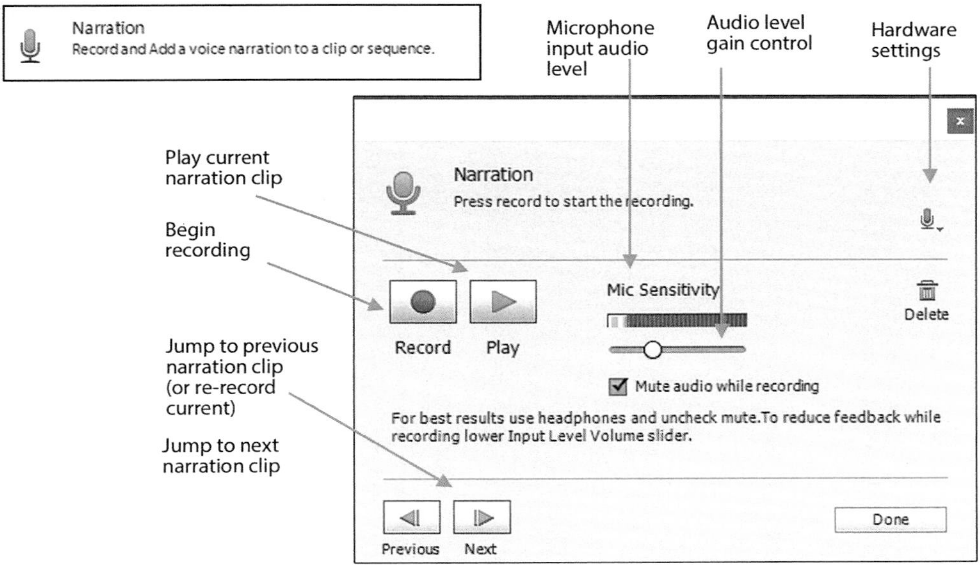

Add Narration

With this tool, you can add narration to your project – and even record it as you watch your video playing.

1 To launch the **Narration** tool, select **Tools/Audio** on the **Toolbar** and click on **Narration**.

The **Narration** panel will open.

If your microphone is properly configured, you should see the audio input level on the **Mic Sensitivity** meter in the center of the panel register as you speak.

You'll want to keep your microphone input level green and full, adjusting the slider as necessary for optimal sound.

Configuring your microphone for Narration

If the **Narration Tool** isn't recognizing your microphone at all (and you'll know, because your voice won't register on the **Narration** panel's input level meter), it could be that your microphone needs to be set up in the program's **Audio Hardware** settings.

Go to Premiere Elements' **Preferences** (under the **Edit** menu on a PC) and select the **Audio Hardware** page. Ensure that your narration microphone is selected as the **Default Input**.

If your microphone is still not detected, click this preference panel's **Settings** button and ensure that your microphone is properly configured in your computer's operating system.

Turn down your computer's speakers, wear headphones or select the option to **Mute Audio While Recording** so that you don't get feedback from your speakers as you record.

2 To record your narration, click the red **Record** button.

The panel will display a three-second countdown and then will begin recording as your movie plays.

3 Click the **Stop** button to stop the recording.

The audio you've recorded will appear as a clip on the **Narration** audio track.

Note that, when you've finished recording, the **CTI** will jump back to the beginning of your narration clip.

This is so that, if you're unhappy with your recording, you can immediately re-record your narration clip. Your new narration will automatically replace your old.

In fact, any narration you record will overwrite whatever audio is currently on **Narration** on the timeline. This is why it's best to reserve this audio track for narration recordings and not use it for music or other audio.

Click the **Play** button or press the spacebar on your keyboard to hear the results.

A good microphone and good, quality sound card are essential to getting a good strong narration recording.

Create a Pan & Zoom motion path

Pan & Zoom
Create quick and easy Pan and Zoom effects in videos and photos.

The **Pan & Zoom Tool** is an easy-to-use tool for creating motion paths – pans and zooms across your photos – using a very intuitive interface. (It's, of course, not the only way to create motion paths. For more information on using keyframes to create your own custom motion paths, see **Chapter 15, Keyframing**.)

Although this tool can also be used on video, the effect will create the best results when used on photos that have a slightly higher resolution than the video project. As we explain in **Use photos in Premiere Elements** on page 56, you'll get the best balance of photo quality and system performance if your photos are no larger than 1000x750 pixels in size for standard DV or DVDs and 2500x1875 pixels for high-def video.)

1 Click to select a still photo on your timeline.

2 Select **Tools/Video** on the **Toolbar** and click on the **Pan & Zoom** tool.

The **Pan & Zoom** workspace will open, as illustrated on the facing page.

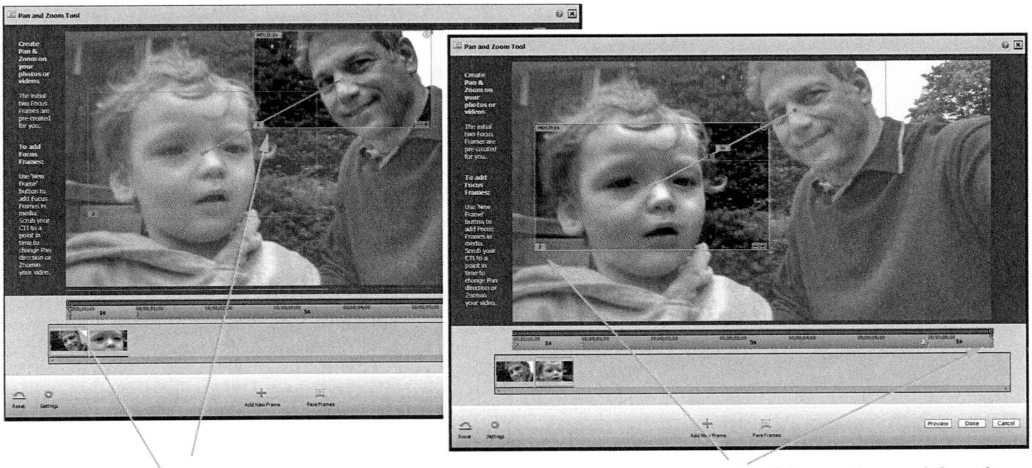

With the CTI at the beginning of the timeline, drag the corner handles to size and position Frame 1 to create the initial composition for your motion path.

Move the CTI to the end of the timeline and then drag the corner handles of Frame 2 to create the composition you'd like your motion path to end on.

Place the CTI at other positions on the timeline and click the New Frame button to create as many additional motion path keyframes as you need (including hold motion frames) to build your motion path.

The concept behind this workspace is a simple one: You indicate the views (**Focus Frames**) you'd like for the beginning and for the end of your pan and zoom and Premiere Elements will create the path of motion between them.

By default, the program will use **Face Recognition** metadata to automatically create a five-second motion path from one face to another with a one-second pause on each face. (For more information on metadata, see **Auto Analyze your media** on page 208.) You may opt to use this proposed motion path or customize it.

3 Customize your initial **Focus Frame.**

Ensure that the **CTI** is at the beginning of the timeline that runs along the bottom of the workspace. (You should see a little, diamond-shaped keyframe on the timeline at the **CTI's** position.)

Drag the corner handles on **Frame 1** (the highlighted green box) to size and position your motion path's initial **Focus Frame.**

4 Move the **CTI** to the end of the timeline.

There will be another diamond-shaped keyframe at this position on the timeline. When you move the **CTI** over this keyframe, **Frame 2** will become highlighted.

Size and position **Frame 2**. (A little blue line will indicate the duration (in seconds) of your motion.) Continue to adjust any other **Focus Frames,** as needed.

Click the **Preview** button along the bottom right of the panel to preview your motion path.

To add more **Focus Frames** to your motion path, move the **CTI** to another position on the timeline and click the **Add New Frame** button below the timeline, as illustrated on the previous page.

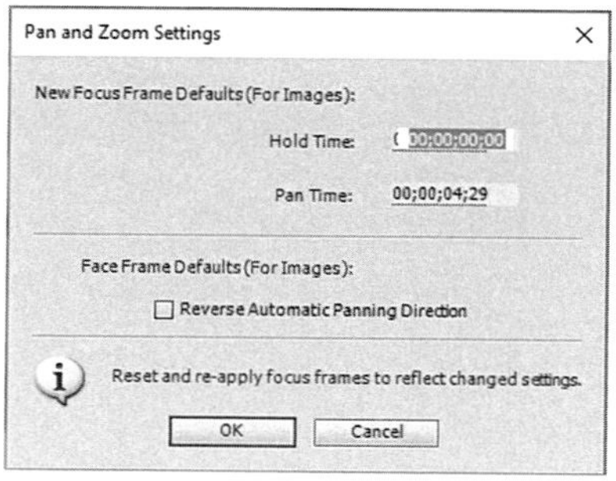

If you'd like to permanently remove the one-second pause at each **Focus Frame**, click the **Settings** button in the lower left of the workspace. On the **Pan and Zoom Settings** panel that opens, change the **Hold Time** to 00;00;00;00. **OK** the change and then click the **Reset** button in the lower left of the workspace.

5 When you are satisfied with your motion path, click **Done** to return to the regular editing workspace.

If you'd like to further customize this motion path, you can do so by opening the clip's **Motion** properties, as described in **Chapter 15, Keyframing.**

Smart Mix your audio

Premiere Elements' **Smart Mix** tool will automatically adjust the levels of several audio tracks to allow one track to dominate over the others.

In other words, if you've got a sequence that includes music, narration and the original audio from a video clip, **Smart Mix** can be set to automatically lower the music and other audio levels whenever there is a narration clip.

1 To set the criteria for your audio clip adjustments, select **Tools/ Audio** on the **Toolbar** and click on the **Smart Mix** tool.

The **Smart Mixer Options** panel displays each audio track in your Premiere Elements project and allows you to indicate, with drop-down menus, which tracks will serve as your audio **Foreground**, which will serve as **Background** and which will be **Disabled** completely. (As illustrated below.)

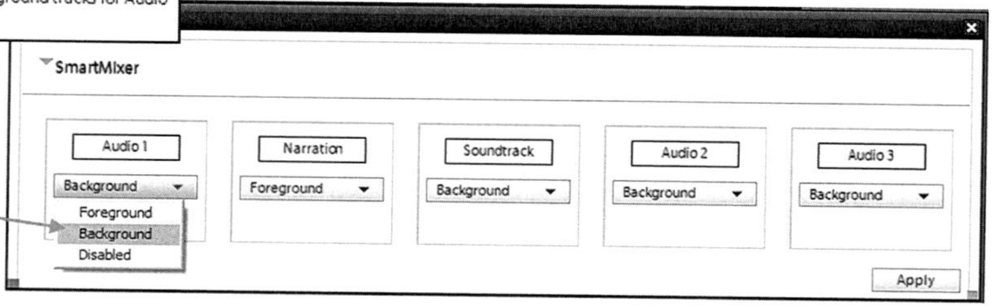

In the SmartMixer, you designate which audio tracks will dominate and which will be lowered or eliminated completely.

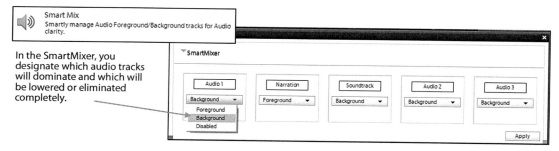

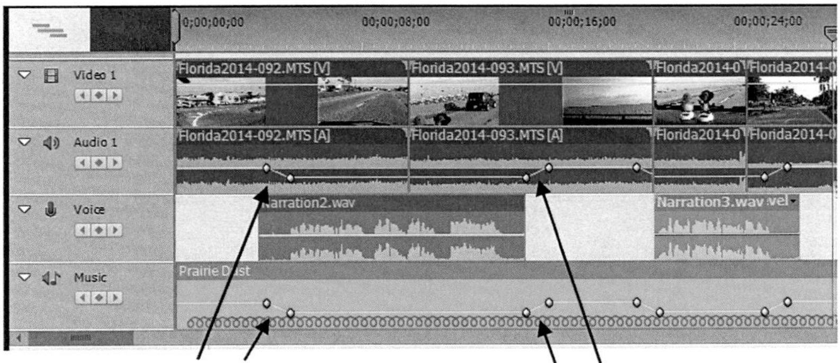

When applied, Smart Trim automatically creates the necessary keyframes to lower the audio on the tracks you've designated as Background.

2 Once you've set your preferences for the tool, activate the **Smart Mix** feature by clicking on the **Apply** button.

The **Smart Mixer** will create the necessary audio keyframes – which appear as little white dots on your audio clip(s) (as seen above) – to lower the volume of the audio clip(s) that you've designated as **Background** audio.

Further, if you move or change a clip you've indicated as your **Foreground** and re-apply **Smart Mix**, the **Smart Mixer** will automatically remove or revise the audio keyframes!

To set preferences for the **Smart Mixer** – including how much the **Background** audio is reduced in volume and if the **Foreground** audio is automatically **Normalized** – go to the Premiere Elements **Preferences** panel (under **Edit**) and select the **Audio** page.

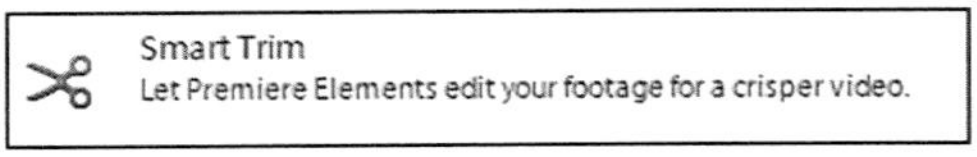

Smart Trim your video

The **Smart Trim** tool analyzes clips you've added to your movie's timeline, indicating which sequences do not meet quality standards, then recommends trims to remove segments from your clips (or automatically trims the sequences for you).

1 To **Smart Trim** your video, select **Tools/Video** on the **Toolbar** and click on the **Smart Trim** tool.

If your video has not already been analyzed in the Element Organizer, the **Auto-Analyzer** will automatically search all of the videos on your timeline and indicate in which segments the lighting is bad, the picture is blurry or the camcorder was not held steady. It will also use **Face Recognition** to identify areas of the clip in which people appear.

These indicated areas – called **Suggested Trimmings** – will appear with blue diagonal lines over them, as illustrated on the following page.

If you hover your mouse over these areas, the program will indicate why it

If you hover your mouse over a Smart Trim Suggested Trimmimg, Premiere Elements will explain why the segment should be removed.

recommends they be removed.

You may then opt to either remove any or all of the **Suggested Trimming** segments or to override the program's suggestion.

2 Click on a **Suggested Trimming** to select it.

The diagonal shading will highlight in light blue.

By dragging on either end of this selected segment, you can trim or extend the length of this **Suggested Trimming** area.

3 Once you've tweaked your **Suggested Trimming** area, **right-click** on this area and select the option to:

Trim, or remove the **Suggested Trimming** segment from your video.

Keep, or opt not to remove the **Suggested Trimming** segment.

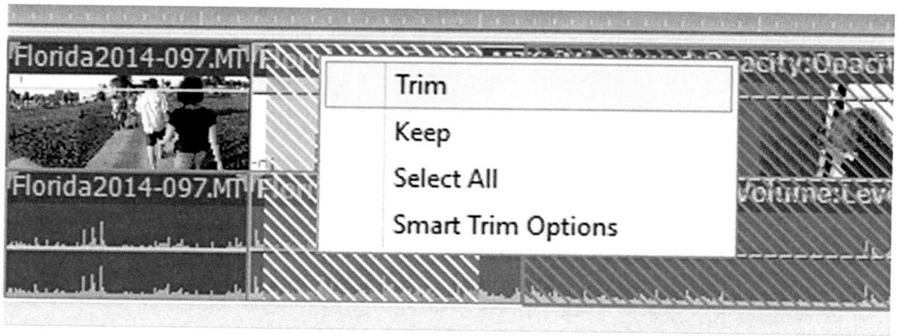

Right-click on a selected Suggested Trimming area to select whether to cut it or to override the recommendation.

Select All of the **Suggested Trimmings** and remove them.

Additionally, this context menu includes access to the **Smart Trim Options** panel.

A pair of sliders on the **Smart Trim Options** panel allows you to set a **Quality Level** and an **Interest Level** for any new clips you add.

Quality automatically checks your clips for issues like blurriness, shakiness, brightness and contrast.

Interest examines the segments recommended for deletion based on your **Quality** setting and re-evaluates their content to see if they're actually worth saving, based on your **Interest** level.

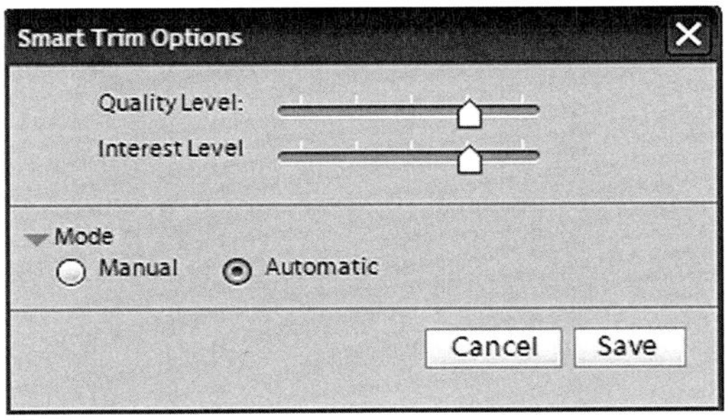

In other words, the **Interest Level** and **Quality Level** balance each other out, according to the levels you set.

On this **Options** panel, you can also set **Smart Trim** to **Automatic** mode, in which case it will automatically remove any **Suggested Trimming** areas from your video timeline as it detects them.

Create cool Time Remapping effects

Time Remapping is one of the newest and most sophisticated tools in the Premiere Elements toolkit.

With **Time Remapping**, you designate a section of a clip on your timeline and the tool will suddenly speed it up or slow it to a crawl – then just as suddenly, bring it back to real time – like it's some cool modern action film.

You can slow your video to as much as one-eighth speed with this tool, by the way, with excellent results. The **Remapping** feature of this tool does an excellent job of blending the motion in between frames so that even extremely slowed action looks smooth and even. (Clicking the **Frame Blending** button, in

the lower left of the workspace, further improves this smoothing.)

The workspace for this effect is very simple, yet also surprisingly powerful.

1 Click to select a clip on your timeline.

2 Select **Tools/Video** on the **Toolbar** and click on the **Time Remapping** tool.

The **Time Remapping** workspace will open. Your clip will be

displayed on a timeline along the bottom of the interface.

3 Create a **Time Zone** by moving the **CTI** to the approximate location of the clip you'd like to remap and either clicking the **Add Time Zone** button in the lower left of the interface or clicking the **+** sign on the **CTI**.

A yellow-green box will indicate the location of the designated **Time Zone** on your clip. The speed of your playback for this **Time**

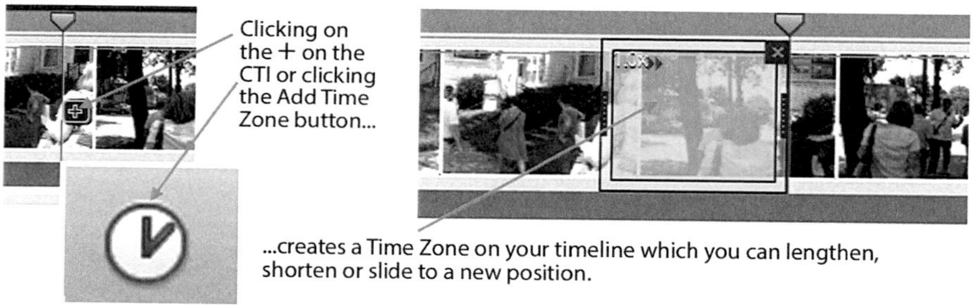

Clicking on the + on the CTI or clicking the Add Time Zone button...
...creates a Time Zone on your timeline which you can lengthen, shorten or slide to a new position.

Zone is indicated by a number in the upper left of this box– which by default reads 1.0x (normal speed).

4 Tweak your **Time Zone's** location or size by dragging on either

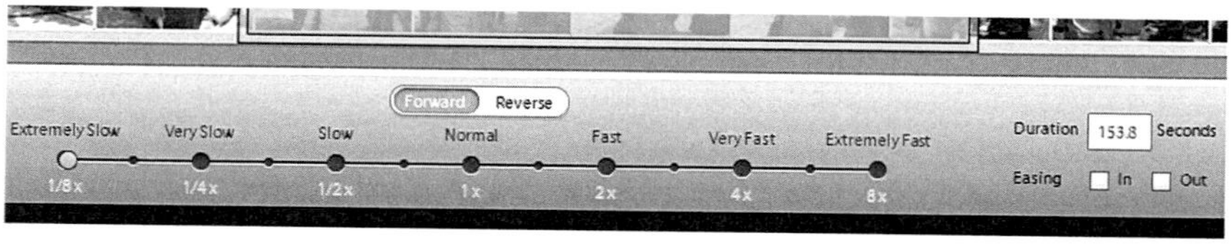

end of this green box. The duration of your **Time Zone** segment is indicated in the lower right of the workspace interface.

5 Select a **Time Remapping** speed using the big slider.

The **X** indicator on the upper left of the green box will indicate the new playback speed of your **Time Zone**, while the **Duration** indicator will list its adjusting playback time. In other words, a 10-second **Time Zone** set to play at 2.0x will have a duration of 5 seconds. Pretty simple, right?

Your **Time Zone** can be mapped to play in forward or reverse, by clicking the toggle above the slider.

You can add several **Time Zones** of varying speeds to a single clip, by the way. Although they can't overlap or double-up on each other.

But note that your audio will not be affected by your speed settings. And, when you click **Done** to leave this workspace, you'll be offered the option of removing the audio completely from your clip. If you elect not to remove your audio, it will remain as a separate clip on your timeline, no longer in sync with your video.

Finally, if the shift to high or low speed and back again seems too abrupt, you can select the option to **Ease In** or **Ease Out** of a **Time Remapping** segment.

Time Stretch your scenes

Time Stretch (available only in Expert View) isn't nearly as sophisticated a tool as **Time Remapping** – but it gets the job done.

Unlike **Time Remapping, Time Stretch** is applied to an entire clip on your timeline at once rather than applied to a designated segment.

To **Time Stretch** a clip:

1. Click to select a clip on your timeline.
2. **Right-click** on your clip and select **Clip** then, from the sub-menu, select **Time Stretch**.

   The **Time Stretch** option screen will open, as illustrated below.
3. Set the amount your clip will be **Time Stretched** by either

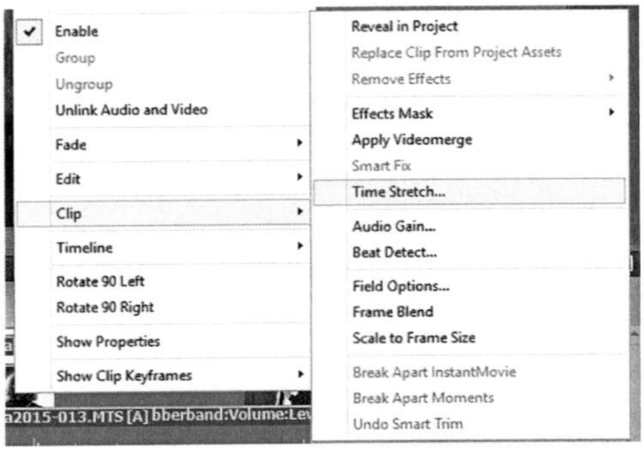

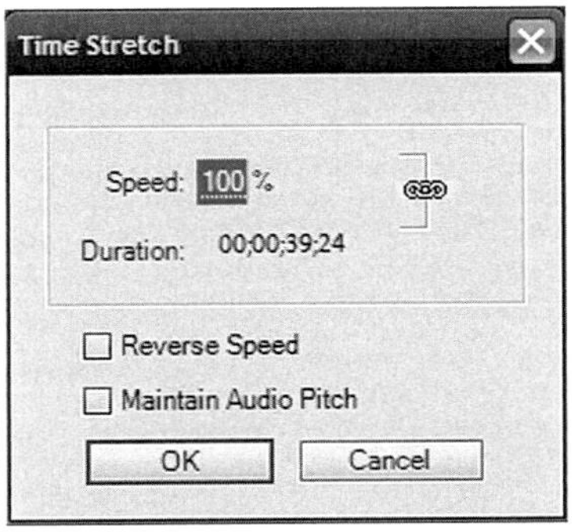

designating the percentage of playback **Speed** or by setting the **Duration** you'd like the clip to extend or contract to. (The shorter the **Duration**, the faster the **Speed**, and vice versa.)

To play a clip in reverse, check the **Reverse** option box.

Select Favorite Moments from your video clip

Favorite Moments is a cool workspace for locating and creating a compilation of your favorite segments from a longer video clip.

Like the **Clip Monitor** (see page 64), the **Favorite Moments** workspace is a tool for previewing and trimming your video clips. But, with the **Favorite Moments** tool, you can select and fine tune *several* segments of a single video clip.

The program will then save your "favorite" segments to the timeline, a simple **Default Transition** between them.

1 Open the **Favorite Moments** workspace.

Click to select a clip on your timeline, then select **Tools/Video** on the **Toolbar** and click on the **Favorite Moments** tool.

The **Favorite Moments** workspace will open, and your clip will be displayed on the workspace's timeline.

2 Start a **Favorite Moments** selection.

There are two ways to create a **Favorite Moments** selection:

Click the + sign on the **CTI** playhead. A yellow, one-second overlay will appear on your clip.

Stretch or trim this overlay by dragging on either end of it until your "favorite moment" is selected.

Alternatively, you can simply play your video through and click the **Star (Mark Moment)** button at the bottom center of the workspace to mark the beginnings and ends of your "favorite moment" selections.

Clicking the **Star** button starts a selection and clicking it again ends it. Using the same process, you can create as many selected segments on your clip as you'd like.

Clicking the **Auto Mark Moments** button will launch the **Auto Analyzer** (page 208), and the tool will then automatically select **Favorite Moments** based on the visual quality of the video and the presence of faces in your clip.

3 Adjust and customize your selection.

Drag either end of a yellow selection overlay to trim, extend or move it. The **Monitor** panel will display your selection's new beginning or end point.

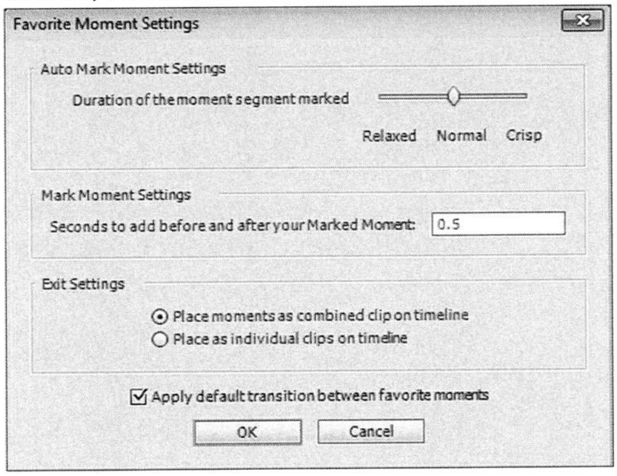

When you are satisfied with the **Favorite Moments** you've selected, click the **Done** button to return to the Premiere Elements timeline.

4 Customize your **Favorite Moments** Settings.

To control how the tool processes your selections, click the **Settings** button in the lower left of the tool's interface.

When the **Favorite Moments** tool generates your finished compilation, it will automatically add a **Default Transition** between your selections. By default, this transition is a **Cross-Dissolve** – however, you can set any transition as your **Default Transition**, as we discuss on page 134.

To turn off the option to add a transition between your selected segments, uncheck the **Apply Default Transition** option on the **Settings** panel.

The **Mark Moments Settings** will optionally add a pre- or post-duration to your selections. This adds a few extra frames to the beginning

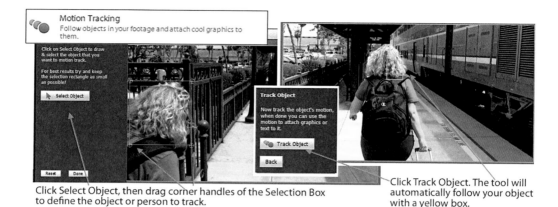

Click Select Object, then drag corner handles of the Selection Box to define the object or person to track.

Click Track Object. The tool will automatically follow your object with a yellow box.

or end of each selection so that a vital part of your selected segment doesn't get lost during the transition between segments.

Finally, the **Exit Settings** allow you to set whether your finished **Favorite Moments** compilation appears as a single clip on your timeline or if the tool creates a separate short clip of each selected segment.

Follow an object or person with Motion Tracking

Premiere Elements' **Motion Tracking** tool will lock onto an object or person you indicate in a clip and follow it, him or her around your video frame.

You can then link a graphic to that object or person and the program will automatically create a motion path so that the graphic moves around the video frame along with the tracked person or object!

You can, for instance, link someone running across your frame with clip art of a hat or a cartoon talk bubble, and that hat or bubble will follow that person throughout the clip.

To use the **Motion Tracking** tool:

1. Click to select a video clip on your timeline. For best results, make sure the **CTI** playhead is positioned at the point in your clip at which you'd like your **Motion Tracking** to begin.

2. Select **Tools/Video** on the **Toolbar** and click on the **Motion Tracking** tool.

   The **Motion Tracking** workspace will open in the **Monitor** panel, as illustrated above.

3. Click the **Select Object** button.

   A selection box will appear on your video. Drag on the box's corner handles to position this box or the person or object in your video that you'd like to track. (The more distinct in color your selected object is from your video's background, the better the tool will work.)

4 Once you've framed the object or person to be tracked, click on the **Track Object** button.

The program will analyze the clip and automatically create the motion keyframes necessary to follow your indicated person or object around your video frame.

When it has finished, if you play or scrub the clip (by dragging the **CTI** back and forth), a yellow box should follow the indicated object or person around your video frame.

When a graphic is linked to the Motion Tracked object, the program creates keyframes so that the clip follows the object across the video frame.

To link a graphic to your **Motion Track**:

5 Click on the **Graphics** button on the bottom of the **Toolbar**, as discussed in **Add a Graphic to your movie** on page 115.

Select a graphic from one of the 13 **Graphics** categories. Drag the graphic onto the **Motion Tracking** yellow rectangle (which will turn temporarily blue) on your **Monitor** panel, at the point in your video in which you'd like this graphic to first appear.

You can size or position this graphic by dragging on its corner handles or by dragging it around the video frame.

Premiere Elements includes a set of animated clips that move or change shape as they follow your Motion Track across your video frame.

The graphics clip will be added to a video track above your current video. When you leave the **Motion Tracking** workspace (by clicking on the timeline, for instance), the tool will create the necessary motion keyframes so that the graphic will follow your object or person.

You can lengthen the duration of most graphics by dragging on one end to extend it on the timeline. However, animated graphics have a fixed duration and can not be extended.

Similarly, you can link a picture-in-picture video or previously-created title to your **Motion Track**:

Click on the **Project Assets** button (which, in Expert View, will now have moved to the upper *right* of the program's interface, as illustrated below).

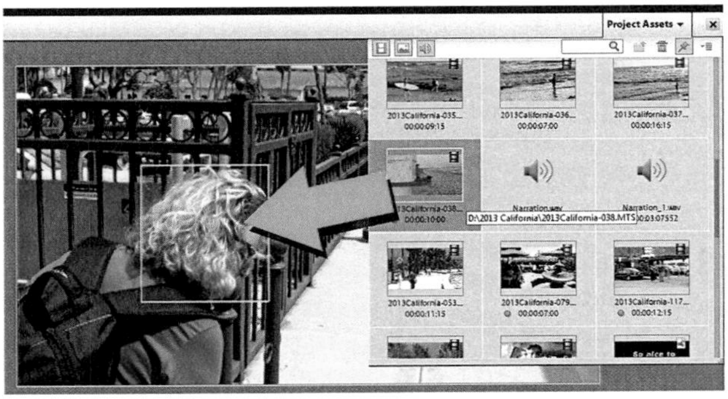

Select a video clip from the **Project Assets** panel and drag it onto the **Motion Tracking** yellow rectangle (which will turn temporarily blue), at the point in your video in which you'd like this graphic to appear.

You can size or position this clip by dragging on its corner handles or dragging it around.

The clip will be added to a video track above your current video. When you leave the **Motion Tracking** workspace (by clicking on the timeline, for instance), the tool will create the necessary motion keyframes so that the graphic will follow your object or person.

Cartoon Thought or Speech Bubbles graphics can be used to follow a person in your video.

Thought and Speech Bubbles are some of the most fun graphics to follow people in your videos with. Like titles, these graphics clips can be opened and customized.

1. Add a graphic from the **Thought and Speech Bubbles** category, as described in **Step 5** above.
2. A pop-up panel will appear. Type in your custom text. (You can modify it, as well as the text's style and font, later.) Click **OK**.

   You can size or position this clip by dragging on the corner handles or dragging it around. The **Thought or Speech Bubble** clip will be added to a video track above your current video. When you leave the **Motion Tracking** workspace (by clicking on the timeline, for instance), the tool will create the necessary motion keyframes so that the graphic will follow your object or person.

Once the program has finished creating the **Motion Track** so that the **Thought or Speech Bubble** follows your selected object or person around your video frame, you can open the **Bubble** and customize it.

3. Select the **Thought or Speech Bubble** clip on your timeline and click the **Adjust** button on the right side of the interface.

   The **Thought or Speech Bubble** will open in the **Title Adjustments** workspace, where you can change the text, the text's style, color, position and color, as described in **Chapter 12, Add Titles & Text**.

   Don't worry that, when you open the **Thought or Speech Bubble** in the **Title Adjustments** workspace, it enlarges to fill your **Monitor** panel, as on the facing page. It does this for editing purposes only. When you close the **Adjustments** panel or click on the timeline to return to the regular editing workspace, the **Thought or Speech Bubble** will revert to the size and position you set for it when you created your **Motion Tracking** graphic.

If you reopen the **Motion Tracking** tool a number of times for the same clip, you may

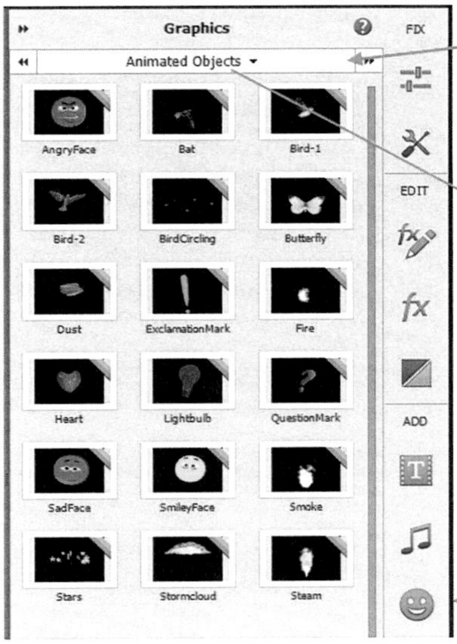

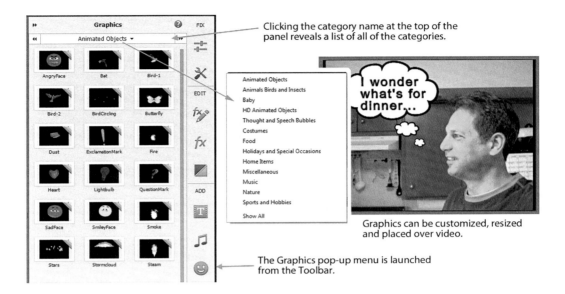

Clicking the category name at the top of the panel reveals a list of all of the categories.

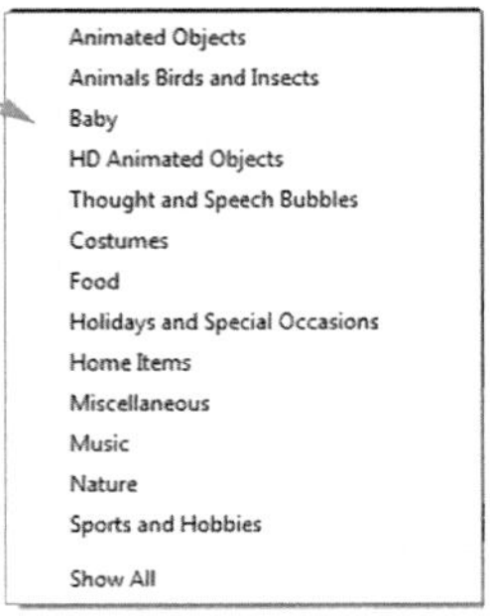

Graphics can be customized, resized and placed over video.

The Graphics pop-up menu is launched from the Toolbar.

find yourself with several yellow rectangles following your object(s) or person(s) around. To remove the extra rectangles, click to select each, then **right-click** and select **Delete Selected Object**.

Add a graphic to your movie

A cool little extra feature that Adobe includes with Premiere Elements is a library of over 350 video graphics in 13 categories, including cartoon characters, food, musical instruments, wigs and costumes and themed graphics for birthdays and holidays, new babies and sports.

And most interesting of all, a number of these graphics are even animated!

These animated graphics include cartoon faces that move, a fluttering butterfly, a storm cloud, fire, steam and a circle of stars.

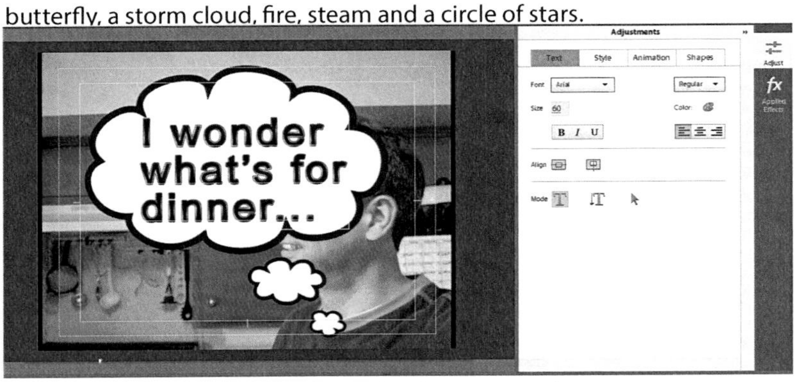

Graphics, like titles, can be edited in the Title Adjustments workspace.

These graphics are transparent, so you can place them right over your video.

To access the Premiere Elements **Graphics** library, click on the **Graphics** button at the far right of the **Toolbar**. To add a graphic to your movie, simply drag it to your timeline – or directly onto your **Monitor**.

Among my favorite graphics are the **Thought and Speech Bubbles**.

Functioning essentially like title templates, a thought bubble or speech bubble is dragged to your timeline on a video track above existing video or directly onto the clip in the **Monitor** panel. You can then size it by selecting the clip in your **Monitor** and dragging in or out on its corner handles.

To edit and customize the text, just **double-click** on the graphic clip on your timeline. The graphic and text will open in the **Title Adjustments** workspace, as described in **Chapter 12, Add Titles & Text**.

Smart Fixing Your Video

Color, Gamma and Lighting Adjustments

Adjusting Color Temperature and Tint

Adjusting Volume, Balance, Bass and Treble

Keyframing Adjustments

Adjustment Layers

Chapter 10

Make Adjustments to Your Video and Audio

Correct and customize your clips' levels

Premiere Elements includes a whole panel of adjustment tools for correcting your videos' colors, lighting and color temperature and for setting your audio's volume and balance.

Even better, thanks to Adobe's simple Quick Fix interface, making these adjustments couldn't be more intuitive!

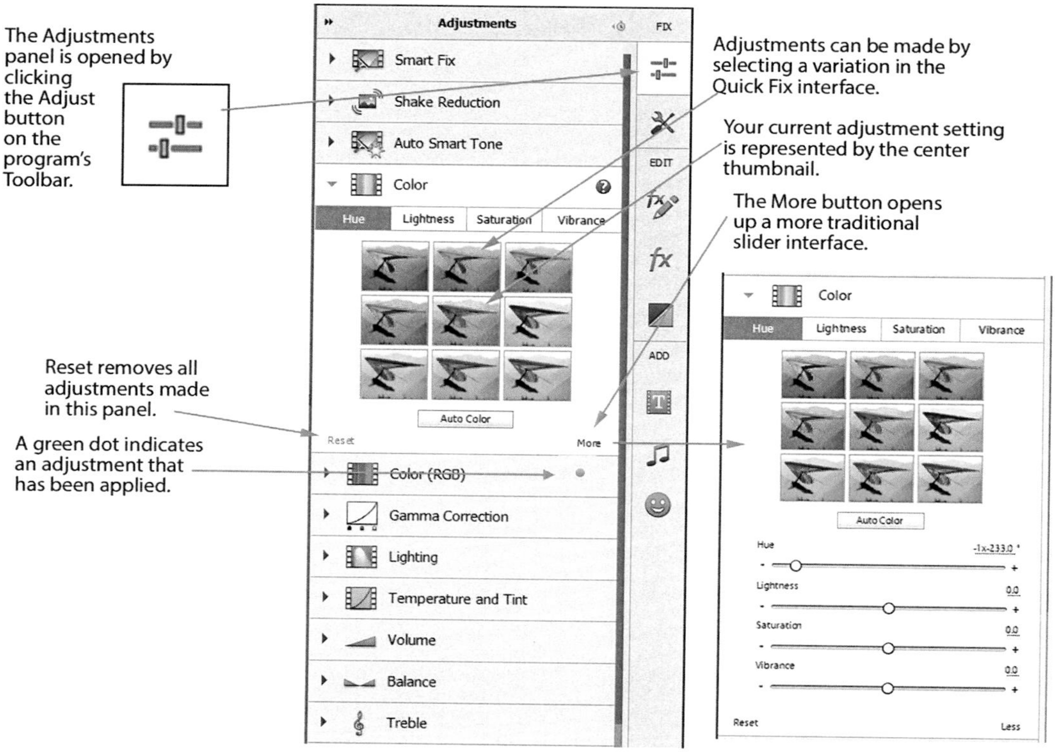
The Adjustments panel is opened by clicking the Adjust button on the program's Toolbar.
Adjustments can be made by selecting a variation in the Quick Fix interface.
Your current adjustment setting is represented by the center thumbnail.
The More button opens up a more traditional slider interface.
Reset removes all adjustments made in this panel.
A green dot indicates an adjustment that has been applied.
Adjustments
FIX
Smart Fix
Shake Reduction
Auto Smart Tone
Color
Hue
Lightness
Saturation
Vibrance
Auto Color
Reset
More
Color (RGB)
Gamma Correction
Lighting
Temperature and Tint
Volume
Balance
Treble
EDIT
ADD
Less

The **Adjustments** panel includes eight powerful video tools and five helpful audio tools for fine tuning the color, lighting, sound and balance levels of your video and audio clips. Which adjustment tools are available depends, of course, on whether the clip you've selected on your timeline includes audio, video or both.

The **Adjustments** pop-up panel is launched by clicking the **Adjust** button on the **Toolbar** along right of the Premiere Elements interface.

Applying an **Adjustment** to a clip is as simple as selecting an audio or video clip on your timeline and selecting an option from the listing in the pop-up menu.

Each video **Adjustment** tool (except **Smart Fix** and the **Shake Stabilizer**) includes an intuitive, picture-based interface as well as a slider-based adjustment tool set (opened by clicking the **More** button, as illustrated above).

On the Tic Tac Toe-style adjustment tool (called the **Quick Fix** interface), your un-adjusted image is represented by the center square thumbnail. Adjustments are applied to your video as you click on one of the surrounding squares. To reset your image's look, click the center square.

Any adjustments can also be undone by clicking the **Reset** button in the lower left of the tool panel (or by, of course, pressing **Ctrl+z** on your keyboard (**⌘+z** on a Mac) to undo the last adjustment applied).

Most of the video **Adjustment** tools include options also for adjusting several individual lighting and color elements. For instance, the **Color Adjustment** tool includes options for fine-tuning **Hue, Lightness, Saturation** and **Vibrance** (as discussed below).

A number of tools also include the option to apply **Auto Levels** or **Auto Fixes**. Once you've applied an **Auto Fix**, you can, of course, further tweak your levels using the **Quick Fix** interface or sliders.

Once any **Adjustments** have been applied to a clip, a green dot will appear on the right end of the **Adjustments** panel next to the applied effect's listing, as illustrated on the facing page.

Smart Fix

Smart Fix is a tool which automatically adjusts the lighting and color in your video and, if necessary, adds the **Shake Stabilizer** effect (see below) to reduce movement in handheld shots.

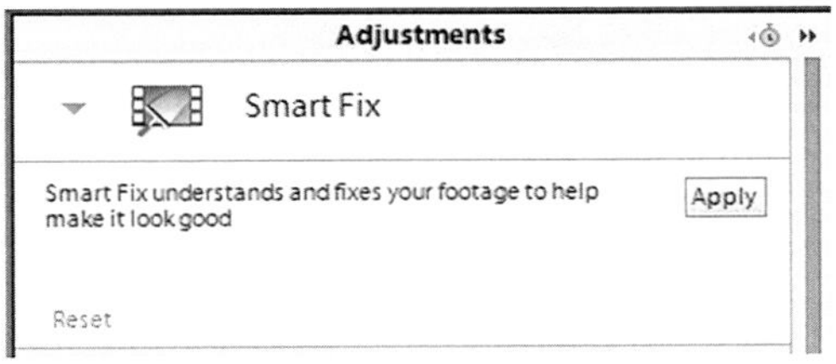

(Note that, if your clip has not yet been analyzed and **Smart Tagged** by the Elements Organizer's **Media Analyzer** (see page 208), the program may need to **Auto-Analyze** the clip before a **Smart Fix** adjustment can be applied.)

When a simple tweak is needed, **Smart Fix** often does a very good job.

The Shake Stabilizer

The Shake Stabilizer locks onto the content in the center of your video and then adds several adjustment keyframes to the position of your video to keep that content in the frame's center. It can be a great tool for taking some of the shake out of your handheld camera shots.

It's not magic – and it can't take the shake completely out of every video – but it is remarkably effective and it can certainly smooth out most of the bumpier bumps.

To use it, simply select the clip you want to stabilize on your timeline, click the **Adjust** button to open the **Adjustments** panel, click on **Shake Stabilizer** and then click the **Quick** or, for more challenging video, the **Detailed** button. The program will analyze the content of your clip, apply the **Shake Stabilizer** effect and make the necessary adjustments.

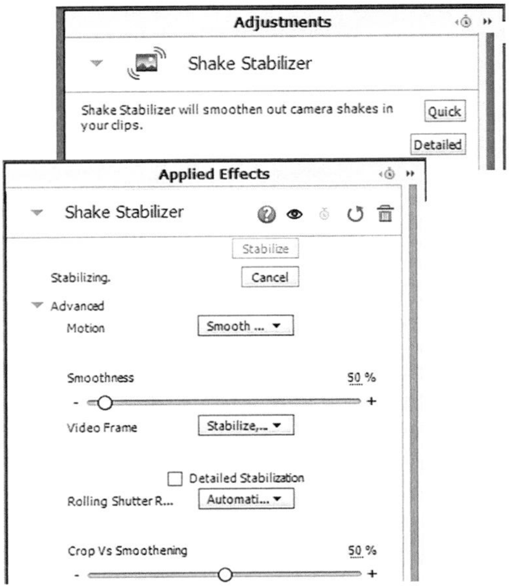

You can further tweak this effect in the **Applied Effects** panel. **In fact, for best results, we recommend going to the Stabilizer's Advanced settings on the Applied Effects panel and using the *minimal* settings (often as low as 10-15% for Smoothness and Crop vs. Smoothening). This will minimize the "over-rezzed" blurring the default settings tend to produce.**

Auto Smart Tone

Like the similarly-named feature in Photoshop Elements, **Auto Smart Tone** allows you to adjust your video clip's color tone levels by intuitively moving a control dot toward previews of various tone variations. (Tone is similar to brightness and contrast, but is somewhat more sophisticated, usually based on the range of individual red, green and blue levels in your video.)

The tool also includes an automatic **Smart Tone** feature, which can be activated by simply clicking the **Apply** button on the **Auto Smart Tone** panel.

To manually adjust your video's color tone:

1 Select **Auto Smart Tone** from the program's **Adjustments** menu, then click **Custom.**

The **Smart Tone** workspace will open.

A grid with a control dot in the center will appear over your video. On each of the four corners of the workspace will appear thumbnails representing tone level variations.

2 Adjust your video's tone.

To adjust your video's tone, drag the control dot toward the thumbnail that best represents the tone you'd like your photo to have.

Smart Tone adjustments are made by dragging the control dot toward the variation that best represents the adjustment you want.

If you check the option to **Learn From This Correction** in the lower left of the workspace, the next time you apply **Auto Smart Tone**, the tool's default setting will be based on the tone levels you've set in the past.

Color

The **Color Adjustments** tool has separate adjustment panels for **Hue, Lightness, Saturation** and **Vibrance**.

Hue is the color mix itself, as imagined on a color wheel with violet in the upper left, magenta in the upper right, cyan in the lower right and green in the lower left. Changing this effect will shift the color hue values of all of the colors in your clip.

Lightness is the amount of white or black mixed with the color.

Saturation is the amount of hue applied (more blue or less blue, for instance).

Vibrance, similar to saturation, is the overall richness or intensity of the colors.

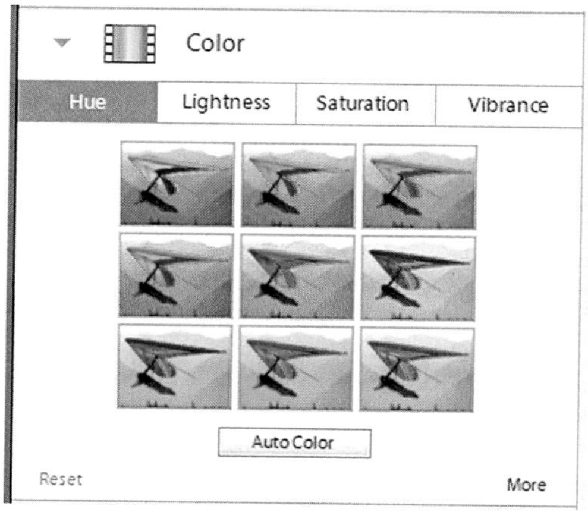

The panel includes an **Auto Color** button for a quick color correction.

Color (RGB)

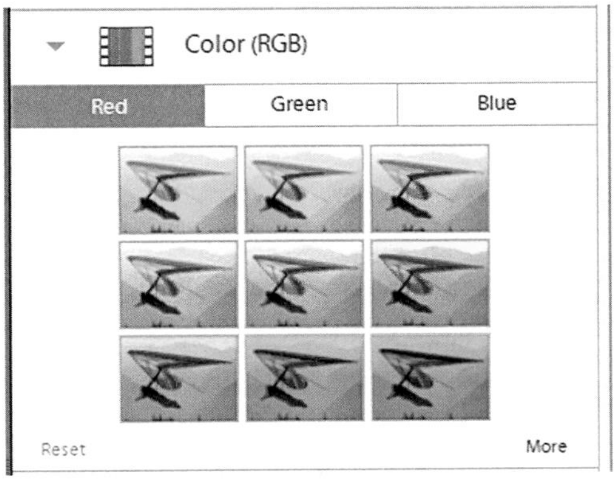

In contrast to the **Color Adjustments**, the **Color (RGB) Adjustments** are concerned only with the levels of **Red**, **Green** and **Blue**, the three primary colors of video.

Selecting one of the squares on each of the color's **Quick Fix** interfaces, or adjusting the corresponding slider, sets an intensity level for that particular color only (on a scale of 0% to 200%) without affecting either of the other two colors' levels.

Gamma Correction

Gamma is basically how bright or dark a picture is. Unlike **Lighting** (below), which bases its changes on the whitest white point and the blackest black point in an image, **Gamma** brightens or darkens an image based on its mid-tones. In other words, **Brightness** and **Contrast** deal with how white or black an image is, while changing the **Gamma** level brightens or dims the image.

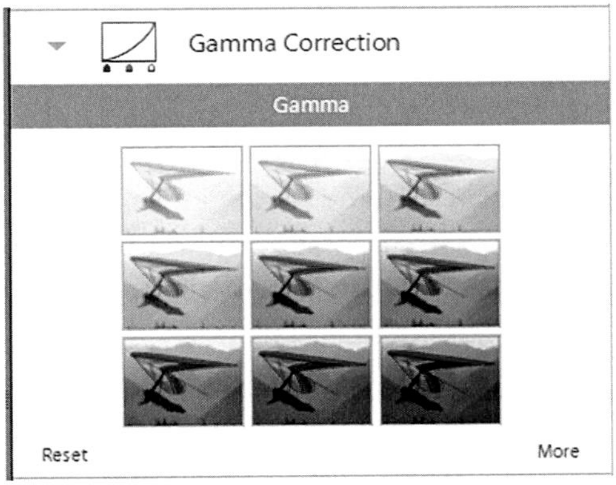

It's a subtle difference, to be sure. But the important thing to understand is that sometimes a video needs its **Lightness** adjusted – and sometimes it needs its **Gamma** adjusted. So, if one doesn't work, try the other. Eventually, you'll come to recognize the difference.

Lighting

Lighting sets the level of the whitest white and the blackest black in your video and/or adjusts the contrast between them. This **Adjustment** includes five separate adjustment panels: **Brightness, Contrast, Exposure, Black** and **White**.

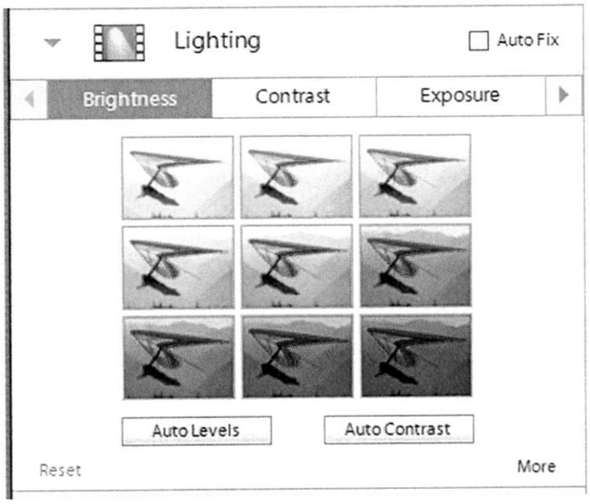

- **Brightness** sets the levels for the blackest black or whitest white point in your video image. The higher the black level, the darker your image will look; the higher the white level, the lighter.
- **Contrast** increases or reduces the difference between the lighter and darker elements in your image.
- **Exposure** simulates lighting adjustments usually made automatically in your camera or camcorder as it takes a picture or shoots your video. This can be a great tool for

fixing a picture shot, for instance, in shade with a brighter background, in which your subject came out too dark.

Black increases or decreases the amount of black in your video image.

White increases or decreases the amount of white in your video image.

(If the **Black** and **White** options aren't visible on your panel, you can scroll to see them by clicking the arrow to the right of the **Exposure** tab along the top of the panel.)

In addition to the **Auto Levels** and **Auto Contrast** buttons, this **Adjustment** tool includes an **Auto Fix** checkbox along the top right of the panel. Checking this box applies a **Lighting Auto Fix** to your video image – however, it also locks out the other tools on this panel from further adjustment.

Temperature and Tint

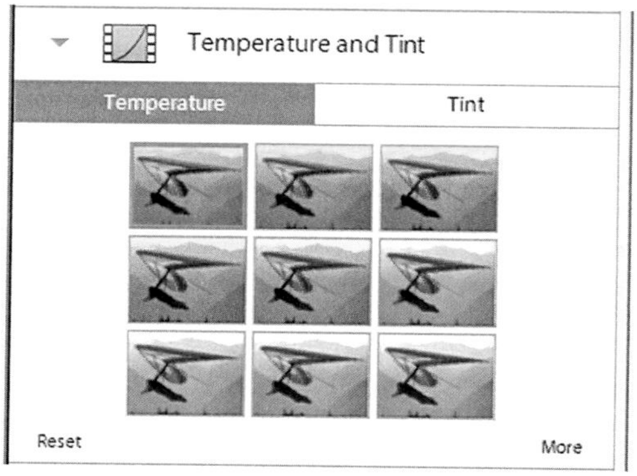

Temperature and **Tint** are color correction tools for compensating for video shot in less-than-ideal lighting conditions – or, of course, for intentionally applying a cooling or warming effect.

Color Temperature refers to the frequency or temperature of light applied to a given scene. Sunlight and outdoor lighting, for instance, has a color temperature of about 6,500 K, which gives pictures shot outdoors a slightly blue tone. Indoor incandescent lights are around 3,000 K, giving your pictures a redder or yellower tone.

In most cases, you don't notice the difference in color temperatures because your eyes – and camcorders – automatically adjust for it.

However, if you've ever shot a video or taken a picture in which a person is lit by indoor lighting while standing in front of a window or an open door, you've seen the difference. The camera adjusts to one or the other color temperature, and you end up with either the person looking orange or the outdoor background looking blue.

This can also happen if you've been shooting indoors and then run outdoors and start shooting before your camcorder has a chance to reset. The leaves on the trees come out all green-blue!

Color temp set too low.

Proper color temp setting.

Color temp set too high.

Temperature adjusts the color temperature of your video image so that the unwanted blue or red/yellow tones are corrected.

Tint, a more primitive way of correcting color, shifts the hue of your video to various levels of red, green and blue.

You can also use these **Adjustments** to intentionally change the tint of your video to create, for instance, a spookier, gloomier tone.

However, to achieve these visual effects, you may find Premiere Elements' great library of **Hollywood Looks** much more effective. For more information on these **Effects**, see page 158.

Volume

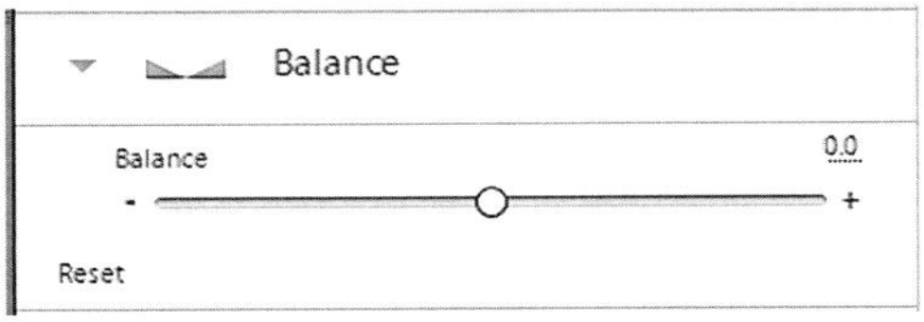

Pretty simply, **Volume** increases or decreases the loudness of your audio clips. This adjustment, by the way, can also be made by raising and lowering the yellow horizontal "**Rubber Band**" line running through the audio clips on the Expert View timeline. These levels can also be adjusted higher or lower at specific points on your timeline using keyframing, as we discuss on page 189.

Balance

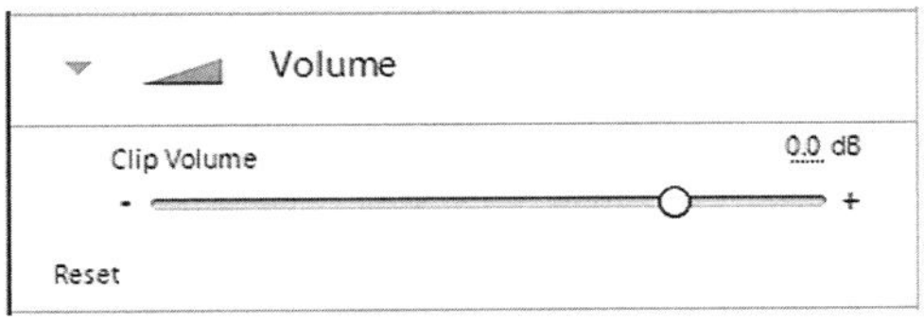

Balance adjusts the levels of your right and left stereo audio channels with respect to each other.

By the way, if you've recorded with a monaural device and you have audio on only one channel, you spread it across both channels equally using the **Fill Left with Right** or **Fill Right with Left Audio Effects**, as discussed on page 168.

Treble and Bass

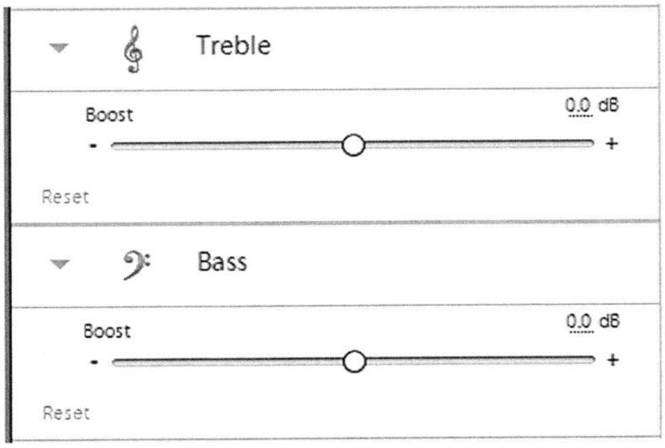

These **Adjustment** tools decrease or increase the levels of specific frequencies on your audio clips.

Treble adjusts the levels of the higher frequency sounds in your audio.

Bass adjusts the levels of the lower frequency sounds.

Audio Gain

While the **Volume** sets how loudly your audio clip plays, **Audio Gain** increases or decreases the loudness of the *original audio* on the clip. The difference is subtle but worth knowing.

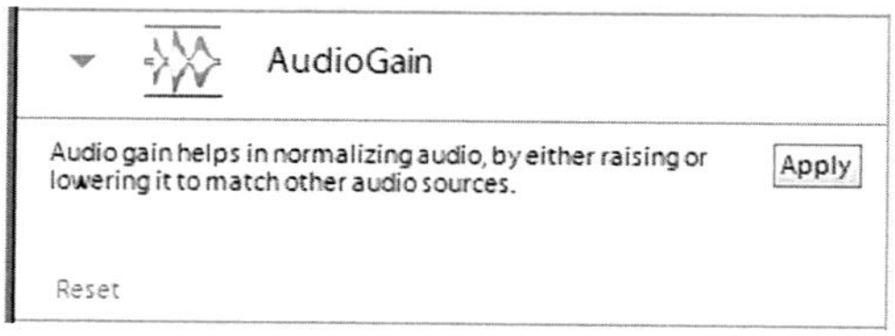

When I've got audio that I've recorded at too low a level and I want to make it louder, **Audio Gain** is my preferred tool for doing so. Increasing the gain tends to make the audio sound richer and fuller in addition to simply louder. At least to my ears.

When you click the **Apply** button on this tool panel, the **Audio Gain** tool launches. For more information on using this tool, see page 190.

Keyframe your Adjustments

By default, changes made in the **Adjustments** panel are applied evenly to your entire clip. In other words, if you change the **Temperature** of a clip, you change it for the entire clip. If you raise the **Volume**, you raise the volume level overall for the entire clip.

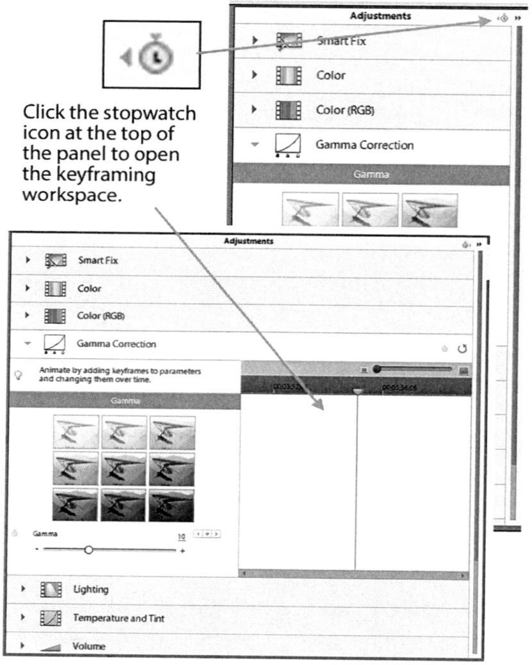

Click the stopwatch icon at the top of the panel to open the keyframing workspace.

However, sometimes you want these **Adjustments** to vary over the course of a clip – if, for instance, your clip includes both video that needs color correction and video that does not, or your audio includes both loud and quiet moments that you want to even out.

To set up your **Adjustments** to vary their levels over the course of a clip, you use a process called **keyframing.** (**Adjustments keyframing** is only available in Expert View.)

To create keyframes that vary the levels of your **Adjustments**:

1 Open the keyframing workspace.

With the panel open for the **Adjustments** tool you want to keyframe, click the stopwatch icon at the top right of the **Adjustments** panel.

The **Adjustments** panel will stretch wide – sliding your **Monitor** way off to the left of the interface – and a mini-timeline will appear to the right of your selected **Adjustments** tool. (By nature of their effects, **Smart Fix** and **Audio Gain** do not have keyframing workspaces.)

The mini-timeline in this keyframing workspace represents the duration of the clip you have selected on your timeline.

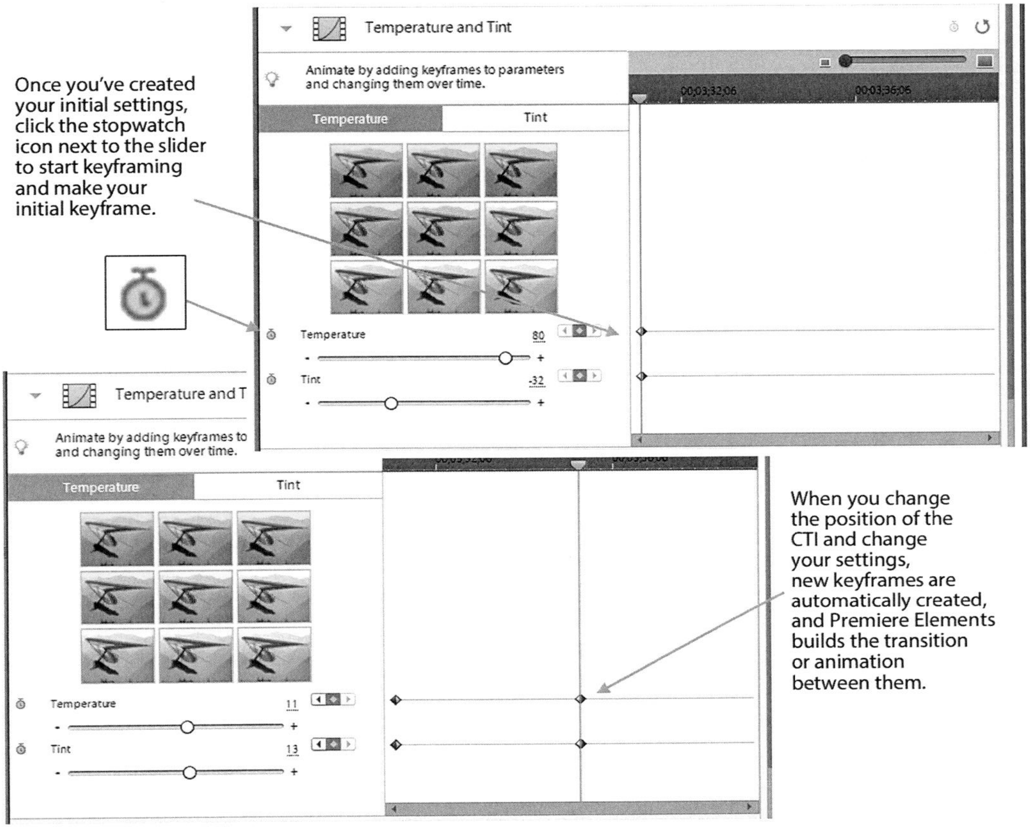
Once you've created your initial settings, click the stopwatch icon next to the slider to start keyframing and make your initial keyframe.
Temperature and Tint
Animate by adding keyframes to parameters and changing them over time.
Temperature
Tint
Temperature 80
Tint -32
Temperature and T
Animate by adding keyframes to and changing them over time.
Temperature 11
Tint 13
When you change the position of the CTI and change your settings, new keyframes are automatically created, and Premiere Elements builds the transition or animation between them.

2 Set your adjustment level.

Drag the **CTI** in the keyframe workspace to the point on your clip's mini-timeline that you'd like your first setting to be applied.

Click the **More** button at the bottom right of your **Adjustment** tool's panel to open the slider interface and make your adjustment. (Although you can make your adjustments using the sliders or the **Quick Fix** interface, you'll need to have the sliders visible to create your initial keyframe.)

3 Create an initial keyframe.

Click the stopwatch icon to the left of the slider or the sliders you've adjusted (as illustrated above) to begin keyframing.

A horizontal line will appear to the right of your adjustment, and a little diamond keyframe at the **CTI's** position will indicate your current adjustment setting.

4 Create a second keyframe.

Move the **CTI** in the keyframe workspace to a new position and change your adjustment(s) setting.

A new keyframe will automatically be created, and the program will automatically create the animation or transition between the two.

You can create as many keyframes as you need to create the effect you want. And you can change, move and remove your keyframes as needed. (Or, by clicking the stopwatch again, remove all keyframes completely.)

Keyframes have many applications in Premiere Elements, from creating motion paths over photos and creating animations and special effects to precisely mixing audio tracks. For more information on this powerful tool, see **Chapter 15, Keyframing.**

For information on using keyframes to precisely control the **Volume** levels on your audio clips, see **Adjust your audio levels at specific points in your video** on page 189.

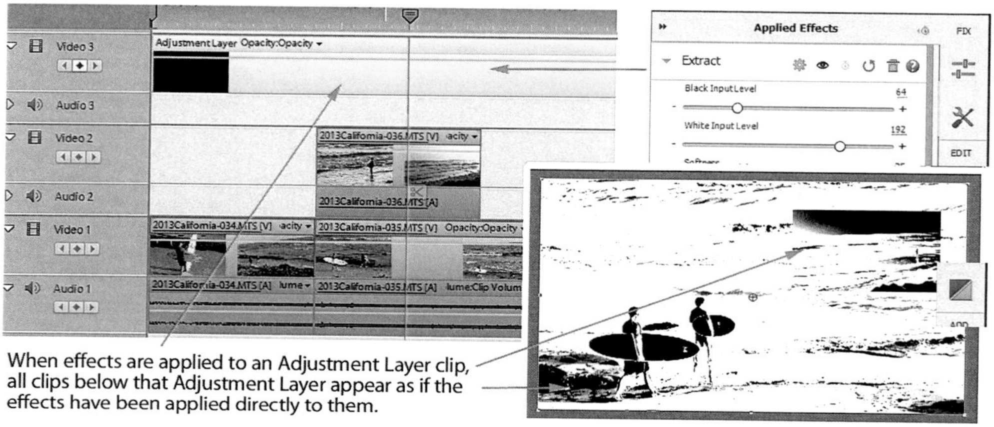

When effects are applied to an Adjustment Layer clip, all clips below that Adjustment Layer appear as if the effects have been applied directly to them.

Add Effects and Adjustments to your movie with Adjustment Layers

Adjustment Layers are a feature that allows you to add all of your effects and adjustments to a null video track, affecting the look of all of the video on tracks below it.

An **Adjustment Layer**, then, can be used to apply an effects or adjustments to an entire sequence or to your entire movie at once.

The effects you add or adjustments you make are made to the **Adjustment Layer** clip rather than directly to your individual video clips.

This could come in handy if, for instance, you wanted to apply the **Old Film** effect or the **Animated FilmLook** overall to your whole, finished movie instead of adding the effect one clip at a time.

Adjustment Layers can be added in both Quick View and Expert View.

To add an **Adjustment Layer** to your movie project:

1 Select an **Effect**.

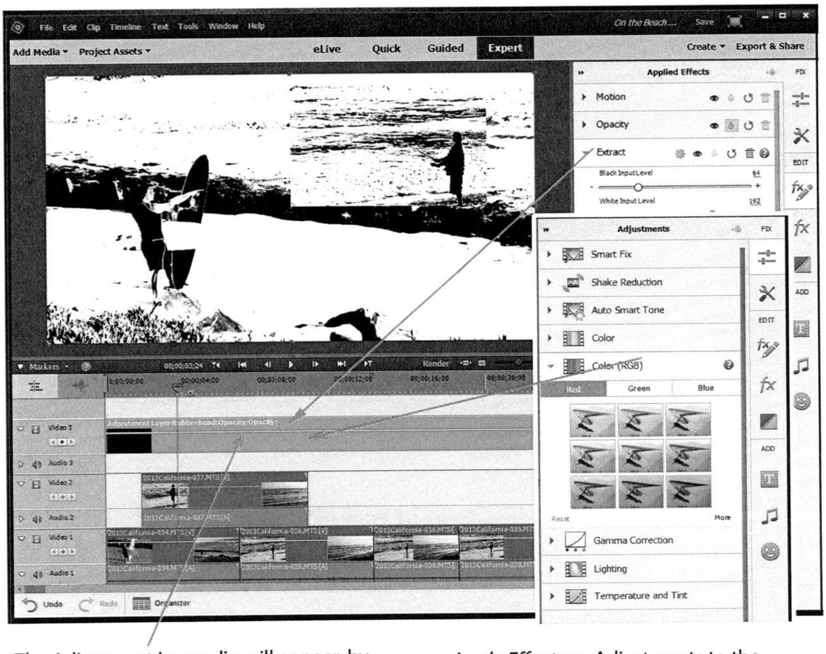

The Adjustment Layer clip will appear, by default, on an upper video track, over your entire movie. (This track will not be visible in Quick View.)

Apply Effects or Adjustments to the Adjustment Layer rather than directly to the video clips on your timeline.

Click on the **Effects** button on the **Toolbar** that runs along the right side of the program.

Select an effect as described in **Chapter 13, Add Audio and Video Effects**. (You can add more effects or adjustments after you create the initial **Adjustment Layer**.)

2 Create an **Adjustment Layer**.

Drag your selected effect onto the **Monitor** panel.

A pop-up panel will ask, **Do you want to apply this effect to your entire movie?** Click **Yes**.

An **Adjustment Layer** clip will be added to your timeline.

(You can also create an **Adjustment Layer** by selecting the **New Item** option from the **Project Assets** panel, as illustrated on page 63).

In Expert View, this **Adjustment Layer** will appear as a clip on an upper video track. This **Adjustment Layer** clip will be, by default, the same length as your movie and will appear over your entire movie, as illustrated above.

In Quick View, you will not see the **Adjustment Layer** on your timeline. However, its effect will be seen throughout your movie.

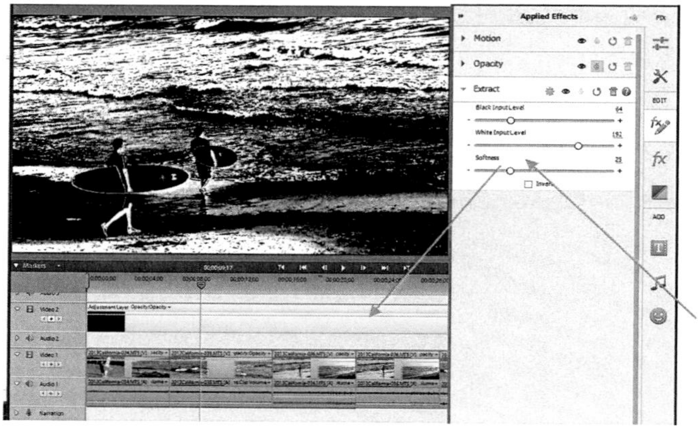

Effects settings or video adjustments will be applied to the entire area covered by the Adjustment Layer.

3 Customize your effect.

Your effect can be customized using the same tools described in **Chapter 14, Adjust Applied Effects**.

Although your movie will reflect these adjustments – any adjustments or changes in effects' settings will be made to the **Adjustment Layer** rather than the individual clips.

4 Apply additional effects or adjustments.

With the **Adjustment Layer** clip selected on your timeline, you can add, remove or customize as many effects or video adjustments as you'd like. Any effects you add or adjustments you make will affect all of the video clips under the **Adjustment Layer**.

5 Trim and position the **Adjustment Layer**.

If you'd like your **Adjustment Layer's** effects to only apply to a segment of your timeline rather than to your entire movie, you can trim and position the **Adjustment Layer** clip as you would any other video clip on your timeline.

To temporarily turn off the effects added and adjustments made to your **Adjustment Layer**, right-click on the **Adjustment Layer** clip on your timeline and uncheck **Enable**.

To permanently remove the effects you've added overall to your movie, simply select and delete the **Adjustment Layer** clip from the timeline.

Customizing Your Transitions

Transitions Defined

How Transitions Work

The Gradient Wipe

Chapter 11

Add and Customize Transitions

Cool ways to get from one scene to the next

Transitions in Premiere Elements are very easy to use.

However, as with most of Premiere Elements' features, there is also a surprising amount you can do to customize them, if you know how.

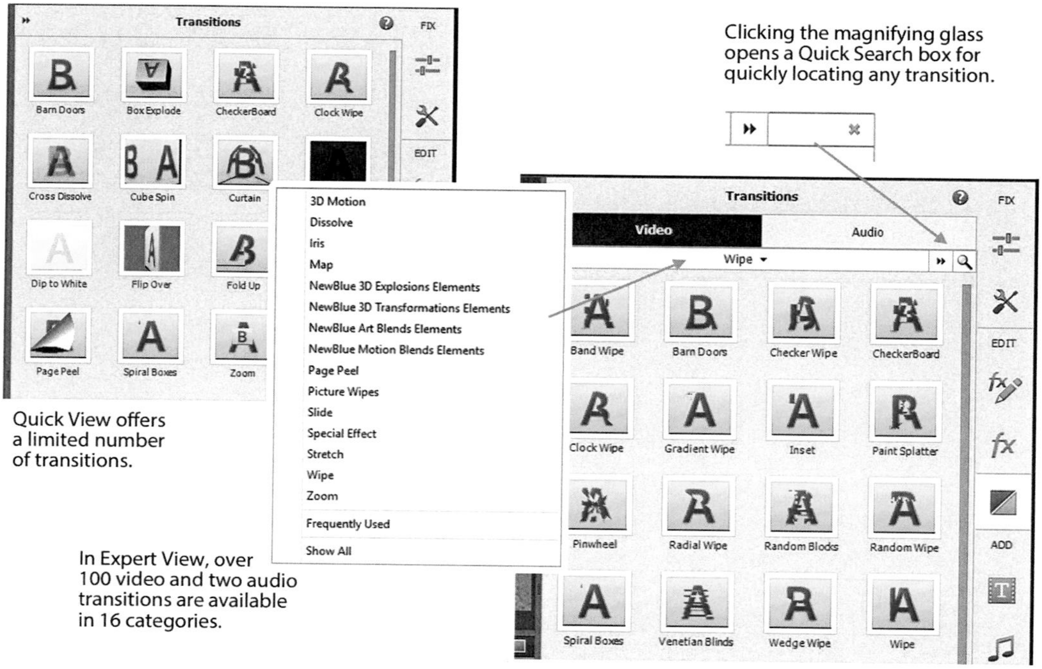

Clicking the magnifying glass opens a Quick Search box for quickly locating any transition.

Quick View offers a limited number of transitions.

In Expert View, over 100 video and two audio transitions are available in 16 categories.

Transitions are added to your timeline from the **Transitions** panel, launched from the **Toolbar** along the right side of the interface.

Whether you're working in Quick View or Expert View, transitions are added to your project essentially the same way. However, Expert View offers a much wider selection of transitions and transition categories.

To apply a transition:

1 Click the **Transitions** button on the **Toolbar** along the right side of the interface.

The **Transitions** panel will open.

Once the panel is open, you can widen it by dragging on its left edge.

2 Browse to a transition.

In Quick View, Premiere Elements offers you about 16 basic video transitions.

In Expert View, you will find over 100 video transitions in 15 categories, plus 2 audio transitions. As illustrated above, you can browse the transition categories by either:

- Clicking on the category title bar at the top of the panel, as illustrated above. A complete list of transition categories will appear, and you can click to select and jump to the category; or

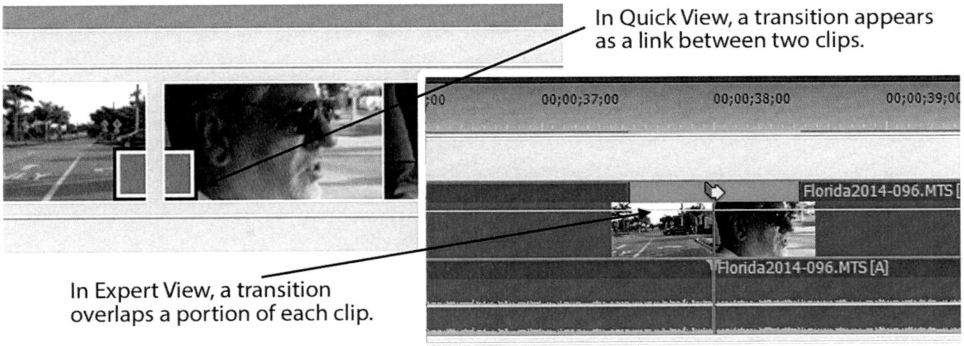

In Quick View, a transition appears as a link between two clips.

In Expert View, a transition overlaps a portion of each clip.

- Clicking on the black arrow to the right or left of the category title bar.

You can also **Quick Search** directly to any transition by clicking on the magnifying glass in the upper right of the **Transitions** pop-up panel (as illustrated on the facing page) and then typing in the transition's name.

3 Apply the transition.

Drag your selected transition onto the intersection of two clips.

A **Transition Adjustments** option panel will open.

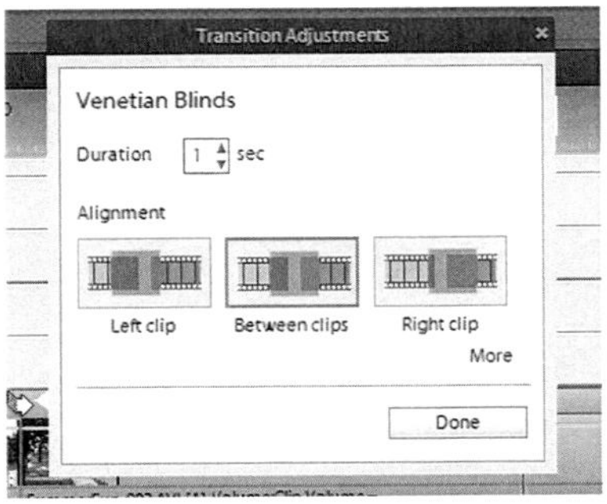

4 Set your transition's **Duration** and **Alignment**.

Your transition will last 1 second by default. You can change the duration by clicking the up or down arrows to the right of the current **Duration** length or you can simply type over the current **Duration**. To set your transition's **Duration** to fractions of a second, use decimal points. For instance, a transition will last two and one-half seconds if you set its **Duration** to 2.5 sec.

Your transition's **Alignment** is, by default, centered between your two clips. However, if you'd prefer (or if you lack adequate "head" or "tail" material [see page 136] on one or the other clip) you can manually set its **Alignment** over the left or the right clip.

Mac transitions: A limited edition

The Mac version of Premiere Elements 15 does not include all of the transitions available in the PC version. For a list of the omitted effects, see page 274 in the **Appendix**.

The **Transitions** panel includes a **Default Transition**, which is used to transition between clips when you use the **Project Assets' Slideshow Creator** (page 67) as well as by the **Add Transition Along the CTI** tool (see **Apply a transition to several clips at once** on page 135).

By default, the **Default Transition** is the **Cross-Dissolve**. However, you can manually set any transition as your **Default Transition**, as discussed on page 134.

Customize your transition

Most transitions include a number of options for customizing their look, animation, borders, colors and other transitional elements.

These options are set in the **Transition Adjustments** panel that appears when you first add the transition to your timeline – or whenever you **double-click** on an existing transition. Click the **More** button on the lower right corner of this panel to access the deeper transitions properties settings, as illustrated below.

At the very least, you'll have a couple of basic customization options available to customize, depending on the complexity of the transition itself. Some transitions have several customizable features. You may need to scroll down in the panel to see all of the options available.

An option available for nearly every transition is **Reverse.** Reversing changes the direction of a transition so that, for instance, it replaces the old clip with the new in a movement from left to right, rather than from right to left.

When you have finished customizing your transition, click **Done**.

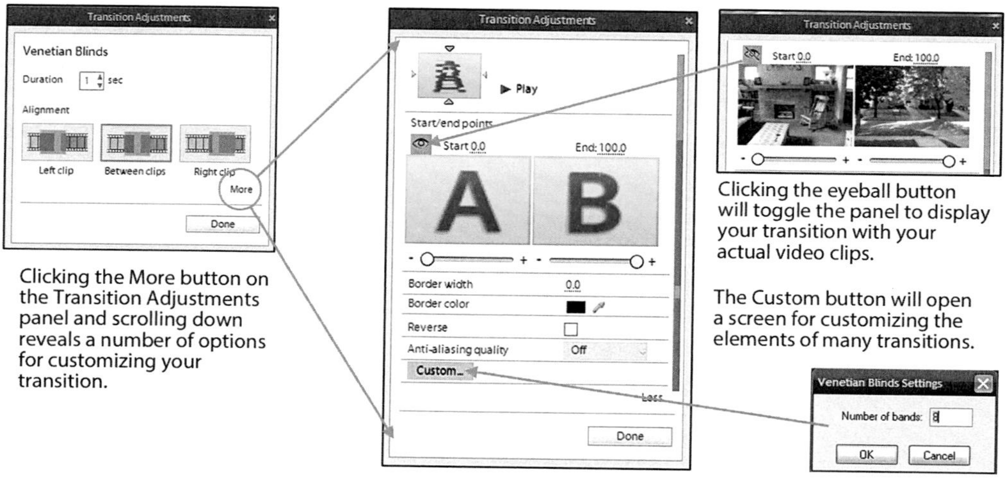

Clicking the More button on the Transition Adjustments panel and scrolling down reveals a number of options for customizing your transition.

Clicking the eyeball button will toggle the panel to display your transition with your actual video clips.

The Custom button will open a screen for customizing the elements of many transitions.

Fade in or out of a clip

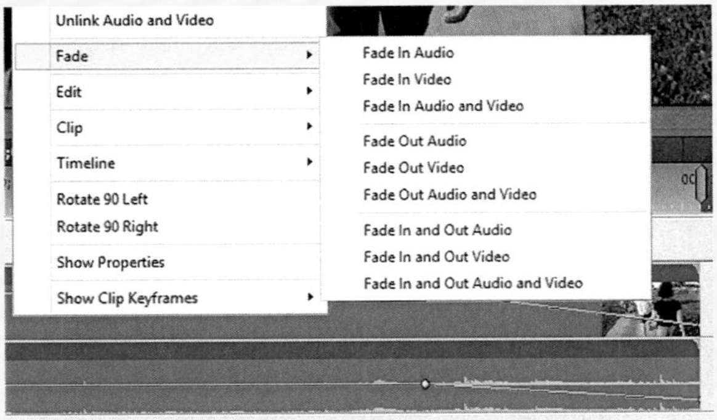

Fades, in and out of a clip, are most easily achieved by **right-clicking** on a clip on your timeline and, from the **Fade** sub-menu, selecting **Fade In, Fade Out** or **Fade In and Out.**

If you've selected a clip that includes both audio and video in Expert View, you'll find separate fade options for the audio and the video. In Quick View, the fade in or fade out is always applied to the both the audio and video on a clip.

Video transitions

Video Transitions are displayed in the **Transitions** panel as thumbnails representing their effect. If you click or hover your mouse over any thumbnail, you will see an animated representation of the **Transition** in action.

The categories of **Video Transitions** are:

3-D Motion. These transitions give the illusion that your video clips are transitioning by turning around or flipping over in three-dimensional space.

Dissolve. **Cross-Dissolve** is the most basic transition, a dissolve from one clip to the next.

The **Dip to Black** transition fades the first clip to black before fading the next clip in from black.

Iris. **Iris** transitions change from one clip to another through a shape.

Map. These transitions map their transitional phase to your clip's luminance values.

NewBlue 3D Explosions, NewBlue 3D Transformations, NewBlue Art Blends, NewBlue Motion Blends. These categories contain very cool effects created by NewBlue, one of the world's top video effects companies.

Page Peel. These transitions give the illusion of a page peeling or rolling away between clips.

Picture Wipes. These transitions use graphics (such as stars, travel signs or wedding dress lace) to transition from one clip to another.

Slide. **Slide** transitions push one clip out of the way so that another is revealed or they transition between clips through sliding boxes or swirls.

Special Effects. A hodgepodge of very showy transitions.

Stretch. These transitions seem to twist or stretch one clip away to reveal another.

Wipe. A variety of transitions that replace one clip with another with a clear line of movement. (See **Create custom transitions with the Gradient Wipe** on page 137 for information on the unique features of this transition.)

Zoom. A collection of high energy transitions that suddenly shrink or enlarge one clip to reveal another.

Audio transitions

To access the **Audio Transitions**, open the **Transitions** panel, click on the **Audio** tab. (Audio transitions are only available in Expert View.)

There are only two **Audio Transitions** – **Constant Gain** and **Constant Power** – both variations of an audio cross-fade.

The difference between the two is minor, having to do with whether the effect transitions from one audio clip to another in a linear fashion or by varying the audio levels as they crossfade.

Of the two, **Constant Power** is generally considered to provide the smoother transitional sound – though, in reality, most people can't really tell the difference.

Set the Default Transition

If you use the **Create Slideshow** feature in Premiere Elements (see page 67), create a compilation of **Favorite Moments** (see page 110) or you **Add a transition to several clips at once**, as discussed on the facing page, the program will place the **Default Transition** between your slides or video clips.

By default, that transition is a **Cross-Dissolve**. However, you can designate any transition in the **Transitions** panel as your **Default Transition**.

To designate a transition as your default, **right-click** on the selected transition in the **Transitions** panel and select the **Set Selected as Default Transition** option.

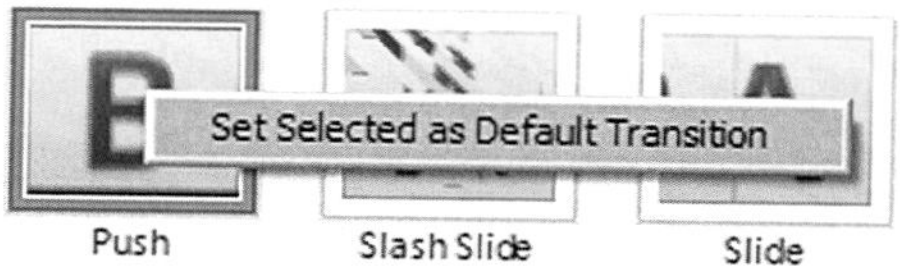

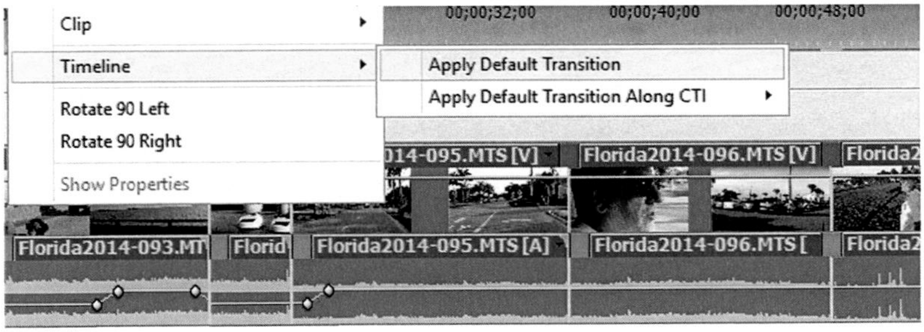

Apply a transition to several clips at once

In Premiere Elements you can add a transition between several clips in one move.

To apply the **Default Transition** to several clips at once:

1. Select your clips, either by holding the **Shift** or **Ctrl** key (⌘ key on a Mac) as you click to select clips on your timeline, or by dragging across your timeline from beyond your clips to "lasso" the clips you would like to select. (You can also use **Ctrl+a** – **⌘+a** on a Mac – to select all of the clips on the timeline.)
2. Once the clips are selected, **right-click** on the group and select **Timeline,** then **Apply Default Transition** from the context menu.

You may get a warning that your selected clips include "Insufficient media. This transition will contain repeated frames."

This means that one or more of your clips lacks enough "head" or "tail" material and that, if you proceed, some of your transitions will be composed of freeze frames. (For more information on why this happens and what you can do about it, see the discussion of **How transitions work** on page 136.) The only alternative to letting the program generate freeze frames is to trim back your clips so that at least one second of transitional material exists beyond the in and out points on each clip.

There is currently no way to add a transition other than the **Default Transition** (or to add random transitions) to multiple clips in one move.

Add a transition automatically

You can quickly apply the **Default Transition** at the position of the **CTI**. To do so, position the **CTI** playhead over the intersection of two clips, **right-click** and select the option to **Add Default Transition Along the CTI**.

Using the **Page Up** and **Page Down** keys on your keyboard, you can quickly jump from intersection to intersection of clips on your timeline, adding transitions along the way.

How transitions work

To create the transitional sequence, the transition must "borrow" extra footage – from beyond the out point of clip 1 and from beyond the in point of clip 2, sometimes resulting in the transition showing frames you've trimmed away.

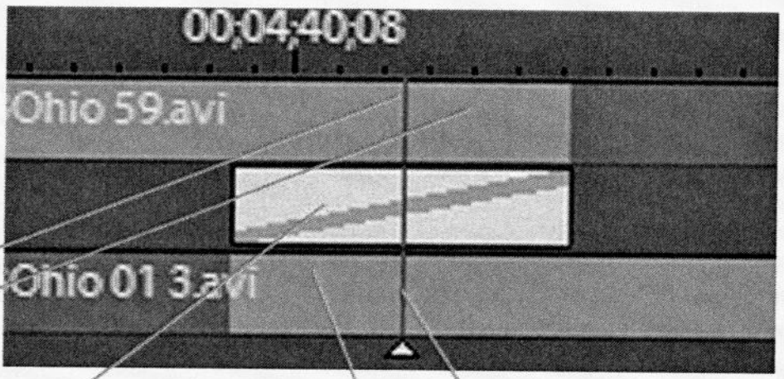

Sometimes transitions seem to behave in mysterious ways. They may show frames of video you've trimmed away – or they may show a freeze frame of your video during the transition. However, once you understand what's actually going on, you may find it easier to work with the process to resolve these issues.

1 In order to create the transitional segment – the segment during which both clips are displayed – the transition that you've added needs *a few extra frames*, beyond one clip's end and the next clip's beginning, as illustrated above.

   Officially these extra frames are called "**head**" and "**tail**" material.

   Unfortunately, this sometimes means that frames you've trimmed away from the end or beginning of a clip will appear during this transitional segment!

   If this happens, you may need to trim a few more frames from the beginning or end of the clip so that, even amidst the transition, these unwanted frames are not displayed.

2 If there are no extra frames beyond the beginning or end of your clips for the program to use to create its transition, the program will create a **freeze frame** of the last available video frame for the clip and use that for the transitional material.

   This, too, can be a bit annoying if you're not aware of why it's happening. Once again, the solution is to trim back the clip so that the transition has at least a second of "head" or "tail" material to work with.

3 You may also find, sometimes, that the transition will not sit evenly between two clips on your timeline but, rather, seems to be entirely over one or the other clip.

   This is because the transition was not able to find the necessary head or tail material on at least one of the clips – so it has positioned itself over the clip that offers the most available transitional footage.

   If this is not what you want, you can go to **Transition Adjustments**, as described on page 127, and set the transition's **Alignment** so that it sits evenly over both clips. However, you may find that this also creates an undesirable effect (such as a freeze frame in the head or tail material of one clip).

   So weigh your options carefully. The default point at which the transition lands is usually the best available position for it.

4 If you're using transitions between several photos (as in a slideshow) or even titles, you may find that the transition regularly rests over one or the other clip entirely. In this case, it's best not to bother to tweak its position since, with a still image, head, tail and freeze frames all look the same.

The Gradient Wipe transition creates a wipe based on a pattern from black to white.

Click the More button on the Transitions Adjustments panel to view the transition's properties.

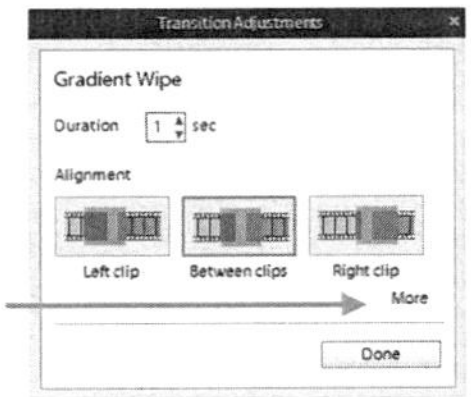

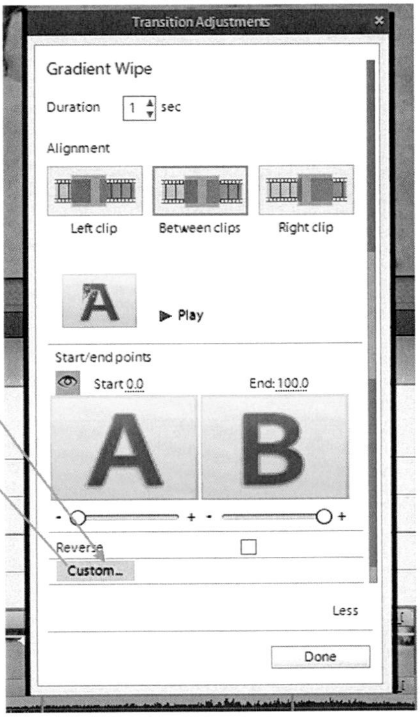

To load a custom pattern, click the Custom button in the Transition Properties panel, then click Select Image in the Gradient Wipe Settings and browse to your image.

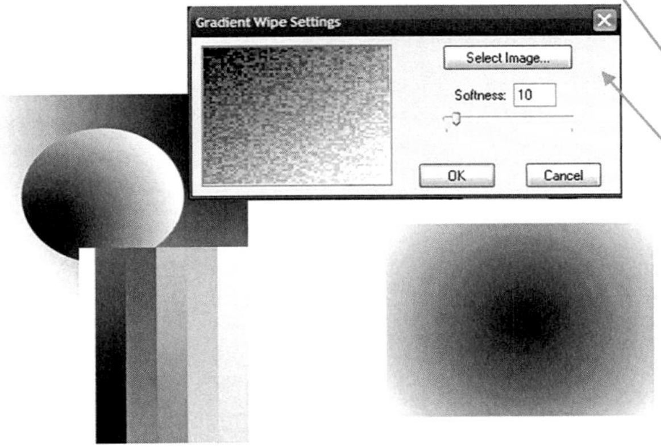

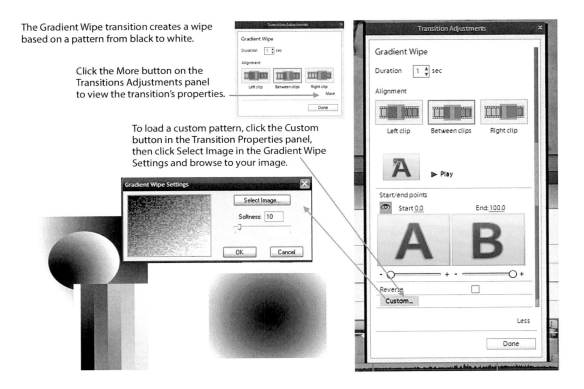

Create custom transitions with the Gradient Wipe

One of the most versatile **Video Transitions** available in Premiere Elements is the **Gradient Wipe** (available in the **Wipe** category).

The **Gradient Wipe** will create a *custom pattern* wipe from one clip to another based on any gradient (black to gray to white) pattern you provide!

When you first drag the **Gradient Wipe** transition onto a point between two clips, the **Gradient Wipe** Settings panel will open.

You can also re-open this panel at any time by **double-clicking** on the transition on your timeline, selecting **More** and then again clicking on the **Custom** button on the **Transitions Adjustments** panel, as illustrated above.

The **Gradient Wipe Settings** panel will display a default gradient pattern along with a slider to adjust its level of softness.

To use any black and white pattern to create your custom wipe, click on the **Select Image** button. A browse screen will open allowing you to locate and apply any image file on your computer.

The **Gradient Wipe** will base its wipe shape and animation on a movement from the blackest area to the whitest area in the graphics file or pattern you've provided.

In other words, by using a grayscale image you've created in Photoshop Elements, you can design virtually any transitional wipe pattern you can imagine!

For more information on the **Gradient Wipe** and how to use it – plus a free pack of several gradient patterns – just search for my *Steve's Tips* article "The Gradient Wipe" and the free "Gradient Wipe Pack" on the products page at Muvipix.com.

Titles and Title Templates

Editing Your Titles

Applying Styles, Graphics and Animations

Rolling/Crawling Options

Adding Graphics to Your Titles

Chapter 12

Add Titles & Text

Using title templates and text

With Titles, you can create opening or closing credits for your movie.

Or you can use them to add subtitles or captions to your videos.

Additional content

art-in-motion_title

You may notice a little blue flag over the upper right corner of a number of title templates.

This blue flag indicates that the template or theme is available but has not yet been installed on your computer. When you select this template or theme, the program will automatically download it for you from the Adobe site – a process that should only take a moment or two.

If you'd like to download all of these templates at once, right-click on any one and select the Download All option.

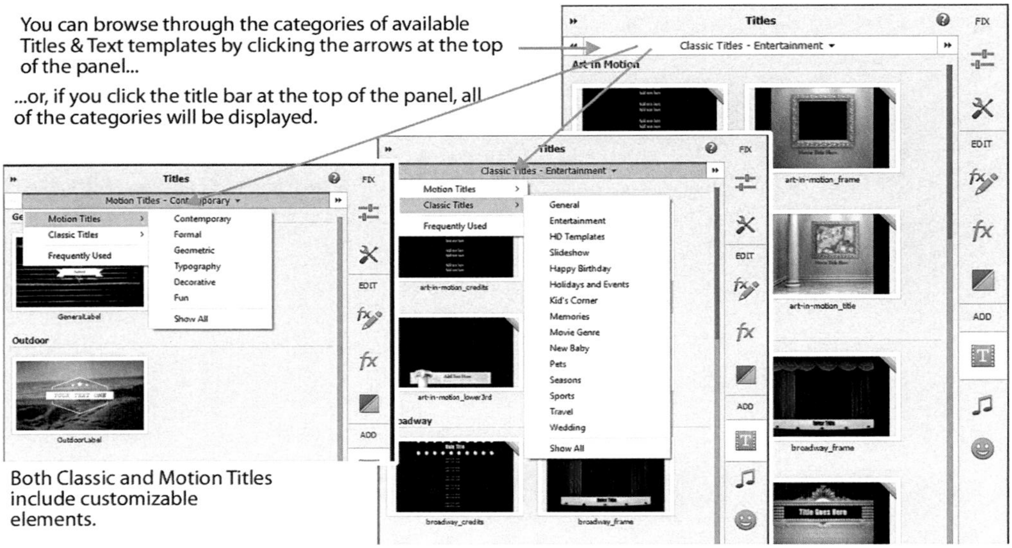

You can browse through the categories of available Titles & Text templates by clicking the arrows at the top of the panel...

...or, if you click the title bar at the top of the panel, all of the categories will be displayed.

Both Classic and Motion Titles include customizable elements.

Titles and other text can be used to help tell your video's story – or to give credit where credit is due.

Premiere Elements comes loaded with hundreds of title templates in several different categories. In addition to **Classic Titles**, stationary illustrations and blocks of text, the program includes **Motion Titles**, animated templates with easily customizable elements. (We show you how to use them on page 148.)

Within each category of **Classic Titles** are sets or themes. Each theme usually includes four template styles:

A still title, usually with stylized text and often accompanied by theme graphics.

A rolling title with a template for a list of names.

A crawling title (which moves left to right or right to left across the screen).

A lower third title, in which the text is positioned in the lower one-third of the video frame.

Many of these templates include custom graphics – which you can reposition or remove in the **Title Adjustments** workspace. And most of the templates that include graphics also include transparent areas (which appear as black on the thumbnails in the **Titles & Text** panel) through which any video placed on a video track below the title will show through.

To add any title or text template to your movie:

1 Click on the **Titles & Text** button on the **Toolbar** that runs along the right side of the program's interface.

The **Titles & Text** pop-up panel will open.

Once the panel is open, you can enlarge it by dragging on the black bar at the top of the panel.

2 Browse to a title.

To browse through the title template theme sets.

- Click on the category title bar and select either the **Classic Title** or **Motion Title** (see page 148) category. A complete list of title template categories will appear. Click to select a specific sub-category; or
- Click on the black double-arrow to the right and left of the category title bar to scroll through the various categories.

Once you've selected a category, scroll down the panel to select a title theme and a specific title.

3 Add your title.

Drag your selected title template onto your timeline.

You can add your template to the **Video 1** track, in which case any transparent areas will appear as black in your video, or you can add it to an upper video track, in which case any transparent areas in the title template will show the video on the track or tracks below it.

Once you've placed your title, the program will open up in the **Title Adjustments** workspace, where you can further customize the look and content of your text and accompanying graphics.

Safe Margins

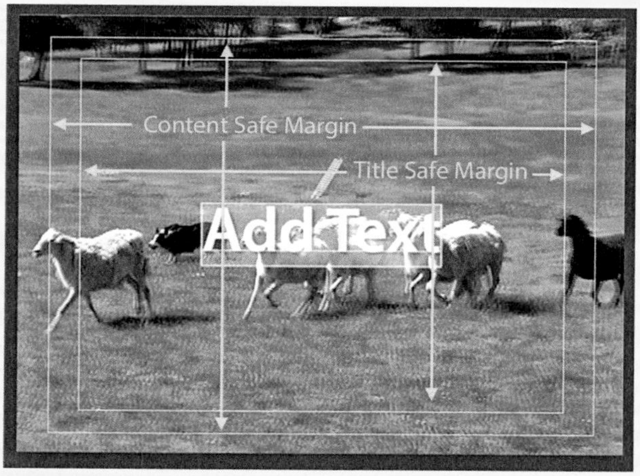

When your title opens in the **Title Adjustments** workspace, you'll notice two concentric rectangles overlaying the **Monitor** panel. These rectangular overlays are called **Safe Margins** – and they are guides for placing important information in your video frame so that they don't become victim's of overscan, television's terrible habit of cutting off up to 10% of the area around the edge of a video frame.

The inner rectangle is called the **Title Safe Margin.**

Keeping all of your onscreen text within the bounds of this inner **Title Safe Margin** ensures that it will always be displayed completely, with no chance of any accidental cut-off.

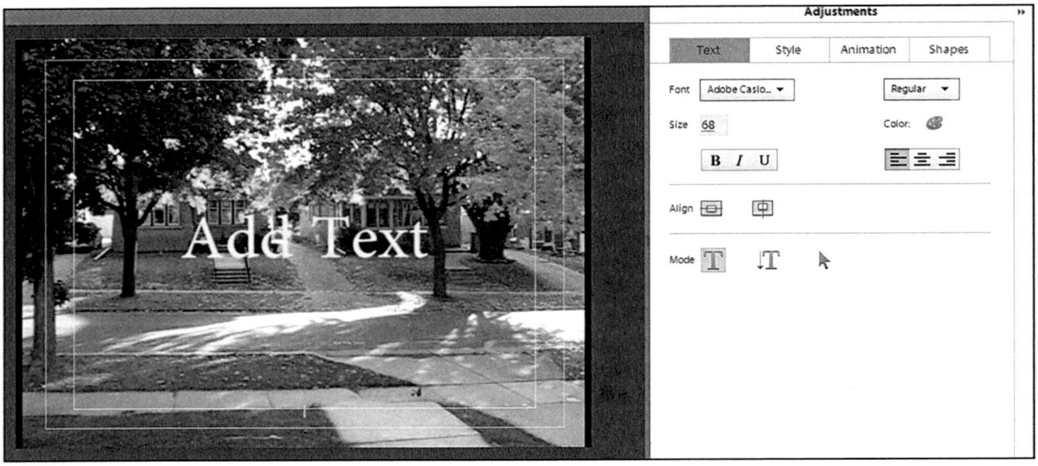

Customize your title in Title Adjustments

When you first add a title or template to your timeline – or any time you **double-click** on an existing title – the program will open into the **Title Adjustments** workspace.

In this workspace, you can customize and color your text, add additional text, draw, add and remove graphics and add a variety of animations.

The **Adjustments** panel in this workspace (illustrated above) is your toolkit for creating and customizing your titles. Its tools are organized under four tabs, as detailed on the next pages:

Text, where you'll find tools for setting your text's font, style and color.

Style, a catalog of more than 80 text styles that automatically apply fonts, colors, strokes and drop-shadows to your text and graphics.

Animation, a catalog of nearly 50 pre-created text animations.

Shapes, a toolkit for creating and coloring basic shapes and selecting and positioning text boxes and graphics in your video frame.

Create a quick title

If you want to just add a plain vanilla text title to your movie – or maybe a basic roll or crawl – without rooting through dozens of templates, you can do so simply by selecting the **New Text** option under Premiere Elements' **Text** menu.

A title, in the default color and font, will be added to your project at the position of the **CTI** and you'll be launched into the **Title Adjustments** workspace, where you can customize your text's font, size and color and/or add animation and graphics.

Edit your title's Text

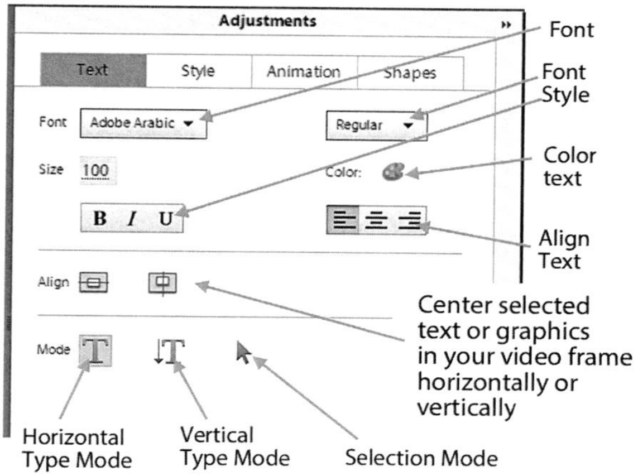

The **Text** panel contains tools for creating, customizing and positioning your text.

The top half of this panel includes tools for setting your text's **Font, Size, Style, Color** and **Left, Center** and **Right** paragraph alignment within its text box. (For more information on coloring your text, see **Color your shape or text** on page 145.)

The **Align** tools will automatically center any selected text boxes or graphics horizontally or vertically in your video frame.

The three **Mode** buttons determine the mode of your cursor.

In the default **Horizontal Type** mode, you can edit existing text or create a new text box by clicking and typing outside of an existing text box.

In **Vertical Type** mode, any text you type will be written down rather than across.

In **Selection mode**, you can use your cursor to select a text box or a graphic, resize it by dragging on its corner handles or drag it to a new position on your title area.

Give your text a Style

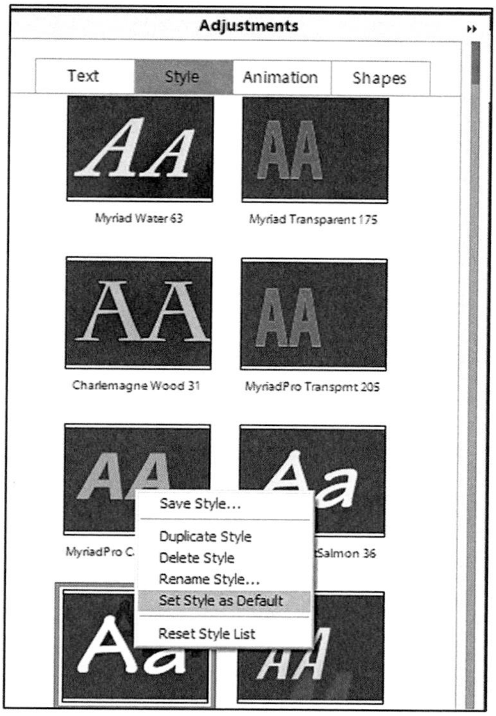

Under the **Styles** tab in the **Title Adjustments** workspace, you'll find over 100 **Text Styles** – combinations of fonts, font styles, colors and, in some cases, drop shadows and glows that can be applied to selected text simply by clicking on it.

If you **right-click** on any of these **Text Styles**, you will find the option to set that particular style as your **Default Style**. This style will then automatically be applied whenever you open a new title.

One other thing worth noting: In order for you to color your text's stroke (its outline) using the **Color Properties** tool on either the **Text** or **Shapes** tab, *you must first have* a **Text Style** *applied to the text or graphic that includes a stroke or outline.* Otherwise, the **Stroke** color option will not be available.

Add a Text Animation

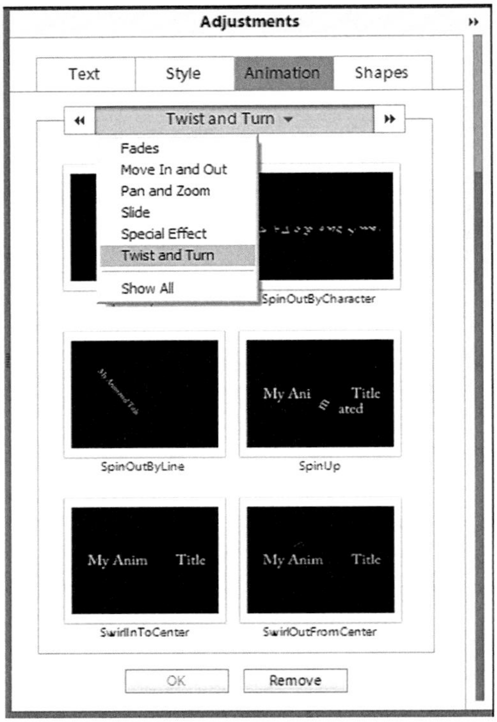

Under the **Animation** tab in the **Title Adjustments** workspace, you'll find over three dozen **Text Animations** – very cool pre-programmed movements for getting your text on and off screen. Some juggle entire words, others dance your titles around one letter at a time.

These **Text Animations** are in several categories, and you can browse the various categories by clicking the title bar at the top of the panel or by using the arrow buttons on either side of the title bar.

Fades bring your text in or out with a fade to or from transparency.

Move In and Out animate your text one letter at a time.

Pan and Zoom animations reveal your text through a slow zoom in or out.

Slide animations slide your text in from off-screen all at once or one letter at a time.

Special Effect is a collection of very interesting ways to reveal your text.

Twist and Turn animations spin and twist in or out your text or individual letters.

To see a preview of how an animation looks when applied, hover your mouse over the animation thumbnail until a **Play** button appears, then click on this **Play** button.

To apply a **Text Animation** to your title:

- Your text or text block must be selected on the **Monitor**;
- Your text block must *not* be more than one line long; and
- A **Text Animation** must be selected.

To apply a **Text Animation** to your text:

1. Select your text on the **Monitor** in the **Title Adjustments** workspace.
2. Click to select a **Text Animation.**
3. Click the **Apply** button at the bottom of the **Animation** panel.
4. To undo a **Text Animation**, select the text again and click the **Remove** button.

The speed of your animation is based on the length of your title. To slow your title's animation, stretch the title longer on your timeline. To speed it up, trim it shorter.

Animations are applied, by the way, to individual text boxes – not to entire titles (which can include several text boxes). So a single title could conceivably include several animated blocks of text!

Add Shapes to your title

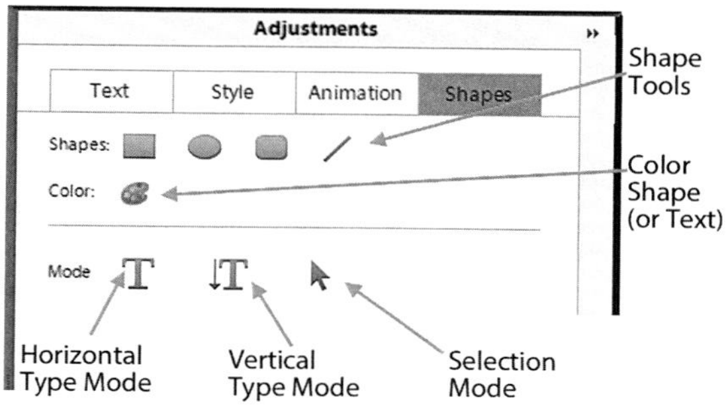

The tools under the **Shapes** tab in the **Title Adjustments** workspace are similar to those under the **Text** tab – except, of course, that the tools under this tab are for drawing basic shapes onto your title.

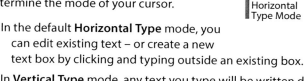

As on the **Text** tab, the three **Mode** buttons determine the mode of your cursor.

In the default **Horizontal Type** mode, you can edit existing text – or create a new text box by clicking and typing outside an existing box.

In **Vertical Type** mode, any text you type will be written down rather than across.

In **Selection mode**, you can use your cursor to select a text box or a graphic, resize it by dragging on its corner handles or drag it to a new position on your title area.

Color your shape or text

Clicking the **Color** button (the painter's palette) on either the **Text** or **Shapes** tabs opens a **Color Properties** panel for setting the color of whatever text or graphic you have selected.

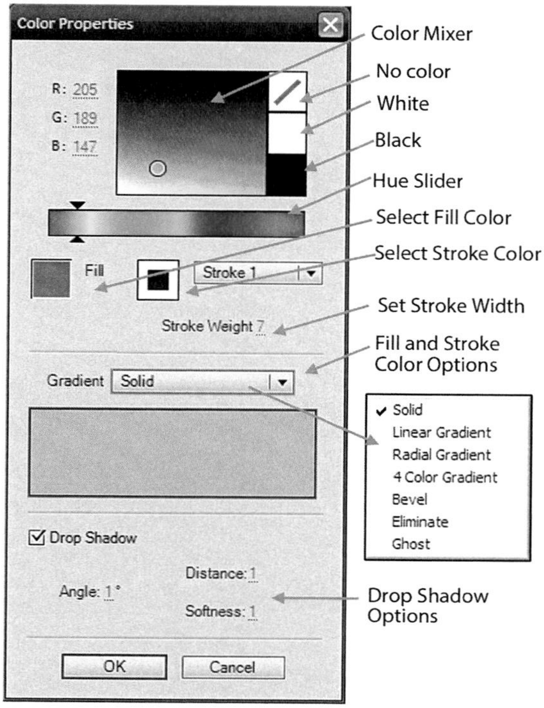

To color your selected graphic or text, click the **Fill** button on the panel and then select a color using the **Color Mixer** at the top of the panel.

A **Stroke** is an outline around your text or graphic. A strange quirk in the program is that you *cannot* add or color your text's **Stroke** in this panel unless a **Text Style** has first been applied to it that includes a stroke (see page 143).

Even stranger, this applies to shapes as well as text: To color a stroke around a shape, you must first apply a **Text Style** that includes a stroke to your shape!

The **Gradient** drop-down menu allows you to color your **Fill** or **Stroke** with either a solid color or any of a number of gradient mixes. (Or, using the **Ghost** option, to make your text or graphic invisible except for its **Stroke** or **Drop Shadow**.)

A **Drop Shadow** can be added to any text or graphic.

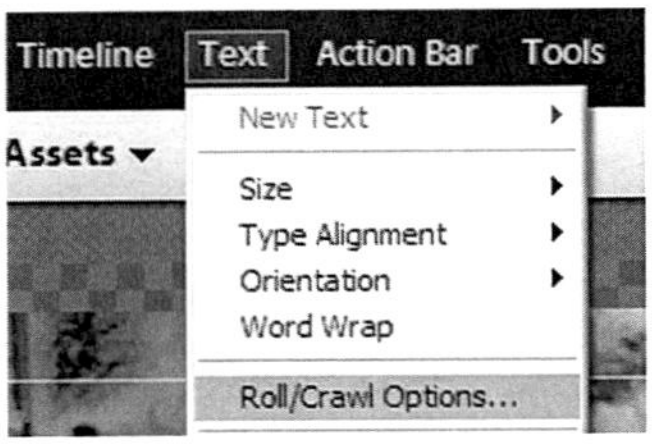

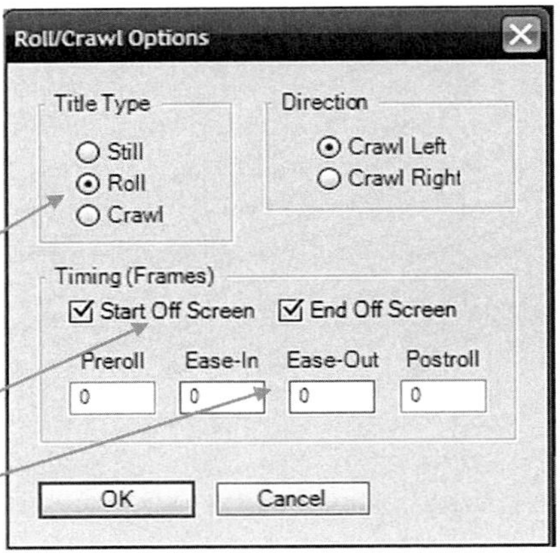

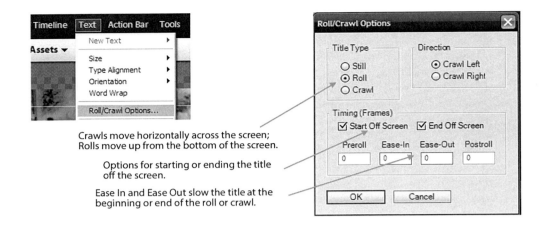

Crawls move horizontally across the screen; Rolls move up from the bottom of the screen.

Options for starting or ending the title off the screen.

Ease In and Ease Out slow the title at the beginning or end of the roll or crawl.

Create rolling or crawling titles

In addition to **Text Animations**, you can use more traditional ways to move your titles on and off the screen. Premiere Elements includes a tool for making any title you create **roll** (move up over a video frame) or **crawl** (move left to right, or right to left) across your video frame.

The **Roll/Crawl Options** panel is launched from the Premiere Elements **Text** menu (as illustrated above) – and, of course, it's only available while you're in the **Title Adjustments** workspace.

The options you select in this panel will apply to the entire title you are currently editing. In other words, whatever else you've got on your title – text animations, graphics, etc. – setting options in the **Roll/Crawl** panel will make it all roll or crawl across your screen. (If you've selected a title template that is already set to roll or crawl, you'll find that, when you open this panel, some of the options on this panel have already been set.)

The settings on the **Roll/Crawl Options** panel are fairly intuitive. If you select **Crawl**, for instance, you have the option of setting it to either **Crawl Left** or **Crawl Right** across the video frame.

The **Timing** options allow you to set if and how your roll or crawl starts and/or ends off screen.

- You have the options of setting your title to **Start Off Screen** and/or **End Off Screen.** Alternatively, you can manually set the **Preroll** or **Postroll** time for how long the title is off the screen before or after it rolls or crawls.
- The **Ease In** and **Ease Out** options allow you to change the rolling or crawling movement from a steady speed to one that begins slowly and then speeds up (**Ease In**), or vice versa (**Ease Out**).

The speed at which the title rolls or crawls is determined by how long the title is on your timeline. Extending (by dragging one end to lengthen) the title on your timeline will **increase its duration and thus slow the speed** of the roll or crawl; dragging in one end of the title to **decrease its duration will increase the speed** of the roll or crawl.

As an alternative to using these automatic roll and crawl options, you can manually keyframe the movement of your title so that it is revealed through any movement, effect or animation you can imagine. To learn more about using keyframing to create animations, see **Chapter 15.**

Add a graphic to your title

To add a graphic, photo or any image on your computer to your title, select the option to add an **Add Image** from the Premiere Elements **Text** menu or **right-click** on the **Monitor** and select the **Image** option there. (This option is only available while you're in the **Title Adjustments** workspace.)

Once you've added the graphic, use the **Selection Tool** to size and position it in your video frame (as discussed in **Add Shapes to your title** on page 145).

You can grab an image from the Premiere Elements **Graphics** collection (see page 115) by browsing to C:/Program Files/Adobe/Premiere Elements 15/Clip Arts/Common on a PC – or, on a Mac, by browsing to Library/Application Support/Adobe/Premiere Elements/15.0/Online/Clip Arts/All_Lang.

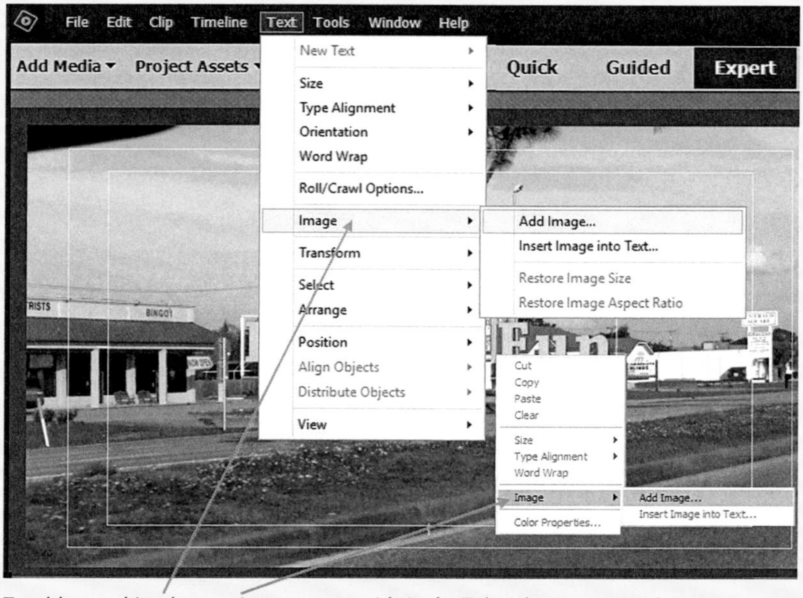

To add a graphic, photo or image to your title in the Title Adjustments workspace, select the option from under the Text menu or right-click on the Monitor and select the option from the context menu.

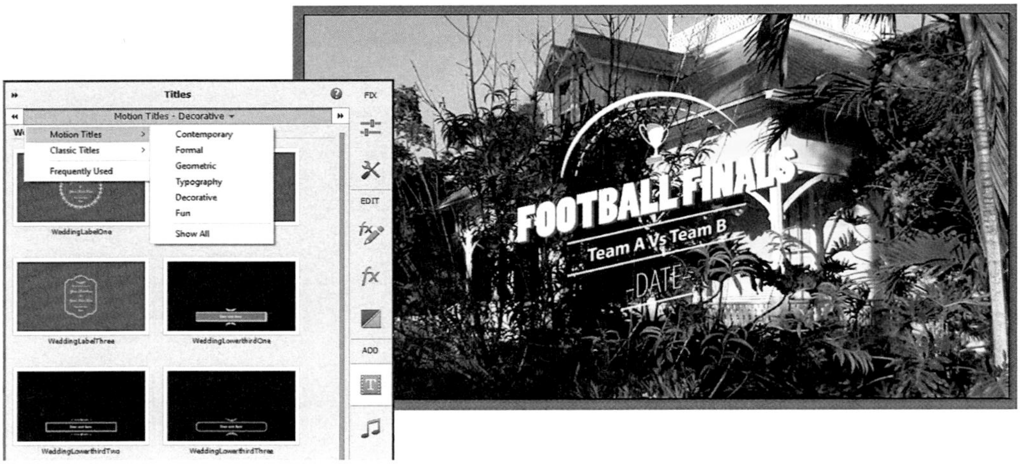

Add a Motion Title to your movie

Motion Titles are animated title templates that include text motion and animated graphics – each of which is easily customizable.

And, if you're happy with your custom elements, you can even save your new title as a template in your own personal library!

Adding a **Motion Title** is similar to adding a **Classic Title**:

1 Click on the **Titles & Text** button on the **Toolbar** that runs along the right side of the program's interface.

The **Titles & Text** pop-up panel will open.

Once the panel is open, you can widen it by dragging on the left edge the panel.

2 Browse to a title.

To browse through the title template theme sets.

- Click on the category title bar (which displays the name of the title category at the top of the panel, as illustrated above) and select the **Motion Title** category. A complete list of title template categories will appear. Click to select a specific sub-category; or
- Click on the black double-arrow to the right and left of the category title bar to scroll through the various categories.

Once you've selected a category, scroll down the panel to select a title theme and a specific title.

3 Add your title.

Drag your selected title template onto your timeline.

You can add your template to the **Video 1** track, in which case any transparent areas will appear as black in your video, or you can add it to an upper video track, in which case any transparent areas in the title template will show the video on the track or tracks below it.

Once you've placed your title, the program will open up in the **Motion Titles Adjustments** workspace, where you can further customize the look and content of your text and accompanying graphics.

Motion Titles include built-in animation for both the text and graphics. You can preview the title's animation at any point by playing your video's timeline. However, because these animation's animation can challenge even the most powerful personal computers, you may want to **Render** the timeline (Press **Enter**, as on page 80) to create a hard render preview before you preview the playback.

You can return to the **Motion Titles Adjustments** workspace at any time by double-clicking on the title on the timeline.

The animation in each **Motion Title** is programmed into the template itself. This means that, even if you customize the text or replace the graphics, the original animation will remain intact.

4 Customize your title's text.

As illustrated below , when you select any block of text in your title, the **Motion Titles Adjustments** panel will display a **Text** option panel, in which you can type in your custom text. The panel will also offers you the option to customize your text's font and color (as on page 143), add a text style (as on page 143) or add a text animation (as on page 144).

You can also change the location of the text block in your title by dragging it into a new position in the **Preview** window.

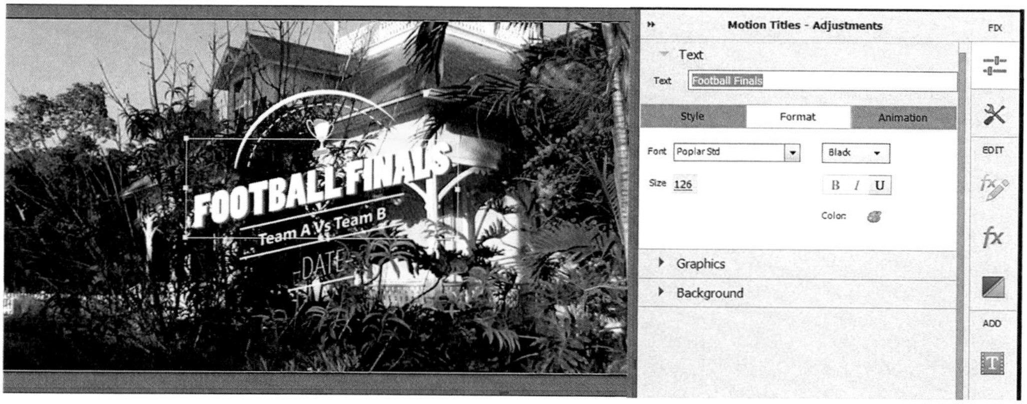

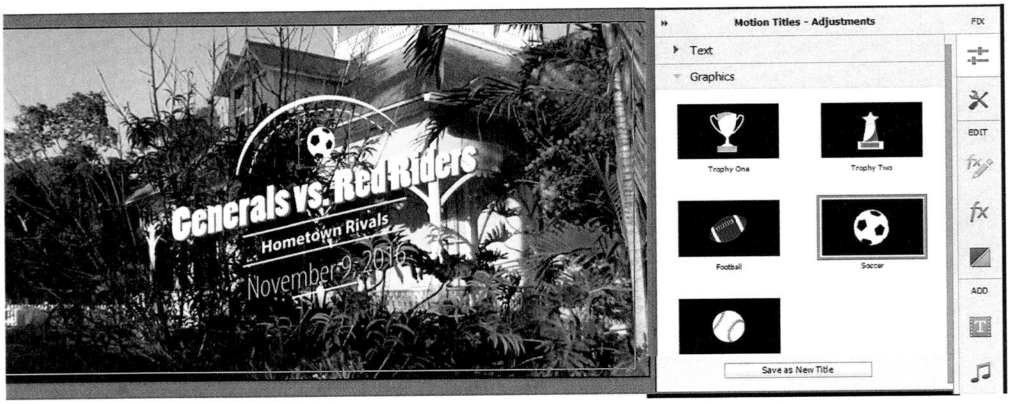

5 Customize your title's graphics.

As illustrated above, when you select a graphic or graphical element on your title, the **Motion Titles Adjustments** panel will display alternative graphics.

To apply the new graphic, **double-click** on it or select the graphic and click the **Apply** button at the bottom of the panel.

The graphic you use to replace the original graphic will display with the original **Motion Title's** animation.

6 Customize your titles background.

When you click on the background of the title displayed in the **Preview** window, the **Motion Titles Adjustments** panel will display a **Background** options drop-down menu. By default this menu is set to **Transparent**, displaying the video, if any, below the title on the timeline.

If you select the **Color Matte** option from this drop-down menu, the **Color Picker** will open, from which you can set the color of your title's background. Once you select a color and close the **Color Picker**, the

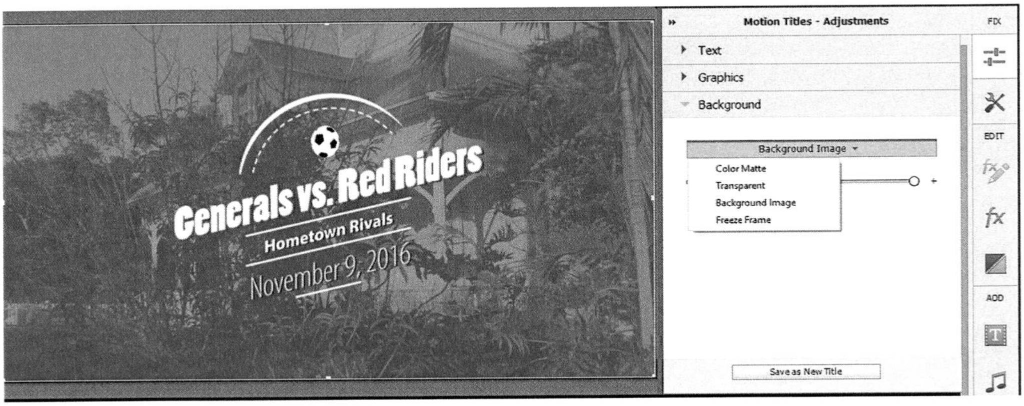

Motion Titles Adjustments panel will display an **Opacity** slider. The higher the Opacity setting, the more this color background will obscure the video, if any, below the title on your timeline.

If you select the **Freeze Frame** option from this drop-down menu, the title will use the current video frame displayed in the **Preview** window as a background. The higher the **Opacity** setting, the more this freeze frame will obscure the moving video below the title on your timeline.

When you're done editing your title, click the **Adjustments** button on the right side of the interface to close the **Motion Titles Adjustments** workspace, or simply click on the timeline.

Be sure to render your timeline (press **Enter**) before playing back your **Motion Title** sequence.

To re-edit the title, simply **double-click** on the title clip on your timeline.

7 Optionally save your title as a new template.

Once you've customized your **Motion Title**, you can save it as a new template. To do so, simply click the **Save as New Title** button on the **Motion Titles Adjustments** panel and name your title.

This new template will then be available on the **Titles & Text** panel for any future project under the **Motion Titles/Custom** category.

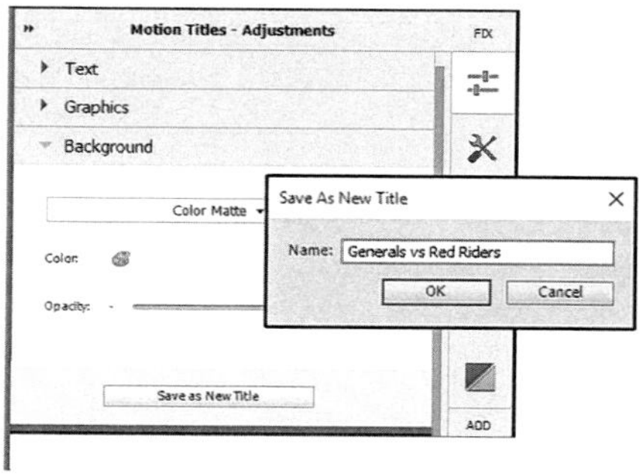

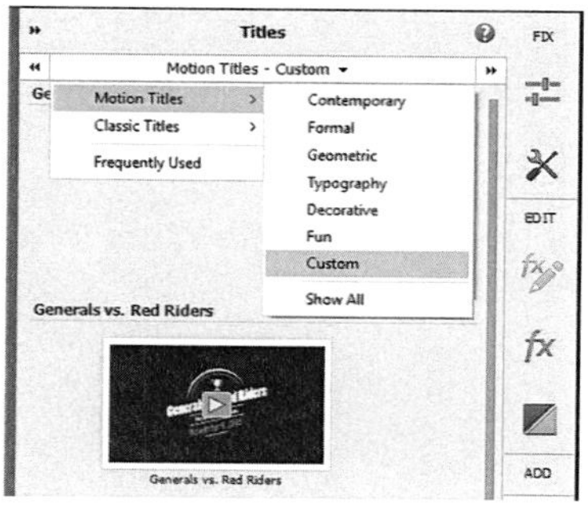

Finish your title

Once you've completed your title, click on the timeline to leave the **Title Adjustments** workspace and return to regular video editing mode. Your new title will appear as a clip on your timeline.

Re-edit a title

If, after you've created a title, you'd like to re-edit it, you can re-open it in the **Title Adjustments** workspace by **double-clicking** it on your project's timeline or by simply clicking to select the title on your timeline and then clicking the **Adjustments** button on the right side of the interface.

To leave **Title Adjustments** and return to timeline editing, click the **Adjustments** button again.

Duplicate a title

If you like how your title looks and you want to re-use the look and style for another title, you can duplicate it and then edit the duplicate.

To duplicate a title, **right-click** on it in the **Project Assets** panel and select **Duplicate**. You can then drag the duplicate title to your timeline and **double-click** on it to re-open its **Title Adjustments** workspace for editing.

It's important that you *duplicate* your title in the **Project Assets** panel rather than merely copying it or doing a copy-and-paste on the timeline.

If you create a *copy* of your title rather than make a duplicate, you've merely created a "clone" – and any changes you make to one title *will be made to both.*

Duplicating a title creates a copy of it, which you can use as a template for a new title. Copying a title, on the other hand, creates a "clone" of your title, such that any changes you make to the original are made to both titles.

And that's likely not how you intend to use the title's copy.

Duplicating creates an *independent* and editable copy of your title.

Render your title

Your title will likely look a bit rough when you first play it back from your timeline. To see a cleaner playback of your title sequence, press **Enter** on your keyboard or click on the **Render** button along the top right of the timeline. Rendering creates a preview video of the segment that smooths your playback and gives you a much better idea of what your final video output will look like. (For more information, see **Render your timeline** on page 80.)

Video Effects

Color Correction Tools

Chroma Key

Videomerge

Preset Video Effects

Audio Effects

Chapter 13

Add Audio and Video Effects

Bringing excitement to your movie

There is an amazing number of effects available in Premiere Elements – too many, in fact, to display on a single panel.

The program includes nearly 90 video and 20 audio effects as well as nearly 275 automatic, or "Preset" effects, that include applied effects as well as keyframed animations – all of which are infinitely customizable.

Adjustment Layers

In addition to applying effects to individual clips, you can also add effects overall to change the look of a whole sequence in your movie or to your entire movie at once using Adjustment Layers.

For more information on using and adding Adjustment Layer clips to your timeline, see page 126.

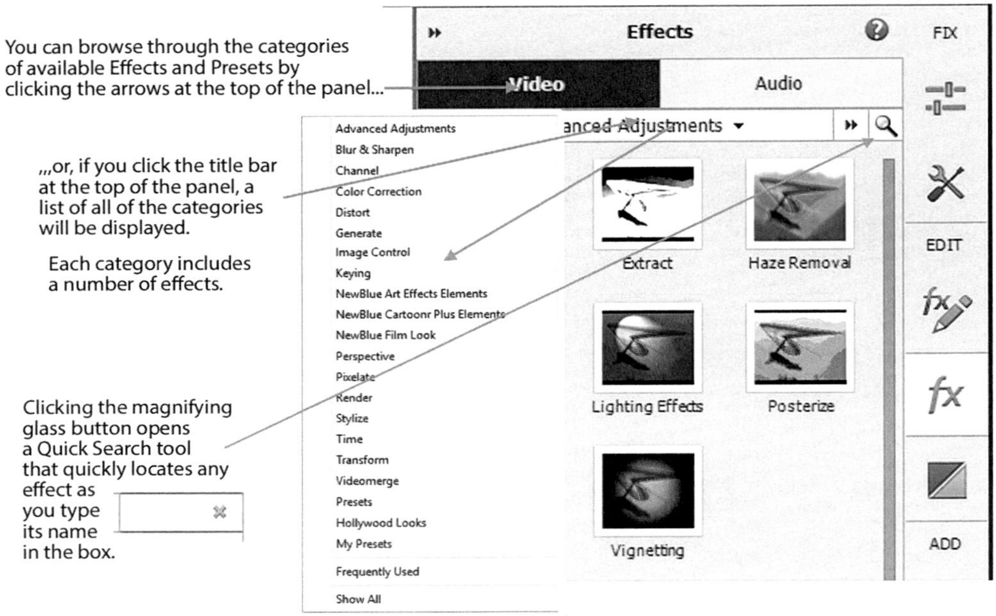

Premiere Elements' **Video Effects** and **Audio Effects** libraries are accessed by clicking the **Effects** button on the **Toolbar** along the right side of the interface.

In addition to its huge catalog of **Video Effects** and **Audio Effects**, the **Effects** panel includes **Presets**, pre-programmed effects (many of them animated), and a **My Presets** folder where you keep your own custom-created effects and animations.

Presets and **Video Effects** display in the panel as thumbnails, demonstrating their effect. Animated **Preset** effects can be previewed by clicking on the thumbnail image. **Audio Effects** appear as speaker thumbnails.

As indicated in the illustration above, you can also quickly call up an effect simply by clicking on the magnifying glass button on the upper right of the panel and typing its name in the search box. As you type, the program will search in real time.

Applying an effect or preset is as simple as dragging the effect from this panel onto a clip on your timeline.

Once an effect has been added to a clip, its settings can be modified, customized and even be animated. (In fact, some effects won't even change your clip much at the default settings.) For more information on customizing these settings – or removing an applied effect completely – see **Chapter 14, Adjust Applied Effects**.

You can apply any number of effects to a clip. In fact, you can even double-up the same effect on the same clip (such as **Channel Volume** on an audio clip) to increase its intensity. Sometimes the way effects interact with each other on a clip can create a new effect all its own.

Video effects can also be applied to an **Adjustment Layer** rather than directly to a clip, as discussed on page 126.

Apply an effect to several clips at once

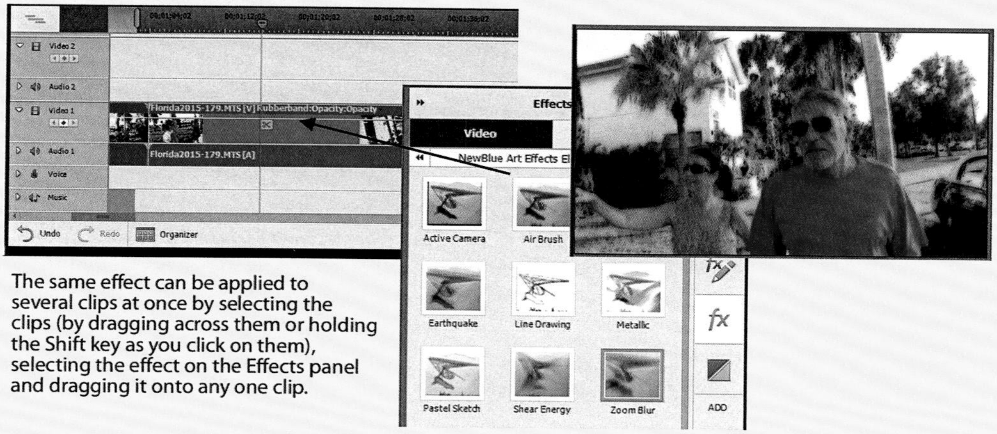

The same effect can be applied to several clips at once by selecting the clips (by dragging across them or holding the Shift key as you click on them), selecting the effect on the Effects panel and dragging it onto any one clip.

Premiere Elements includes the ability to apply an effect to several clips at once.

To apply an effect to several clips in one move:

1 Select your clips, either by holding the **Shift** or **Ctrl** key (⌘ key on a Mac) as you click to select clips on your timeline or by dragging across your timeline from beyond your clips to "lasso" the clips you'd like to apply the effect to. (You can also use **Ctrl+a** on a PC or **⌘+a** on a Mac to select all of the clips on the timeline.)

2 Once several clips are selected, go to the **Effects** panel and locate the effect you want to apply.

Drag the effect onto any one of your selected clips.

The effect will be applied to all of your selected clips.

You can fine-tune the effects in the **Applied Effects** panel (one clip at a time). For more information on adjusting effects settings, see **Chapter 14, Adjust Applied Effects.**

To create and customize an effect on one clip and then apply the same effect and settings to several other clips, use the **Paste Effects and Adjustments** feature, as we also discuss on page 178.

Mac video effects: A limited edition

The Mac version of Premiere Elements 15 does not include all of the effects available in the PC version. For a list of the omitted effects, see page 274 in the **Appendix**.

Premiere Elements' video effects

Premiere Elements' video effects are arranged in categories. To jump to a category, click on the category title bar at the top of the panel, as illustrated on page 154, and select your category from the drop-down menu. To browse the categories, use the arrow buttons to the right and left of the category title bar.

Here are the various categories as well as brief descriptions of how some of the key effects in that category work.

Advanced Adjustments. Advanced Adjustments can be used to effect or correct a clip's color, tint or lighting with a **Channel Mixer** or **Image Control**.

The **Shadow/Highlight** effect is a great way to decrease contrast in a clip (e.g., the sky is too bright and the shade is too dark). Also available in Photoshop Elements is **Shadow/Highlight,** one of my personal favorite picture-saving effects!

The Vignette effect.

The **Vignetting** effect, illustrated to the right, which makes your video lighter toward the center and darker around the sides.

Posterize reduces the number of colors in your clip, making it appear more cartoon-like.

Lighting Effects impose a spotlight-like effect on your clip.

And new to this category is the **Haze Removal** effect, discussed below.

Blur & Sharpen. These effects soften or sharpen your picture.

The **Ghosting** effect leaves a very cool trail behind objects that are moving in your clip.

Channel. Invert, the single **Channel** effect, turns your video's picture into its negative.

Haze Removal

New to version 15 is an easy-to-use tool for reducing haze and fog in your videos.

Haze Removal is found in the **Advanced Adjustments** category of **Effects.**

Once it is applied to clip, you can elect to use **Auto Dehaze** or to manually adjust the effect's **Haze Reduction** and **Sensitivity.**

Color Correction. The effects in this set – **HSL Tuner, Split Tone** and the **Three-Way Color Corrector** – are advanced tools for enhancing and correcting the color in your video. We take a close-up look at the **Three-Way Color Corrector** on page 161.

Distort. The **Distort** effects warp, twist and/or bend your video image.

Generate. The **Lens Flare** effect in this category adds a bright, white flare to a spot on your video picture, as if a light is being shone back at the camcorder.

Image Control. These effects offer tools for color, contrast and light adjustments. Among this set are tools for tinting, replacing and even removing the color completely from your video.

Keying. **Keying** effects remove or make transparent a portion of your video's picture.

A powerful tool in this category is the **Chroma Key** effect, which we discuss in detail on page 158. Other effects in this category are essentially the **Chroma Key** preset applied to certain colors (**Green Screen Key, Blue Screen Key**). Others, like the **Garbage Mattes**, create transparent areas in a clip that can be shaped with user-defined corner handles.

Note that the Chroma Key, Green Screen Key and Blue Screen Key effects are not available on the Mac version of Premiere Elements. On a Mac, the alternative keying effect is Videomerge, as discussed on page 164.

NewBlue Art Effects, NewBlue Film Look, NewBlue Motion Effects. These effects categories include high-level image effects created by NewBlue, one of the world's top video effects companies.

One of the most popular of these is the **Old Film** effect, a highly customizable effect which makes your video look like a damaged, worn, old movie.

NewBlue Cartoonr Plus Elements. This effect makes your videos look cartoon-like, as in the illustration above right!

The very cool, new NewBlue Cartoonr effect.

Perspective. These effects can be used to make your video image look as if it is floating or rotating into space.

Pixelate. The **Facet** effect in this category reduces your video picture to a group of large color blocks.

Render. The **Lightning** effect is great fun, although it takes a lot of computer power to create and customize it!

The **Ramp** effect fades your video out across the screen in a gradiated pattern.

Stylize. The effects in this category, as the category name implies, can be used to create a highly stylized video.

Time. Effects in this category change how your video displays motion by reducing or affecting the look of the frame rate.

Note that this is *not* the place to go if you want to slow down or speed up a clip. That's the **Time Stretch** effect (see page 109), available in the tool kit launched from the **Tools** button on the **Toolbar**.

Transform. A real hodgepodge of effects, this category includes some stylized effects, some 3D transformations and, for some reason, **Clip** and **Crop**, two effects for trimming off the sides of your video picture.

(For the record, **Clip** trims away the sides of your video and replaces them with color while **Crop** trims away the sides and replaces them with transparency – a significant difference, if you're using your cropped clip on an upper video track with another clip on a track below it).

To learn more about using the **Crop** tool (or **Clip** tool, since you use the same method to adjust both) see **Types of effects settings** on page 176 of **Chapter 14, Adjust Applied Effects.**

Videomerge. This effect is essentially a more automatic version of the **Chroma Key** effect. When applied to a clip, it removes what it interprets to be the background in a single step. We take a **Close-Up** look at how to use it on page 162.

For information on changing settings for effects, see **Adjust settings for effects and properties** in **Chapter 14, Adjust Applied Effects.** For information on animating effects to change over time, see **Chapter 15, Keyframing**.

Apply a Hollywood Look to your video

Relatively new to Premiere Elements are **Hollywood Looks**, a collection of 16 very cool color grading presets that automatically give your video the moody look of an artsy Hollywood production (or of a cheap home movie).

Included in this set are effects for shifting colors, tinting your videos, brightening them or making your videos look dark and creepy.

The **Hollywood Looks** included with Premiere Elements 15 are:

Comic uses the **NewBlue Cartoonr Plus** effect to make your movie look like an animated cartoon.

Cross Process desaturates the color in your video, reducing it to shades of gray, blue and yellow.

Crushed Color washes out the color in your video. Great for doing *Cold Case*-style flashbacks.

Deep Copper makes your video black & white with a cold, coppery tone.

Dreamy applies an ethereal **Gaussian Blur** effect.

Hollywood Movie increases the blue levels of your video to give it a more filmic look.

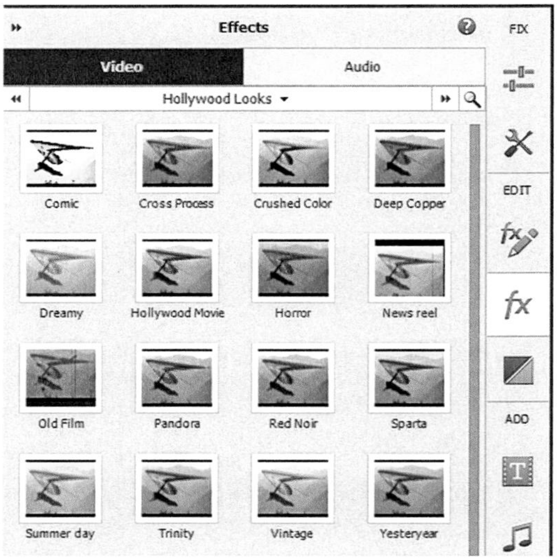

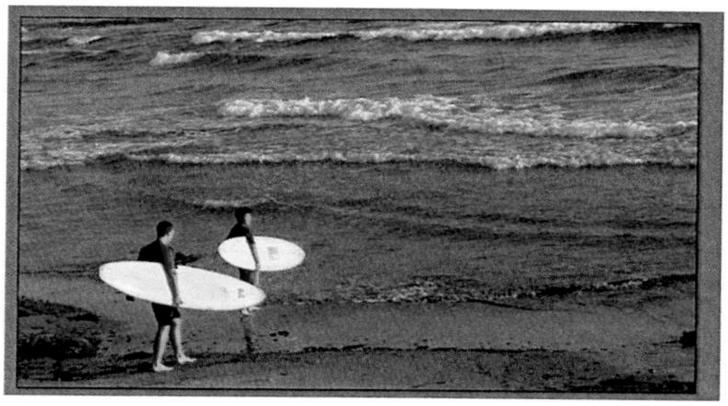

Hollywood Looks change the visual tone of your movie by applying preset effects and adjustments in a single move.

Comic

Cross Process

Crushed Color

Deep Copper

Dreamy

Hollywood Movie

Horror

News Reel

Old Film

Pandora

Red Noir

Sparta

Summer Day

Trinity

Vintage

Yesteryear

Horror desaturates the color to give your video a dull, deadly look.

Newsreel and **Old Film** lower or remove your color levels and "damage" the video to make it look older and worn.

Pandora turns everyone's skin blue (like the Na'vi characters in *Avatar*).

Red Noir desaturates all of the colors except for a few spots of red.

Sparta gives your video a surreal, golden look.

Summer Day washes out your video's color with yellow "sunshine".

Trinity shifts your video's tint to mystical green shades.

Vintage makes your video look like an old home movie.

Yesteryear shifts the tint of your video toward orange and green to create the mood of a faded memory.

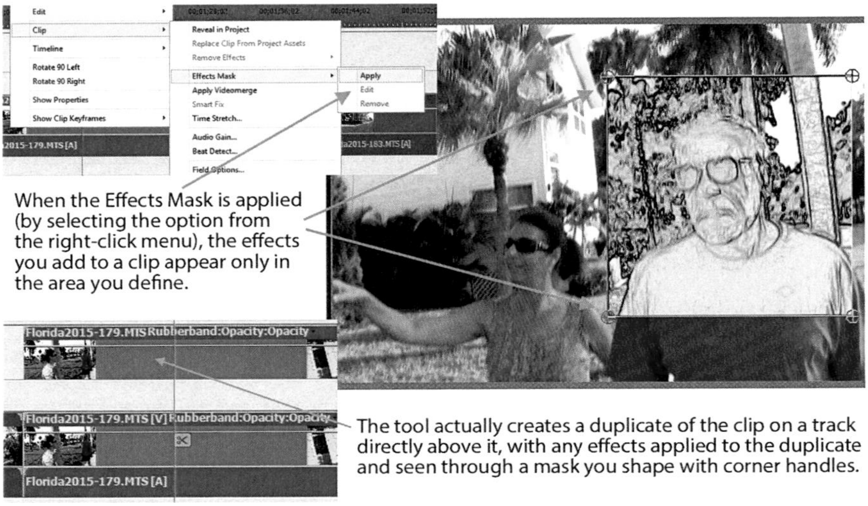

When the Effects Mask is applied (by selecting the option from the right-click menu), the effects you add to a clip appear only in the area you define.

The tool actually creates a duplicate of the clip on a track directly above it, with any effects applied to the duplicate and seen through a mask you shape with corner handles.

Isolate an effect area with the Effects Mask

The **Effects Mask** enables you to isolate an area of your video and apply an effect to it without affecting the other areas of the clip. (This effect is only available in Expert View.)

For example, with the **Effects Mask**, you can define a rectangular area any place in your video frame and apply the **Black & White** effect to it. The area within the defined rectangle will be black & white while everything in the video frame outside this rectangle will remain in color.

To create an **Effects Mask**:

1 **Right-click** on a clip on your timeline and, from the **Clip** sub-menu, select **Effects Mask** and then **Apply**, as illustrated above.

   A duplicate of your clip will appear on the Video 2 track and a rectangle, with four active corner handles, will appear in the **Monitor** panel.

2 Click and drag the corner handles to define the mask area.

This area can be moved and re-shaped later, if you'd like.

3 Click on the **Effects** button on the **Toolbar,** then select and apply an effect to the clip on Video 2 (or simply drag it onto the **Monitor**).

   The effect will be applied only to the area defined by the rectangular mask.

To fine tune the effect, select the clip(s) (they'll be grouped, and when you select one, you'll select both) and open the **Applied Properties** panel, as described in **Chapter 14, Adjust Applied Effects**.

Adjust your added effect as described in **Adjust an effect or property** on page 174.

- To re-edit the position and shape of the **Effects Mask**, **right-click** again on the clip on your timeline and select **Effects Mask** then **Edit** from the context menu. The corner handles will again become active and you will be able to drag them, or the mask box, to any new position on the **Monitor** display.
- To remove the **Effects Mask**, **right-click** on the clip on your timeline and select **Effects Mask** then **Remove**. The duplicate clip will be removed from the Video 2 track and any effects you've added will be applied to the entire original clip.

  The effect(s) can then be removed from the original clip by **right-clicking** on the clip and selecting the **Remove Effects** option.

Close Up: The Three-Way Color Corrector

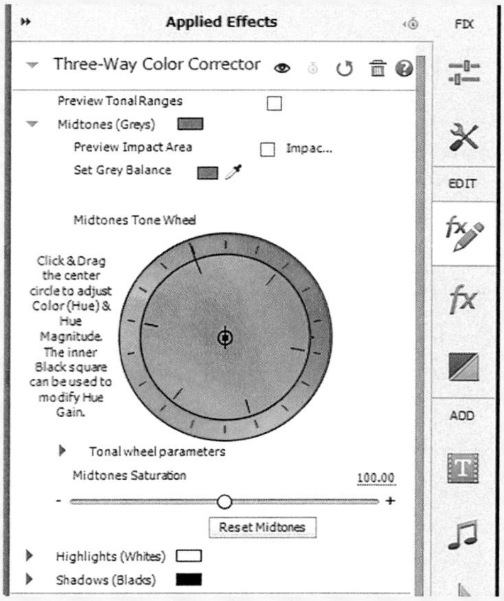

Premiere Elements includes exciting, professional-style effects for correcting and enhancing the colors in your videos (located in the **Color Correction** category of **Effects**).

One of the most advanced is the **Three-Way Color Corrector.** Modeled after color correctors in professional video editing software, this effect allows you to adjust the hue, saturation and lightness for your video's individual **Shadows (Blacks), Midtones (Grays)** and **Highlights (Whites)**.

To adjust the effect's levels, open the **Applied Effects** panel (as discussed in **Chapter 14**).

Locate the **Color Corrector** listing on the **Applied Effects** panel. Under each of the effect's three tonal levels, you will find a color wheel.

To adjust that tonal level's hue and lightness, drag the center circle point around within the color wheel. To adjust the hue's saturation, move the slider below the wheel.

To see which areas of your video image are being affected with each adjustment, check the **Preview Impact Area** checkbox.

For best results, we recommend you adjust **Shadows (Blacks)** first, then **Highlights (Whites)**, then **Midtones (Grays)**.

Close-Up: Chroma Key

Whether you're aware of it or not, you've encountered **Chroma Key** (and its variations in **Green Screen** and **Blue Screen**) countless times.

Place your foreground clip on the Video 2.

Place your new background on the Video 1 track, directly below the Video 2 clip.

Apply the Chroma Key effect to the clip on Video 2.

Every time you've watched a televised weather report – the weather person apparently standing in front of satellite video and moving maps – you've actually seen a **Chroma Key** effect. That weather person is, in reality, standing in front of a plain green screen, electronics removing this green background and replacing it with the weather graphics for the broadcast.

Virtually every movie that includes scenes of live actors interacting with special effects is using some form of **Chroma Key** – as those actors, like the weather person, perform in front of a green or blue background, which is later swapped out with some new background or effect.

Creating the effect is fairly simple. And once you understand how it works (and maybe how to combine it with keyframed motion), you'll be able to create many of these same big-screen Hollywood effects at home. **(Sadly, this effect is not available on the Mac version of the program. However, the Videomerge effect [page 164] serves nearly the same function.)**

Here's how it works: You shoot your subject standing in front of an evenly-colored screen – usually bright green or blue (colors that are not present in human skin tones). This clip is placed on an upper video track. Your new background is placed on a lower video track, directly below it on your timeline.

The **Chroma Key** effect is then applied to the clip on the upper track and its "key" color is set to the color of the background. **Chroma Key** then renders that "key" color transparent, revealing through it the video on the track below – making it appear that your subject is standing in front of whatever video you've placed on the lower video track!

The **Chroma Key** effect actually appears in a couple of forms in the **Keying** category of Premiere Elements' **Effects**. Also known as the **Blue Screen Key** and the **Green Screen Key**, though the function of the effect is essentially the same – a designated color, or range of colors, on a clip is made transparent. The **Green Screen** and **Blue Screen Keys** are merely preset to the two most commonly used "key" colors.

To create a **Chroma Key** effect, you'll need two things: A video clip that has been shot with a subject standing in front of an evenly-colored, evenly-lit green or blue background and a second clip with a background you'd like to swap in.

By the way, you can only effectively do a **Chroma Key** effect in Expert View, because it requires two video tracks, as shown in the illustration.

Continued on facing page

Chroma Key (continued)

1 Place the video you shot in front of a green or blue screen (we'll call it your **Key Clip**) on the Video 2 track, as illustrated on the facing page.

Place the video or still of the background you want to swap in on the Video 1 track, directly below the **Key Clip**.

2 Apply the **Chroma Key** effect to your **Key Clip.**

3 With the **Key Clip** selected on your timeline, click the **Applied Effects** button to open the **Applied Effects** panel.

4 In the **Applied Effects** panel, click the **Chroma Key** listing to open its properties, as illustrated.

5 On the **Applied Effects** panel, click to select the little **eye dropper** icon next to the color swatch (technically called the **Color Sampler**). Your cursor will become an **eye dropper**.

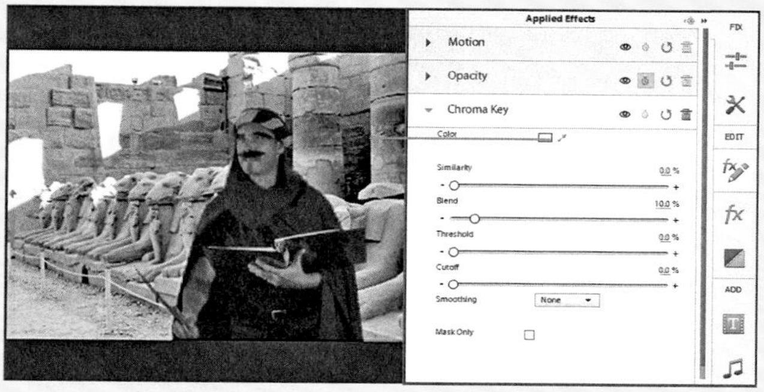

On the Applied Effects panel, locate the Chroma Key effect listing. Click to select the Sampler (eye dropper) and use it to sample the green background on the clip in your Monitor. It will become transparent – revealing the new background on Video 1.

Use this eyedropper to click on the green or blue colored background in your **Key Clip** in the **Monitor**.

6 Once you've selected your **key color**, most of the **Key Clip**'s background will become transparent, revealing the background clip you've placed on Video 1.

You'll likely need to do some fine-tuning with the sliders in the **Chroma Key** properties to remove the **Key Clip**'s background completely and smooth the edges between the keyed area and the subject in the foreground.

One very effective way to fine-tune your **Chroma Key** is to check the **Mask Only** option in the **Chroma Key** properties.

This will display your keyed foreground as a white silhouette so that you can focus on removing the keyed area while maintaining the integrity of your foreground subject.

It's usually best to adjust only the **Similarity** and **Blend** levels in **Mask Only** mode. Once you've got these properties adjusted as well as possible, uncheck the **Mask Only** box to return to regular view before adjusting the other properties.

You may also find that the **Green Screen Key, Blue Screen Key** or even **Videomerge** (page 164) will work more effectively for your particular needs or situation than the **Chroma Key** effect.

Don't be afraid to experiment and see which **Keying** effect works best for your situation!

Close-up: Videomerge

As with **Chroma Key, Videomerge** works by making areas on a clip transparent – and it tends to do this fairly automatically.

You'll find access to the **Videomerge** effect in several places throughout the program:

- **When you drag a potential "key" clip to your timeline** – If you drag to your timeline a clip that includes a flat, evenly-colored background, the program will launch a pop-up panel asking if you'd like **Videomerge** to be applied to the clip.
- **On the Effects panel** – Like **Chroma Key, Videomerge** can be applied to a clip by dragging the effect from the **Effects** panel (from the **Videomerge** category) onto a clip.
- **Right-click on a clip** – **Right-click** on any clip on the timeline, in the **Clip** sub-menu, you'll find the option to **Apply Videomerge.**
- **On the Monitor** – If you drag a clip onto the **Monitor** while holding down the **Shift** key, the pop-up menu will offer you the option of adding the clip to the track directly above the currently-displayed video clip and applying the **Videomerge** effect to it.

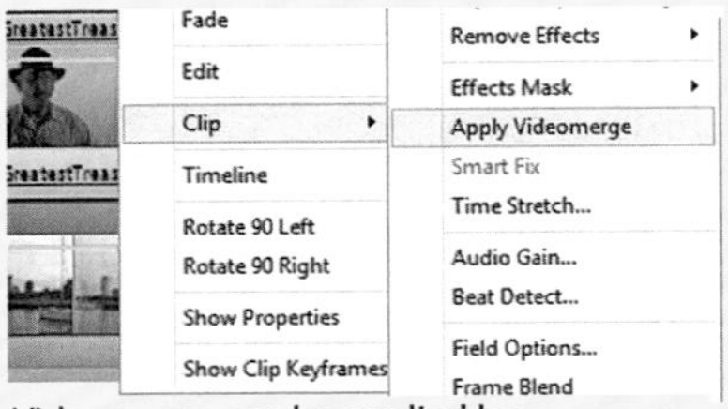

Videomerge can be applied by right-clicking on the clip on your timeline.

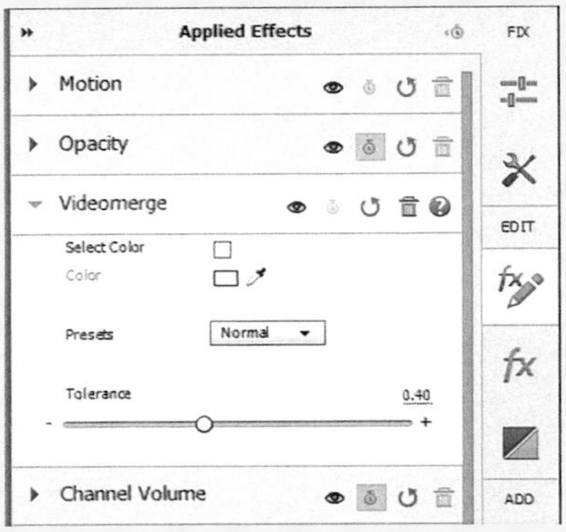

The settings for Videomerge are much simpler than those for Chroma Key.

Once applied to a clip, the **Videomerge** effect has a greatly simplified "key" adjustment tool.

Click the **Applied Effects** tab on the right side of the interface to open the **Applied Effects** panel for the clip. Click on the **Videomerge** listing to open its settings control panel.

The **Videomerge** effect's control panel includes only a few simple adjustments:

- An **eyedropper** for designating the color to be keyed. (Check the **Select Color** box to use the eyedropper to sample your clip's background color on the **Monitor**.)
- **A drop-down Preset list** for controlling how detailed the **Videomerge** key is.
- A **Tolerance** slider for setting the range of colors to be keyed.
- The option to **Invert Selection**, which makes the clip transparent *except for* the designated key area.

In our experience, **Videomerge** is easy to use and surprisingly effective. In many situations, it's a great alternative to the **Chroma Key, Blue Screen** and **Green Screen Key** effects.

And, as the Mac version of the program does not include **Chroma Key, Green Screen Key** or **Blue Screen Key**, it is the only way to create this type of effect on the OSX platform.

Preset Effects

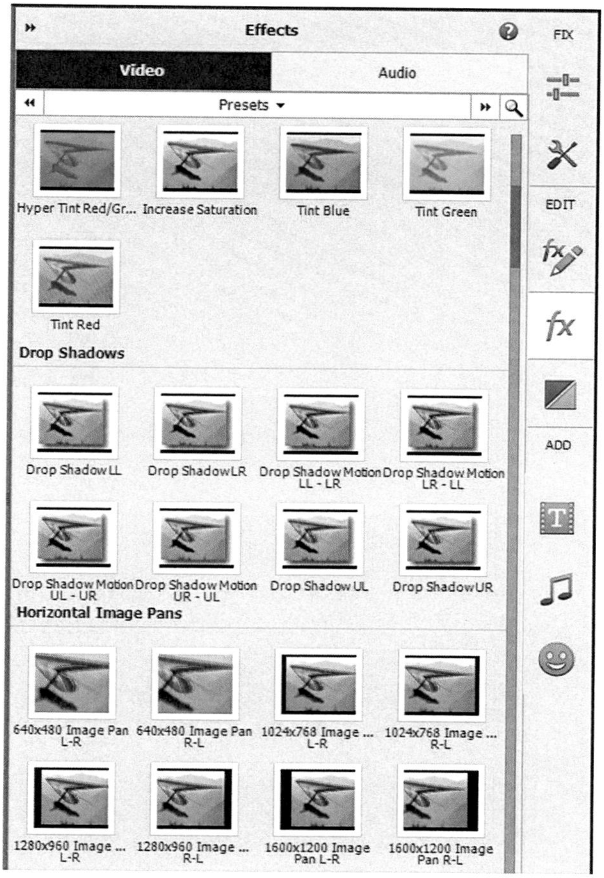

The Preset category includes hundreds of pre-set up effects and effect animations in a dozen sub-categories.

Although they appear as a separate category of effects on the **Effects** panel, **Presets** are, actually, effects to which settings have already been applied. Some of these presets change the size or texture of your video clip, or create a **Picture-in-Picture** effect. Others include animated effects so that your video image moves or changes size or an effect's settings change over the course of the clip. (For more information on motion paths and animated effects, see the **Chapter 15, Keyframing**.)

Presets are represented as thumbnails on the panel and, if you hover your mouse over those that are animated, a preview of the animation will play.

Once you apply a **Preset** to a video clip, you can open the clip's **Applied Effects** panel and customize the settings or animations. (For information on making these adjustments, see **Adjust an effects or property** on page 174.)

To apply a preset effect to a clip, just drag the preset from the **Presets** panel to your clip on the timeline or onto the **Monitor** panel.

The nearly 275 **Presets** fall into a number of categories.

Bevel Edges. These presets create the illusion of a raised edge along the sides of your video clip.

Blurs. Animated **Blur** presets go from blurry to clear or clear to blurry, and can be applied to the beginning or end of a clip.

When using multi-track editing (See **Use L-Cuts, J-Cuts and multiple tracks** on page 78 of **Chapter 7, Edit Your Video in Expert View**), you can use these keyframed blurs as transitions between video tracks.

Color Effects. These presets can be used to tint your clip or to increase the color saturation.

Presets are pre-set Effects, often with keyframed motion.
Applying a Picture-In-Picture preset to a clip on Video 2 is a quick and easy way to create a Picture-in-Picture composite of the clips on Video 1 and Video 2.

Drop Shadows. These presets reduce your clip's scale and create a shadow effect so that your clip appears to be floating – an effect that's most effective when applied to a clip on the Video 2 track, casting a shadow over a clip on the Video 1 track.

Some of these presets use motion paths so that the shadow moves around over the course of your clip.

Horizontal Image Pans, Horizontal Image Zooms, Vertical Image Pans, Vertical Image Zooms. These presets are pre-programmed motion paths for panning and zooming around your photos – their names describe which size photo they are preset to pan or zoom across.

They'll do the job in a pinch, but you'll have much more control over the process if you use keyframing to create your own motion paths, as explained in **Chapter 15, Keyframing**.

The biggest challenge to using these preset pans and zooms is that they are designed for specific sizes of photos (as indicated in each preset's name). If the photo you are panning and zooming around is smaller than the effect, for instance, the effect may pan right off the edge of your photo!

With **keyframing** – and even the **Pan & Zoom Tool** (page 102) – you have the ability to control *precisely* how your motion path behaves.

Mosaics. These animated presets go to or from a mosaic pattern and can be applied to the beginning or end of your clip.

Picture-in-Picture (PiP). The **PiP** presets, when applied to a clip on the Video 2 track with another clip on the Video 1 track under it, automatically reduce the scale of the clip on the Video 2 track and reposition it in the video frame, such that both it and the clip under it are on screen at the same time (as illustrated above).

Create a custom preset

You can easily create your own presets, saving your custom effects settings, animations or motion paths for future use.

To create a custom preset, **right-click** on the effect it represents in your clip's **Applied Effects** panel and select the **Save Preset** option, as illustrated above.

Once you have saved the preset, it will be available in the **My Presets** category on the **Effects** panel.

Applying a custom preset to a clip is just like applying a default preset.

Click to select the clip on your timeline and then drag the preset onto it from the **My Presets** category on the **Effects** panel.

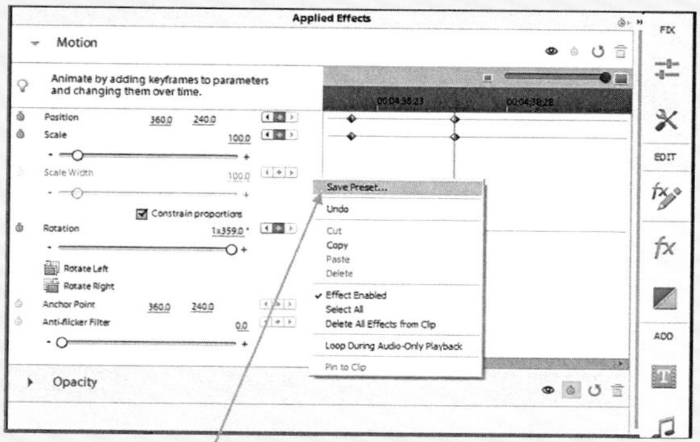

Once you've created settings for an effect or created a keyframed effect or motion path, you can save it as a custom preset effect by right-clicking on it (Ctrl-clicking on a Mac) in the Applied Effets panel and selecting the option to Save Preset.

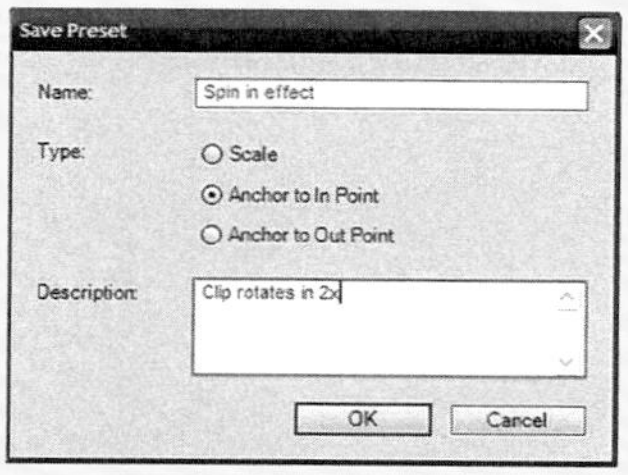

When you Save Preset, you can name it, set it to apply to the beginning or end of a clip and give it a description.

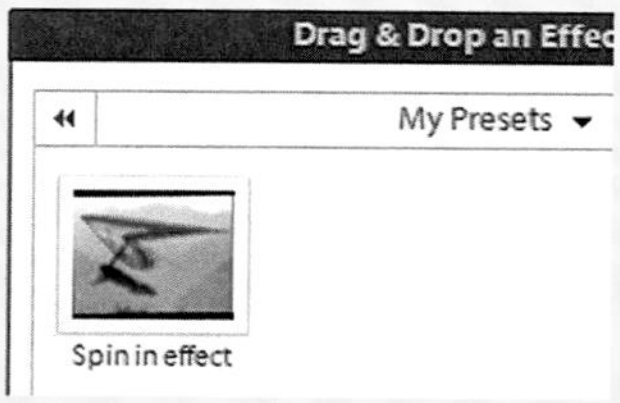

Once saved, your preset will appear in My Presets in the Effects panel for all of your Premiere Elements projects.

Some **Picture-in-picture** presets will even add motion, changing the scale or position of **PiP** over the course of the clip – sometimes even incorporating an elaborate animation effect, such as spinning.

Solarizes. These animated presets go to or from a bright **Solarize** effect, and can be applied to the beginning or end of a clip.

Twirls. These animated twirling effects can be applied to the beginning or end of a clip.

Audio effects

Premiere Elements includes 19 effects in its **Audio Effects** category. (The Mac version includes a slightly reduced set, as discussed on page 274.)

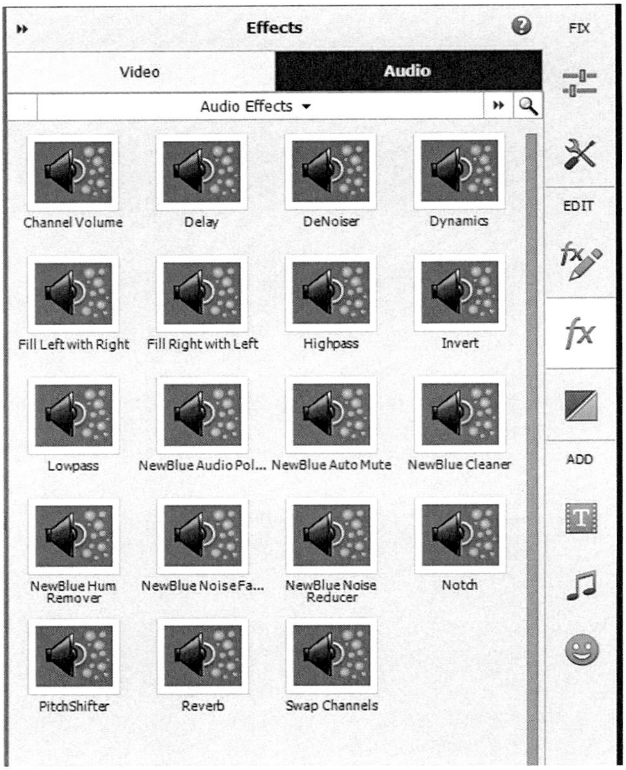

These effects are designed for adding special effects to your audio files or for filtering the sounds in your movie. (More basic audio effects, such as **Channel Volume, Bass** and **Treble** are found on the **Adjustments** panel, as described on page 123.)

A number of these effects (**DeNoiser, Highpass, Lowpass** and **Notch**) are filters for removing sounds at certain frequencies.

The **DeNoiser** effect reduces noise in your audio clip. The **DeNoiser** is primarily designed to clean up tape hiss that may have crept into your audio.

Dynamics is a processor for cleaning and "sweetening" your movie's sound.

The **Dynamics** effect can be used to compress the sound of your audio by reducing the difference between the highest and lowest levels in a clip. **Dynamics** also lets you "sweeten" the sound by removing some background noise, reducing distortion or otherwise balancing the dynamic range. Well-tuned dynamics can give your video a richer, more professional, more big-screen movie-like sound. Premiere Elements also includes six audio enhancement effects from NewBlue – high-end, professional-style tools for reducing noise and sweetening your audio: **NewBlue Audio Polish, NewBlue Auto Mute, NewBlue Cleaner, NewBlue Hum Remover, NewBlue Noise Fader** and **NewBlue Noise Reducer**.

Fill Left with Right and **Fill Right with Left** are very helpful effects for those times when you have an audio clip with audio on only one of your stereo channels (as when you record with a monaural microphone). Applying **Fill Right with Left** or **Fill Left with Right** to the clip takes the mono audio from one channel and uses it for both the right and left stereo channels.

Delay and **Reverb** create echo effects.

And just for fun, there's the **PitchShifter**, which changes the pitch of an audio track, usually in very unnatural and often comic ways, as indicated by some of the names of some of its presets: **Female Becomes Secret Agent, Cartoon Mouse, Boo!, Sore Throat, A Third Higher, Breathless, Slightly Detuned, A Quint Up** and **A Quint Down**.

As with video effects, the intensity or other settings for your audio effects can be applied constantly, over the entire duration of a clip, or variably, using keyframes – adding an echo to one portion of a clip but not another, for instance.

For more information on changing settings for effects, see **Adjust an effect or property** on page 174 of **Chapter 14, Adjust Applied Effects.**

For information on keyframing effects to specific settings at specific points in your movie, see **Chapter 15, Keyframing**.

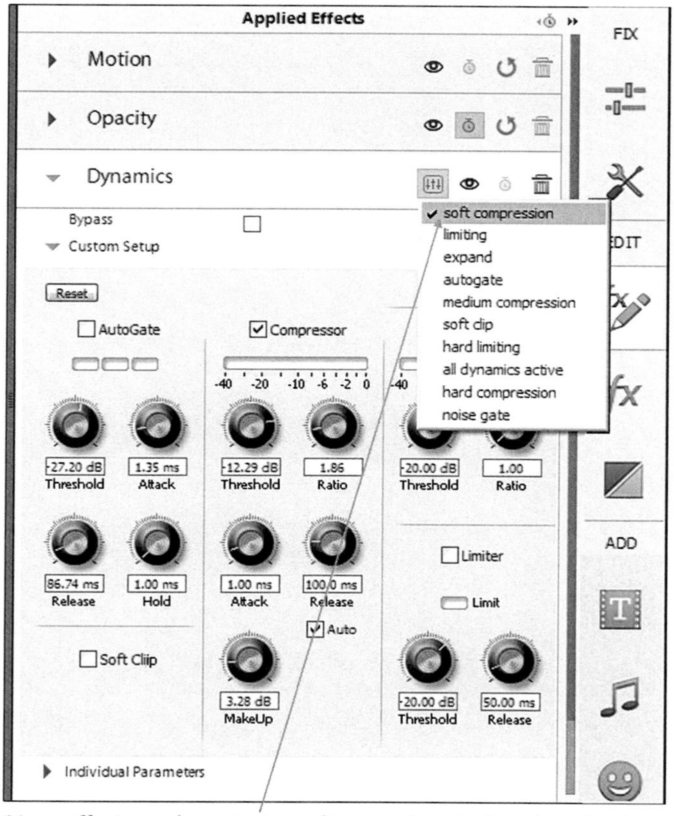

Many effects can be set using adjustment controls or by selecting a preset from the drop-down menu.

Cool Tricks & Hot Tips for Adobe Premiere Elements 14

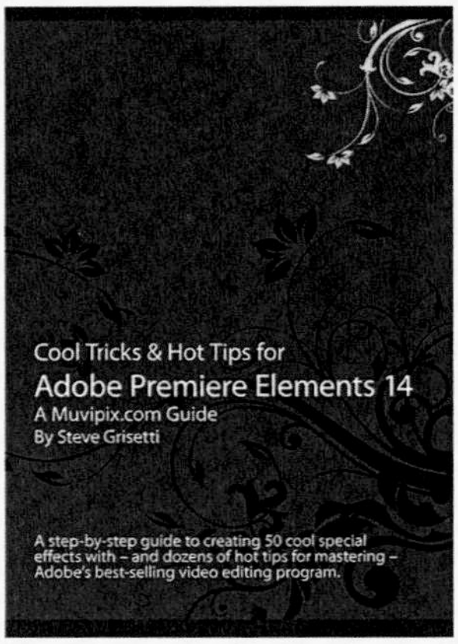

Cool Tricks & Hot Tips for
Adobe Premiere Elements 14
A Muvipix.com Guide
By Steve Grisetti
A step-by-step guide to creating 50 cool special effects with – and dozens of hot tips for mastering – Adobe's best-selling video editing program.

There is practically no limit to the special video and audio effects you can create with Premiere Elements.

If you'd like to learn some advanced tricks – like creating explosions in the sky or making a person appear to confront his identical twin, making your photos look three-dimensional or creating amazing titling effects – check out our *Cool Tricks & Hot Tips for Adobe Premiere Elements 14.* (And, yes, it also works with versions 12, 13 and 15, of course).

Full of bright, colorful illustrations and step-by-step instructions for creating 50 very cool special effects, with dozens of helpful "Hot Tips" thrown in for good measure, it's a book that will show you the amazing potential of this simple, inexpensive program.

The book is available through major online bookstores, like Amazon.com, as well as at the Muvipix.com store.

For more information, as well as examples of some of the effects you'll learn to create and free tutorials, see Muvipix.com/cooltricks14.php.

Opening the Applied Effects Panel

Default Clip Properties

Adjusting Effects

Copying Effect Attributes

Chapter 14

Adjust Applied Effects

Customizing your effects' settings

The Applied Effects panel is second only to the timeline as the most powerful and important workspace in Premiere Elements.

The timeline may be where you assemble, trim and order your clips, but the Applied Effects panel is where you make the movie magic happen!

It's where the effects are customized and sometimes even animated. It's where motion paths and many special effects are created.

Once an effect has been applied to a clip on your timeline, the settings for that effect can be adjusted in the Applied Effects panel.

After you've applied a video or audio effect to a clip on your timeline, you'll want to tweak its settings to customize how it affects your clip.

This customization is done in the **Applied Effects** panel.

The **Applied Effects** panel will list all of the effects added to your clips (as well as a couple of default properties, as discussed on the facing page). These effects and properties each include individual settings for customizing the way the effect behaves.

These custom settings can be made overall, affecting the look or sound of an entire clip, or they can be keyframed, creating an animated effect.

Keyframing is the process of creating animated effects or effects that change settings over time (such as a **Crop** effect in which the cropped area changes shape or a **Ripple** effect that shows actual, moving ripples across your clip). For a more detailed discussion of created animated effects, see **Chapter 15, Keyframing**.

Open the Applied Effects panel

Click to select a clip on your timeline and then click on the **Applied Effects** button on the right side of the program's interface, as illustrated above.

The **Applied Effects** panel will display a list of any effects applied to your selected clip as well as a couple of default video properties, as illustrated at the top of the facing page.

To access the individual settings for any applied effect, click on that effect's listing.

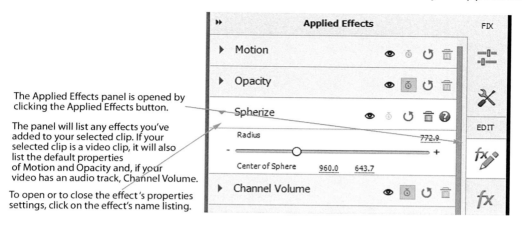

The Applied Effects panel is opened by clicking the Applied Effects button.

The panel will list any effects you've added to your selected clip. If your selected clip is a video clip, it will also list the default properties of Motion and Opacity and, if your video has an audio track, Channel Volume.

To open or to close the effect's properties settings, click on the effect's name listing.

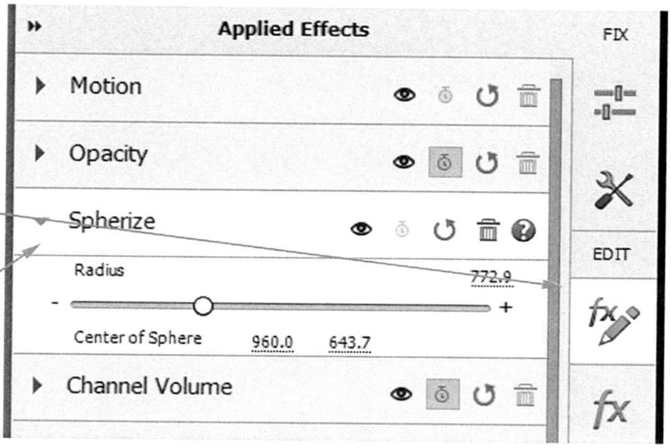

Clip effects and properties

The **Applied Effects** panel lists any effects you've added to a selected audio or video clip.

In addition, there are two default properties that will appear on this panel for every video clip – **Motion** and **Opacity.**

Click on the **Motion** or **Opacity** listing to open that property's individual settings, illustrated below right.

Motion. Includes individual settings for **Position, Scale** and **Rotation** – the settings used to keyframe pan & zoom motion paths over photos. (See **Chapter 15, Keyframing** for detailed information on how to create motion paths using these properties.)

Position is the location of a clip in your video frame, based on its center point, measured in pixels. For a 720x480 video frame, default center is 360, 240. For a 1920x1080 frame, default center is 960, 540.

Scale is the size of your clip, listed as a percentage, 100% being the default.

Rotation is a measure of degrees of angle imposed on your video image.

The settings for a clip's **Motion** properties can be changed in this panel or, more intuitively, by clicking on the video image in the **Monitor** panel and dragging it or its corner angles to change its position, resize the clip or rotate it (as discussed on page 175).

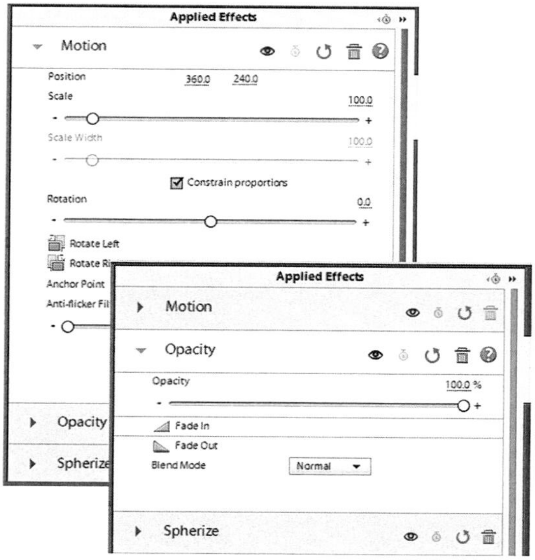

Opacity. Opacity is the transparency level of a clip. (Well, technically "opacity" is the *non*-transparency level of a clip.)

A **Fade In** or **Fade Out** transition is, technically, a function of the clip's **Opacity** property. Because of that, a **Fade In** or **Fade Out** can be added to a selected video clip by selecting the option here in the panel as well as by selecting the option from the **right-click** menu, as discussed on page 76. (A **Fade In** or **Fade Out** uses **Opacity** keyframed animation to bring the clip from transparency/black to 100% opaque or vice versa.)

The **Opacity** property settings also include an option for setting the clip's **Blend Mode**. **Blend Modes** are a bit beyond the scope of this book, but basically they're a high-level way of setting how a selected clip reacts with the video tracks below it on your timeline. In the vast majority of your work, you'll likely leave it set to **Normal**. But if you'd like to explore this advanced "bonus" tool Adobe has included, you can place a video on a track below your selected video and experiment with the interesting effects the different **Blend Modes** produce.

Many effects can be added to a single clip, and you can even add multiple instances of the *same* effect to increase its intensity. For instance, several **Channel Volume** effects can be added to the same clip, each adjusted to full volume, to raise the sound level of a clip several times.

Adjust an effect or property

Once you've opened the **Applied Effects** panel for a clip, you'll see a list of all of the effects added to that clip as well as the default properties of **Motion** and **Opacity,** as applicable.

To open up the individual settings for an effect listed in the panel, click on the effect's listing.

A few effects, such as the **Black & White** effect, have no settings at all. They are either on or off.

Some effects (such as **Lightning**) offer dozens of settings for customizing the effect. Others (such as **Posterize**) may offer only a few – or even a single "intensity adjustment" slider.

A number of effects (**Spherize**, for instance), when first applied to a clip, may not show a significant change at their default settings. You need to adjust the effect's settings in the **Applied Effects** panel to see any real change.

There are always several ways to adjust the settings for an effect.

Numbers – The numbers that represent an effect can, depending on the effect, represent the effect's **Position** (measured in pixels across the frame), percentage (as in **Opacity**) or intensity. To change a number, click on it and type in a new amount.

Alternatively, you can click and drag right or left ("scrubbing") over a number to increase or decrease its level.

Adjusting Applied Effects

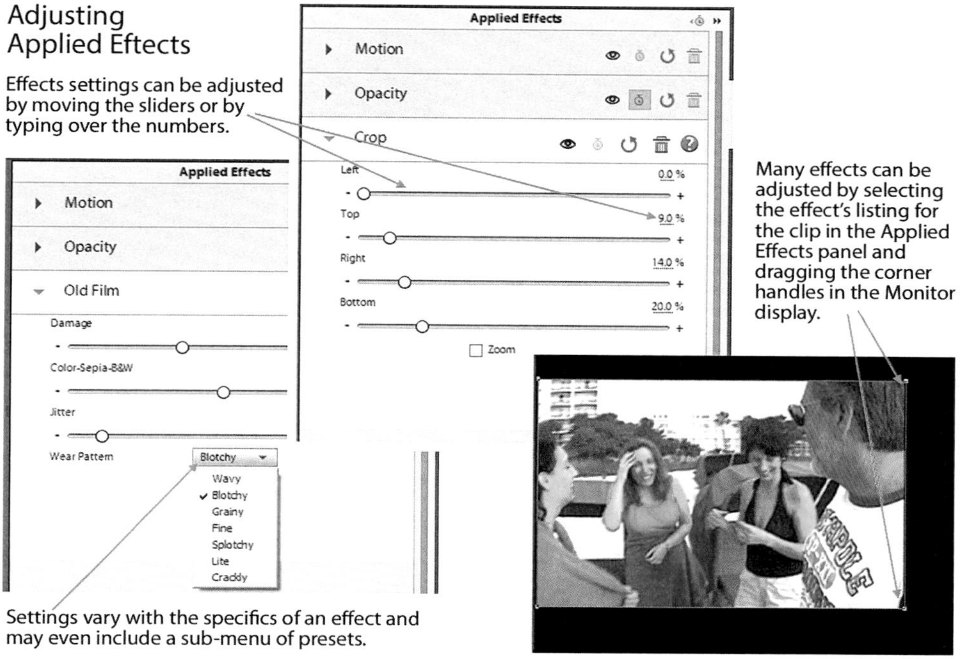
Effects settings can be adjusted by moving the sliders or by typing over the numbers.
Applied Effects
Motion
Opacity
Crop
Left
0.0 %
Top
9.0 %
Right
14.0 %
Bottom
20.0 %
Zoom
Applied Effects
Motion
Opacity
Old Film
Damage
Color-Sepia-B&W
Jitter
Wear Pattern
Blotchy
Wavy
Blotchy
Grainy
Fine
Splotchy
Lite
Crackly
Many effects can be adjusted by selecting the effect's listing for the clip in the Applied Effects panel and dragging the corner handles in the Monitor display.
Settings vary with the specifics of an effect and may even include a sub-menu of presets.

Sliders – The intensity or percentage settings for a large number of effects settings can be increased and decreased by moving its sliders back and forth.

On the Monitor – For a number of effects, the most intuitive way to change the effect's settings is to click and drag right on the video displayed in the **Monitor**.

When the effect's listing is selected in the **Applied Effects** panel, a position marker or corner handles will appear on the clip in the **Monitor**, as illustrated above. You can then click on this marker or corner handle and drag them into your desired positions.

For effects that involve motion (such as repositioning, rotating or resizing the video image) dragging a corner handle in the **Monitor** will move, rotate or resize the image.

For effects that involve shaping or sizing (such as scaling, cropping or using one of the garbage mattes) dragging the corner handles will reshape the image or affected area.

Once you change your effect's settings, the changes will be immediately displayed in your **Monitor** panel. (If they're not, it's because the **CTI** playhead isn't positioned over the clip you're adjusting on your timeline.) The exception is the **Lightning** effect, which is so intensive and erratic that you'll need to play back the clip to see how your adjusted settings have affected the clip.

Disable or remove an effect

Once you've adjusted the settings for an effect, you can do a before-and-after comparison by temporarily turning off – or disabling – the effect.

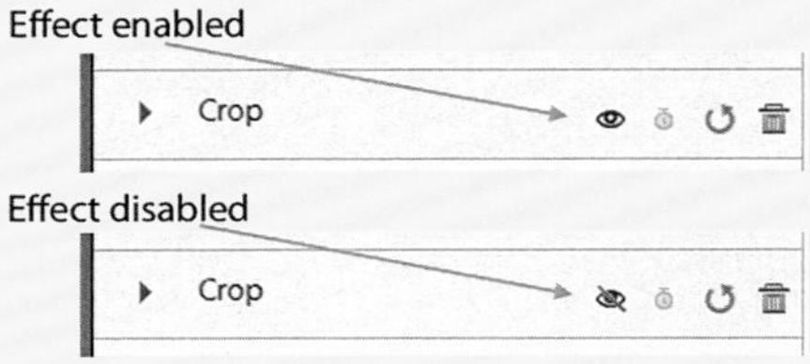

To temporarily turn off the effect, click on the eyeball icon to the right of the effect listing in the **Applied Effects** panel.

When you disable the effect, the eyeball icon will appear with a slash through it, and the effect's change on your video image will disappear.

To re-enable the effect, click on the same spot. The eyeball icon will return and the effect will once again be applied to your clip.

To remove an effect from a clip, click on the trashcan icon on the right end of the effect's listing. (The **Motion** and **Opacity** properties can not be removed.)

To remove all effects and adjustments from a clip, **right-click** on the clip on your timeline and select **Remove Effects/All Effects**.

Types of effects settings

Because effects change your clips in different ways (some that shift colors, some that create transparency [see **Chroma Key** and **Videomerge** in **Chapter 13, Add Audio and Video Effects**], some that reshape or distort your video image), each effect has its own unique settings.

Some settings increase the intensity of an effect. Some add optional elements to the effect. Other settings, depending on the effect, may shift color or define which areas on your video image are affected.

The **Crop** effect is an example. The settings for the crop effect define the percentage of the video image that will be cropped from each side. Dragging a slider representing any side will crop away that side of the clip.

Additionally, an effect's settings can be set to vary as the clip plays, creating an animated change, as illustrated on page 185.

- The **Basic 3D** effect, for instance, can be keyframed to create the illusion that your video image is tumbling back into space.
- The **Crop** effect can be animated using keyframes so that the amount of the video image that is cut away changes, opening or closing the cropped area over the course of the clip.
- **Fast Blur** and **Gaussian Blur** can be set to blur and then come back into focus.

For more information on how to create these types of motion paths and animated effects, see **Chapter 15, Keyframing** .

Save a custom Preset

Once you've adjusted, or even keyframed an effect or property, you can save its custom settings as a **Preset** so that you can use it on another clip at any time, even in another project.

To save your customized effect or keyframed animation as a **Preset, right-click** on the effect's listing in the **Applied Effects** panel and select **Save Preset...**

An option screen will then prompt you to name your preset, as illustrated below.

If your effect includes an animation, the screen will ask you if you'd like to set this animation to be applied to the beginning or end of the clip it is applied to.

You can also include a description of the effect, if you'd like.

Click **OK** to save the **Preset.**

The new **Preset** will be available in the **My Presets** category on the **Effects** panel. You can then apply this preset to a clip just as you would apply any effects, by selecting the clip on your timeline and dragging your **Preset** onto it.

When a **Preset** is applied to a clip, it adds the effect, your settings and any animations you included with it.

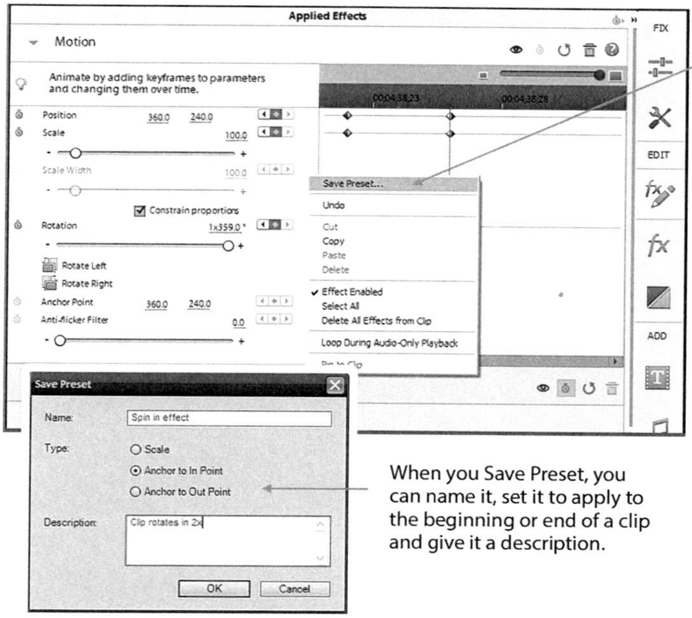

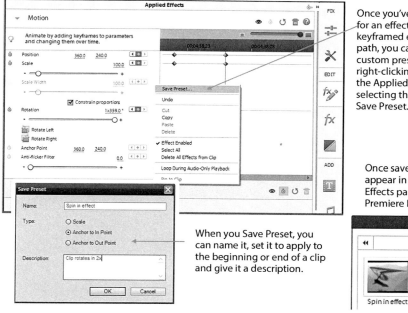

Once you've created settings for an effect or created a keyframed effect or motion path, you can save it as a custom preset effect by right-clicking on it in the Applied Effects panel and selecting the option to Save Preset.

When you Save Preset, you can name it, set it to apply to the beginning or end of a clip and give it a description.

Once saved, your preset will appear in My Presets in the Effects panel for all of your Premiere Elements projects.

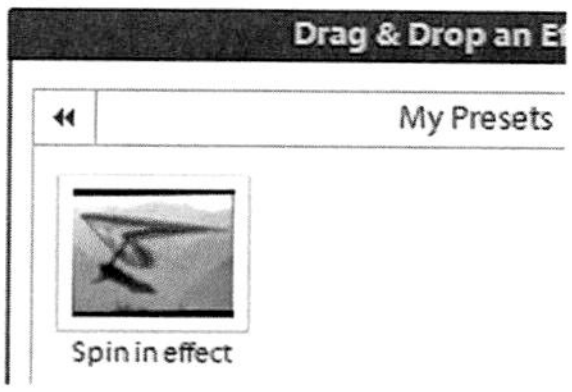

Paste Effects and Adjustments

If you've customized the settings for an effect – or created a keyframed animation – for one clip, you can easily apply it to another or even several other clips with just a few clicks using the **Paste Effects and Adjustments** feature.

Right-click on a clip on your timeline to which you've added your effect or keyframes and select **Copy** from the context menu.

Then select another clip – or even a group of clips – **right-click** on this group of clips and select **Paste Effects and Adjustments.**

All of the original clip's effects, adjustments and keyframed actions will automatically be applied to your selected clips!

Basic Keyframing

Creating a Pan & Zoom Animation

Advanced Keyframing Effects

Chapter 15

Keyframing

Animating effects and creating motion paths

Keyframing is the system that Premiere Elements uses to create motion paths, and to create and control effects that animate or change their settings over time.

With keyframing, you can control the level of an effect or the scale and/or position of a clip at precise points throughout the duration of the clip.

You can raise and lower the audio level at precise points; you can create panning and zooming around a photo; you can even animate, at precise points in any clip, the intensity or movement of a video or audio effect.

The principle is a simple one: You indicate which two or more points (**keyframes**) on your clip represent settings for a position, scale, effect or level of an effect and the program automatically generates the transitional animation between them. (Note that keyframing in the **Applied Effects** panel is only available in Expert View.)

You can, for instance, set **Scale** and **Position** settings in the **Motion** property to create one keyframe point displaying a close-up of one corner of a still photo, and then set the **Scale** and **Position** settings of a second keyframe point so that the entire photo is displayed. Premiere Elements will automatically create the smooth animation between those two positions, seeming to zoom out from the corner to a view of the entire picture.

With Premiere Elements, you can add any number of keyframes to a clip, creating as much motion or as many variations in your effects' settings as you'd like.

But the real power of this tool is in how easy it is to revise and adjust those positions and settings, giving you, the user, the ability to fine tune your motion path or animation until it is precisely the effect you want to achieve.

Although there are other workspaces in which you can create and edit keyframes (See **Adjust the audio levels at specific points in your video**, on page 185), most of your high level keyframing animation will likely be done on the **Applied Effects** or the **Adjustments** panel.

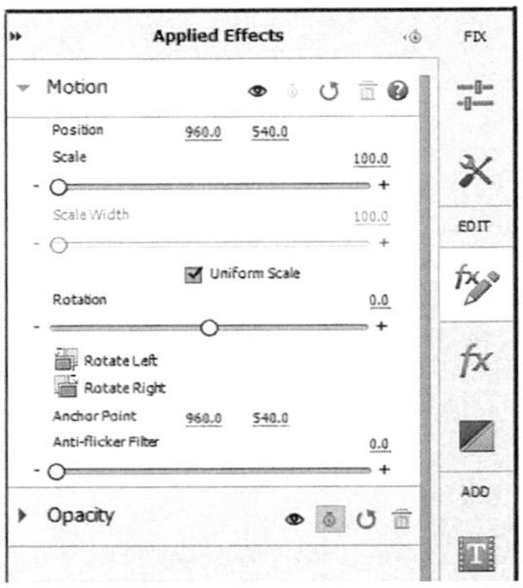

The Pan and Zoom Tool

In addition to its traditional keyframing workspace, Premiere Elements includes a very intuitive workspace for creating pan and zoom motion paths over your photos, accessible by way of the **Tools** button on the **Toolbar**.

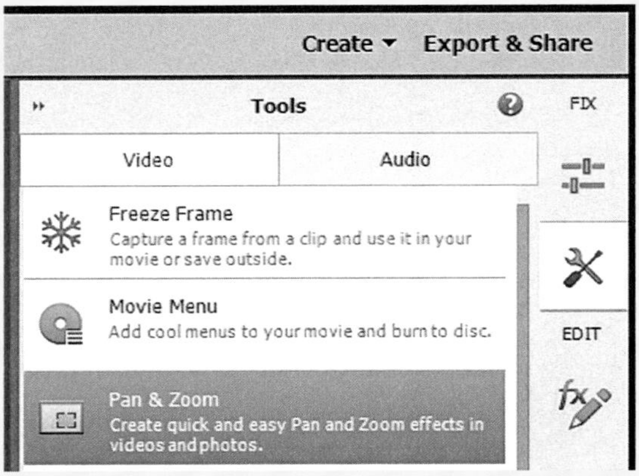

For more information on this new **Pan and Zoom** workspace, see **Create a Pan & Zoom motion path** on page 102 of **Chapter 9, Use the Premiere Elements Toolkit**.

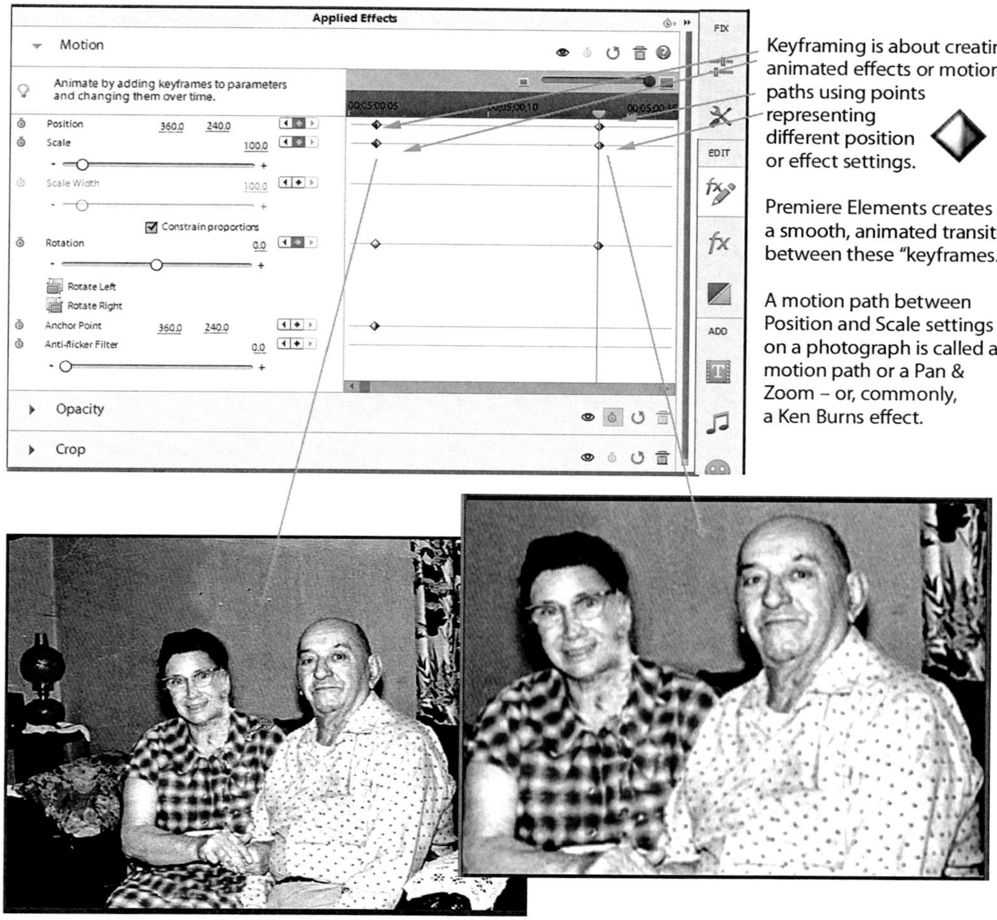

Keyframing is about creating animated effects or motion paths using points representing different position or effect settings.

Premiere Elements creates a smooth, animated transition between these "keyframes."

A motion path between Position and Scale settings on a photograph is called a motion path or a Pan & Zoom – or, commonly, a Ken Burns effect.

Keyframing vs. adjusting an effect's settings overall

Until you begin a keyframing session (by clicking the **Toggle Animation** button, as described below), any positioning, scaling or settings you make for an effect or property in the **Applied Effects** panel will apply to your *entire* clip.

In other words, if you change the **Scale** to 50% in the **Motion** properties, your entire clip will appear at 50% of its size.

However, once you click **Toggle Animation** (the little stopwatch icon) and turn on keyframing, every change to the effect or property you make will generate a **keyframe point** at the position of the **CTI** (Current Time Indicator) on your timeline.

It becomes a sort of "waypoint" for your effect or motion path.

When you create another keyframe point later in the clip and apply new settings to the effect or property, the program will create a path of motion, animation or transition between the two points.

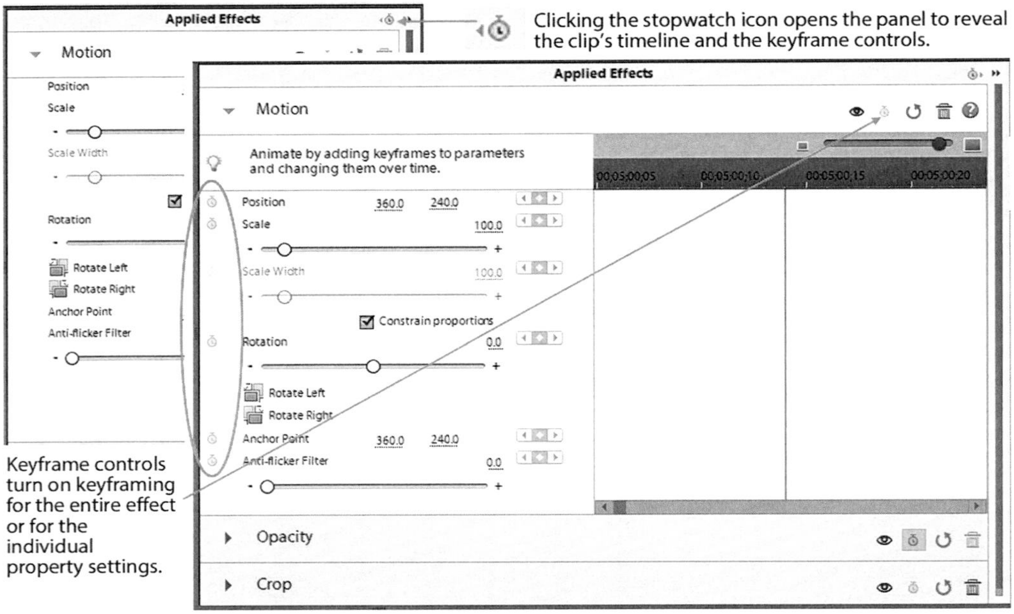

Clicking the stopwatch icon opens the panel to reveal the clip's timeline and the keyframe controls.

Keyframe controls turn on keyframing for the entire effect or for the individual property settings.

Open a keyframing session

When you first open the **Applied Effects** panel for a clip, the keyframing workspace is hidden.

To reveal this workspace (the **keyframing timeline**), click on the **Show Keyframes** button (the stopwatch icon with the arrow pointing left) in the upper right of the panel, as illustrated above. (Expert View only.)

The **keyframing timeline**, which appears to the right of your settings, is your workspace for creating, adjusting and editing your keyframes.

The time positions on this timeline represent positions, in time, on the clip itself. In fact, if you're editing in timeline mode, you'll notice that, as you move the **CTI** on the **keyframing timeline,** the **CTI** on your project's main timeline will move in sync with it.

Create a simple motion path using keyframes

To demonstrate how to use keyframes, we'll create a simple motion path – a pan and zoom across a photo.

1 With the **Applied Effects** panel open and a still photo clip selected on your timeline, click on the **Motion** property listing to reveal the settings for **Motion** – **Position**, **Scale, Rotation** and **Anchor Point**.

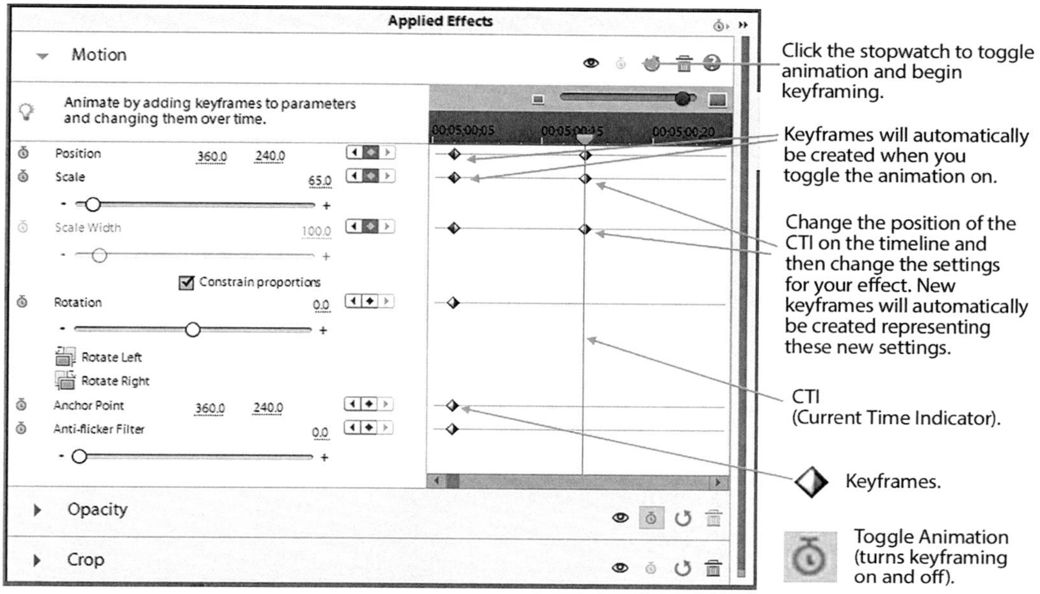
Applied Effects
Motion
Animate by adding keyframes to parameters and changing them over time.
Position 360.0 240.0
Scale 65.0
Scale Width 100.0
Constrain proportions
Rotation 0.0
Rotate Left
Rotate Right
Anchor Point 360.0 240.0
Anti-flicker Filter 0.0
Opacity
Crop
Click the stopwatch to toggle animation and begin keyframing.
Keyframes will automatically be created when you toggle the animation on.
Change the position of the CTI on the timeline and then change the settings for your effect. New keyframes will automatically be created representing these new settings.
CTI
(Current Time Indicator).
Keyframes.
Toggle Animation
(turns keyframing on and off).

2 Turn on keyframing for the **Motion** property by clicking on the **Toggle Animation** button (the stopwatch at the top right end of the **Motion** property listing, as illustrated above).

When you click the **Toggle Animation** button, a keyframe point – or set of keyframe points – will automatically be created at the position of the **CTI** representing the current settings for that effect.

3 Move the **CTI** to a new position, a few seconds to the right, on the clip's **keyframing timeline.** Then change the **Position** and **Scale** settings, by changing the setting numbers or by clicking on the clip in the **Monitor** panel and either dragging the screen image to a new position or dragging on its corner handles to resize it.

As you change the settings at this new **CTI** position, new keyframe points will automatically be generated on the **keyframing timeline**. (You can also manually create new keyframes by clicking on the diamond-shaped **Make Keyframe** buttons to the right of each effect's setting, as detailed on the following page.)

You have just created a simple motion path!

If you play back the clip, you will see how the program creates an animated movement between your two sets of keyframe points, using your keyframed settings to define the path.

A Simple Motion Path Created with Keyframes

Clicking Toggle Animation creates keyframe points for all settings for the Motion property.

CTI at the beginning of the clip.

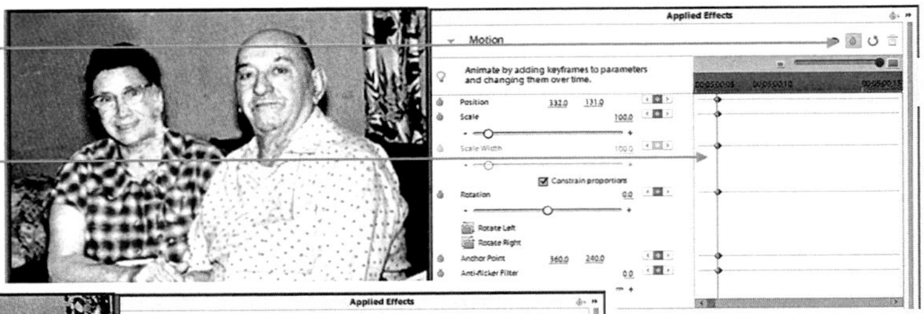

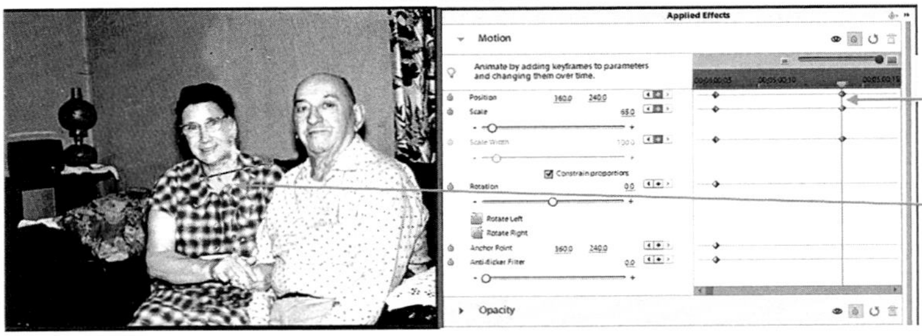

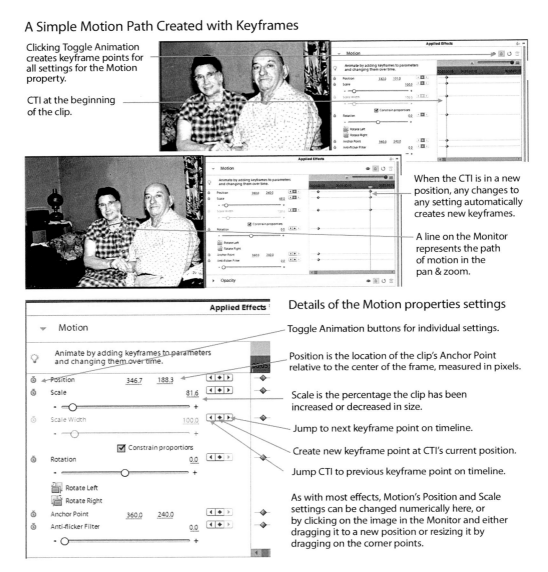

When the CTI is in a new position, any changes to any setting automatically creates new keyframes.

A line on the Monitor represents the path of motion in the pan & zoom.

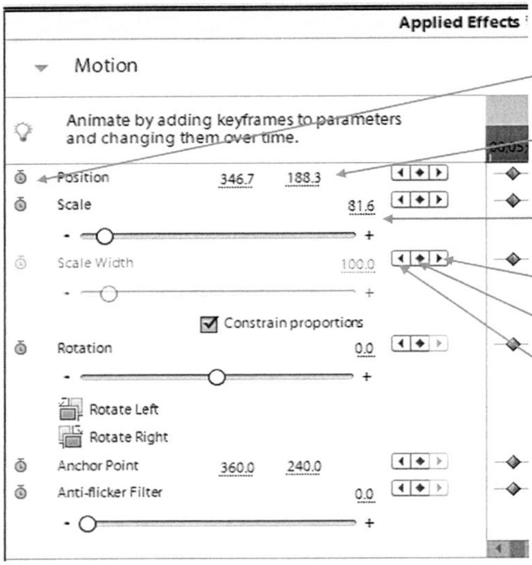

Details of the Motion properties settings

Toggle Animation buttons for individual settings.

Position is the location of the clip's Anchor Point relative to the center of the frame, measured in pixels.

Scale is the percentage the clip has been increased or decreased in size.

Jump to next keyframe point on timeline.

Create new keyframe point at CTI's current position.

Jump CTI to previous keyframe point on timeline.

As with most effects, Motion's Position and Scale settings can be changed numerically here, or by clicking on the image in the Monitor and either dragging it to a new position or resizing it by dragging on the corner points.

Edit your keyframes

The beauty of the keyframing tool is that any motion path or effects animation you create with it is infinitely adjustable.

By dragging the keyframe points closer together or further apart on the **keyframing timeline**, you can control the speed at which the motion occurs. (The closer the keyframes are to each other, the faster the animation.)

You can add more keyframe points and/or delete the ones you don't want. And, if you really want to go deep, **right-clicking** on any keyframe point accesses you the option to **interpolate** the animation movement or use **Bezier** control handles to change the shape of the motion path or vary the speed of the motion.

Many applications for keyframing

Keyframing has many applications in Premiere Elements. (It's also a feature of Premiere Pro, After Effects and virtually every professional video editing system.) It can turn pretty much any effect into an animation. And it can be used to vary audio effects and levels as well as video.

Using Keyframes to create animated effects

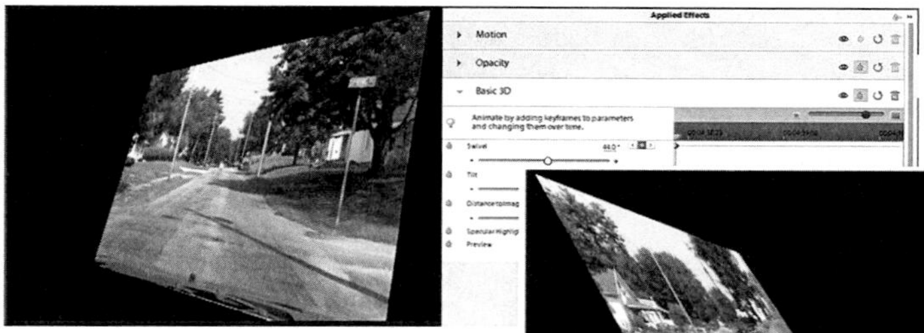

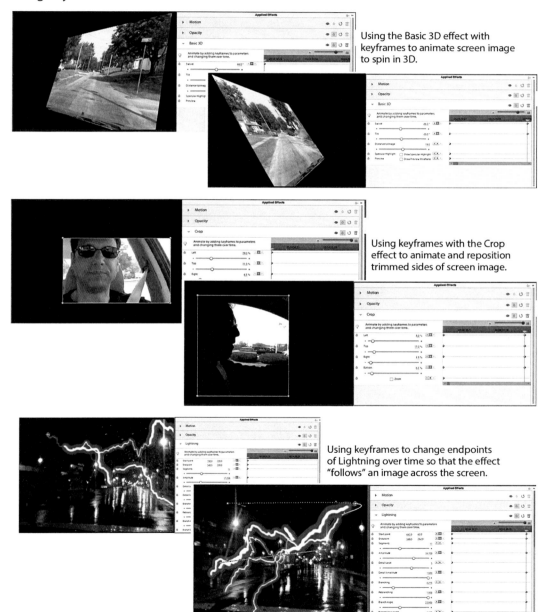

Using the Basic 3D effect with keyframes to animate screen image to spin in 3D.

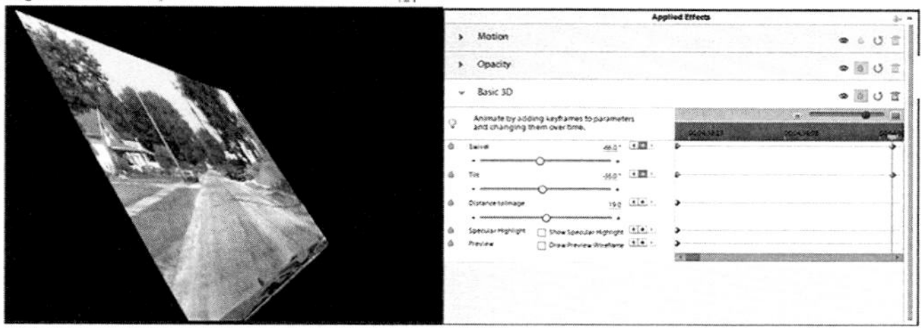

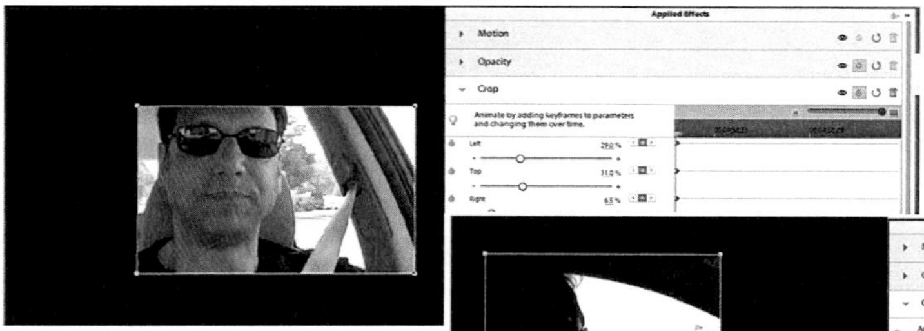

Using keyframes with the Crop effect to animate and reposition trimmed sides of screen image.

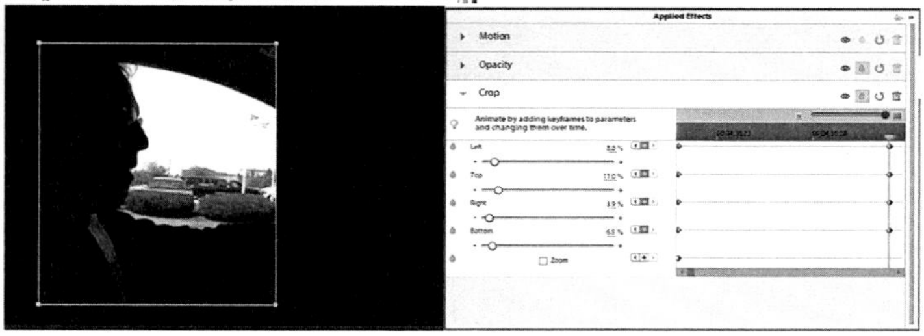

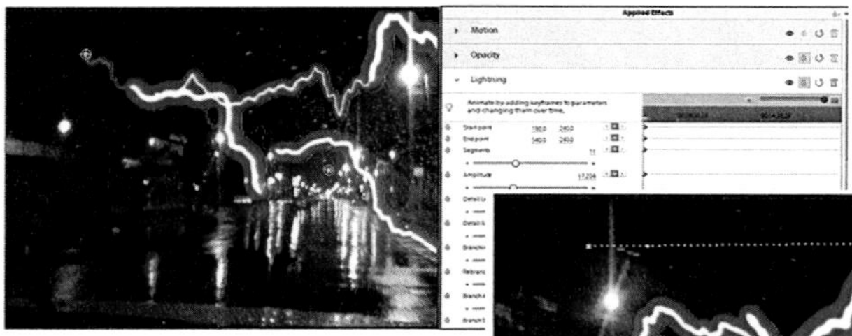

Using keyframes to change endpoints of Lightning over time so that the effect "follows" an image across the screen.

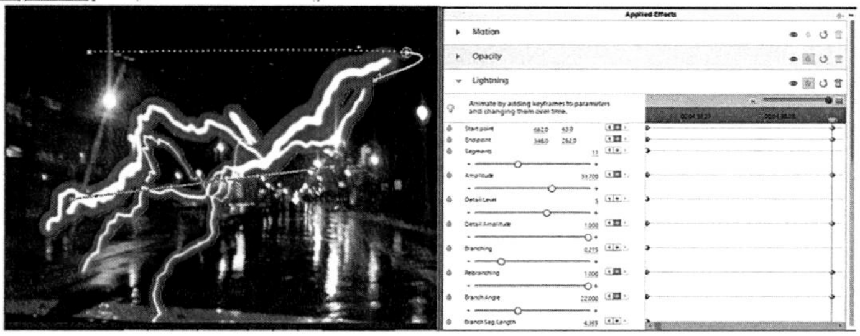

The Adjustment panel (Chapter 10) also includes a keyframe control timeline so you can, for instance, keyframe your Saturation level to make your video shift from color to black & white.

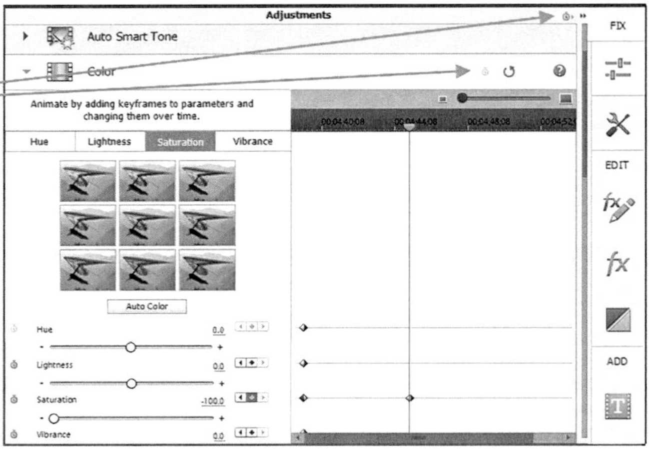

Keyframing can be used to control audio volume levels at precise points in your video project. (For more on controlling audio levels with keyframes, see **Adjust the audio levels at specific points in your video** on page 189 of **Chapter 16, Mix Your Audio and Add Music**.) You can also keyframe audio and video **Adjustments**, as we show you on page 124.

With keyframing, you can control effects, such as **Crop**, so that the area of your image that's cropped widens, narrows or changes position as the clip plays, as illustrated on page 185.

Or you can very precisely increase or decrease the intensity of an effect on a clip or animate a **Picture-in-Picture** effect. (See **Use L-cuts, J-cuts and multiple tracks** on page 78.)

You can even use keyframes to create an animated 3D movement for your video image using the **Camera View** or **Basic 3D** effect so that your video images seems to tumble head over heels in space.

Indeed, mastering the keyframing tool is the key to getting to the deeper aspects of Premiere Elements (or Adobe After Effects, Premiere Pro and even Apple's Final Cut programs).

It may not seem intuitive at first. But, once you develop a feel for how it works, you'll soon find yourself able to see all kinds of applications for it in creating and refining all manner of visual and audio effects.

For more information on some of the deeper aspects of keyframing and their applications, see my *Steve's Tips* articles "Advanced Keyframing: Editing on the Properties Panel Timeline" and "Advanced Keyframing 2: Keyframing Effects," available for our subscribers on the products page at Muvipix.com.

There is practically no limit to the special video and audio effects you can create with Premiere Elements.

Adjusting Audio Levels with Keyframes

Normalizing Your Audio Gain

Creating Custom Music Tracks with Adobe Scores

The Premiere Elements Sound Effects Library

Detecting Beats in Your Music

Chapter 16

Mix Your Audio and Add Music

Working with sounds and music

Great sound is as important as great visuals in your video project. And Premiere Elements includes a number of tools for adding and enhancing your audio and music files.

Premiere Elements even includes Scores, an amazing tool for creating musical tracks – based on your custom specifications – for your movies!

Additional content

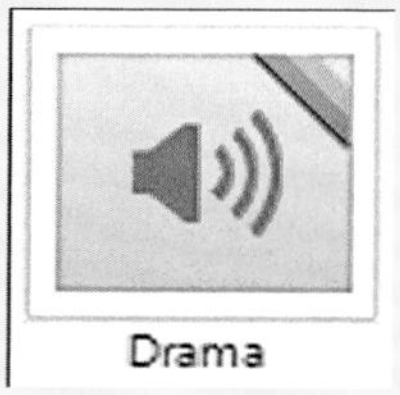

You may notice a little blue flag over the upper right corner of a number of music Scores.

This blue flag indicates that the template or theme is available but has not yet been installed on your computer. When you select this template or theme, the program will automatically download it for you from the Adobe site – a process that should only take a moment or two.

If you'd like to download all of these templates or Scores at once, right-click on any one and select the Download All option.

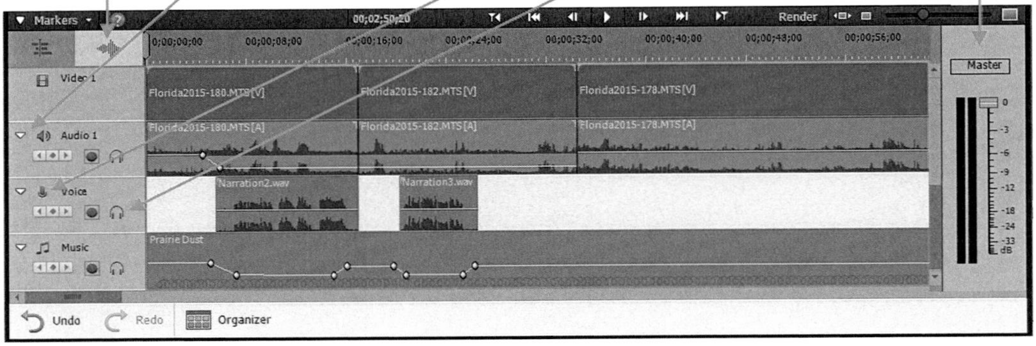

Your audio is as at least as important to your movie as your video. And Premiere Elements includes a number of powerful tools for creating custom music tracks, monitoring and adjusting your audio levels and mixing the levels of your various audio sources.

Audio View

Premiere Elements includes an **Audio View** workspace, where you can focus on the audio aspects of your production. To switch between **Classic View** and **Audio View**, click the toggle at the top left of the **Timeline** panel, as illustrated above.

When you're in **Audio View**, you'll be able to monitor the overall audio level for your movie using a **Master** VU meter to the right of the timeline. (To monitor and adjust the audio levels for specific tracks, we recommend you use the **Audio Mixer**, as discussed on page 99.)

It is very important that your audio levels do not peak in the red on your VU meter! Overmodulation can result in poor and distorted audio for your movie.

Collapsed view vs. full view

By default, your audio tracks are collapsed in order to conserve vertical space. To toggle open a track, click the little white triangle on the left side of the track.

In the fully open view, you'll be able to see the waveforms for your clips' audio and adjust the audio levels for each track (as discussed on the facing page).

Solo and Mute an audio track in Audio View

Muting a track means to temporarily disable its audio. Soloing a track means muting all other tracks so that only the selected "solo" track can be heard.

To Mute a track, click on the audio icon on the track header.

To Solo a track, click on the headphones button on the audio track.

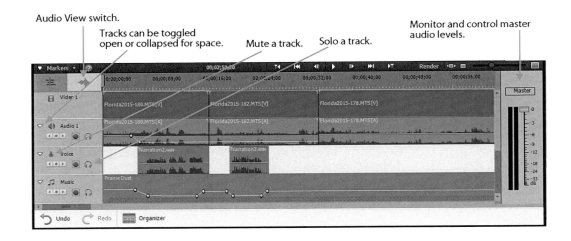

Clicking the red button on any track allows you to record narration to that track. For more information on recording into your Premiere Elements project, see **Add Narration** on page 101 of **Chapter 9, Use the Premiere Elements Toolkit**.

Adjust your audio levels at specific points in your video

In Expert View, with your audio tracks toggled open (see page 73), yellow lines (officially called **Rubber Bands**) running horizontally through your clips represent the clips' volume levels, as illustrated below. Raising or lowering a clip's volume level is as easy as dragging a **Rubber Band** up or down. (Also see **Monitor and mix your audio levels** on page 99.)

But what about if you want to raise and lower the audio levels for a clip at specific points?

Say you want to fade your music down for a few seconds so that your narration track can dominate? Or you have a conversation recorded in which one person speaks very quietly and you need to raise the audio level for his part of your clip, while leaving the audio level for the rest of the clip as is?

That's when you use audio keyframes.

Create audio volume keyframes on your timeline

To create **keyframes** for your audio clips:

1. Click to select an audio or audio/video clip on your Expert View timeline and position the **CTI** (Current Time Indicator) playhead over the approximate spot where you want to add a keyframe.

   (A clip must be selected and the **CTI** positioned over it in order to create a keyframe on the timeline.)

2. Click on the little, diamond-shaped **Make Keyframe** button on the track header, left of the video or audio track, as illustrated.

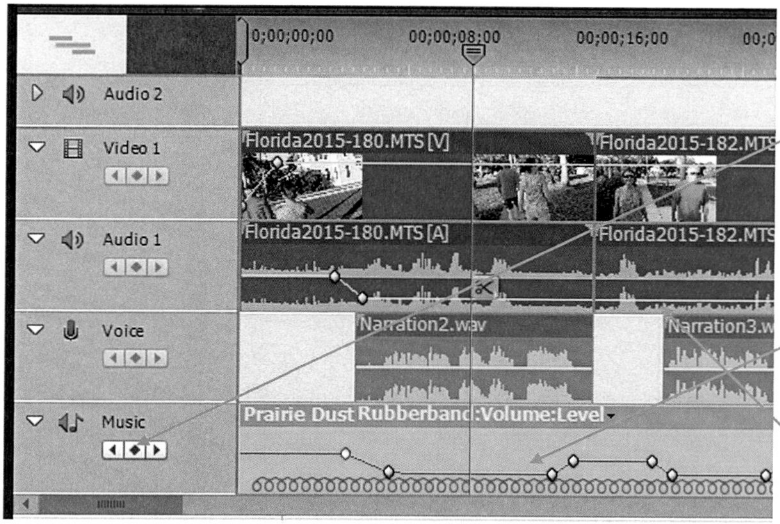

Audio keyframes adjust audio levels at specific points

When a clip is selected (clicked on), audio keyframes can be added with the timeline's Add/Remove Keyframe button.

Keyframes are added at the position of the CTI, but can be dragged to any position.

Dragging the keyframes higher raises the clip's audio level; dragging them lower reduces the audio level.

Dragging the yellow line with no keyframes applied raises or lowers the audio level for the entire clip.

This will create a keyframe point, which will appear as a white dot on your audio clip's **Rubber Band** at the position of the **CTI**.

You can drag this dot to any position on the clip, or change or delete it at any time.

3 Adjust the keyframe point's position to adjust the clip's volume levels.

- Positioning the keyframe higher on the clip increases the audio volume level at that point.
- Lowering it decreases the audio volume level.

In the illustration on the previous page, the audio level on the **Music** track has been temporarily lowered so that the narration can be heard.

You can create as many keyframes as you need, using several to set the audio levels higher for some segments, and lower for other segments, on your clips.

To delete an audio keyframe, **right-click** on the white diamond keyframe point and select **Delete** from the context menu.

Audio **Volume** keyframes can also be created and adjusted in the **Adjustments** panel (as discussed on page 124 of **Chapter 10**).

Normalizing and raising your audio's gain

There's a slight but significant difference between raising your audio's volume and raising it's gain. Volume is the amplification applied to your clip's audio. It makes whatever sound is on the clip louder.

Gain, on the other hand, refers to the level of audio on the clip itself. Raising a clip's gain makes its waveform on your timeline bigger and thicker. And increasing the gain can add a richness and fullness to the increased sound level that raising the volume doesn't. Well, at least to my ears anyway.

The **Normalize** tool is designed to automatically raise whatever sound is on your clip to a good, full level.

To use the **Normalizer**, **right-click** on your audio clip, select **Clip/Audio Gain** from the right-click menu. On the **Clip Gain** panel that opens, click the **Normalize** button.

If the **Normalize** tool doesn't automatically raise your clip's gain level enough, you can also manually raise the sound level yourself by typing a **db** number in the **Gain** box. I've rescued some very low-level audio by applying a **Gain** of 10 db or more to it.

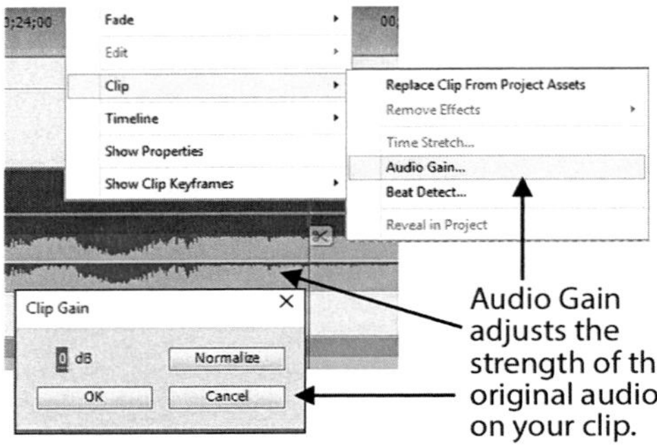

Audio Gain adjusts the strength of the original audio on your clip.

Create custom music clips with Scores

Scores is Premiere Elements' built-in tool for creating and customizing your movie's music.

The **Scores tool** creates royalty-free music tracks. That means you can use the music this tool generates in any project – even a professional or work-for-hire project – without concern about copyright or rights management. **Scores** are yours to use any way you'd like (short of re-selling the music, of course).

Scores are accessed by clicking the **Audio/Music** button on the **Toolbar** that runs along the right side of the program. It includes over 50 musical clips in 7 categories:

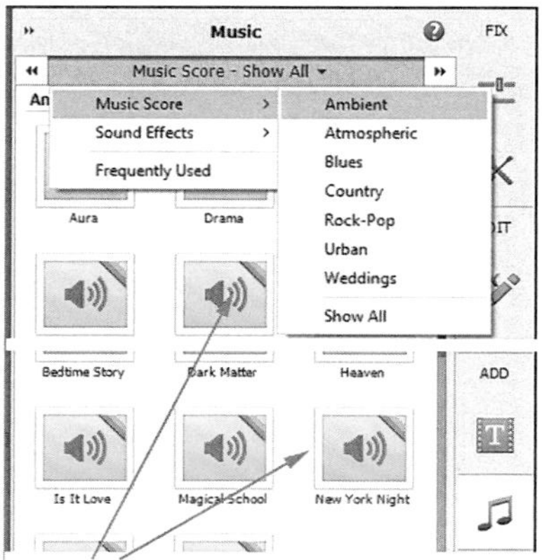

Content with a blue banner over the upper right corner will be downloaded when and as you use it.

Ambient – Gentle, subtle music scores that set the mood of a scene by playing quietly in the background.

Atmospheric – Scores designed to less subtly set a scene's mood, from dark to magical.

Blues – Cool, bluesy musical scores.

Country – Rural scores, representing everything from mountain music to traditional country to rockabilly.

Rock-Pop – Upbeat brassy or guitar-based rockers.

Urban – R&B scores with strong rhythms and funky tones.

Weddings – Traditional wedding scores, including the *Canon in D* and *Wedding March.*

You can sample any **Score** by hovering your mouse over the thumbnail on the **Audio** panel until a **Play** button appears, then clicking on it.

Like most additional content in the program, **Scores** are downloaded to your computer as you use them in a Premiere Elements project. Scores that have not yet been downloaded to your computer are indicated with a blue banner over the upper right corner, as in the illustration above.

Although the program comes with a wide selection of musical options, the real beauty of **Scores** is that it will generate custom music to fit your specific needs.

In other words, once you've placed a **Score** on your timeline and you've trimmed it to whatever length you need, the program will *re-generate* the **Score** so that, at your custom length, the clip has a natural beginning, middle and end.

When you first add a **Score** to your timeline (and once it's been downloaded to your computer, if necessary), a **Score Property** panel will offer you the option of setting the **Score's** intensity (which you can preview before finalizing) and for automatically setting your clip to trim itself to the length of your movie.

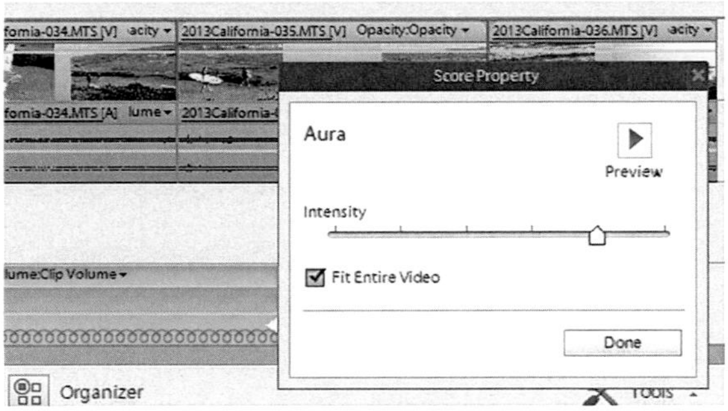

When you add a Score to your timeline, you'll have the options of setting and testing its intensity and of setting it to automatically extend itself to the length of your movie.

Your Score will automatically generate a natural beginning, middle and end for the clip based on the settings you've selected.

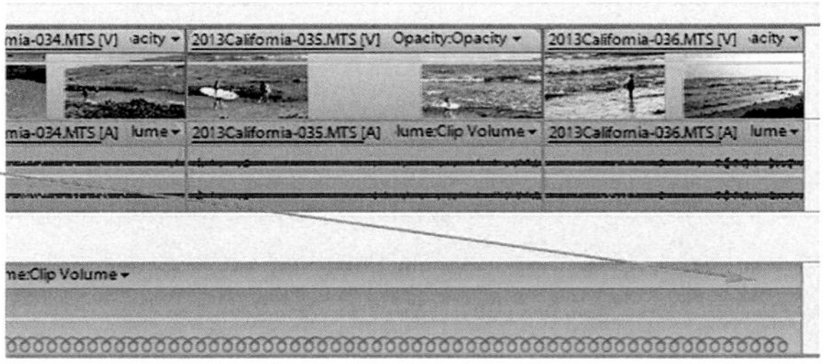

When you click **Done**, the program will generate your custom musical track and add it to your timeline. Even after you've created your musical track, you have the option of manually trimming or extending the length of your **Score** clip. The program will automatically re-generate the musical clip based on the length and properties you've selected.

The **Score Properties** panel can be re-opened at any time by **double-clicking** on the music clip on your timeline.

Add Sound Effects to your movie

As a very cool added-value bonus, Premiere Elements comes bundled with a library of over 260 sound effects in 13 categories. These range from ambient sounds, like a **Basketball Game** or **Auto Shop** to weather to science fiction to animal sounds.

It's really a terrific library of high-quality sounds!

You'll find them sharing the panel with **Scores** under the **Audio/Music** button on the **Toolbar** along the right side of the program.

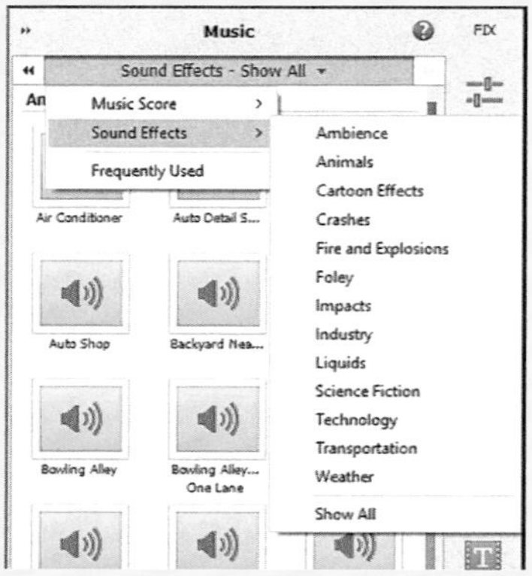

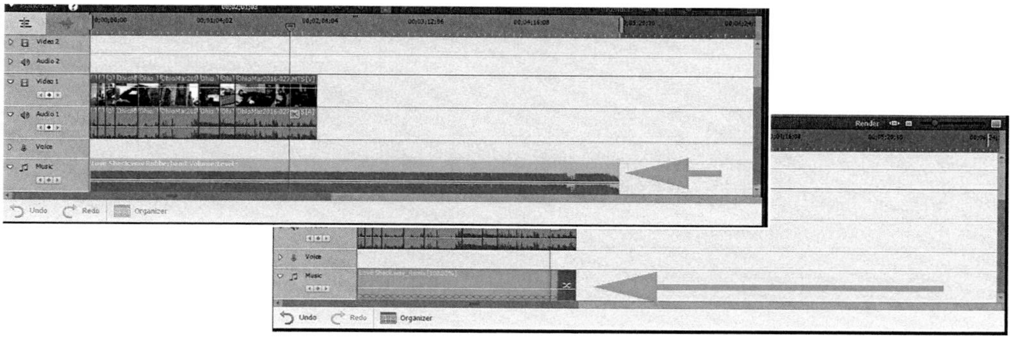

Create custom-length musical clips with Music Remix

A cool new feature in version 15 is **Music Remix**, a tool that rebuilds trimmed musical clips to create custom-length music from pretty much any musical source. As with **Scores**, your remixed music clip will have a natural beginning, middle and end.

This tool works best with clips trimmed to a duration of no shorter than one minute. This is because the tool works by, more or less, blending the beginning and end of the song with its middle. The longer your clip, the more natural this blend will sound.

To remix your music.

1 Place any musical clip on the **Music** track on your timeline.

Note that this feature is only available on the lower-most Music track on the timeline, in either Quick and Expert View.

As we've discussed earlier in this chapter, the ideal audio format to use in Premiere Elements is the WAV format. (**Audacity**, a free download we recommend on page 275 of our **Appendix** will convert pretty much any audio to a WAV file.)

And, as we discuss in the sidebar on page 55, music purchased from iTunes often includes very strict copy protection software that may prevent you from using any iTunes-purchased music in a video editing project. (It will throw up an error code.) Music purchased from other sources (like Amazon) does not have such tight restriction on its usage.

2 Hover your mouse over the end of the audio clip.

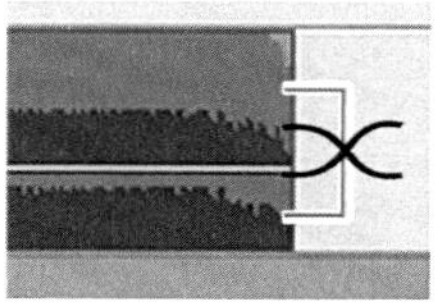

A **Remix Handle** will appear. As illustrated to the right, this **Handle** looks similar to but distinct from the **Trim Handles** that appear when you hover over the ends of other media clips (see page 75).

3 Trim your music clip.

Drag left to trim the music clip to your desired length.

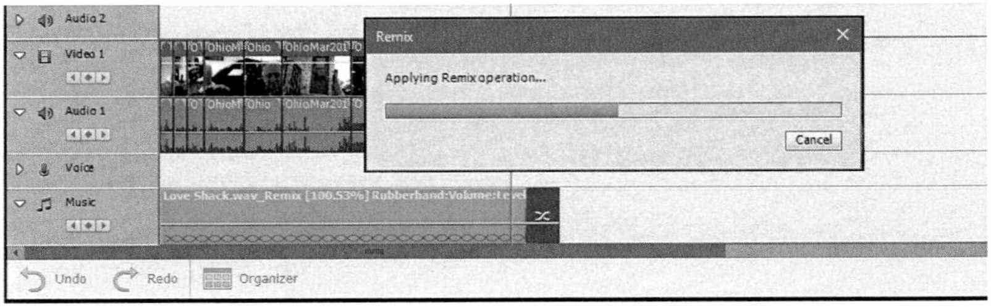

4 Set the **Remix Music Settings.**

Once you've trimmed the clip, a context menu will appear, inviting you to set the **Remix Music Settings**.

(This option panel can be re-opened at any time by double-clicking on the darker-colored "mixed" area at the end of the musical clip.)

The more the slider is set to **Shorter**, the more the song will be broken into to shorter, repeating segments. The more the slider is set to **Longer**, the more the song will remain intact, with the end of the song naturally mixed into the middle.

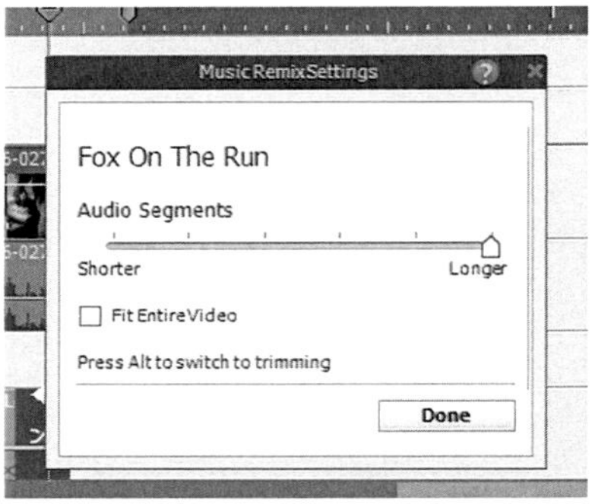

Once you've selected your **Settings** and clicked **Done**, the program will remix the track.

Before you play your timeline, the program will "render" it – essentially creating a finalized version of the remix. (The program will warn you if the trimmed music clip is too short to properly remix.)

The remix should be such a natural blend of beginning, middle and end that most of viewers will be unaware that an edit has been made to the song.

The **Remixed Music** will also appear, in its shortened form, inside a **Remix** folder in your **Project Assets** panel.

Some music lends itself better to this tool than other music.

Most popular songs that follow standard patterns of verses and chorus work very well with this tool. Music with several movements or more irregular patterns may not remix quite as smoothly.

The **Music Remix** feature can be disabled by going to the program's **Preferences** (under the **Edit** menu on a PC) and, on the **Audio** page, setting the **Remix Options** drop-down menu from **Remix** to **Trim**.

The Beat Detect Tool

Adjust settings as needed for your music.

Click to select your musical clip on the timeline, then select Beat Detect from the right-click menu (or the Tools menu at the top of the interface).

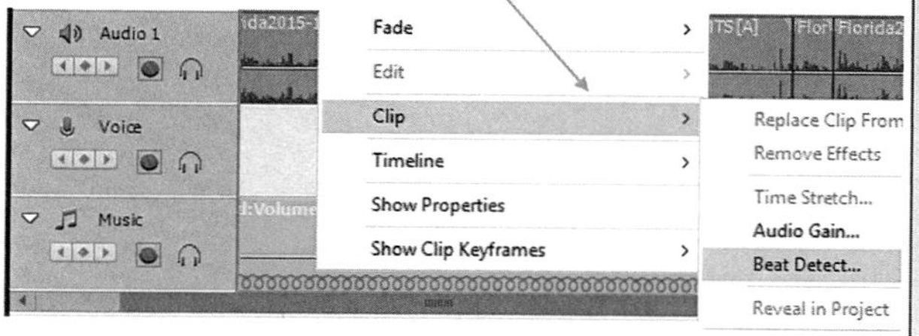

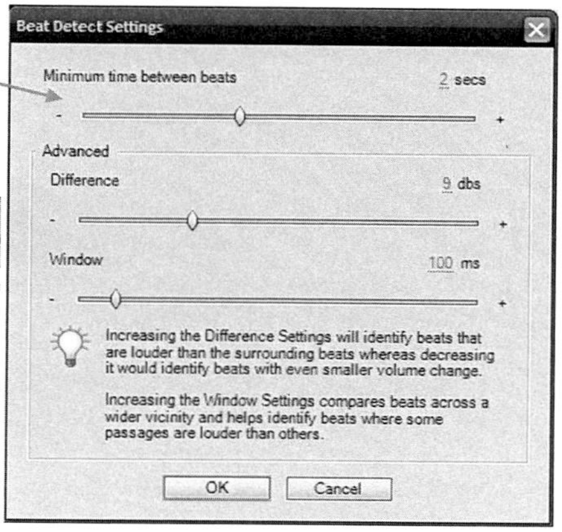

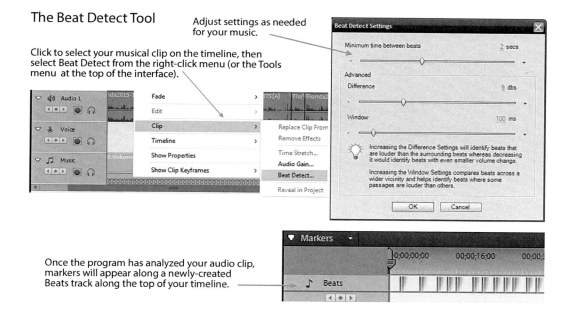

Once the program has analyzed your audio clip, markers will appear along a newly-created Beats track along the top of your timeline.

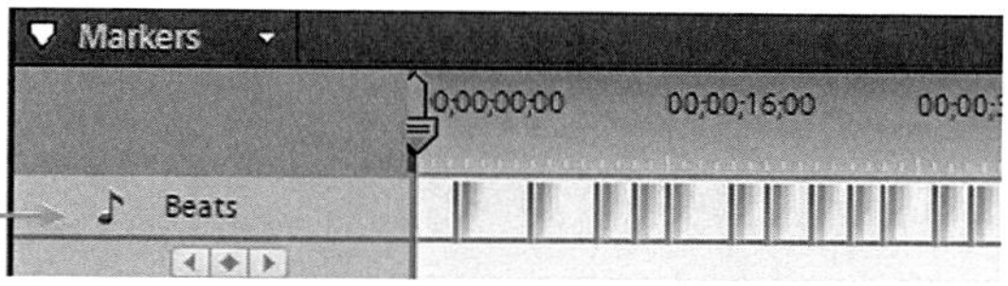

Detect beats in your music

This cool tool can be used as part of the process of creating a slideshow so that your slides change in rhythm with your music. (Note that the **Beat Detect** tool is only available in Expert View.)

To use the **Beat Detect** tool:

1. Click to select a music clip on your timeline or sceneline.

   When a clip is detected on your timeline, it will be highlighted.

2. Click on the **Tools** menu at the top of the program's interface or **right-click** on the clip and select **Clip**, then **Beat Detect**.

   The **Beat Detect Settings** option screen will open, as illustrated above.

3. Set the sensitivity and limitations of your beat detection.

4. Click **OK**.

The tool will then analyze your music clip and create a series of markers, representing your music clip's rhythm, on a newly-created **Beats** track along the top of the timeline.

Once these markers have been created, you can use them as indicators for the **Create Slideshow** tool in the **Project Assets** panel so that your slides will change in rhythm with the music.

For information on using the **Create Slideshow** tool, see page 67 of **Chapter 6, Explore the Project Assets Panel**.

Additional Audio Tools

Premiere Elements offers several other tools for adding to and mixing your movie's audio, some of which are discussed in greater detail in **Chapter 9, Use the Premiere Elements Toolkit**:

The **Audio Mixer** is a tool for monitoring your movie's audio levels and for mixing your volume levels on the fly, as your movie timeline plays. For more information on using it, see **Mix and monitor your audio levels** on page 99.

Smart Mix will automatically mix your movie's audio, based on the criteria you select. In other words, you can set **Smart Mix** to make narration your foreground audio and your music your background. The program will automatically set the music on your timeline to play at regular volume, then lower the music's volume automatically whenever it encounters a narration clip. For more information on this tool, see **Smart Mix your audio** on page 104.

The **Narration** tool lets you record a narration track right into your movie, even while watching the movie play! For more information on this tool, see **Narration** on page 101.

The **Adjustments** panel includes tools for raising and lowering your clips' **Volume**, adjusting the **Balance** of your stereo channels and raising and lowering the levels of **Bass** and **Treble**. For more information on these tools, see page 123 of **Chapter 10, Make Adjustments to Your Video**.

And, finally, the program includes several great **Audio Effects** for sweetening your audio, reducing noise, adding echo effects and filtering certain frequencies to clean your audio or creating special audio effects. You'll find out all about them on page 168 of **Chapter 13, Add Audio and Video Effects**.

Part IV

The Elements Organizer

File Management with the Organizer

The Media Browser

Keyword Tags and Metadata

Smart Tags and the Media Analyzer

Storing Your Media in Albums

Identifying People, Places and Events

Chapter 17

Manage Your Files with the Organizer

Getting to Know the Media Browser

The Elements Organizer, which comes bundled with both Photoshop Elements and Premiere Elements, is Adobe's media file management tool.

It's a way to organize, to search and to create search criteria for your audio, video and photo files.

It also includes a number of great tools for creating everything from slideshows to DVD case covers from your media files!

A companion program to both Premiere Elements and Photoshop Elements, the Elements Organizer is a media file management system. It includes several interesting ways for you to organize and search your still photo, video, music and audio files

Additionally, the Organizer includes a number of tools for working with your media files to create photo projects, like calendars, scrap books and slideshows, as we discuss in **Chapter 18, Create Fun Pieces** and **Chapter 19, Share Your Photos and Videos**.

The Elements Organizer links directly to both Premiere Elements and Photoshop Elements and it can be launched from the **Welcome Screen** of either program – or by clicking the **Organizer** button on the bar along the bottom left of either program's interface.

Think of your Elements Organizer as a giant search engine that can be programmed to store and retrieve the audio, video and still photo files on your computer, based on a wide variety of criteria – some of which you assign, some of which are assigned automatically and some of which are inherently a part of your photo, sound and video files when they're created.

Adaptive Grid vs. Details View

The **Media Browser** in the Organizer displays your files by default in **Adaptive Grid View**, an efficient way to view and browse the media files on your system. Unfortunately, it doesn't give you easy access to information about your media files or even display the file names.

To display more detailed information about your media files, go to the program's View menu and select **Details.**

You can also toggle between these **Details View** and **Adaptive Grid View** by pressing **Ctrl+d** on your keyboard (**⌘+d** on a Mac).

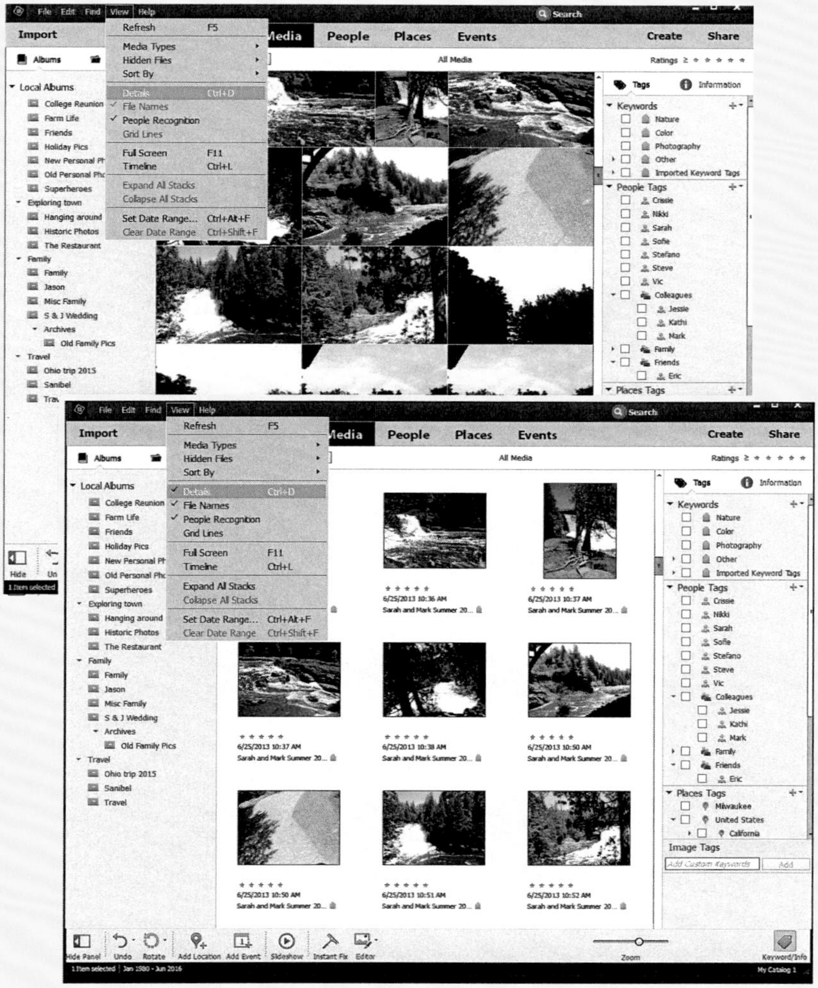

These search criteria aren't limited to obvious details – such as the type of media or the date it was saved to your computer.

Search criteria can include **Keyword Tags** – or it can be minute technical details, such as the type of camera that was used to shoot a photo or whether the photo was shot with a flash or natural light.

Additionally, the Organizer includes features that support other tools and functions in both Premiere Elements and Photoshop Elements. The **Media Analyzer/Auto Analyzer**, discussed on page 208, for instance, prepares your video files for use with the **Smart Fix** and **Smart Mix** tools in Premiere Elements.

Your Elements Organizer's media files can also be assigned **Tags**, categorized according to the **People** in them or the **Places** they were shot, or identified by the **Events** they represent.

The Media Browser area

The main area of the Organizer's interface, in which your media files are displayed as thumbnails and which dominates the Organizer workspace, is called the **Media Browser**.

There are several types of media files, and they are each represented by slightly different thumbnail images in the **Media Browser**, as illustrated to the right:

- **Video files** are represented as image thumbnails with a filmstrip icon on the upper right corner.
- **Photo files** are represented by a plain thumbnail of the image file.
- **Audio files** are represented by gray thumbnails with a speaker icon on them.

Video file

Photo file

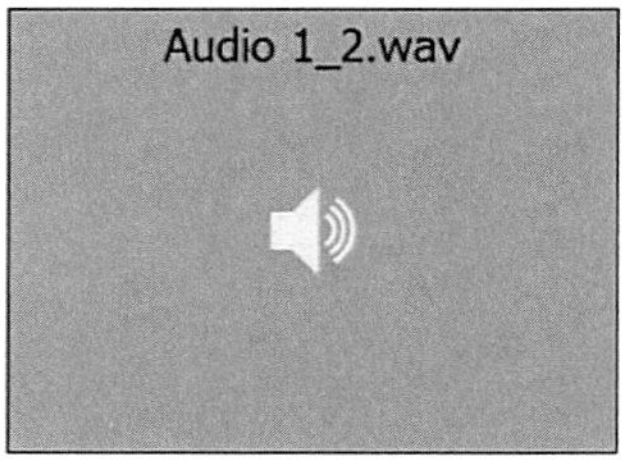

Audio file

The size of these thumbnail images in the **Media Browser** is controlled by the slider at the bottom right of the interface.

Under the **View** drop-down on the Organizer menu bar, in the **Media Types** sub-menu, you can filter which file types are displayed in the **Media Browser**.

Using the tabs along the top of the interface, you can set whether the **Media Browser** displays your files as categories of **People, Places** or **Events** – categories we'll show you how to build later in this chapter.

The Back or All Media buttons

Whatever tags or filters you've applied, you can always work your way back to a display of all the media in your **Catalog** by clicking the **Back** or **All Media** button in the upper left of the **Media Browser**.

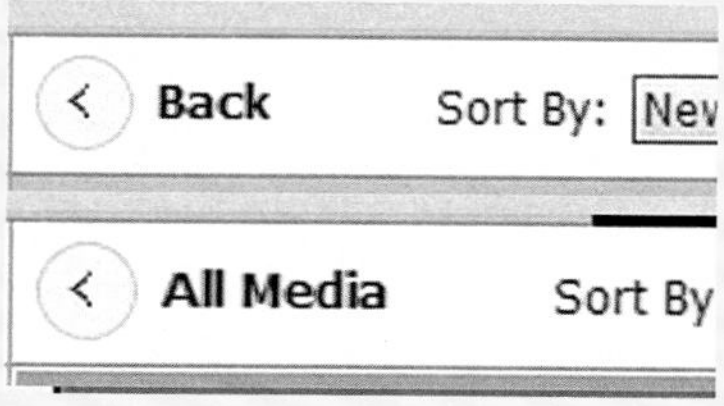

In **Detail View** (see page 201) media file **Details** (such as the date the file was created or its **Star Rating**) as well as its **File Name** can be displayed under its thumbnail in the **Media Browser.**

Although by default the files are listed according to the date they were created – most recent to oldest – you can display them in a couple of different orders. To change the order your files are displayed in, select an option from the **Sort** menu at the top left of the **Media Browser**.

Oldest or **Newest** lists your files according to the date they were saved to your computer, either most recent first or least.

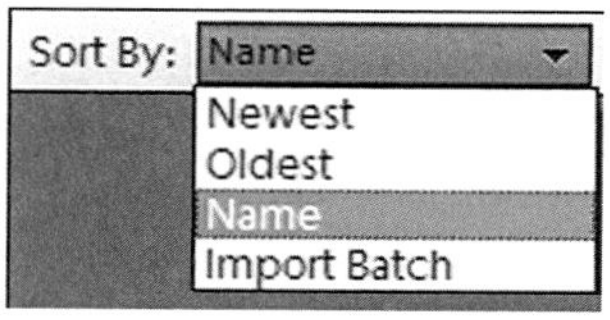

Name lists your files alpha-numerically, according to their names.

Import Batch lists only the files which have been added recently to your Elements Organizer **Catalog**.

The Organizer Catalog

The media files that the Organizer manages and displays, as well as the metadata that defines them, are said to be in the Organizer's **Catalog**. Some files and information are added to this **Catalog** automatically, while others may be added to the **Catalog** manually.

The Elements Organizer's **Catalog** is a file that includes data and metadata on all of the video clips, audio clips and photo files in your computer's **managed** folders (see page 206) as well as any media files that you've edited with Premiere Elements or Photoshop Elements.

If you download or capture video or photos to your computer using any of the tools in Premiere Elements or Photoshop Elements, they too are automatically added to your Organizer's **Catalog**.

Manually add to and update your Organizer Catalog

The first time you launch the Elements Organizer, it will offer to search your computer for media files in order create to your initial **Catalog**. (If you've had a previous version of the Organizer installed, the program will offer to simply update your existing **Catalog**.) If you're running the program on a Mac, it may even offer to build its initial **Catalog** from the data in your iPhoto catalog.

Import media files into your Catalog

You can manually add files to your **Catalog** by clicking the **Import** button in the upper left of the interface.

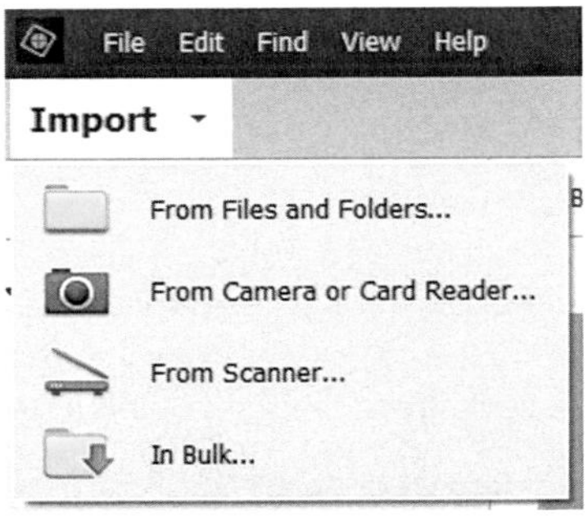

- To manually add files, and folders full of files, to your Organizer's **Catalog**, select **From Files and Folders**. Browse to the folder or files you would like to add and then click **Get Media**.
- To download media **From a Camera or Card Reader** or (on a Windows PC) to add images **From a a Scanner**, select the respective option.
- When you select the option to import **In Bulk**, a panel will open in which you can designate folders to search. The program will locate any unlisted files in these directories and offer you the option of adding them to your catalog.

Your **Catalog**, by the way, does not actually *contain* your media files. It's merely a data file with links to and metadata for your media files. A **Catalog** file is actually a relatively small file – and, in fact, you can create several catalogs and manage them under the program's **File** menu.

Resync media in or remove media from your Catalog

If you move, delete or change files using Windows Explorer, Finder or a program other than one of the Elements programs, you may find your Organizer's **Media Browser** will indicate some thumbnails as having broken or outdated links to the **Catalog**.

To update these connections manually or to remove the thumbnail of a deleted file from the Organizer **Catalog**, go to the **File** menu and select the option to **Reconnect/All Missing Files**.

The Organizer will update your links and indicate for you all of the thumbnails in the **Media Browser** that do not have files linked to them, offering you the options of re-connecting the links or of deleting these dead thumbnails.

To avoid the program losing track of the links to your media, it's best to use the Elements Organizer to move or remove files from your computer:

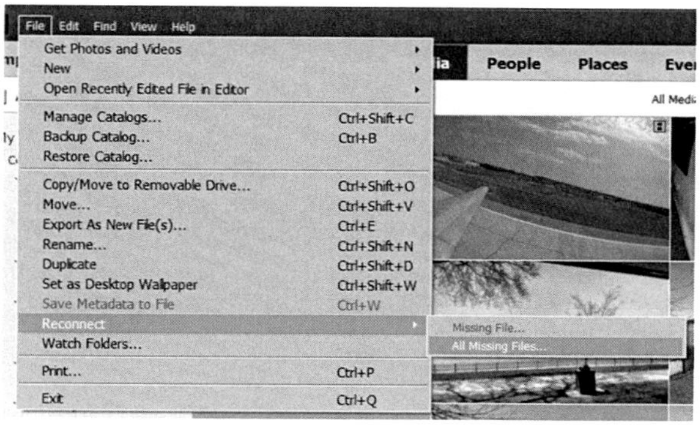

- To delete a file using the Organizer, **right-click** on the file(s) and select **Delete from Catalog.** You will then be given the option of merely removing the file from the **Catalog** or removing it completely from your hard drive.
- To move a file to a new location on your computer using the Organizer, click to select the file(s) in the **Media Browser** and, from the **File** drop-down, select the option to **Move,** then browse to the new location.

Switch between Album and Folder Views

By default, the **Media Browser** displays your files according to the dates they were saved, from most recent to oldest.

The panel along the left side of the interface displays a list of the **Albums** you've created, (if any). If you click on an **Album**, the **Media Browser** will display only the media in that **Album**. (For more information on creating and managing **Albums**, see page 211.)

If you click on the **Folders** tab at the top of this panel, the panel will display a list of the "**managed**" folders on your computer's hard drive(s). (For information on managing your computer's folders, see page 206.)

The **Folders** panel will display your managed folders as a **List** or, if you select the **Tree** option, it will display your computer's entire file directory.

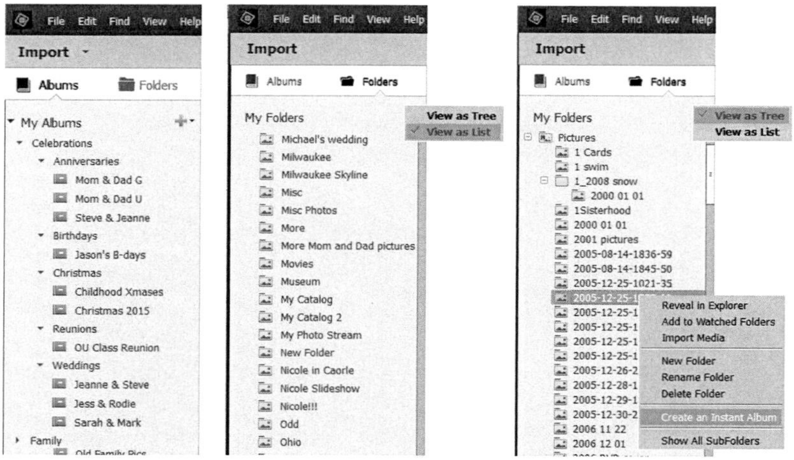

Managed, Unmanaged and Watched Folders

As far as your Organizer's **Catalog** is concerned, there are three types of folders on your hard drive. These folders are listed when the left side panel is in **Folder** view (see the bottom of page 205).

Unmanaged Folders are folders whose contents do not have any links to the Organizer. The folder either does not contain any media files or the media files have not yet been added to the **Catalog**.

Unmanaged Folder

Managed Folders are folders whose contents have been added to the **Catalog** and whose media files can be viewed and searched by the Organizer.

Managed Folder

Watched Folders have a dynamic link to the Organizer's **Catalog**. As media files are added to a **Watched Folder**, they are automatically added to the **Catalog**.

Watched Folder

(Note that any media files which are used in a Premiere Elements project or are edited and saved in Photoshop Elements are *automatically* added to the **Catalog**, regardless of where they are stored.)

The very first time you launch the Organizer, it will search your computer for media files and automatically convert a number of folders into **Managed Folders**.

You can also manually designate a folder as a **Managed Folder** or a **Watched Folder** by setting the left side panel to **Folder** view (see the bottom of page 205) and selecting the **Tree** display option (to view your computer's entire file directory). **Right-click** on any folder you'd like to manage and select either **Import Media** (which will convert the folder into a **Managed Folder**) or **Add to Watched Folders**.

What is metadata?

Metadata is the hidden information embedded into virtually every computer file, including when the file was saved, who modified it last, what program created the file, etc.

The Elements Organizer uses metadata to manage, order and search your media files.

All of your media files carry some metadata. By default, your files are displayed in the Organizer's **Media Browser** according to the date created – most recent first. (To see the file's title, created date, etc., go to the **View** menu and select **Details**.)

"**Date saved**" is the simplest display of metadata and the most basic way to manage your media files – but it's far from the only way. Virtually any metadata can be used to search, organize or gather your media.

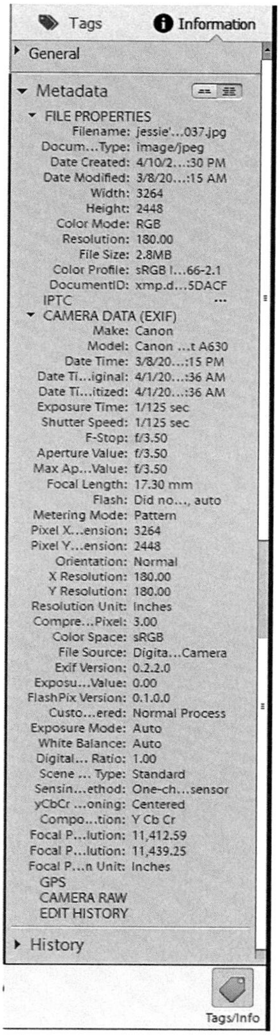

You might be surprised to learn how much metadata is added to your photos and video files by your camera or camcorder automatically.

If the **Keyword Tags/Information** panel isn't displayed to the right of the **Media Browser**, click the **Tags/Info** button in the lower-right corner of the interface. Select the **Information** tab at the top of the panel and select a photo that you've downloaded from a digital camera in the **Media Browser.**

If you open the **Metadata** section of this panel, as illustrated on the right, and then click on the button in the upper right of this panel to display the **Complete** metadata, you'll see an amazing amount of information – from the date and time the photo was shot to the photo dimensions, the make, model and serial number of camera that was used to take the photo, the shutter speed, if a flash was used, what settings and F-stop setting was used, if it was shot with manual or automatic focus and so on.

All of this is metadata. And it can be used – along with any additional metadata you assign to your photos and video manually – as search and sort criteria in the Elements Organizer.

To search by metadata, go to the **Find** drop-down on the Organizer Menu Bar and select the option to search **By Details (Metadata)** as illustrated below.

In the option screen that opens, you can set up a search to find, for instance, all photos shot on a specific date or at a specific time, at certain camera settings – in fact, you can search by pretty much any of the metadata attached to your photo or other media file!

Also under this **Find** drop-down menu, you'll find many more search methods for your files. One of the most amazing search functions, in my opinion, is the Organizer's ability to locate files that contain **Visual Similarity with Selected Photo(s) and Video(s)** (under **Visual Searches**).

That's right: If you have a picture of the beach or the mountains or even of an individual, the Organizer will find for you all of the other photos in your collection that have similar color schemes and visual details!

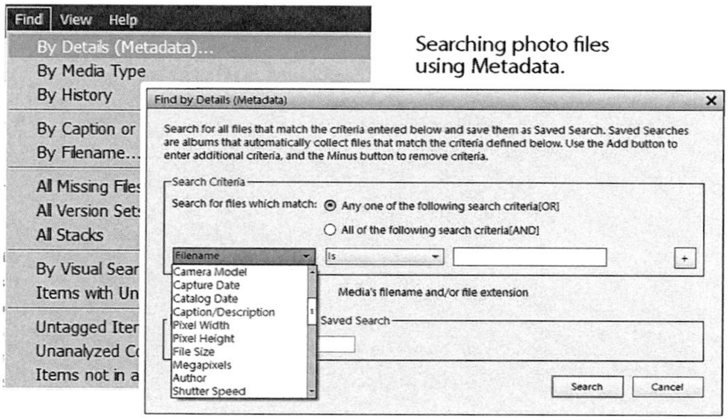

Searching photo files using Metadata.

Add your own Metadata

There are a number of ways to add searchable metadata to your media files. You can, for instance:

Your media files can be categorized by keyword, date, people, place or event.

- Place your media in an **Album** (as discussed on page 211).
- Add **Keyword Tags** (as discussed on page 212).
- Apply one to five **star ratings** to your clips by dragging across the stars that appear under the thumbnail in the **Media Browser**. (If you don't see stars under your clips, go under the **View** menu and select **Details** and/or zoom into the displayed thumbnail using the slider in the program's lower right.)
- Identify your photos by the **People** in them (a process the program does semi-automatically, as discussed on page 213).
- Tag your photos and videos with the **Place** they were shot (as discussed on page 215) . (This data is automatic if your camera has a GPS.)
- Associate your media with a **Date** or an **Event** (as discussed on page 217).

Using both metadata that you supply and metadata supplied automatically by the camera or other device you've recorded your media with, the Organizer provides you with a wide variety of ways to organize and search your media files – including applying **Search** filters, as discussed on page 210.

Auto Analyze your media

The **Media Analyzer** (also called the **Auto Analyzer**) is a key feature of the Organizer that works silently in the background, analyzing and logging information about your photos, video and audio files.

As it analyzes your media files, it records metadata about a number of your media files' qualities, including information on the content of your video or photos (for instance, if there are close-ups, if your photos or video includes faces), information on flaws in your media files (for instance, if your picture is too dark or too light or if your video includes a lot of jiggle) and even, amazingly, information on the content or subject matter in your photos. This metadata is saved as **Auto Tags**.

These **Auto Tags** can be used, along with your manually added metadata, as **Search** filter criteria, as discussed on page 210.

Auto Analyzer metadata is used by various "**Smart**" tools in Premiere Elements to make automatic corrections to your video or photos:

Premiere Elements' **Smart Fix** tool (see page 119) uses data gathered by the **Media Analyzer** to make automatic adjustments to your video's brightness or contrast or to automatically apply video stabilization.

The **Smart Trim** tool (see page 105) uses data gathered by the **Media Analyzer** to recommend cuts to remove poorer quality sequences.

The **Motion Tracking** tool (see page 112) uses data gathered by the **Media Analyzer** to build motion tracks based on objects in your video.

The **InstantMovie** tool (see page 84), **Video Story** tool (see page 86) and the **Auto Mark Moments** feature in the **Favorite Moments** tool (see page 110) use information provided by the **Media Analyzer** to make editing decisions.

The **Analyzer** includes **Face Recognition** technology, identifying faces in your photos and, when possible, identifying the people based on their faces.

This technology not only plays a role in helping you manage and search your files based on the **People** in the pictures (see page 213), but it also provides **Face Recognition** metadata to the Premiere Elements' **Pan & Zoom** tool so that it can automatically generate a motion path from one face to another in your photos (see page 102).

To disable the **Media Analyzer's Face Recognition** feature, go to the Organizer's **Preferences** (under the **Edit** menu on a PC) and, on the **Media Analysis** page, uncheck **Run Face Recognition Automatically**.

More preferences for controlling how the **Analyzer** works – including the option to disable the **Media Analyzer** completely – are found on the **Auto Analyzer** page of Premiere Elements' **Preferences**.

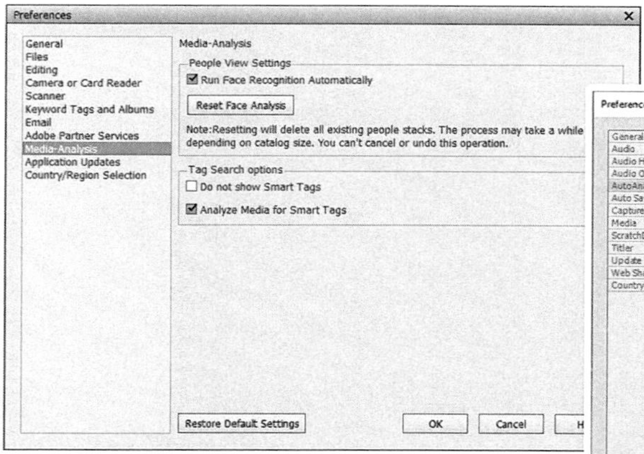

Organizer Media-Analysis preferences.

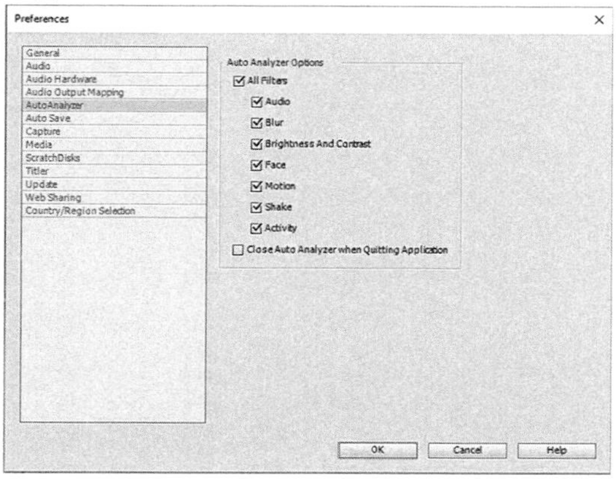

Premiere Elements AutoAnalyzer preferences.

Search your catalog using Filters

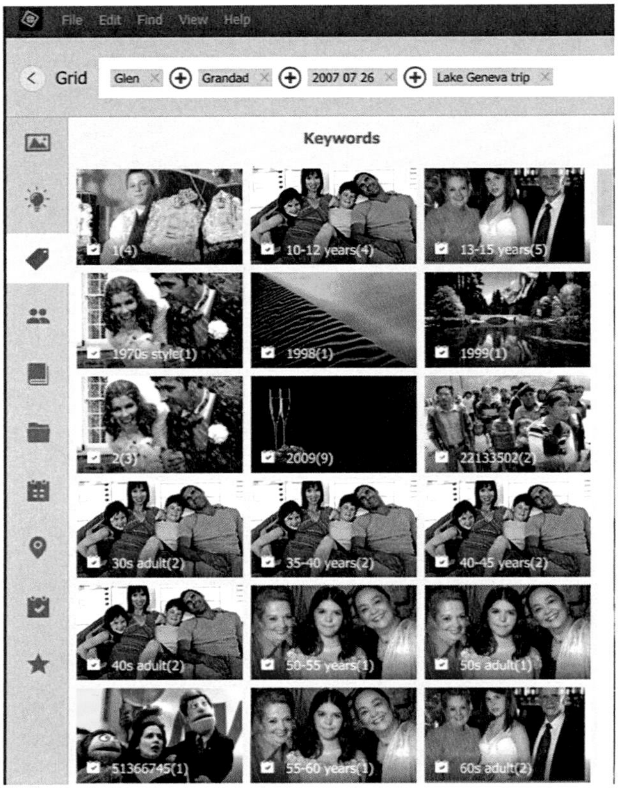

In version 15, the **Search** system in the Organizer has been given a major overhaul.

When you click the **Search** button in the upper right of Organizer's interface, the program opens into a very sophisticated **Search** workspace.

Along the left side of this workspace, you'll find several icons. These icons represent **Filters** for determining which media files are displayed in the **Media Browser**.

These filters include: **Media Type** (page 202), **Auto Tags** (page 208), **Keyword Tags** (page 212), **People** (page 213), **Albums** (page 211), **Folders** (page 205), **Calendar** (page 217), **Places** (page 215), **Events** (page 218) and the **Star Rating** you've assigned the media file.

As you select specific **Albums, Tags, People,** etc., these filter criteria will appear in the **Search Bar** along the top of this workspace, as illustrated above.

By clicking on the symbol between each filter listed, you can set your search filter to display your media based on whether the media files displayed are based on one filter **AND** another, **OR** another or **WITHOUT** another.

In the search illustrated below, I have set my filters to find pictures in either the **Dale's Old Slides** or **Florida** albums that include **Dad** but do not include **Diane**.

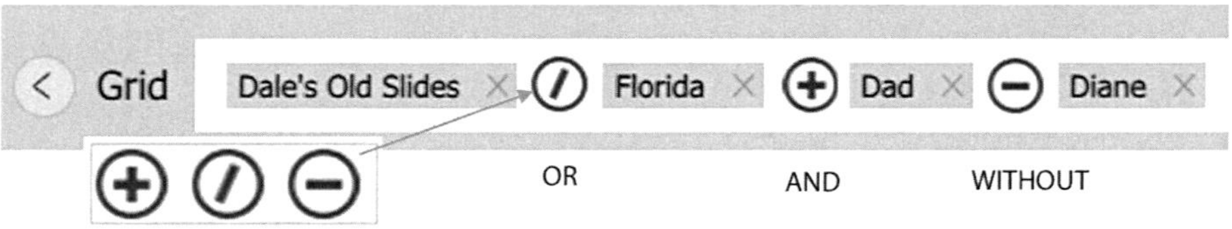

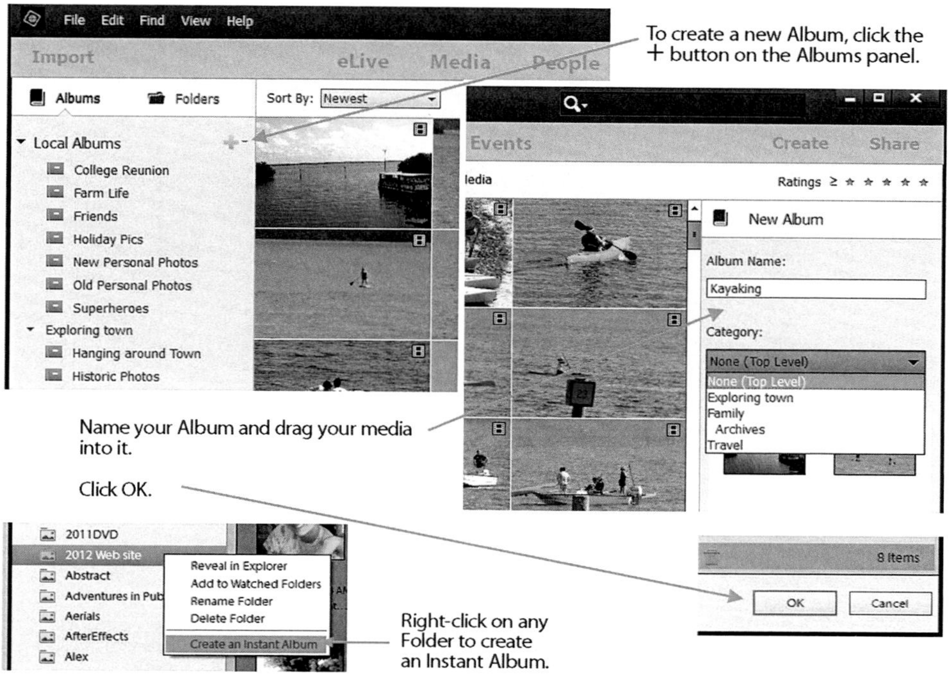

Assign your media files to Albums

Albums are collections of media files that you create and assign your photos and videos to.

When an **Album** is selected in the panel to the left of the **Media Browser**, only the files assigned to that **Album** appear in the **Media Browser**.

Albums are a simple way to gather photos, for instance, for creating slideshows or to gather media for a photo or video project.

To create an **Album**:

Select the media files you'd like to add to your **Album** in the **Media Browser** (by holding down the **Shift, Ctrl** or, on a Mac, the ⌘ key as you click on the files). Click the green **Create Album** button at the top right of the **Albums** panel, as illustrated above. An **Edit Album** panel will open to the right of the **Media Browser**, from which you can name your **Album**, select a sub-category for it and add files to it or remove files from it. When you're done, click **OK**.

If you switch to **Folder** view (see page 205), you can also turn any **Folder** into an **Album** just by **right-clicking** on it and selecting the **Instant Album** option.

Additional media files can be added to an **Album** by dragging the photo or video from the **Media Browser** onto that **Album's** green folder icon in the **Albums** panel on the left. To re-open an **Album** in the **Edit Album** panel, **right-click** on it and select **Edit**. (And, yes, a media file can be in more than one **Album** at the same time.)

To delete an **Album, right-click** on it and select **Delete**.

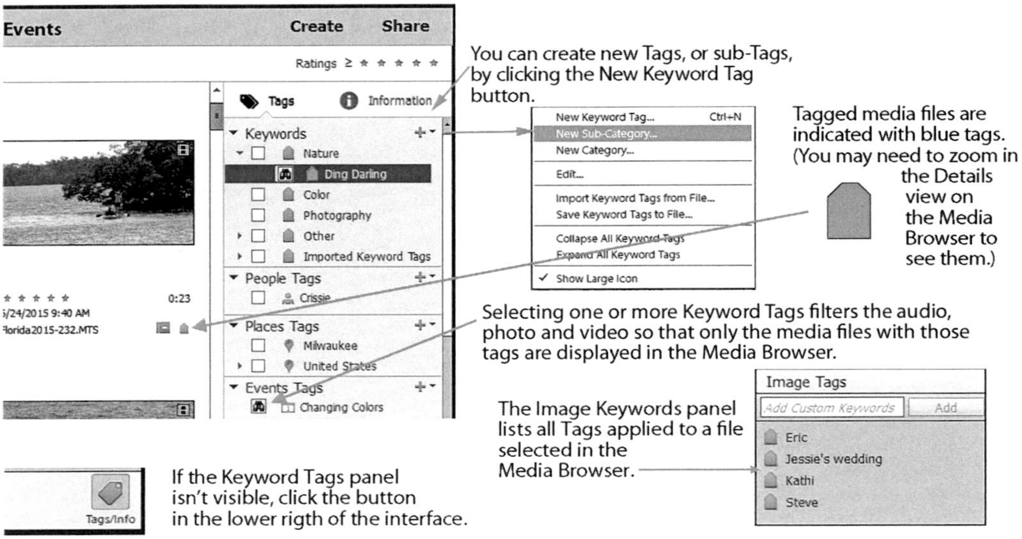

Manage your files with Keyword Tags

Tagging is a way to manually add custom search metadata to your media files.

At first adding **Keyword Tags** to hundreds of accumulated digital photos and videos may seem like a lot of housekeeping – but the payoff is great!

Creating a new **Tag** is as simple as clicking on the **+** symbol at the top right of this panel. You can create as many **Tags** and as many **Categories** – and **Sub-Categories** under them – as you'd like. You can, for instance, create a **Sub-Category** under Places and name it France. Then, within that **Sub-Category**, create **Tags** for Cousin Pierre, Landmarks, The Louvre, etc. (You can also drag your **Keyword** sub-categories in an out of categories on the **Keyword Tags** panel!)

To assign a **Tag** to a media file, drag the **Tag** from the **Keyword Tags** panel onto the selected file or files in the **Media Browser** (or drag selected media files onto the **Keyword Tag**). You can assign as many **Tags** as you'd like to a file. And you can assign the same **Tag** to as many files as you'd like.

In addition to **Keyword Tags**, the Organizer also includes **People, Places** and **Events Tags**. As you assign a media file to a person, place or event (as discussed on the following pages of this chapter) your file will automatically be tagged in the corresponding category.

And, as the **Auto Analyzer** works its way through your photo library, it will add its own **Auto Tags** (see page 208) to your media. These **Auto Tags** include information about the content of your photos including the presence of children and seniors, if the photos show celebrations or religious ceremonies and if the photos are portraits or are pictures of scenery. These **Auto Tags** will appear under **Auto Tags** in the **Tags** panel.

If you check a checkbox next to a **Tag** in the **Tags** panel, only the photos, video or audio files assigned to that **Tag** to will appear in the **Media Browser.** If you checkbox a major category of **Tags**, the files assigned to all of that category's sub-categories of **Tags** will appear.

To further refine your search, you can checkbox several **Tags** at once.

Find People in your files

One of the most powerful tools for managing and searching your photo files in the Elements Organizer – and one which Adobe has clearly invested a lot of effort into developing – is **Face Recognition**.

Face Recognition and the **People Finder** will work with you to identify the people in your photos (identifying as many as it can on its own) so that you can easily locate all of the photos that include one or several individuals.

Once you've identified the faces in your photos, you'll be able to retrieve any photos identified with any name or names by using the **Keyword Tag** filter, as discussed on the facing page.

It can take a while to work through all of your photos, but it's actually kind of fun – and the program does a lot of the work for you!

To begin the process:

1 Click the **People** tab at the top of the **Media Browser**.

Under the **Named** tab, the **Media Browser** will display photos grouped by people you've identified.

Under the **Unnamed** tab, the **Media Browser** will display photos grouped by faces the Organizer thinks are similar. (If faces are not displayed, uncheck the **Hide Small Stacks** option in the upper left of the workspace.)

2 Identify **Unnamed** people.

To identify a face in the **Unnamed** workspace, click on **Add Name** below the photo and type in a name.

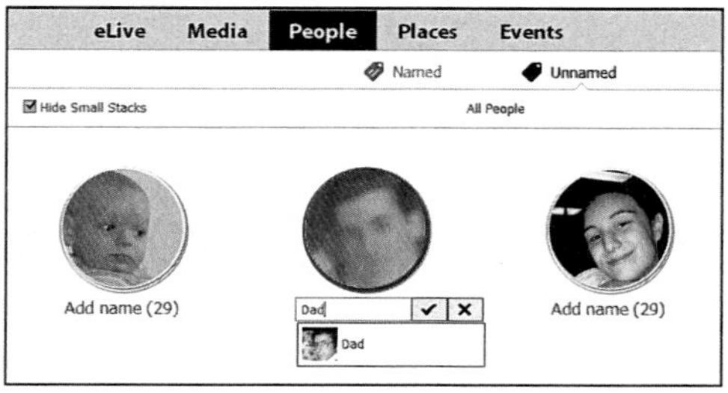

If the name you are typing has already been tagged to photos in your catalog, the program will offer it to you has an option. Select the name from the list offered.

If you type a name and then click the check mark (or press **Enter** on your keyboard), the name will be added to your list of **People**. If you type in a name of someone already in your **People** list and click the check mark rather than selecting the name from the list the Organizer offers, an additional instance of that name will appear in your **People**.

If you'd like this face not to be added to your list of **People**, **right-click** on the face displayed and select **Ignore This Person**.

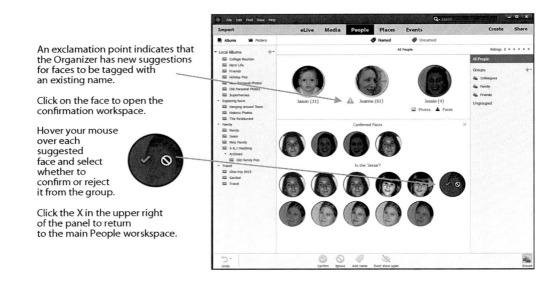

An exclamation point indicates that the Organizer has new suggestions for faces to be tagged with an existing name.

Click on the face to open the confirmation workspace.

Hover your mouse over each suggested face and select whether to confirm or reject it from the group.

Click the X in the upper right of the panel to return to the main People worskspace.

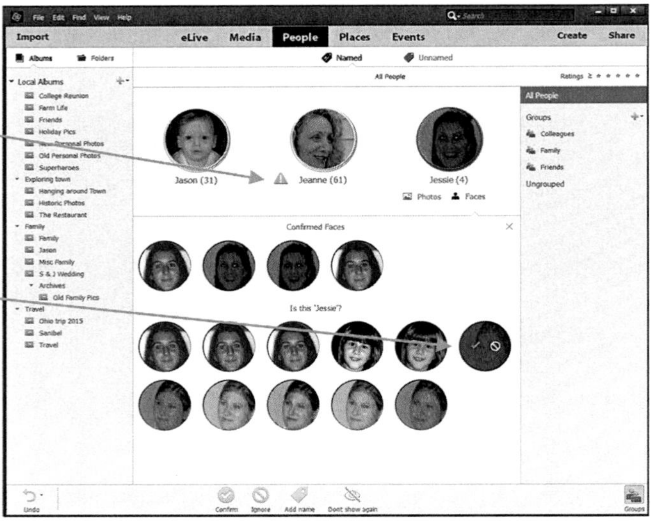

Unnamed people in photos are continually "discovered" by the Organizer's **Auto Analyzer** (see page 208) as it works in the background while you're not using your computer.

The Organizer will "suggest" photos of faces that it thinks belong to a named person.

3 Confirm **Named** people.

As you add **People** to your **Named** files, you may notice that occasionally the **Media Browser** will display an exclamation point inside an orange triangle next to a name, as illustrated above.

This is an indication that the Organizer has found more faces that it thinks should be tagged with an existing name.

Double-click on the face above the name and a workspace will open up in which you can confirm or reject the Organizer's selections.

To remove faces from this list, hover your mouse over each face and click the **Remove** indicator.

When you're happy with the faces that appear under a given name, click the **X** in the upper corner of the confirmation workspace to return to the main **People** workspace.

The Organizer actually "learns" from its mistakes, and it gets more accurate the more you help it identify **People**.

You can begin or end a work session at any time. The Organizer always saves all your work as you work.

Add People to Groups

Your **People** stacks are listed in alphabetic order. But, to make them a bit easier to manage (especially if you've got dozens of them!) you can also arrange them into **Groups.**

The groups **Colleagues, Family** and **Friends** are listed by default. To add someone to an existing **Group**, drag the **Group** onto his or her face.

To create a new **Group**, click the **Add Group** button at the top right of the **Groups** panel.

An option panel will open in which you can name your new **Group** and select whether it will be a main **Group** (select **None**) or it will be a sub-category of an existing **Group**.

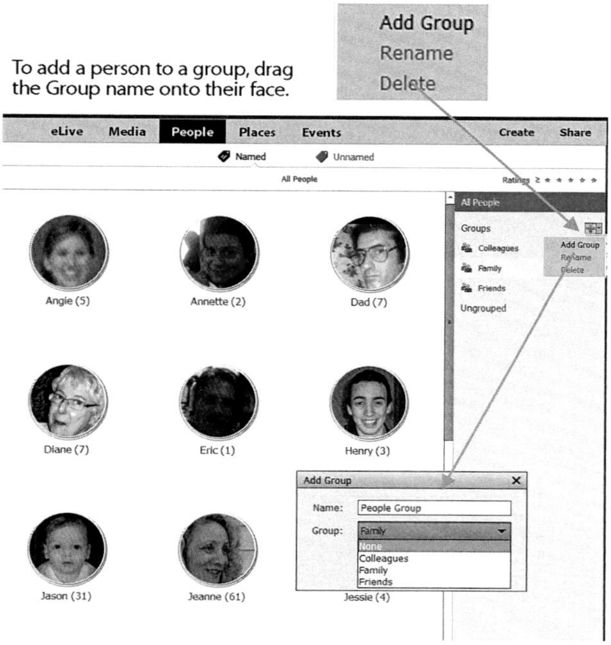

To add a person to a group, drag the Group name onto their face.

To see the **People** in a specific **Group**, click the **Group's** name in the **Groups** panel.

Manage your photos by Place

Just as you can manage your photo files using **Albums, Keyword Tags** and the **People** in them, you can also manage your photos or video by the location at which they were shot. Locating media shot at a given location is as simple as clicking on a pin on a map.

Even cooler, if your camera has a built-in GPS (and virtually all smartphone cameras do!), the Elements Organizer will read this metadata and add the media to your map automatically!

To tag photos or video with a **Place**:

1 Click the **Places** tab at the top of the interface.

A map will be displayed on the right side of the **Media Browser.**

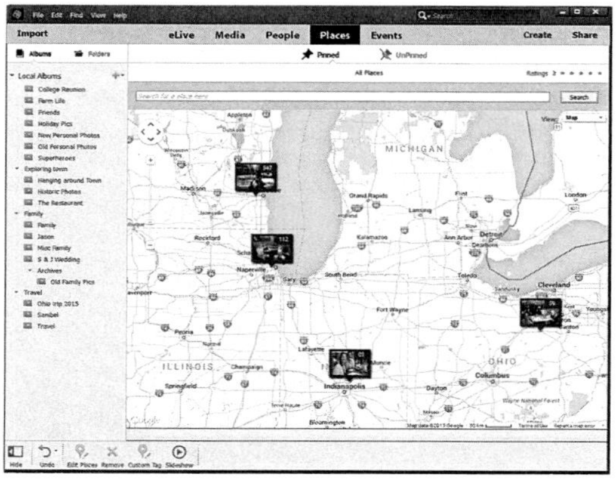

If you select the **Pinned** tab, media files already tagged with **Place** metadata will appear on the map as thumbnails. The number on each thumbnails indicates the number of photos tagged to a given **Place**.

The more you zoom in on the map, the more precise their placement will be displayed.

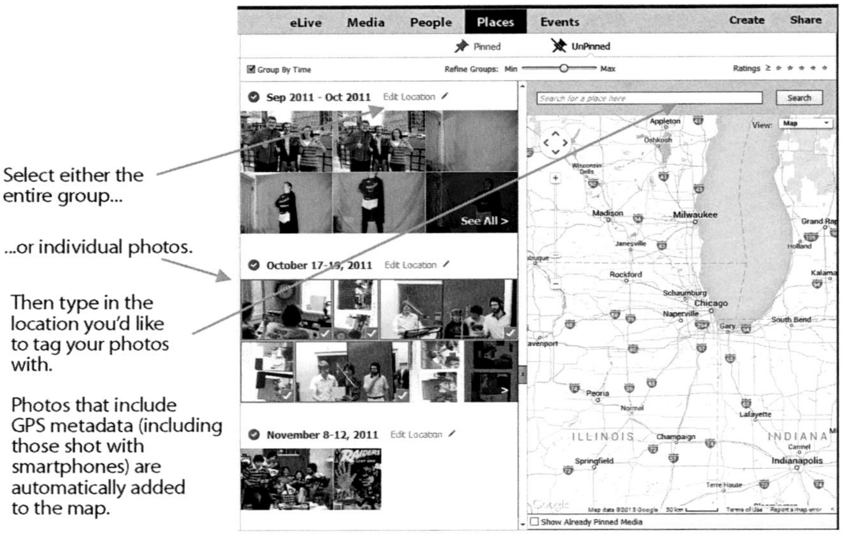
Select either the entire group...
...or individual photos.
Then type in the location you'd like to tag your photos with.
Photos that include GPS metadata (including those shot with smartphones) are automatically added to the map.
eLive
Media
People
Places
Events
Create
Share
Pinned
UnPinned
Group By Time
Sep 2011 - Oct 2011
Edit Location
See All >
November 8-12, 2011
Search
ILLINOIS
INDIANA
Show Already Pinned Media

If you click on the **Unpinned** tab, you'll have option to tag either a group or specific media files to a **Place**.

2 Select photos or videos you'd like to assign to a **Place**.

Under the **Unpinned** tab, the **Media Browser** will display media files not yet assigned to **Places**, grouped by the date they were shot.

To assign an entire **Time Group** of photos or video to a **Place**, click on the **Add Location** link above the group.

To assign individual photos or video files in a **Time Group** to a **Place**, uncheck the **Group by Time** box in the upper left of the interface. All unassigned media files will be displayed in the **Media Browser**. (You can switch between the **Adaptive Grid** and **Details** view of these media files [see page 201] by pressing **Ctrl+d** on a PC or **⌘+d** on a Mac.)

Select the photos or video files you'd like to assign to a **Place**. A checkmark will appear on your selected media files. To select several files, hold down the **Shift** or **Ctrl** key (the ⌘ key on a Mac) as you click.

3 Indicate a **Place**.

Enter the name of the location you'd like to assign to your media files in the **Search For A Location** box above the map – then click **Search** (or press **Enter** in your keyboard). You can enter the name of a city, a zip code or even a specific street address!

As you type, the search box will suggest locations. Click to select the correct location.

Your photo(s) will be added to that location and tagged with that **Place** metadata

Alternatively, you can simply drag your selected photos onto a location on the map – although this may not be as precise as typing in the location information manually.

Once you've tagged your photos will **Place** metadata, you can locate all photos shot at that location by zooming in on the map or by filtering the location **Keyword Tags**, as described on page 212.

Manage your media files by Date or Event

Finally, you can manage your media files according to specific dates or events.

1 Click the **Events** tab at the top of the interface.

If you have media files tagged to **Events**, they will appear as stacks under the **Named** tab.

Under the **Suggested** tab, the **Media Browser** will display media files not yet assigned to **Events**, grouped by date.

By adjusting the **Number of Groups** slider or by selecting options from the **Calendar** menu to the right, you can adjust how precisely the **Suggested** media files are displayed by date.

To tag **Suggested** media files by **Event**:

2 Select the media files you'd like to add to an **Event**.

To add an entire group of media files to an **Event**, click on the **Add Event** link above the group.

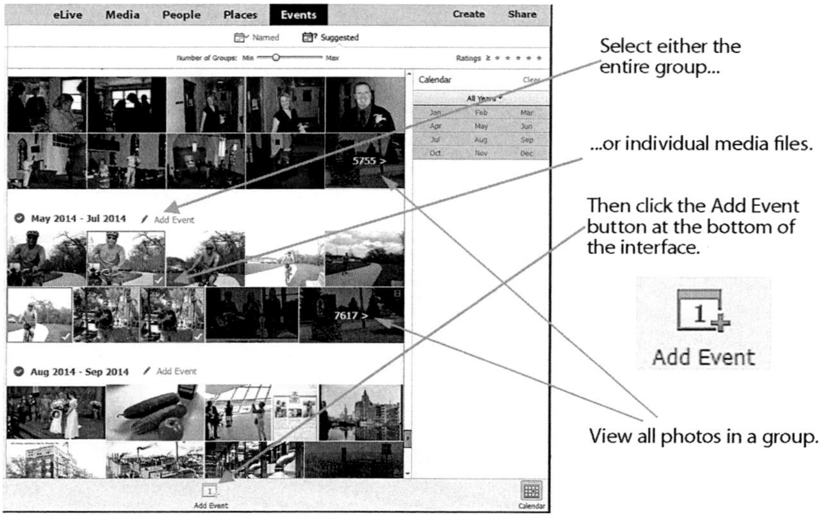

To add an individual media file or files to a location, click on the thumbnail(s) displayed or click on the **000>** thumbnail to view all of the photos in a group.

A checkmark will appear on your selected media file(s). To select several files, hold down the **Shift** or **Ctrl** key (the ⌘ key on a Mac) as you click.

3 Name the **Event**.

Once you've selected the media files, click the **Name Event(s)** button at the bottom of the interface.

In the **Name Event** option panel that opens, you can add the name of the event, the range of dates the event represents and a description of the event.

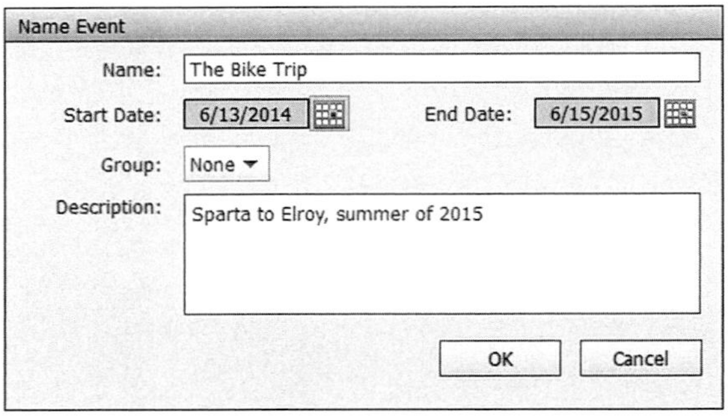

Once you've tagged your media files with **Event** metadata, you can gather all photos related to that event by clicking on the stack under the **Named** tab or by filtering the **Event Keyword Tags**, as described on page 212.

Instant Fix a photo

In addition to all of the file management tools built into the program, the Organizer also includes a fairly powerful **Instant Fix** workspace for cleaning up and adding effects to your photos.

To open this workspace, select a photo or several photos in the Organizer's **Media Browser** and then click the **Instant Fix** button along the bottom of the program.

If you've selected more than one photo, you can apply effects or adjustments to one photo in the selected group or all of the photos at once. (Some fixes – **Flip, Crop** and **Red-Eye Removal** – can only be applied to one photo at a time.)

When you have a group of photos open in the workspace, you can toggle between group and individual views by selecting the option at the top of the program. You can switch back and forth between applying effects and adjustments to the group or individual photos at any time.

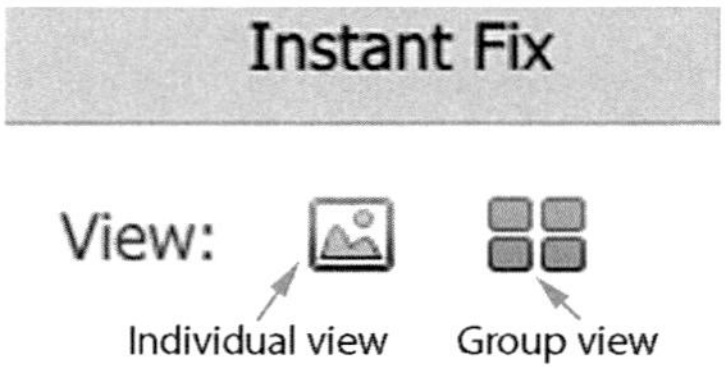

Effects and adjustments can be undone by clicking the **Undo** button in the lower left of the workspace or by pressing **Ctrl+z** (⌘**+d** on a Mac) on your keyboard.

Instant Fixes include:

Flip Photo Horizontal (Available only for one photo at a time).

Crop (Available only for one photo at a time), when selected, will display a library of pre-set crop sizes as well as the option to create a custom crop.

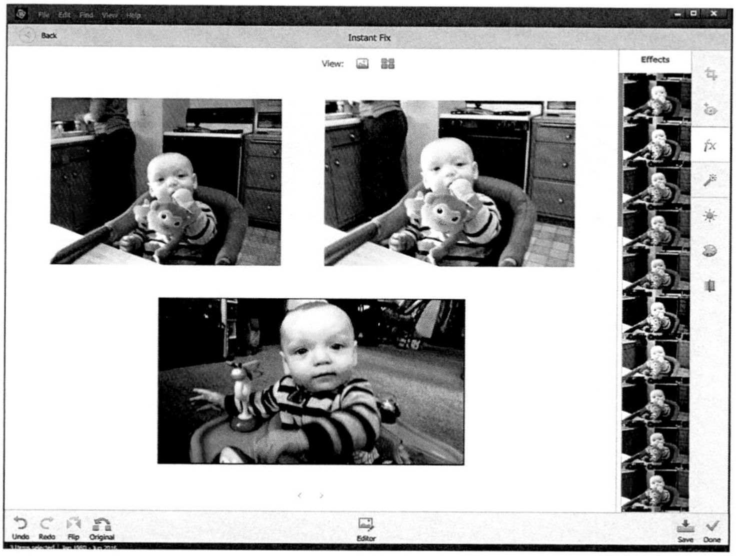

Red-Eye Removal (Available only for one photo at a time) is a fully automatic fix.

Effects/FX, when selected, will display a library of photo effects which can be added to one photo or the group with a single click.

Smart Fix will apply instant color, light and sharpness fixes to one photo or to the group.

Light, when selected, will display previews of lighting adjustments which can be added to one photo or the group with a single click.

Color, when selected, will display previews of color level adjustments which can be added to one photo or the group with a single click.

Clarity, when selected, will display previews of sharpness/softness adjustments which can be added to one photo or the group with a single click.

To save your changes, click the **Save** button in the lower right of the program. Your original photo(s) will not be overwritten. Rather, your photo will appear in the Organizer's **Media Browser** as a **Version Set**.

To access previous versions of your photo, including the original photo, **double-click** on it in the **Media Browser** to open it in a photo preview window. **Right-click** on the photo and select the **Version Set** sub-menu.

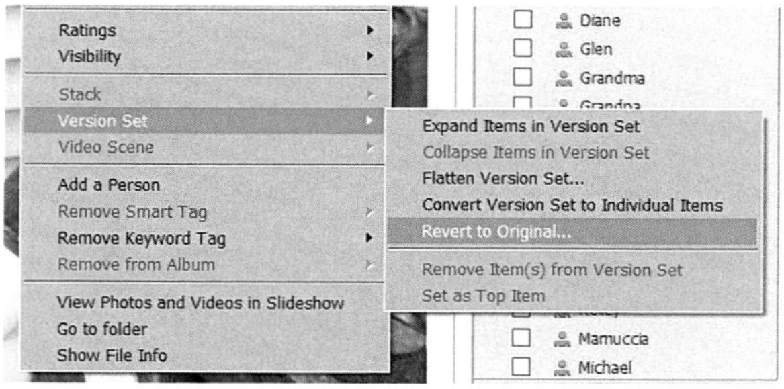

In the **Version Set** sub-menu, you'll find options to **Flatten** the versions into one photo, **Convert the Version Set Into Individual** photos and to **Revert to the Original** photo.

Chapter 18

Create Fun Pieces

The Organizer's project templates

The Elements Organizer includes a number of tools for creating everything from a photo scrapbook to a greeting card, DVD cover or a CD or DVD disc label.

Using the templates and wizards in the Organizer (and sometimes Photoshop Elements), creating these photo pieces is as simple as selecting your artwork and following the prompts.

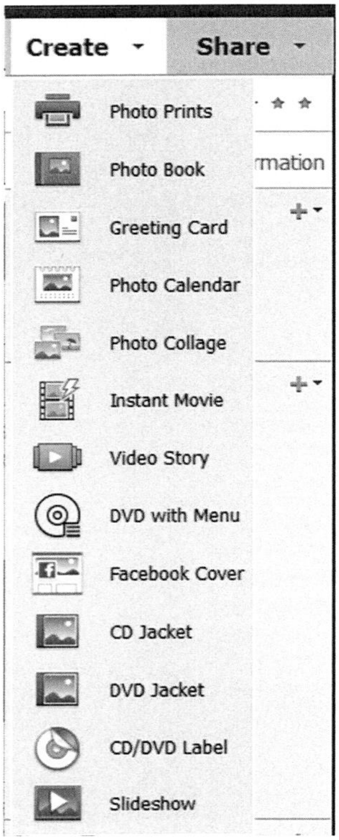

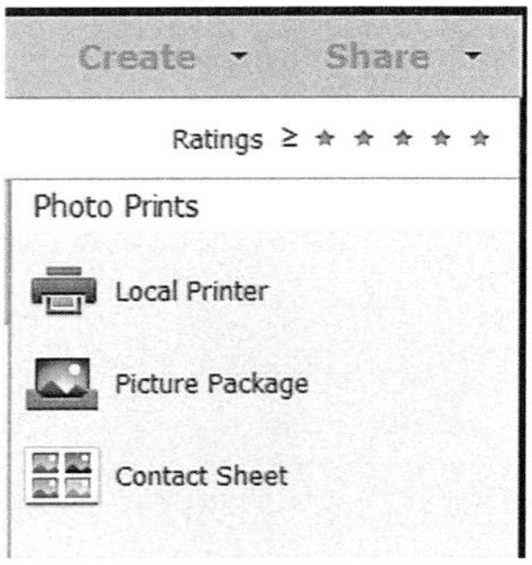

The **Create** tab on the upper right of the Elements Organizer's interface gives you access to an array of tools for creating projects from your media files.

A number of these options are actually links to tools in Premiere Elements or Photoshop Elements, and selecting them will launch the workspace in that program. In fact, **if you do not have Photoshop Elements installed on your computer, some of these options may not be available to you.**

Create Photo Prints

The **Photo Prints** option under the **Create** tab gives you access to several ways to output your photos.

Print Individual Prints on your local printer

As you'd expect, this option sends your selected photo(s) to your printer. But you may be surprised at the number of possible print layouts this option screen includes!

1 Select the photo or photos you'd like to print in the **Media Browser** and click to select the **Photo Prints** option under the **Create** tab.

Then, on the **Photo Prints** option panel that appears, select **Local Printer,** as illustrated to the left.

The **Prints** preview panel will open. The program will automatically arrange the photos you've selected so that it can print as many as possible on each page printed out.

How many photos it fits on a page depends on the **Print Size** you've selected for photos (as in **Step 2**, below).

The complete set of photos you've selected to print are displayed as thumbnails along the left side of the panel, and you may add or remove photos from this list.

2 Select your photo print-out options.

As illustrated on the facing page, the **Select Print Size** drop-down allows you to set how large each photo prints. You can also select from this menu the option to print each photo at its **Actual Size**.

Whenever you print any photo, it's important to consider the resolution of the image. Printing photos smaller than their actual size will usually not be a problem. However, if you set your photo to print at a size in which its final output resolution is less than 150-200 ppi, you will likely see reduced quality and fuzziness in your output. This could definitely be a problem if you selected the **Individual Print** option and you then selected a print size much larger than the actual photo.

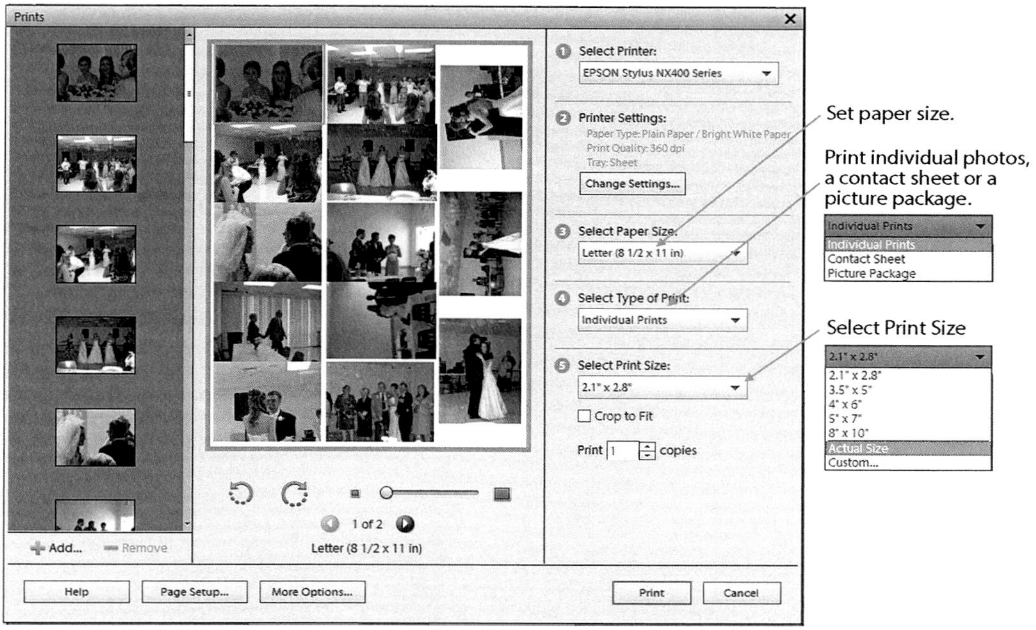

The Print preview panel includes settings for printing your photos in a variety of sizes and layouts as well as options for adding cool custom frames.

Select Type of Print

The **Type of Print** menu on the **Prints** option panel (illustrated above) arranges the photos in your print-out page in one of three patterns.

Individual Prints prints photos to your printer at the size you designate.

Picture Package sends an arrangement of photos to your printer based on the number of photos you designate per page. This **Type of Print** also gives you the option of printing these photos with a **Frame** around each.

Contact Sheet prints proof-style thumbnails of your photos, according to the layout settings you provide.

Print a Picture Package or Contact Sheet on your local printer

The main difference between the **Picture Package** and the **Individual Prints** print-out options is in how you set the size and number of photos that will appear on your print-out page.

When **Type of Print** is set to **Individual Prints**, you will have the option of selecting the *size* your photos will print out at. When you set the **Type of Print** option to **Picture Package** (or **Contact Sheet**), you will have the option of selecting the *number* of photos you want to print on each page.

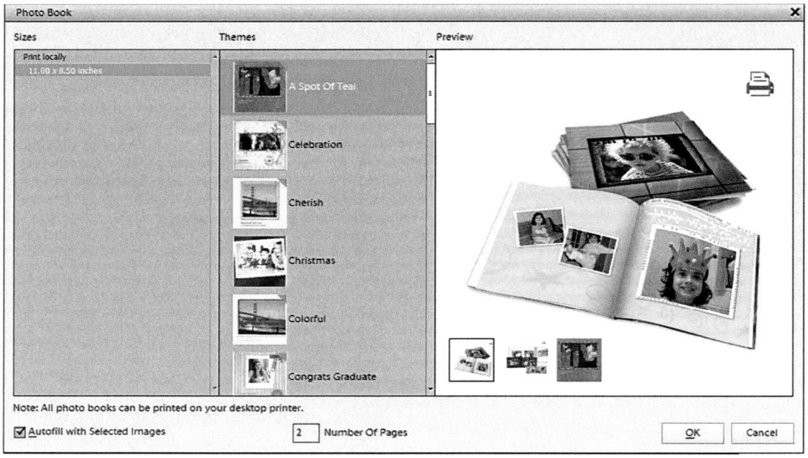

The Photo Book option panel.

Create a Photo Book

A **Photo Book** is a collection of photos laid out in 20 to 80 custom-designed pages. The wizard takes you through the basic steps of setting up the book. Once the book is initially set up, you can add more photos to it and tweak the design and layout. (This tool is only available if you have Photoshop Elements.)

1. Select the photos in the **Media Browser** you'd like to include in your **Photo Book.** Then select the **Photo Book** button under the **Create** tab.

   (You can add, swap out and delete photos later.)

   The **Photo Book** option panel will open in Photoshop Elements.

2. Select a size and output options for your book from the **Photo Book** option panel (illustrated above).

3. On this same panel, select a **Theme** for your book.

   You can assign any number of pages to your book and you can add and remove pages later as needed..

   Click **OK**

The photos you have selected when you launch this tool will automatically be loaded into your **Photo Book** in the order that they appear in the **Media Browser.**

The first of your selected photos will become your **Title Page Photo.**

The program will fill as many pages as possible with the photos you've selected.

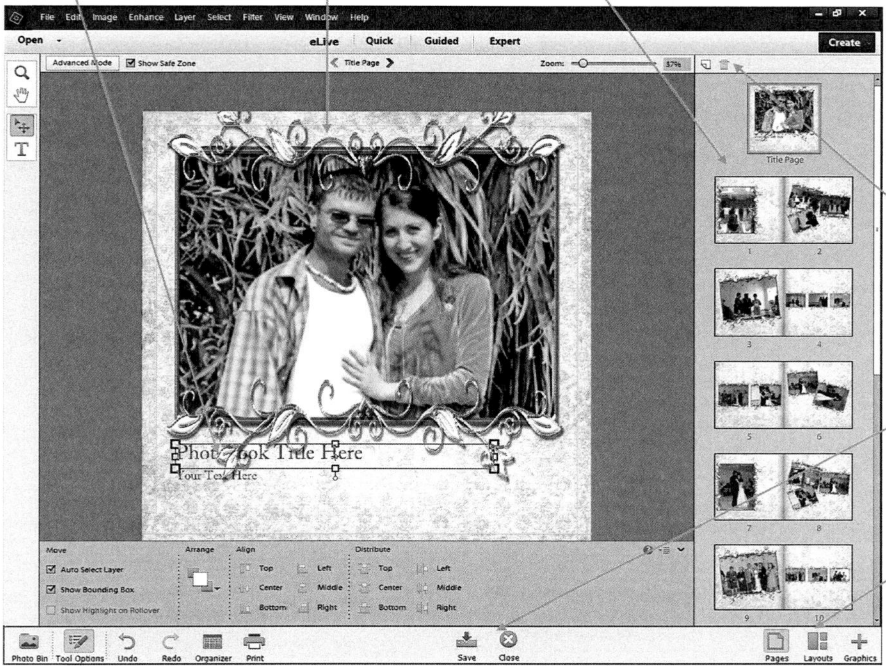

Click a block of text to customize it.
Right-click on photo to modify or replace it.
Select a page for editing from the Page bin.
Add or remove pages.
Click to finish and send to printer.
Select graphics and page layouts.

You can add pages to or remove pages from your book by clicking the icons in the top left of the **Page Bin**.

You may also change the theme and/or frames for the individual pages or add graphics by selecting options at the bottom right.

To add, edit or replace photos, **right-click** on the photo frame:

- If the frame is blank, you'll be prompted to browse for a photo on your hard drive.
- If a photo is already in the frame, options will be displayed to resize the photo or **Position Photo Within Frame**, rotate it or replace it.

By dragging on their corner handles, photos and their frames can be resized and repositioned on the page.

To send your finished book to your home printer, click the **Print** button along the bottom of the workspace.

On the **Print Preview** page, you will also find the option to **Print** (save) your **Photo Book** as an Adobe PDF file under **Select Printer**.

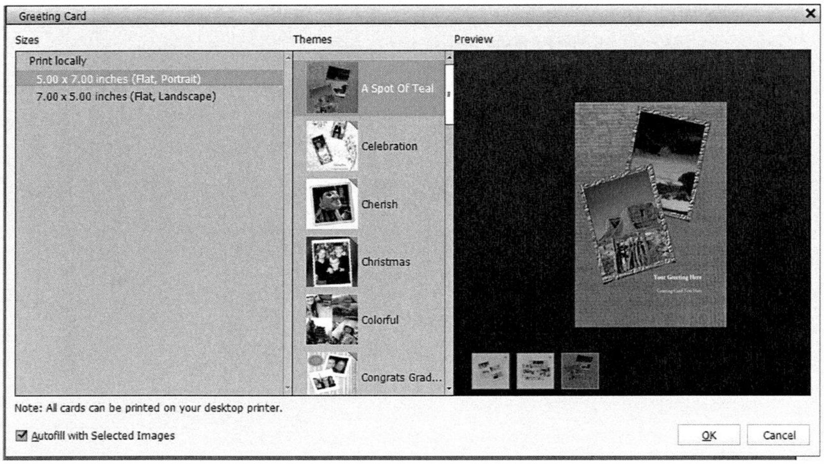

The Greeting Card option panel.

Create a Greeting Card

Once completed, your **Greeting Card** can be printed on your home printer. (This tool is available only if you have Photoshop Elements.)

1 Select the **Greeting Card** button under the **Create** tab.

   The photos you have in your **Project Bin** – whether because they are open in the **Editor** or selected in the **Organizer** – will automatically be loaded into your **Greeting Card.** Photos may also be added or removed after the book is created.

2 Select a size and output option for your book from the **Greeting Card** option screen (illustrated above)..

3 On this same panel, select a **Theme** for your card. (These features can be modified later.)

   Click **OK**.

The program will generate your card.

As with the **Photo Book**, you may swap out photos and modify your **Greeting Card's** layout, graphics or text, as described on page 225.

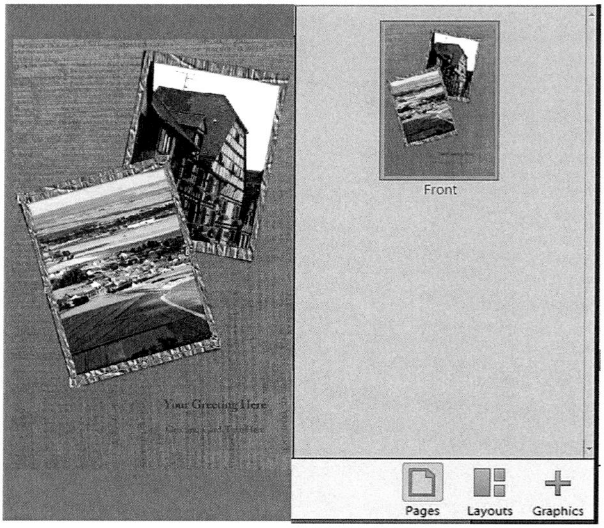

After the program generates your card, you can modify its theme, text, photos and effects.

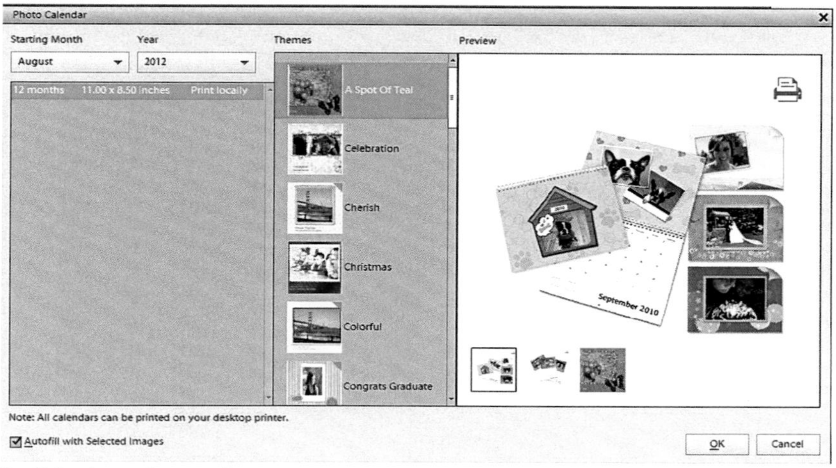

The Calendar option panel.

Create a Photo Calendar

Once completed, your **Photo Calendar** can be printed on your home printer. (This tool is only available if you have Photoshop Elements.)

1. Select the photos you'd like to use in your calendar in the **Media Browser**
2. Select the **Photo Calendar** button under the **Create** tab.
3. Select a starting date, size and output options for your book from the **Photo Calendar** option screen (illustrated above).
4. On this same panel, select a **Theme** for your card. (These features can be modified later.)

   The photos you have in your **Media Browser** will automatically be loaded into your **Photo Calendar.**

   Photos may also be added or removed after the book is created.

   Click **OK**.

The program will generate your card.

As with the **Photo Book**, you may swap out photos and modify your **Photo Calendar's** layout, graphics or text, as described on page 225.

After the program generates your calendar, you can modify its layout, graphics, text and photos.

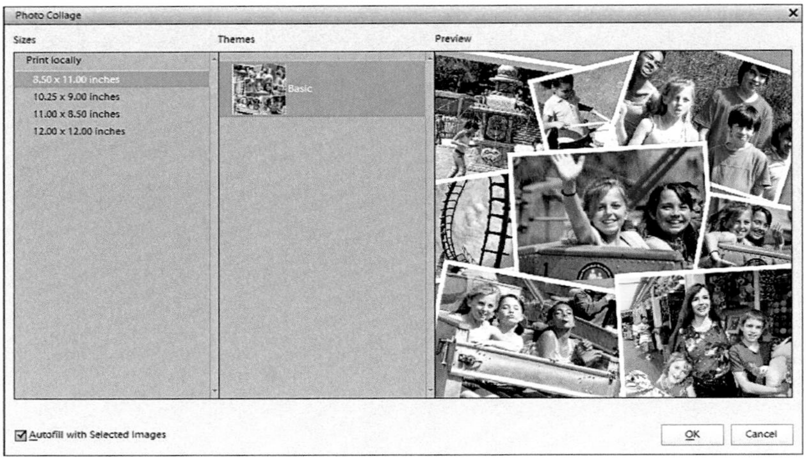

The Photo Collage option screen.

Create a Photo Collage

A **Photo Collage** is an arrangement of photos gathered together in an artful or playful way. Once you create your **Photo Collage**, you'll be able to print it out on your home printer. (This tool is only available if you have Photoshop Elements.)

1 Select the photos you'd like to use in your collage in the **Media Browser**

2 Select the **Photo Collage** button under the **Create** tab.

3 Select a size for your **Photo Collage** from the option screen (illustrated above).

4 On this same panel, select a **Theme** for your collage. (These features can be modified later.)

Click **OK**.

The photos you have in your **Media Browser** will automatically be loaded into your **Photo Collage.** Photos may also be added or removed after the book is created.

As with the **Photo Book**, you may swap out photos and modify your **Photo Calendar's** layout, graphics or text, as described on page 225.

Create an InstantMovie

Selecting the option to create an **InstantMovie** gathers the photos and video clips you've selected in the Organizer's **Media Browser** and ports them to Premiere Elements, where an **InstantMovie Theme** is applied. For more information on **InstantMovies** and **Themes**, see **Chapter 8, Create an InstantMovie, Video Story or Video Collage**.

Create a Video Story

Selecting the option to create a **Video Story** gathers the photos and video clips you've selected in the Organizer's **Media Browser** and ports them to Premiere Elements and into the **Video Story** workspace. For more information on the **Video Story** tool, see **Chapter 8, Create an InstantMovie, Video Story or Video Collage**.

Create a DVD with Menu

Selecting the option to create a **DVD With Menu** gathers the photos and video clips you've selected in the Organizer's **Media Browser** and ports them to a Premiere Elements project for further editing. For information on adding a menu to a DVD or BluRay disc project, see **Chapter 20, Create Movie Menus**.

Create a Facebook Cover

Selecting the option to create a **Facebook Cover** opens a Photoshop Elements workspace for creating a cover illustration for your Facebook home page. For more information on the tools in this workspace, see the sidebar on page 233.

Create a CD Jacket

This tool creates a 9¾" x 4¾" image that you can print out and fit into a CD or DVD "jewel case." (Note that disc jewel cases are 4¾" x 4¾", so this artwork is designed to wrap around the case and includes a ¼" spine.)

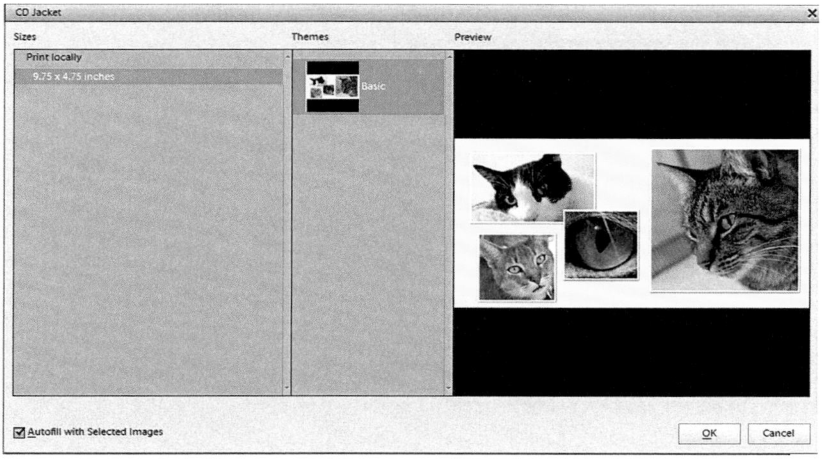

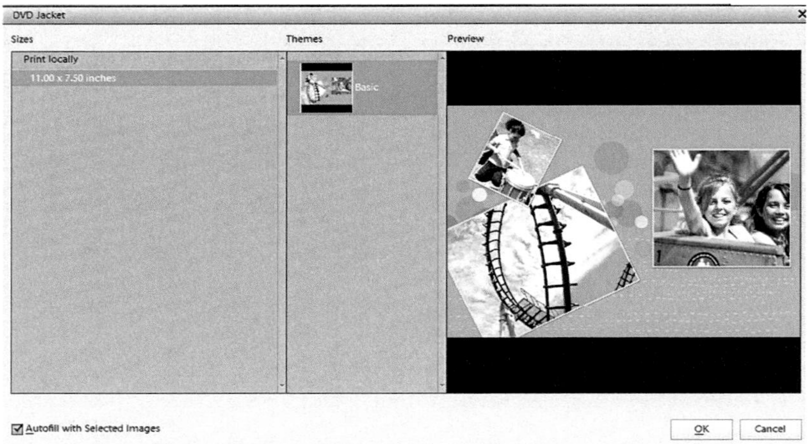

The DVD Jacket template creates an image that wraps around a DVD case that has 5.25" x 7.50" faces and a 0.5" spine.

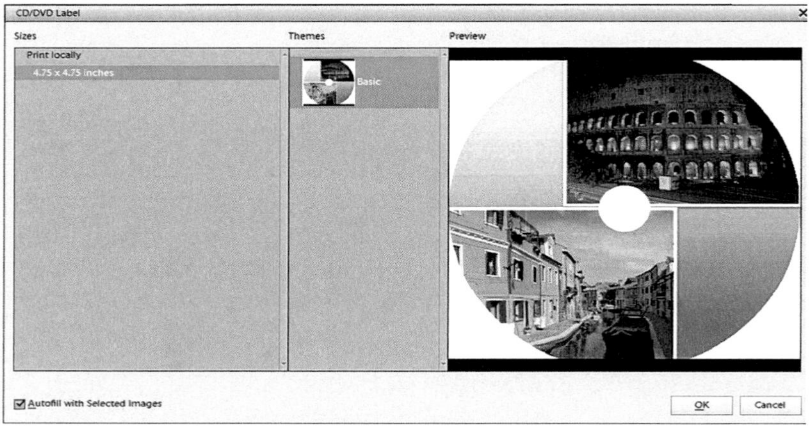

The CD/DVD Label template creates art that can be printed onto a 4.75" disc.

Create a DVD Jacket

This tool creates an 11" x 7½" label for a DVD case. This template is made to fit a 5¼" x 7½" case with a ½" wide spine.

Print a CD/DVD Label

This tool creates 4¾", circular-shaped artwork for printing onto discs. It includes the necessary spindle hole through the center.

(At Muvipix, we recommend never using glue-on labels for your DVDs and CDs. They can cause any number of problems. This tool is best used with printable discs and inkjet printers designed to print on them.)

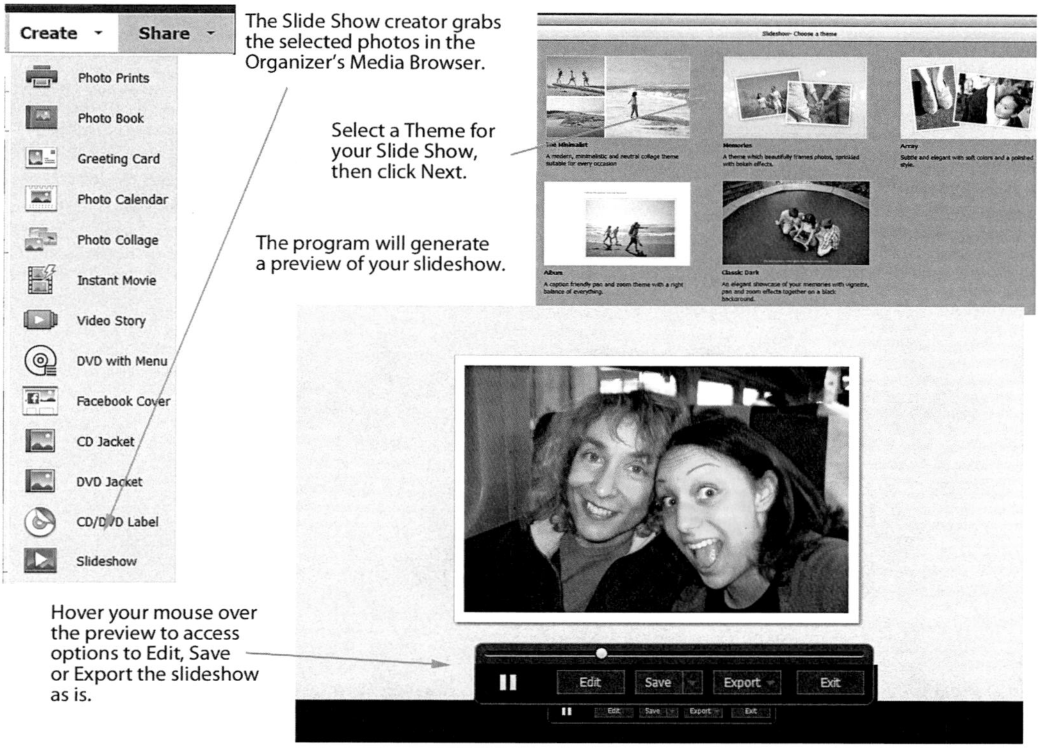
Create
Share
Photo Prints
Photo Book
Greeting Card
Photo Calendar
Photo Collage
Instant Movie
Video Story
DVD with Menu
Facebook Cover
CD Jacket
DVD Jacket
CD/DVD Label
Slideshow
The Slide Show creator grabs the selected photos in the Organizer's Media Browser.
Select a Theme for your Slide Show, then click Next.
The program will generate a preview of your slideshow.
Hover your mouse over the preview to access options to Edit, Save or Export the slideshow as is.
Edit
Save
Export
Exit

Create an Organizer Slideshow

There are actually several ways to create a slideshow in Premiere Elements and Photoshop Elements (including using the tool in the **Project Assets** panel, as we discuss on page 67.) But the Organizer's new and improved **Slide Show creator** is perhaps the most intuitive option – and includes some very nice looking themes to give your slideshow a real professional look!

1. Select the photos you'd like to include in your slideshow in the **Media Browser**. (You can add or remove photos later.)
2. Select the **Slide Show** option from under the Elements Organizer's **Create** tab.

   A **Theme** library window will open.
3. Select a **Theme** for your slideshow.

   Click **Next**.

   The tool will generate a preview of your slideshow.

   Hover your mouse over the slideshow preview.

An option panel will appear, as illustrated above.

Click **Exit** or **Edit** to leave the preview.

4 Edit your slideshow in the **Slideshow Builder** workspace.

Drag your slides in the **Slideshow Builder** to rearrange their order.

Click the **Add Media** button in the upper left of the panel to add more slides.

Right-click on any slide to **Remove Image** from the slideshow.

5 Add production elements.

As illustrated above, click **Add Text Slide** to add a title slide.

Click the **Audio** button to add custom music to your sideshow and select a timing option from the **Speed** drop-down menu.

6 Output your slideshow.

Click **Save** to save your slideshow in a format that will allow you to re-open it and re-edit it later.

Click **Export** to upload your slideshow to Facebook or to output it as an MP4. MP4s can be played on your computer, uploaded to a web site or used in a Premiere Elements project.

Create a Facebook cover page

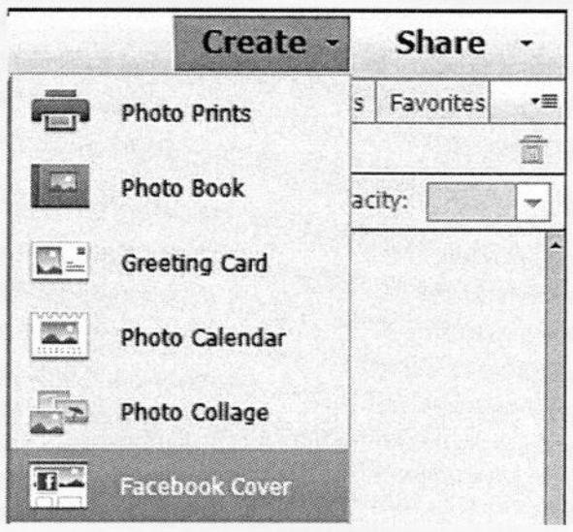

Available only if you have Photoshop Elements installed, the **Create Facebook Cover** workspace offers you templates and tools for creating your own stylish cover illustration for your Facebook home page.

To use this tool, click the **Create** button in the upper right of the interface and select **Facebook Cover**. An option screen will offer you a number of customizable templates for your cover page. Select one and click **OK**.

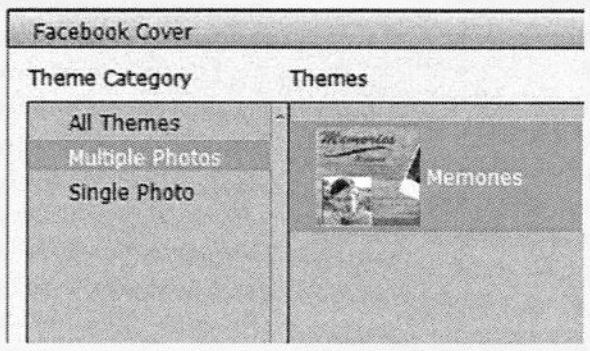

Add photos to the template by clicking on one of the photo placeholders and browsing to a photo on your hard drive.

A zoom slider at the top right the workspace can be used to zoom in and out on your work. **Double-clicking** on a photo that you've added to the template launches a tool for changing the scale and orientation of your photo, as in the illustration below.

The **Text** tool on the left side of the workspace can be used to add custom text, and the **Move** tool can be used to select, reposition and remove any of the template's elements. The **Graphics** button in the lower right opens a library of clip art options.

When you're ready to upload your finished cover to Facebook, click the **Upload** button on the bottom center of the workspace. (The first time you use this tool, you'll need to follow the prompts to authorize the program's link to your Facebook account.)

Chapter 19

Share Your Photos and Videos

The Organizer's output tools

The Elements Organizer includes a number of tools for outputting your photo and video files – from posting them online or e-mailing them to creating a DVD or PDF slideshow.

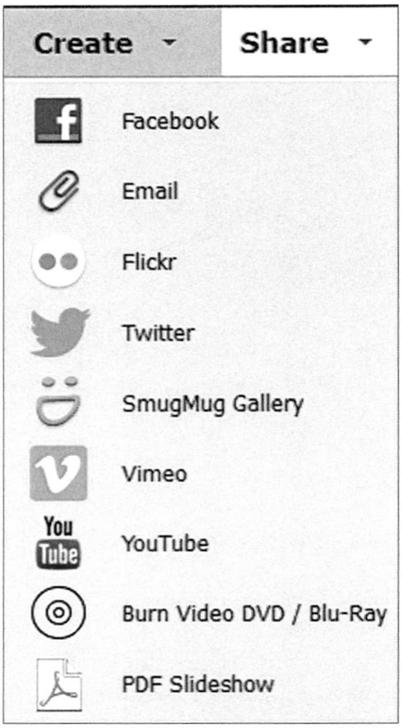

In addition to tools for creating photo and video projects, the Elements Organizer includes a number of tools for sharing your photos and videos.

Share your photos and videos on Facebook

If you have a Facebook account, you can upload your photos and videos directly from the Organizer's **Media Browser** to your page.

To upload to Facebook:

1 Select a video, photo or several photos in the **Media Browser**, then select the **Facebook** option under the **Share** tab.

The Organizer will prepare and optimize your file(s) for upload.

If this is the first time uploading to Facebook from the Organizer, an option screen will ask you to **Authorize** the upload. (It will also ask you if you want to download your Facebook friends to your Organizer **Contacts**. This is, of course, optional.)

2 Click **Authorize**.

After you click the **Authorize** button, your web browser will open to your Facebook page. If you are already logged into Facebook, you're done with the authorization. You can close your web browser now. If not, you will need to log in first.

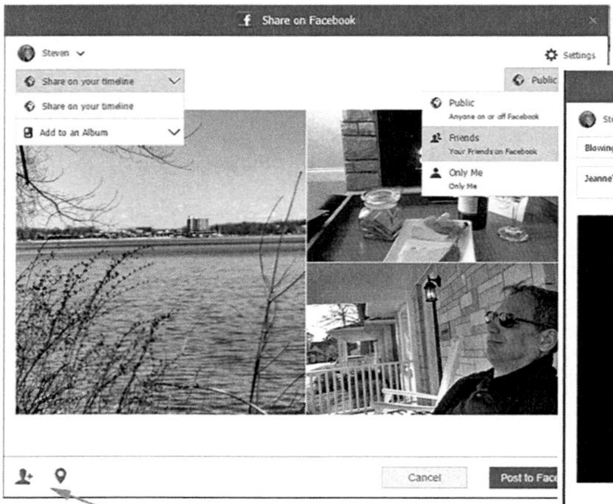

The Facebook Share screen for photos.

Optionally, you can include your People and Place tags with your photos.

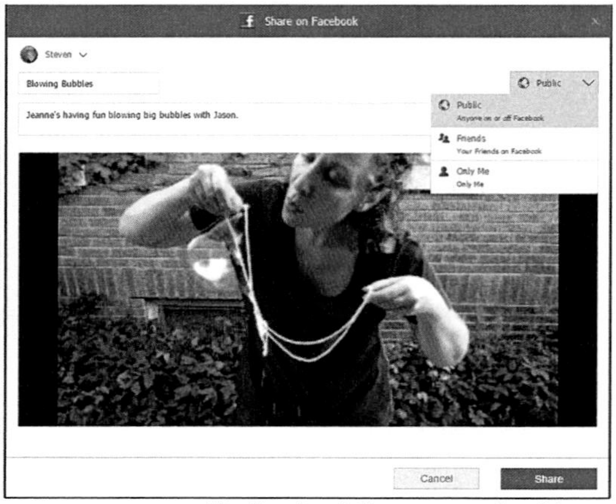

The Facebook Share screen for videos.

3 Back in the Organizer, click the **Complete Authorization** button.

The program will finish preparing your file(s). An option panel will then open, asking you to name your file(s) and set who can see them.

4 Once you've set your options, as illustrated on the facing page, click **Upload**. Your file(s) will load to your Facebook page.

Share your photos via e-mail

The **E-mail sharing** option optimizes your selected photo files and then sends them off, with a brief note, to the person or group of people you designate as **Recipients**.

As with any **Share** tool, you can pre-select your media files before starting the tool or add your media files later.

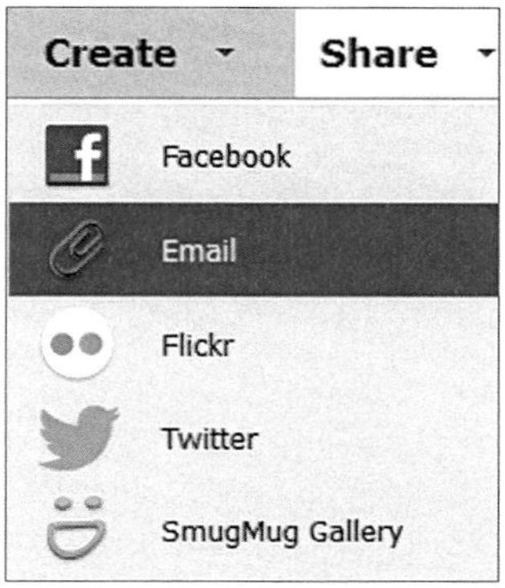

1 Select the photo(s) you want to attach to your e-mail in your **Media Browser**.

2 Select the **E-mail** option under the **Share** tab in the Organizer.

The **E-mail** share panel will open.

3 Drag any more photo(s) you'd like to add to your e-mail attachments from the Organizer's **Media Browser** into the **E-mail Attachments Items** bin.

Remove any photos you'd like to delete by selecting them in the panel and clicking the **trashcan** button below the photos.

You can add photos in any file format. The program will convert whatever you add to this bin into a JPEG for e-mailing.

Set the **Photo Size** and **Quality** by using the slider and selecting a photo size from the **Maximum Photo Size** drop-down menu.

Set up e-mail sharing for the Elements Organizer

In order to use the Elements Organizer's e-mail **Share** options, you must have an active e-mail profile and address listed on the **Email** page of the Organizer's **Preferences** (under the **Edit** drop-down on the Organizer Menu Bar on a PC).

On this **Email Preferences** page, under **Configure Email Client**, select a name for your **Email Profile**, then fill in your e-mail address and password.

Click the **Validate** button. The program will indicate if your validation was successful.

E-mails sent directly from the Organizer will use this e-mail address as their output path.

Naturally, the more photos you're including in your e-mail, the more you'll need to decrease the photo size or quality.

The panel displays an **Estimated Size** and, in order to ensure your e-mail doesn't choke your recipients' e-mail services, you'll probably want to keep your total e-mail size below 1 megabyte or so.

When you are happy with your settings for this panel, click **Next**.

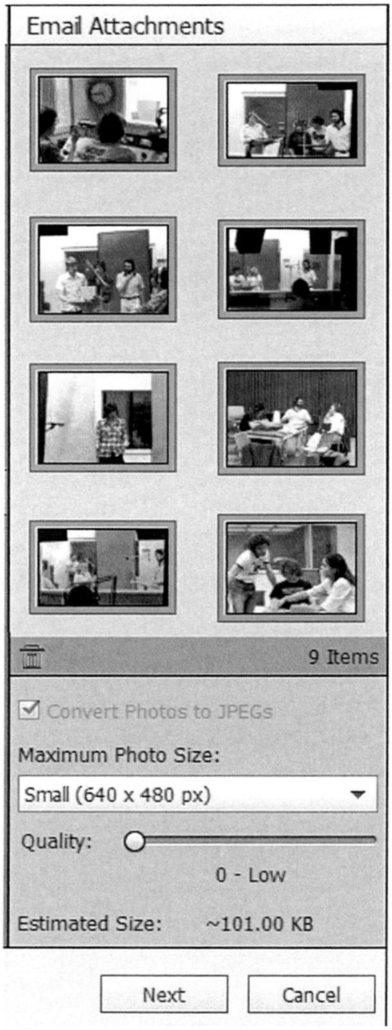

4 Create a message to accompany your photos and then **Select Recipients** from your list of contacts.

(See the sidebar on page 240 – **Create an Elements Organizer Contact Book** – for information on creating your **Contacts** list.)

When you are happy with your settings for this panel, click **Next**.

Your e-mail and optimized attachments will be sent to your selected recipients.

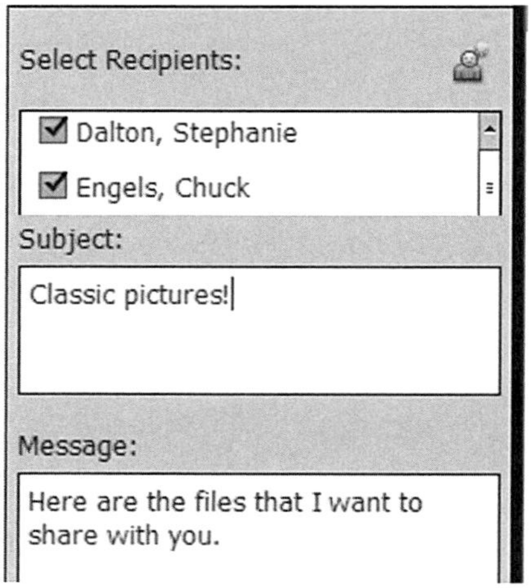

Share your photos on Flickr

When you select photos in your **Media Browser** and select the **Flickr** option under the **Share** tab, your photos will be prepared, then uploaded to your account at www.flickr.com – much like the process described in **Share Your Videos and Photos to Facebook** on page 236.

The first time you use the tool, you will need to log in to Flickr and **Authorize** the upload, as described in **Share Your Videos and Photos to Facebook**.

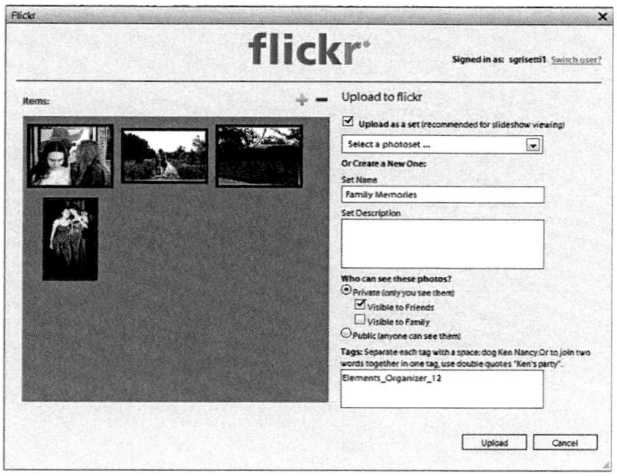

Share your photos on Twitter

When you select photos in your **Media Browser** and select the **Twitter** option under the **Share** tab, your photos will be prepared, then uploaded to your account at www.Twitter.com – much like the process described in **Share Your Videos and Photos to Facebook** on page 236.

The first time you use the tool, you will need to **Authorize** the upload, as described in **Share Your Videos and Photos to Facebook**.

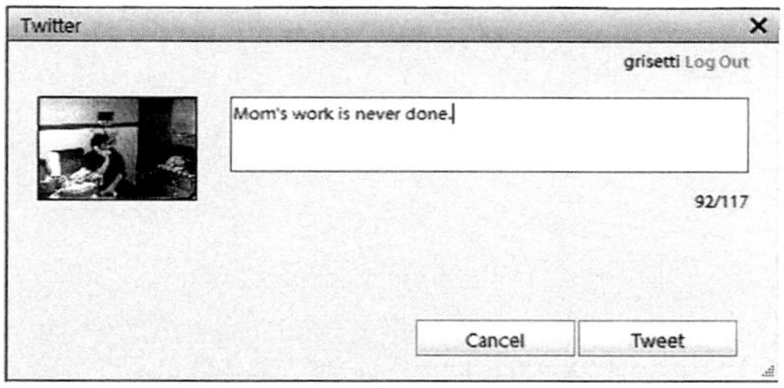

Share your photos in a SmugMug Gallery

A higher-end gallery for displaying your photos, SmugMug offers a wide variety of attractive and stylish templates for displaying your pictures. SmugMug offers their services at prices ranging from $39.95 to $149.95 per year.

When you select your photos in the **Media Browser** and then select the **SmugMug** option under the **Share** tab and follow the prompts, your photos will be displayed as an online slideshow – at a quality worthy of a professional portfolio.

Share your video on Vimeo

When you select a video in your **Media Browser** and select the **Vimeo** option under the **Share** tab, your video will be prepared, then uploaded to your account at www.vimeo.com – much like the process described in **Share Your Videos and Photos to Facebook** on page 236.

The first time you use this tool, you will be prompted to log in to Vimeo and **Authorize** the upload, as described in **Share Your Videos and Photos to Facebook**.

Share your video on YouTube

When you select a video in your **Media Browser** and select the **YouTube** option under the **Share** tab, your video will be prepared, then uploaded to your account at YouTube – much like the process described in **Share Your Videos and Photos to Facebook** on page 236.

Create an Elements Organizer Contact Book

In order to have the options to **Select Recipients** for your **E-mail Attachments,** you will need to have these potential recipients listed in your Elements Organizer's **Contact Book.**

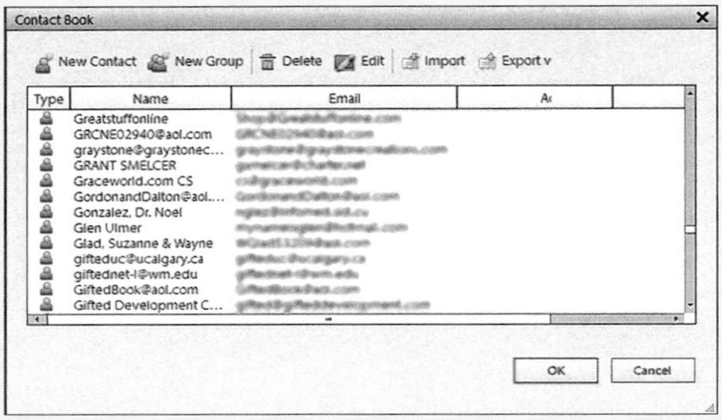

Before you can send out Photo Mail or an e-mail using Adobe's services, you'll need to build a Contact Book, an option available under the Organizer's Edit menu.

To create and add your contacts to this book, go to the **Edit** drop-down on the Organizer Menu Bar and select **Contact Book:**

- Click **New Contacts** to manually add your contacts' names and e-mail addresses.
- Or export your selected contacts from your e-mail program as a **Vcard**, or .vcf file, then click the **Import** button on the Organizer **Contact Book** panel.

Once they have been added to your **Contact Book, these names** will be listed under **Select Recipients** whenever you select the **E-mail Attachment** or **Photo Mail** option.

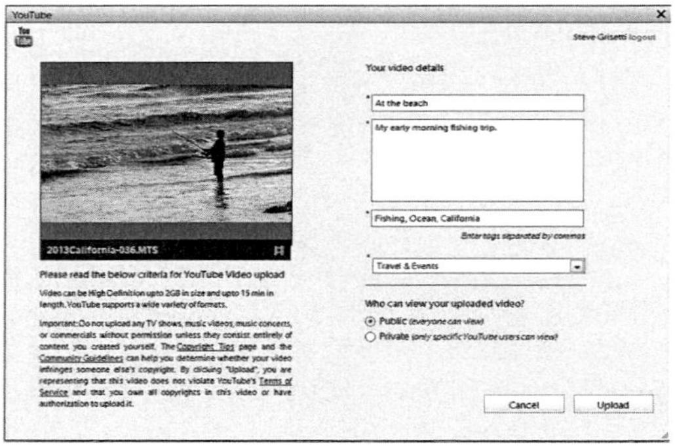

The first time you use the tool, you will be prompted to log in to YouTube and **Authorize** the upload, as described in **Share Your Videos and Photos to Facebook**.

Videos created in Premiere Elements can also be uploaded to YouTube using Premiere Elements' **Export & Share/Online** option described on page 266.

Burn a Video DVD or BluRay disc

When you click on the **Share** option to **Burn Video DVD/BluRay disc**, the program will launch Premiere Elements and the files you have selected in the Organizer's **Media Browser** will be ported to a Premier Elements project.

For information on creating menus for a DVD or BluRay disc in Premiere Elements, see **Chapter 20, Create Movie Menus**.

Share as a PDF Slide Show

Selecting the **PDF Slide Show** option under the **Share** tab creates a dynamic slideshow of the photo files you have selected in the **Media Browser** and outputs them in the PDF (Portable Document File) format, which it then e-mails to your selected recipients.

The slideshow can be viewed on any computer using the free utility Acrobat Reader.

Part V

Export & Share Your Videos

Adding Menu Markers

Selecting a Menu Template

Customizing Your Menu's Background and Music

Customizing Your Menu's Text

Adding Media to a Menu's "Drop Zone"

Chapter 20

Create Movie Menus

Authoring your DVDs and BluRay discs

Once you've finished your Premiere Elements video project, you'll want to share it in the most attractive package possible.

Premiere Elements includes over 70 templates for creating DVD and BluRay disc menus for your videos. And it includes tools for customizing them in a variety of ways!

Additional content

You may notice a little blue flag over the upper right corner of a number of Movie Menu templates.

This blue flag indicates that the template or theme is available but has not yet been installed on your computer. When you select this template or theme, the program will automatically download it for you from the Adobe site – a process that should only take a moment or two.

If you'd like to download all of these templates at once, right-click on any one and select the Download All option.

Although the DVD and BluRay menu authoring system in Premiere Elements isn't as advanced as it is in many standalone disc menu authoring programs, you can do a surprising amount to personalize your disc menus just by using Premiere Elements' library of disc menu templates and its fairly powerful menu customization features.

Once you've applied and customized your disc menus, you can then create a DVD, AVCHD or BluRay disc using the options under the **Export & Share** tab, as described in **Chapter 21, Export & Share Your Video Projects.**

Add Menu Markers to your movie project

The **Set Menu Marker** tool is a very important part of the DVD and BluRay disc authoring process in Premiere Elements.

The **Menu Markers** you place on your timeline will link to buttons on your disc's main menu and scene menu pages.

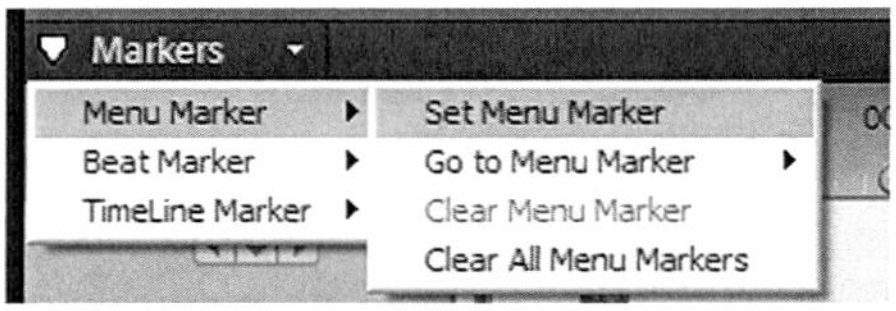

To create a **Menu Marker,** position the **CTI** (Current Time Indicator) on your timeline at the approximate position you'd like your marker to appear. (You don't have to be precise. You can drag the marker to a new position later.) Then click **Markers** at the top left of the timeline and, from the drop-down menu, select **Menu Marker**, then **Set Menu Marker**, as illustrated above.

When you select this option, a **Menu Marker** option panel will open. (You can reopen this panel at any time by **double-clicking** on an existing menu marker on your timeline.) This panel allows you to name your marker as well as determine the role the marker will play in your disc.

As indicated by the **Marker Type** drop-down menu (and detailed along the bottom of the panel), there are three different types of **Menu Markers:**

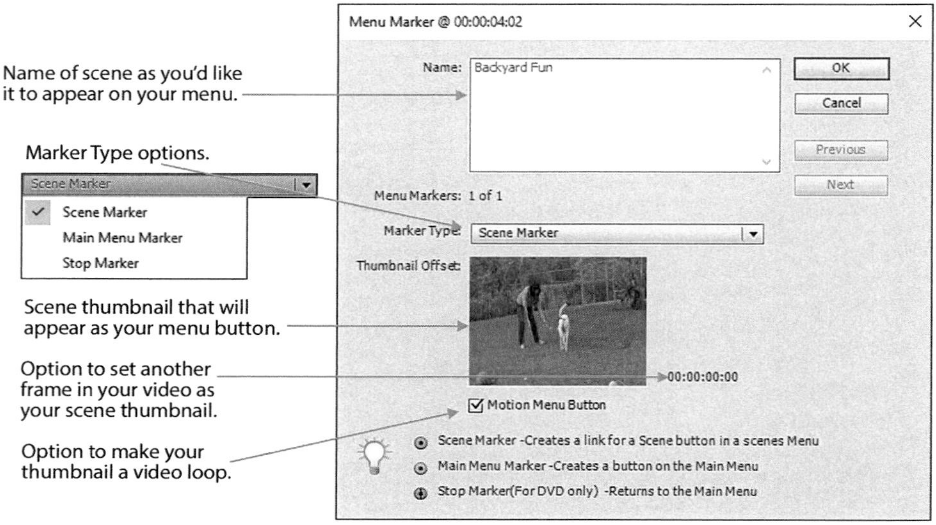

Green **Scene Menu Markers** will be linked to scene buttons on your DVD or BluRay disc's **Scene Menu** page(s).

Blue **Main Menu Markers** will be linked to scene buttons on your DVD or BluRay disc's **Main Menu** page(s).

Red **Stop Markers** stop your movie's playback and return your viewer to your disc's **Main Menu** page. By using these **Stop Markers**, you can create a disc with a number of short movies on it, your viewer returning to the main menu at the end of each.

1 Type a name for your marker in the space provided. This name will automatically appear as the name of the linked button on your disc's main or scene menu.

2 The image from your movie displayed in the **Thumbnail Offset** window is what will appear as your menu button thumbnail on your menu page.

   Changing the timecode that appears to the right of this thumbnail – either by typing in new numbers or by clicking and dragging across the numbers – will change which frame from your video is displayed as the button link. (Although changing this thumbnail image will *not* affect the location of the marker itself on your project's timeline.)

Clicking and dragging over the timecode for the Thumbnail Offset numbers changes the thumbnail image that is displayed for the Menu Marker on your disc menu without changing the marker's position.

3 Checking the **Motion Menu Button** checkbox will cause your button to appear as a short video loop rather than a freeze frame from your video.

For more information on how to create and use **Menu Markers**, see my *Steve's Tips* article "DVD Markers," available on the products page at Muvipix.com.

Add Menu Markers automatically

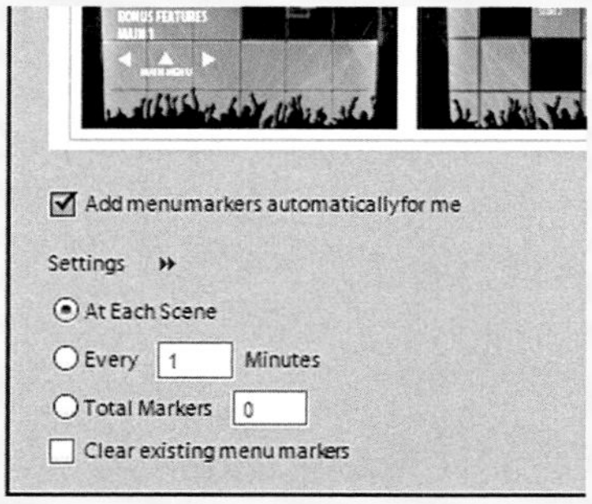

When you select the **Movie Menu** option on the **Tools** pop-up panel on the **Toolbar**, you'll find an additional option, in the lower left corner of the panel, for adding menu markers automatically to your timeline.

If you check this option and click **Settings**, you'll find options to:

- Add menu markers at each scene.
- Designate regular time intervals at which markers will be added; or
- Designate the total number of markers you'd like added to your movie and let the program set them at even paces throughout your movie.

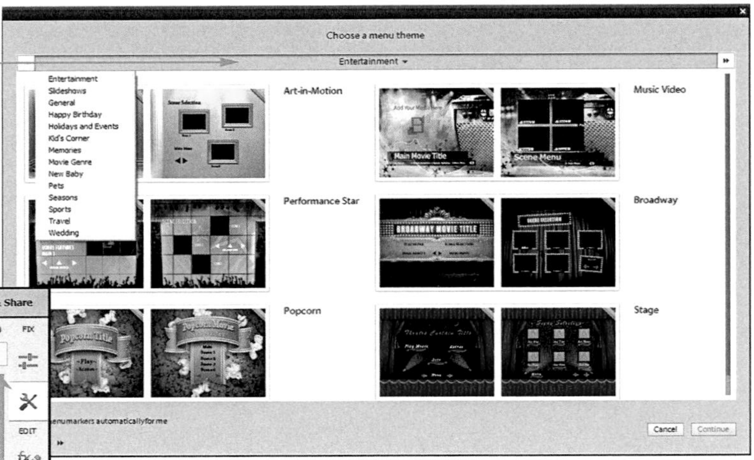

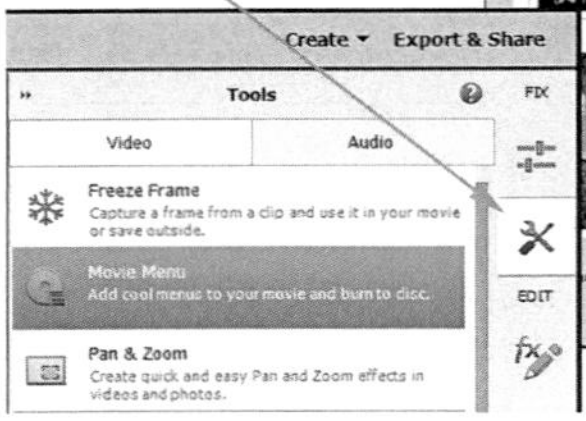

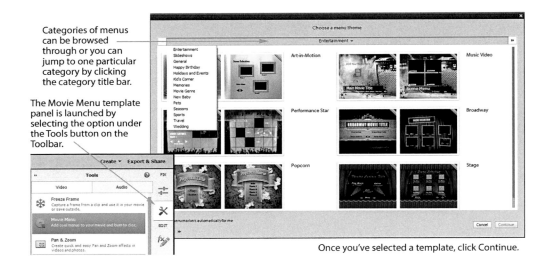

Categories of menus can be browsed through or you can jump to one particular category by clicking the category title bar.

The Movie Menu template panel is launched by selecting the option under the Tools button on the Toolbar.

Once you've selected a template, click Continue.

Add a Movie Menu

After you've added menu markers to your timeline, your next step is to apply a **Movie Menu** template to your movie.

Premiere Elements comes bundled with over 70 standard and hi-def disc templates, in 14 categories, ranging from Entertainment to Travel to Sports to Kids to Birthdays and Weddings – from playful to serious to silly to artistic.

Many of these templates come complete with audio and/or video background loops that add life to your menu pages. These animated templates are indicated with a little media icon on the upper right corner.

Also, many of these templates include a "drop zone," a designated area on the menu page into which you can place a video clip or still. (More about that on page 253.)

Apply a DVD or BluRay movie menu template

To add a Movie Menu template to your project:

1. Click the **Tools** button on the **Toolbar** along the right side of the interface and select **Movie Menus**.

   The **Movie Menus** templates option panel will open, as illustrated above.

2. Select a template.

   The templates are in 14 different categories. You can browse each category by clicking the forward and backward arrows on either side of the **Category** title bar at the top of the panel (which opens to "Entertainment"). Alternatively, you can click on the **Category** title bar and a pop-up menu will list all of the templates categories. Click to select the category you'd like to jump to.

   Once you've selected a template, click the **Continue** button at the lower right corner of the panel, as illustrated above.

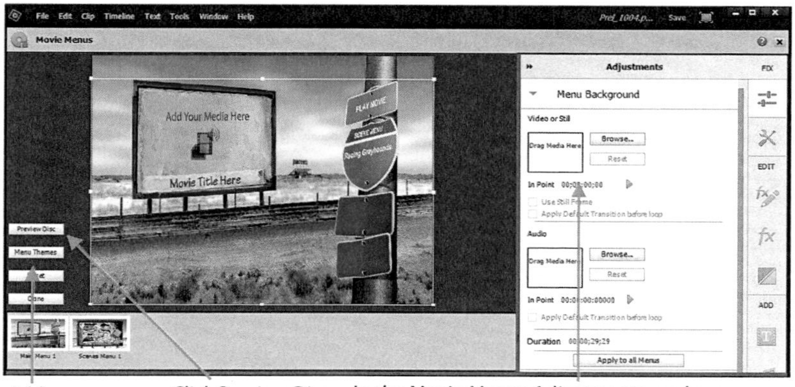

Add a different disc template.

Click Preview Disc to test drive your menus.

In the Movie Menus Adjustments workspace, you can customize the way your menu pages and scene buttons look and function.

The **Movie Menus Adjustments** workspace will open. The **Main Menu** page of your movie's disc menu will be displayed in the big **Movie Menus Layout** window, and thumbnails of each page of your **Main** and **Scene Menus** will appear along the bottom.

Your movie will always have a **Main Menu**. If you've added scene menu markers, it will also include a **Scene Menu**. The program will add as many extra pages as necessary to accommodate all of your scene and main menu markers.

Clicking on any of the thumbnail menu pages along the bottom of the preview window will bring that menu page up in the **Movie Menus Layout** window so that you can customize its individual elements.

As mentioned in **Add Menu Markers**, on page 246, the names you give to your main and scene menu markers will appear as the names of the scene menu links and main menu links on your disc menus. (To change these names, **double-click** on a scene button, as described at the bottom of page 251.)

To see your menu system in action and test drive the links embedded in it, click the **Preview Disc** button at the top right of the workspace.

An important note about **Preview Disc**: The purpose of the preview is to allow you to see a *representation* of how your menu elements will come together and to allow you to test the navigation buttons.

*It is not meant to be a representation of the **quality** of your final menu template.* And, in fact, you'll probably be a bit disappointed with the quality of the picture onscreen. **Preview** is merely an opportunity for you test your navigation buttons.

So don't panic. Once your project is rendered and encoded as a disc, the quality will be up to DVD or BluRay standards.

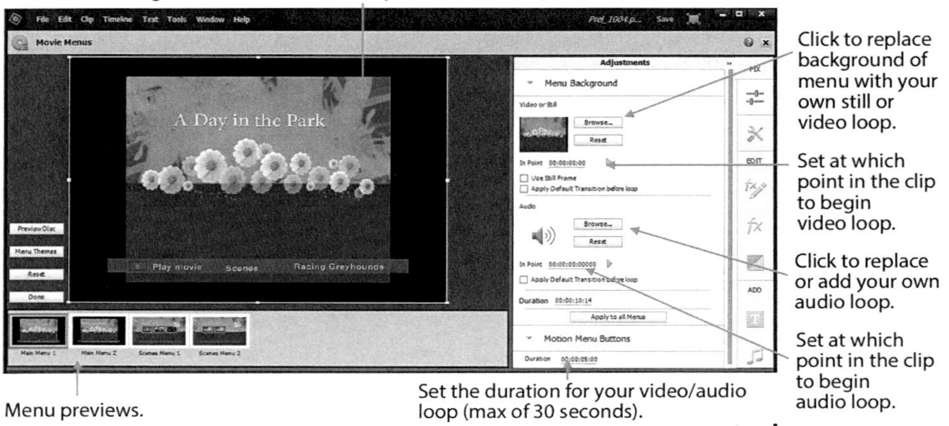
Click on the background in Movie Menus Layout window to open the background replacement options.
Movie Menus
A Day in the Park
Play movie
Scenes
Racing Greyhounds
Adjustments
Menu Background
Motion Menu Buttons
Click to replace background of menu with your own still or video loop.
Set at which point in the clip to begin video loop.
Click to replace or add your own audio loop.
Set at which point in the clip to begin audio loop.
Set the duration for your video/audio loop (max of 30 seconds).
Menu previews.

Customize your menus

Adobe has made it very easy to customize your menu pages right in this **Movie Menus** workspace. As a matter of fact, once you've applied a template, as described on the previous pages, the **Adjustments** panel will open to the right of the **Movie Menus Layout** panel and will display options for customizing your menu pages and scene buttons, as illustrated above.

Which customization options are available in this panel depends on which elements you have selected on the **Movie Menus Layout** window.

- **If you have the menu background selected** in the **Movie Menus Layout** panel, the **Adjustments** panel will display options for replacing the menu background with a still, video and/or audio clip, as discussed in **Customize a menu background** below.
- **If you have a block of text selected** in the **Movie Menus Layout** panel, the **Adjustments** panel will display options for customizing the text's font, style and color, as discussed on page 252.
- **If you have a menu button selected** in the **Movie Menus Layout** window that includes a thumbnail image, the **Adjustments** panel will display options for replacing or customizing the thumbnail image as well as options for customizing the accompanying text's font, style and color, as illustrated on page 252.

Customize a menu background

When you have the menu page background selected in the **Movie Menus Layou**t window, the **Adjustments** panel will display options for replacing the background with a still or video, and/or replacing or adding a music or audio clip, as illustrated above.

Some **Movie Menu** templates allow you to replace the entire background of the menu page. (The **Elegant** template, illustrated above, in the **Wedding** category is an example.)

If your template has a **Drop Zone** in it – indicated with an **Add Media Here** emblem – replacing the background will add your video or photo in a way that integrates it with the menu template, as discussed on page 253.

If you're using a video clip as your menu background:

- You can use the **In Point** timecode (either by dragging your mouse across the numbers or by playing to a particular point and then pausing) to set your video loop to begin at a specific point in the clip.
- You can set the **Duration** of the video loop for any length up to 30 seconds.

You can also add or swap in audio or music loops that play as your menus are displayed. Additionally, you can set the **In Point** for your audio clip such that the audio loop begins playing at any point in the song or clip.

To revert back to your menu's default background, music or sound, click on the corresponding **Reset** button.

Above is the same menu seen on the facing page, but with a new background image swapped in.

When a text block is selected in the Layout window, the Adjustment displays options for changing the font, style and text color. (Double-click on a text block to change its content.)

Customize your text

Double-click on a text block or menu button to edit or replace the text.

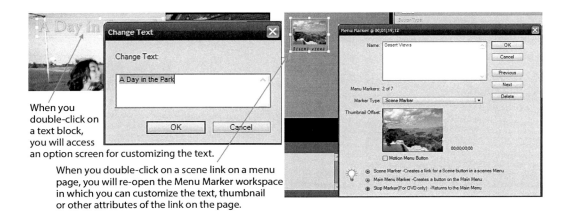

When you double-click on a text block, you will access an option screen for customizing the text.

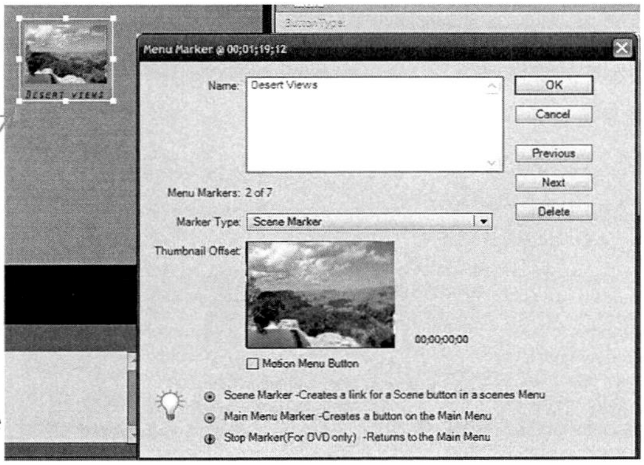

When you double-click on a scene link on a menu page, you will re-open the Menu Marker workspace in which you can customize the text, thumbnail or other attributes of the link on the page.

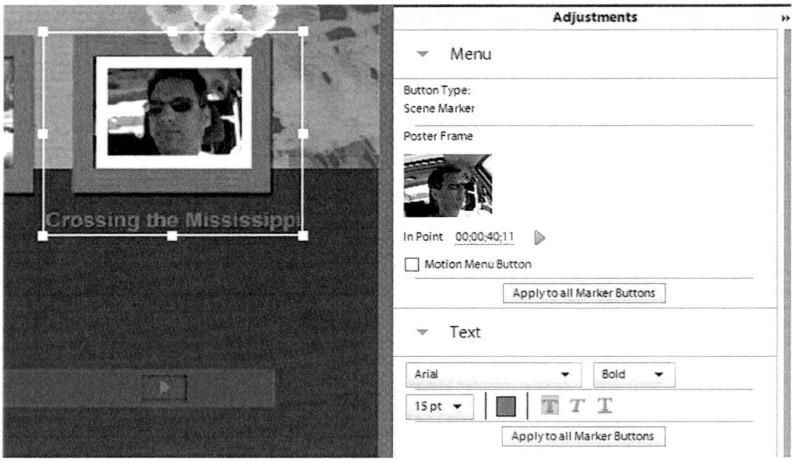

When a scene button or text block is selected, the Adjustments panel will display options for customizing the text font, style and color as well as for customizing the button thumbnail with a still or video loop (motion menu).

Customize your text styles

When you click to select a text block in the **Movie Menus Layout** window, the text customization workspace will display in the **Adjustments** panel.

Using this menu, you can change the font, font size and even color of the text.

The **Apply to All Text Items** button will apply your current font and text style to all of the text that appears on this menu page.

Once you've customized the look of your text, you can also customize its position on the menu page.

Click on the text block or button on the **Movie Menus Layout** window and drag it to where you'd like it to appear.

Two Main Menu pages customized from the same Movie Menu template.

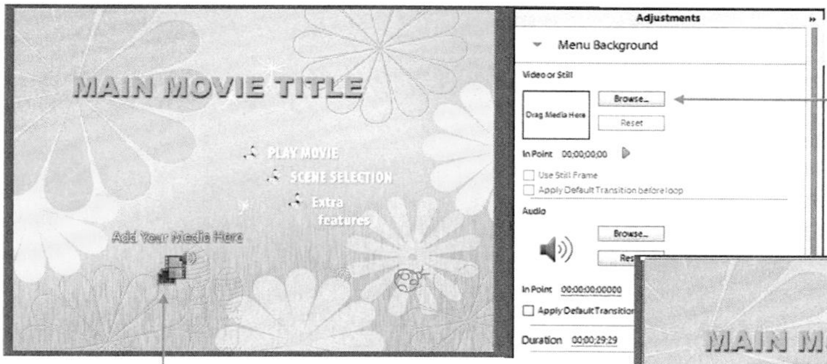

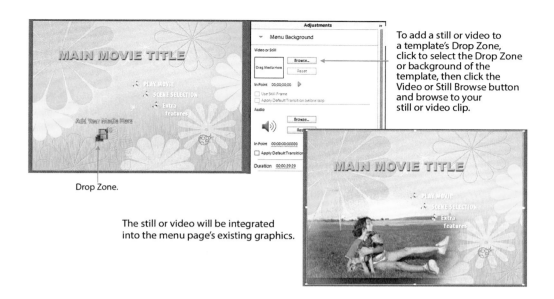

To add a still or video to a template's Drop Zone, click to select the Drop Zone or background of the template, then click the Video or Still Browse button and browse to your still or video clip.

Drop Zone.

The still or video will be integrated into the menu page's existing graphics.

Add a photo or video clip to a menu page "Drop Zone"

A number of **Movie Menu** templates include a "**Drop Zone**" – a designated area on the template into which you can place your own pictures or videos.

Templates that include **Drop Zones** (and most of them do) will be indicated with the **Add Media Here** graphic.

Adding a still or video file to a **Drop Zone** is essentially the same process as replacing a menu background with a still or video: You select the **Drop Zone** or background in the **Movie Menu** Layout window and then click the **Video or Still Replace** button on the **Adjustments** panel and browse to your clip.

The difference is that, rather than replacing the entire background, your photo or video will be integrated into the existing design of the menu page's graphics, as illustrated above.

A number of templates (the **Entertainment** category's **Art-in-Motion**, and the **Memories** category's **Yearbook** and **Family Memories**, for instance) will drop your still or photos into an existing design so that it appears to be a painting on the wall or a photo in a photo album.

Overlapping scene buttons

If, in the process of arranging your scene buttons on your menu (or, occasionally, if you've added lots of text), your buttons display with a red frame around them, this is an indication that you have two buttons sharing the same space or overlapping.

If you move the buttons apart (or even resize the buttons by dragging in on their corner handles), the red frames should disappear.

Overlapping buttons are not a big deal, if you're playing your disc on a DVD or BluRay player. The player reads each button individually. But, if you play your disc on a computer, overlapping buttons can make it difficult to select one button or the other since their hyperlinks share the same space. Because of this, **the program will not let you create a DVD, AVCHD or BluRay disc if any scene buttons are overlapping.**

Sharing Your Movie as a Computer File

Sharing Your Movie to a Portable Device

Sharing to a DVD or BluRay Disc

Sharing Your Movie Online

Chapter 21

Export & Share Your Video Projects

Outputting from Premiere Elements 15

Once you've finished your video masterpiece, you're ready to output your video and share it with the world.

There are many ways to output from Premiere Elements, and a surprisingly large number of formats you can output to.

The **Export & Share** panel in Premiere Elements 15 is designed to be intuitive and workflow-based.

You choose the destination and the format, and Premiere Elements will provide you the most optimized video file.

The **Export & Share** categories include:

Quick Export – A quick, general-purpose video output.

Devices – Share your finished video as a computer file or as an optimized file for viewing on a TV or mobile device (as discussed on page 260). This destination also saves video that can be used in another project or which can be ported to a third-party DVD or BluRay authoring program like Adobe Encore or Sony DVD Architect (see the sidebar on page 262).

Disc – Burn DVD, BluRay and AVCHD discs (as discussed on page 255).

Online – Upload your video to Facebook, Vimeo or YouTube (as discussed on pages 266).

Audio – Output the audio only from your movie. Output options are available in standard Windows format (WAV), Mac format (AIFF) and compressed AACs and MP3s.

Image – Output a frame of your video as a picture file (as discussed on page 268).

The **Devices/Computer** category of outputs also includes options for creating your own custom output presets.

The Quick Reference chart on page 270 shows you the best output settings to use for a number of common situations.

Quick Export

Although Premiere Elements offers you options to create specific video formats, optimized for specific situations, sometimes you just want to output a quick, simple, general-purpose movie.

The **Quick Export** share option creates a video that you can display on your computer, watch on a mobile device or upload to a website like YouTube, Vimeo or Facebook. In a pinch, you can even use it as source video in another video project.

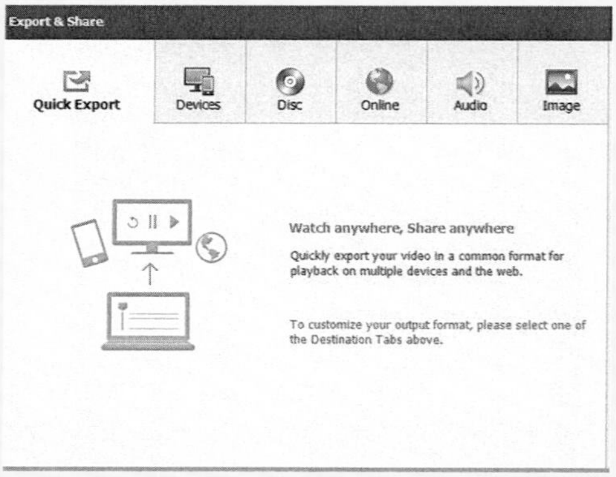

The video produced by **Quick Export** is a 1280x720 24 progressive frames per second MP4 with an 8 Kbps variable bit rate and compressed AAC audio. Although not optimized for every situation, these specs produce a nice-looking, compact, general purpose movie.

Scroll to see all Resolution options.

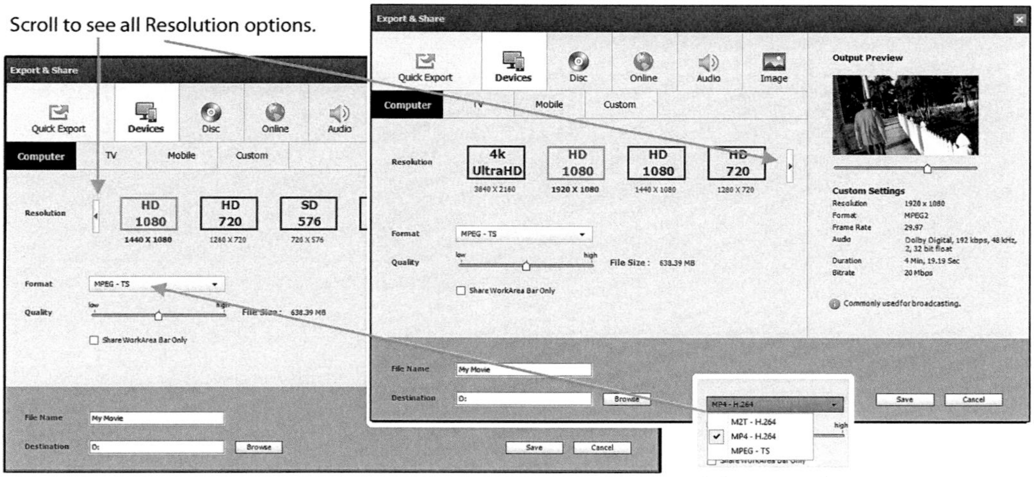

Select option to output Work Area Only.

Select export format.

Output your movie for playback on a computer, for posting online or for use in another project

The **Export & Share** to **Devices/Computer** category is far and away the most powerful category of output options. In this category you'll find options for saving your videos to your computer and for creating optimized files for TV players and mobile devices. Selecting the proper output is as easy as just selecting your destination or device and the resolution you want your video file to be.

Export & Share a computer file

Under **Export & Share/Devices/Computer**, you'll find the greatest number of movie output options.

Files output to **Computer** can, of course, be played on your computer's media player – but they can also be used as source media in another editing project.

This is where you'll find the option to output a standard definition **DV-AVI** (full quality video) file (on PCs) and **DV-MOV** (on Macs), as explained in **Output video to be used in another video project** on page 259. This is also where you'll find the option to output **4K UHD** (Ultra High Definition XAVC-S), a format with four times the resolution of high-definition TV (3840x2160 pixels). (As illustrated above, you may need to use the left and right arrows to scroll through all of the output **Resolutions** available.)

Some **Resolutions** can output to more than one format. **HD 1080** (1920x1080) for instance, can be output as an M2T, MOV, MP4 or MPEG-TS file.

The chart on page 258 indicates the best use for each output, resolution and format. A discussion of each video format can be found on page 270.

Computer Output Formats		
4K UltraHD 3840x2160	**MP4-XAVC**	3840x2160 30p fps ultra high-definition video, ideal for UHD display or uploading to video sharing sites like YouTube.
HD 1080 1920x1080	**M2T-H.264**	Ideal format for saving video for use in a 1920x1080 24p fps AVCHD project or for outputting video for a BluRay disc authoring project in a program like Adobe Encore or Sony DVD Architect.
	MOV-H.264	Ideal QuickTime 1920x1080 24p fps video for Mac playback and uploading to sites like YouTube or Vimeo.
	MP4-H.264	Ideal MP4 1920x1080 24p fps video for uploading to sites like YouTube.
	MPEG-TS	1920x1080 24p fps high-definition saved in MPEG format.
HD 1080 1440x1080	**M2T-H.264**	Ideal format for saving video for use in a 1440x1080 (non-square pixels) AVCHD project.
	MP4-H.264	Ideal 1440x1080 24p fps (non-square pixels) video for uploading to sites like YouTube or Vimeo.
	MPEG-TS	1440x1080 24p fps (non-square pixels) high-definition saved in MPEG format.
HD 720 1280x720	**M2T-H.264**	1280x720 24p fps video, ideal for uploading to video sharing sites like YouTube.
	MOV-H.264	1280x720 24p fps QuickTime video, ideal for Mac playback or uploading to video sharing sites like YouTube or Vimeo.
	MP4-H.264	1280x720 24p video, ideal for uploading to video sharing sites like YouTube or Vimeo.
	MPEG-PS	1280x720 24p fps video, a good format for using in a 1280x720 video project.
SD 576 720x576	**AVI-DV**	The PC-based PAL format for standard definition TV. Ideal for use in a PAL standard def 4:3 video project.
	MOV-DV	The Mac version of the PAL format for standard 16:9 definition TV. Virtually identical to the AVI-DV and, for the most part, can be used interchangeably with DV-AVIs in a Premiere Elements project.
	MP4-H.264	25p fps optimized for 720x576 onscreen or online viewing.
	MPEG-PS	Ideal format for outputting 16:9 widescreen video to be used in a PAL DVD authoring project in a program like Adobe Encore or Sony DVD Architect.
	WMV-VC1	Standard definition PAL file in the Windows Media format. (Not available on a Mac.)
SD 480 720x480	**AVI-DV**	The PC-based NTSC format for standard definition TV. Ideal for use in a NTSC standard def 4:3 video project.
	MOV-DV	The Mac version of the NTSC format for standard definition 16:9 TV. Virtually identical to the AVI-DV and, for the most part, can be used interchangeably in Premiere Elements project.
	MP4-H.264	30p fps optimized for 720x480 onscreen or online viewing.
	MPEG-PS	Ideal format for outputting 16:9 widescreen video to be used in a NTSC DVD authoring project in a program like Adobe Encore or Sony DVD Architect.
	WMV-VC1	Standard definition NTSC file in the Windows Media format. (Not available on a Mac.)

Some HD formats are available to output as 1920x1080 or 1440x1080. 1440x1080 is an older high-definition format that uses non-square pixels (see page 268) while the more standard 1920x1080 uses square pixels. The video in either pixel format is virtually identical – both produce high-definition 16:9 video frames. But, for the most part, 1440x1080 is considered somewhat obsolete (relatively speaking) while 1920x1080 is considered the current HD standard.

To export only a segment of your project, indicate that segment with the **Work Area Bar** and check the **Share Work Area Bar Only** option. (For more information, see **Output a segment of your video using the Work Area Bar** on page 77 of **Chapter 7, Edit Your Video in Expert View**.)

Output your video for use in another video project

Working on a long project in short pieces

You'll often find a longer project much easier to work on if you work on it in shorter pieces. Doing this can minimize system lugging and maximize program responsiveness as well as reduce the likelihood that you'll run into problems when you try to output your finished movie. Once each segment is finished and output, open a new project and combine the segments into a final mix.

In order to do this with minimal loss of quality and maximum performance, you'll want to output each segment in its ideal video format – a format that the program is designed to work with natively and won't have to re-render. Instructions for outputting each of these ideal video formats is found below.

For standard definition video

If you'd like to export your video project – or even a portion of your project – so that you can use the output video as media in a standard definition Premiere Elements video project on a Windows computer, use **Export & Share/Computer/SD 480** (or SD 576 for PAL) in the **AVI-DV** format. The file you output will have an **.avi** suffix.

The Macintosh equivalent to the **DV-AVI** file is the **DV-MOV**. To output a **DV-MOV** file from your project, use **Export & Share/Computer/SD 480** (or SD 576 for PAL) in the **MOV-DV** format. The file you output will have a **.mov** suffix.

For high-definition video

If you'd like to export your video project – or a portion of your project – from an HDV (tape-based high-definition) project for use as media in another HDV project, use **Export & Share/Devices/Computer/HD 1920x1080** in the **MPEG-TS** format.

If you're working on a 1920x1080 AVCHD project, output your video using **Export & Share/Devices/Computer/HD 1920x1080** in the **M2T-H.264** format.

Both forms of high-definition video will output with the **.m2t** suffix.

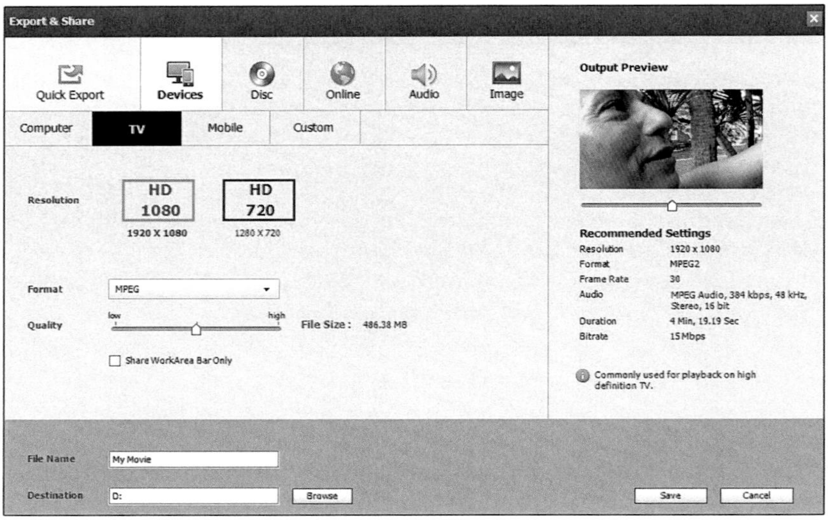

Output your movie for playback on a TV

The outputs available under **Export & Share/Devices/TV** are optimized for playback on an HDTV.

This video is saved in the MPEG format, and the outputs can also be used as source media if you are porting your video over to a BluRay authoring program like Adobe Encore or Sony DVD Architect.

TV Output Formats		
4K UltraHD	MP4	3840x2160 24p fps video optimized for viewing on a 4K UltraHD TV.
HD 1080 1920x1080	MP4	1920x1080 24p MP4 for viewing on HDTV.
	MPEG	1920x1080 24p MPEG video optimized for playing on an HDTV or outputting for BluRay disc authoring.
HD 720	MP4	1280x720 24p MP4 for viewing on HDTV.
	MPEG	1280x720 24p MPEG for viewing on HDTV.

To export only a segment of your project, indicate that segment with the **Work Area Bar** and check the **Share Work Area Bar Only** option. (For more information, see **Output a segment of your video using the Work Area Bar** on page 77 of **Chapter 7, Edit Your Video in Expert View**.)

Output your movie for a mobile phone or portable device

The outputs available under **Export & Share/Devices/Mobile** are optimized for playback on smartphones and other portable devices – from iPods, iPads and iPhones to Android phones and tablets.

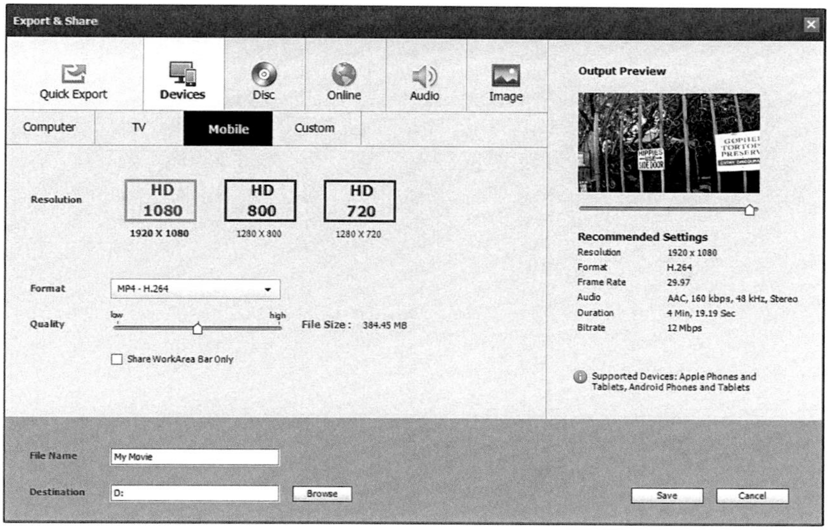

This video is saved in the H.264 (MP4) format, a high-quality compressed video format that is playable on virtually any portable device, smartphone or tablet.

Mobile Output Formats		
HD 1080 1920x1080	MP4-H.264	1920x1080 24p fps format optimized for smartphones and mobile devices.
HD 800 1280x800	MP4-H.264	1280x800 24p fps format optimized for smartphones and mobile devices. Unlike most HD formats, this outputs 4:3 rather than 16:9 widescreen video.
HD 720 1280x720	MP4-H.264	1280x720 24p fps format optimized for smartphones and mobile devices.

To export only a segment of your project, indicate that segment with the **Work Area Bar** and check the **Share Work Area Bar Only** option. (For more information, see **Output a segment of your video using the Work Area Bar** on page 77 of **Chapter 7, Edit Your Video in Expert View.**)

Create a custom output preset

If none of the standard video formats or codecs meets your needs, Premiere Elements offers you the option of creating your own custom output preset under **Export & Share/Devices/Custom.**

When you click the **Advanced Settings** button on this panel, you'll access a panel from which you can choose any of a dozen video, three still photo or four audio **Formats** in a wide variety of codecs (including an uncompressed video file and an animated gif).

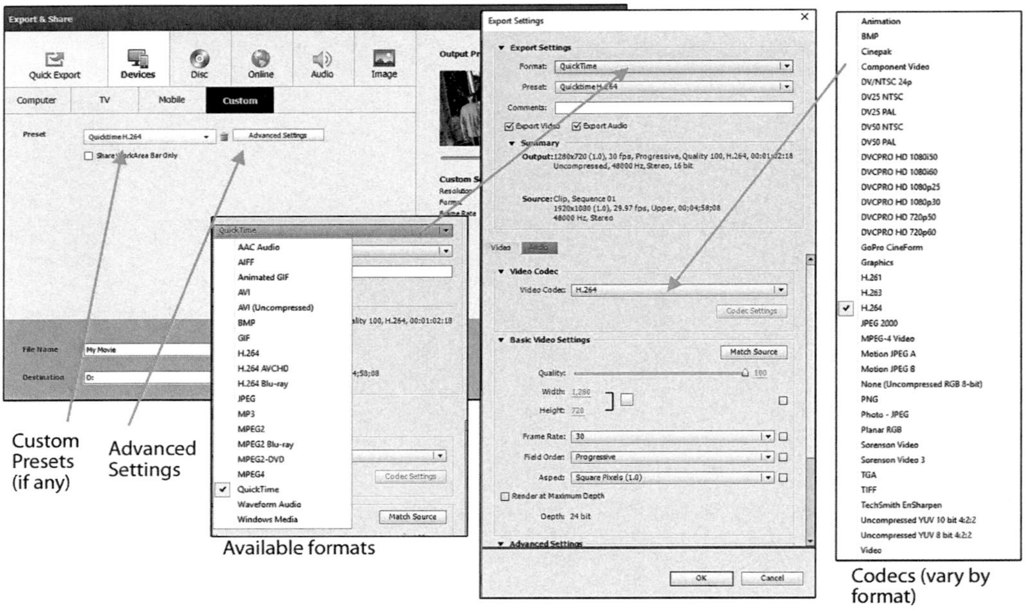

You'll also find options for setting your own resolution, quality level and bitrate and frame rate as well as if this frame rate is interlaced or progressive.

The **Match Source** button will create an output that matches the specs of your original video.

Once you've set up your preset and you click **OK**, you'll be prompted to name your preset. This preset will then be available for any future project.

Output your video for use in a third-party disc authoring program

Premiere Elements is designed to be a total package video editor, taking you all the way from capturing your video to outputting a finished DVD or BluRay disc, complete with menus and scene markers.

But some find the disc authoring tools in Premiere elements a bit limiting. And if you count yourselves among those, you can still use Premiere Elements to edit your videos – and then use a third-party disc authoring program like Adobe Encore or Sony DVD Architect to create your menus and discs.

As indicated in the chart on page 258, to output the ideal of video for these programs, use the following **Export & Share** options:

For a DVD project, use **Export & Share/Devices/Computer/SD 480** (or SD 576 for PAL) and the MPEG-PS format with the **Quality** slider pushed all the way to High.

For a BluRay project, use **Export & Share/Devices/Computer/HD 1080** (1920x1080) and the M2T-H.264 format with the **Quality** slider pushed all the way to High.

Burn your movie to a DVD or BluRay Disc

One of the most popular ways to share movies from your Premiere Elements projects is to burn them as a DVDs or high-definition BluRay discs.

Premiere Elements will burn to both single-layer and dual-layer discs and to both DVD and BluRay formats. (The program automatically scans your system to see which disc burner hardware you have and if you have a disc in the drive.)

Disc Output Formats		
DVD	SD 576	Burns your video as a standard definition disc in the PAL format.
	SD 480	Burns your video as a standard definition disc in the NTSC format.
Blu-Ray	HD 1080 1920x1080	Burns your video as a high-definition BluRay disc in standard 1920x1080 HD.
	HD 1080 1440x1080	Burns your video as a high-definition disc in less standard 1440x1080 HD.
AVCHD	HD 1080 1920x1080	Burns your video as a high-definition disc in standard 1920x1080 HD.
	HD 1080 1440x1080	Burns your video as a high-definition disc in less standard 1440x1080 HD.

DVDs are standard definition video discs and can be played in both DVD and BluRay disc players. As a rule of thumb, you can fit about 70 minutes of full-quality video onto a standard (4.7 gigabyte) DVD at full video quality and about double that on a dual layer disc.

BluRays are high definition video discs that can only be played in BluRay disc players. A BluRay disc (which can store 25 gigabytes of data) can hold about two hours of high-definition video, while a dual-layer BluRay disc can hold about twice that.

AVCHD discs are essentially BluRay video files burned to a DVD disc. Since BluRay discs cost a bit more than DVDs, this can save you some money – although the storage capacity of a DVD limits you to about 20-30 minutes of high-def video.

Note that AVCHD discs, despite using DVD disc media, can *not* be played in DVD players! Since their data is essentially BluRay, AVCHD discs can only be played in BluRay disc players.

If you put more than these recommended capacities on a disc, Premiere Elements will automatically reduce the quality of the video as needed if you have the **Fit Contents** option checked. (This reduced quality may not be noticeable unless you try to squeeze considerably more content onto the disc than the optimal capacity.)

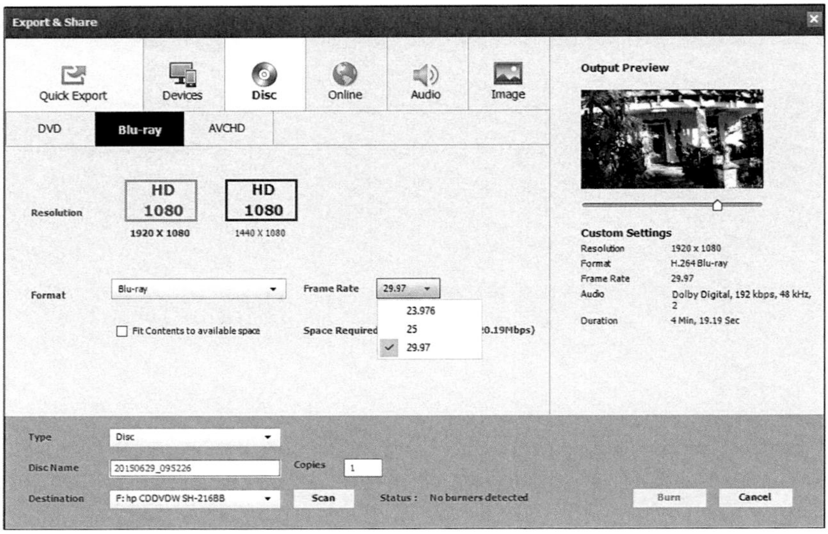

1 Under the **Export & Share** tab, select **Disc.** On the **Disc** option screen, select the type of disc you want to burn.

2 Although DVDs can only be output from Premiere Elements at standard interlaced frame rates, BluRays and AVCHD discs can be set to output video at either NTSC (29.97), PAL (25) or 23.976 frames rates. Many people feel that the 23.976 (24p) frame rate provides a much more cinematic viewing experience.

Disc files saved as an **ISO file** can be archived to your hard drive. A third-party program like ImgBurn (a free download) or your operating system's disk utilities can then be used to output copies of your DVD or BluRay from this image file as needed, as discussed on page 277.

3 Click the **Burn** button.

The challenge with home-burned DVDs and BluRays

Although this is becoming less of an issue as home-burned DVDs and BluRay discs have grown in popularity, it's important to realize that not all DVD and BluRay players can play home-burned discs. This is because the process used to create commercial discs (pressing) is very different than the process you use to create discs on your computer (a chemical process).

Manufacturers have recognized the growing popularity of home-burned DVDs and BluRay discs and have been making their players more and more compatible with them. But be prepared for the occasional friend or client who simply can't play a disc you've created!

Burn your disc files to an ISO image file

In addition to giving you the ability to burn your video directly to a disc, Premiere Elements also gives you option of saving your disc files as an ISO image file. An ISO file is a package that includes all of the video and menus for your DVD or BluRay disc in a single file.

To access this option, open the **Type** drop-down menu for your DVD, BluRay or AVCHD.

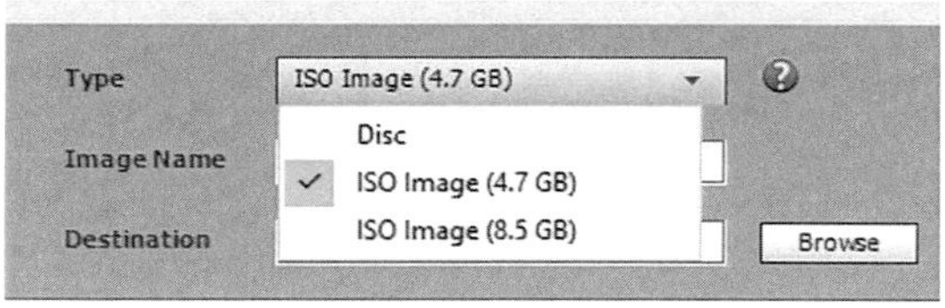

Set **Destination** to the location you'd like your files saved in.

The folder you save your ISO file to should have no other files in it.

Once a DVD or BluRay image file has been created, you can use your computer's disc burning software (Nero, ImgBurn, etc.) or your computer's disk utilities to burn a DVD or BluRay disc from this ISO file.

We show you how to do this in **Burn a DVD or BluRay disc from an image file** on page 277 of the **Appendix**.

Why save your disc files as an ISO?

At first, the idea of burning your DVD, BluRay or AVCHD disc to a file on your computer rather than directly to a disc may seem like an unnecessary workaround. After all, if you're eventually going to burn these files to a disc, doesn't burning them to a file just take more time and add extra steps to the process?

But there are a couple of advantages to burning your files to your hard drive:

Burning your DVD, BluRay or AVCHD disc files to a file on your computer archives your finished disc. In other words, it saves a library of your work. Disc files are relatively small compared to raw footage and, should you need to grab footage from one of your finished projects, it will be readily available on your hard drive.

It makes outputting several copies of your discs very easy. The least preferred way to make several copies of a DVD or BluRay disc is to burn one master and then make several copies of it. It usually works okay, since it's a digital copy – but it's a sketchy way of doing things. Like typing onto carbon paper.

When you've stored your disc files on your computer's hard drive, on the other hand, every disc you output from your **ISO** is essentially an *original*!

It can save you a world of heartache. The process of burning a DVD or BluRay directly to a disc sometimes fails. And the point at which is most often fails is during the during disc burn. In other words, if something goes wrong at the point the computer is transferring your transcoded files from the temp storage to your disc, you lose everything. Saving your DVD, BluRay or AVCHD disc files to your hard drive dodges that risk. You know your disc files are safe and complete. All that's left to do is write them to a disc.

By the way, the process of saving your files to your computer and then writing them to a disc takes virtually no more time than burning your Premiere Elements project directly to a disc. So there's no cost whatsoever.

Which is why writing your DVD, BluRay and AVCHD disc files to your hard drive rather than burning directly to a disc is pretty much standard operating procedure for most video editors I know.

Labeling discs

At Muvipix, we recommend that you *never* stick a label onto your DVD or BluRay disc.

Labels can throw the spin and balance off when the discs are loaded into a player and the glue and label can damage the media itself. If you'd like to customize your discs, we recommend that you buy printable discs and use a good inkjet printer with disc printing capabilities. Epson and HP make very nice printers with this feature for under $100.

Upload your video to Facebook, Vimeo or YouTube

To upload your video to directly to a social media site:

1 On the **Export & Share** tab, select **Online**, then select the site you'd like to upload your video to.

2 Select a resolution and quality.

In most cases, you'll probably want to select the highest resolution available. For Facebook and Vimeo, this will be 1280x720. Files destined for YouTube can be as large as 1920x1080.

Likewise, in most cases you'll choose the **High** quality option. However, particularly if you've got a longer movie, reducing the quality to Standard can reduce your upload time.

3 Click the **Begin Share** button.

If this is the first time uploading to Facebook, Vimeo or YouTube from the program, an option screen will ask you to **Authorize** the upload.

Click the **Authorize** button. Your web browser will open to the Facebook, Vimeo or YouTube authorization page.

If you are already logged into the site, you're done with the authorization. You can close your web browser and return to the program to finish the authorization.

Otherwise, log in to the site and, when prompted, close your browser and return to Premiere Elements.

4 Give your video a title and description. If you are uploading to Vimeo YouTube, you will also have the option of adding search word tags.

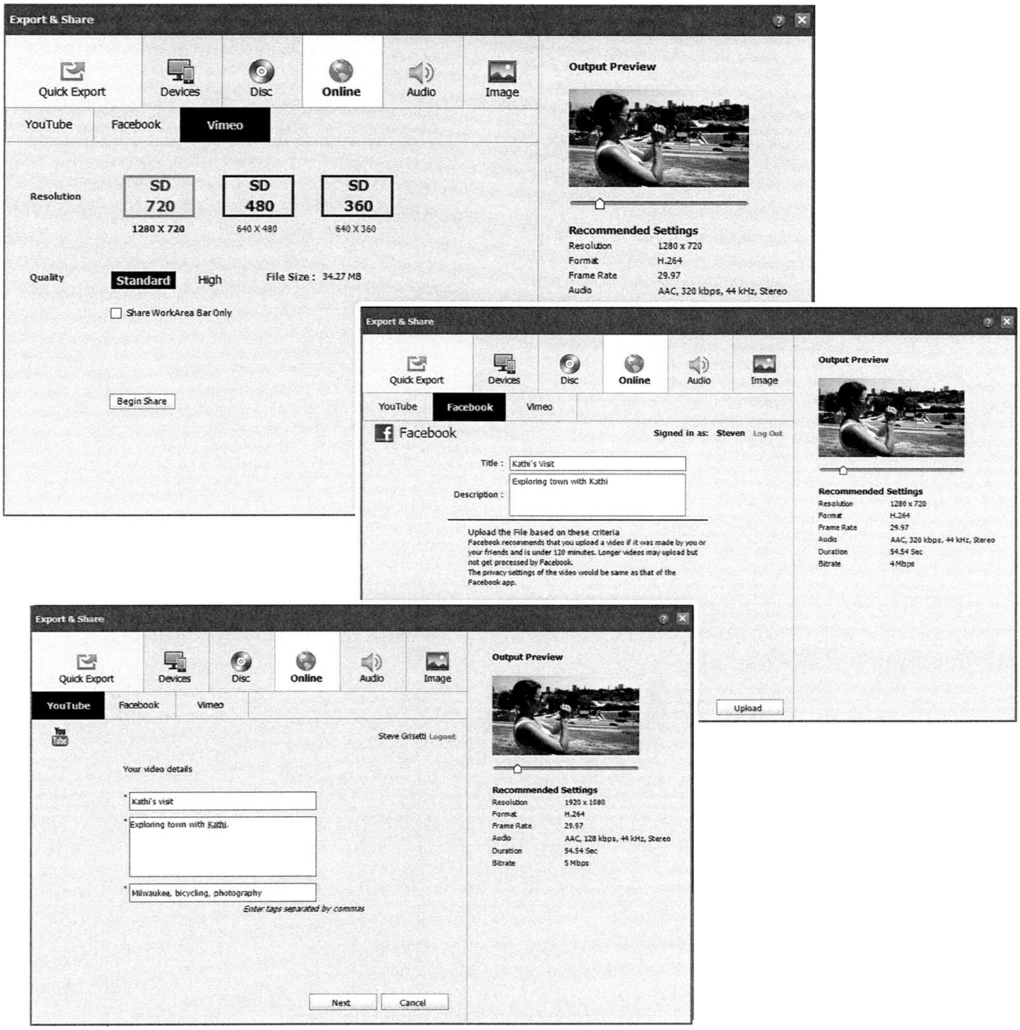

5 If you are uploading your video to Vimeo or YouTube, click **Next** and then select a category for your video and set whether it is for public or private viewing.

Click **Upload.** Your video will be rendered and uploaded to the site.

What if uploading directly to YouTube, Vimeo or Facebook doesn't work?

There are a number of reasons this can happen, including (and most commonly) because the web site has changed something at their end. But, regardless, it's no big deal. You can still just output your video from Premiere Elements as an MP4 and then use the site's tools to upload the video manually.

To output a high-definition video for uploading to YouTube, Vimeo or Facebook, use **Export & Share/Device/Computer 1920x1080** with the **Format** set to **MP4-H.264**, as we show in the chart on page 271.

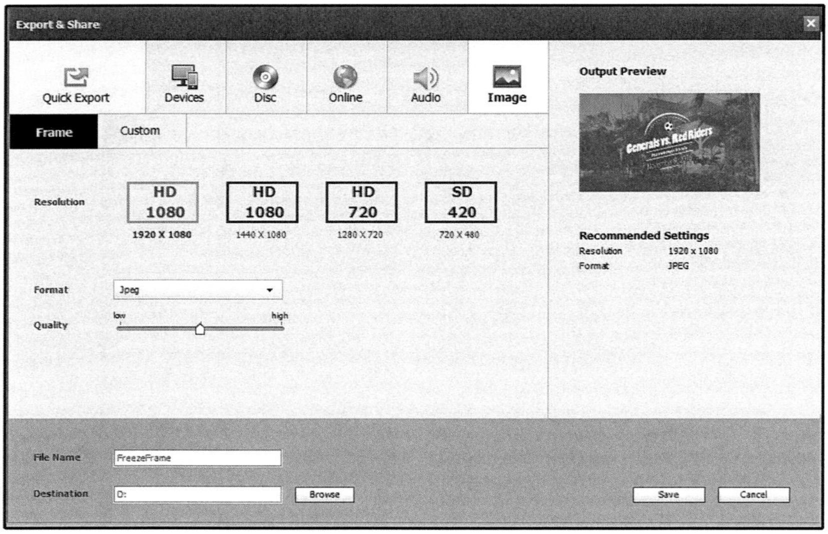

Output a still image of your current video frame

The **Export & Share/Image** screen give you the option to output **a frame of** your video as a **JPEG Image**. This **Image** can be saved as high-definition 1920x1080, 1440x1080 or 1280x720 or as standard definition 720x480.

The **JPEG** output option here makes this a great alternative to the **Freeze Frame** option available in the program's **Tools** (discussed on page 100 of **Chapter 9, Use the Premiere Elements Toolkit**) since this tool includes more options for customizing the settings of your output.

The 1920x1080 and 1280x720 resolutions create still photos with square pixels from your high-definition videos. The 1440x1080 and 720x480 resolutions will produce still photos with non-square pixels, which can look a bit oddly stretched in some applications. We show you how to create your own custom 640x480 square pixel preset for outputting still photos from 4:3 standard definition video in the sidebar on the facing page.

Non-square pixels

Pixels are the tiny blocks of color that make up your digital photos and video.

For reasons that date back to the early days of television, the vast majority of television video is made up of **non-square pixels**. This is true for PAL as well as NTSC video.

In standard NTSC video, these pixels are approximately 90% as wide as they are tall. Thus a 720x480 pixel video image becomes a 4:3 aspect ratio video (the equivalent of a 640x480 *square-pixel* video). A widescreen video is made up of the *same number of pixels* – however, because these pixels are 120% as wide as they are tall, a 720x480 pixel widescreen video has a 16:9 aspect ratio.

Some high-definition camcorders shoot their video in 1440x1080 *non-square* pixels. This produces exactly the same size video as a camera that shoots in 1920x1080 *square* pixels.

Create a custom JPEG output preset

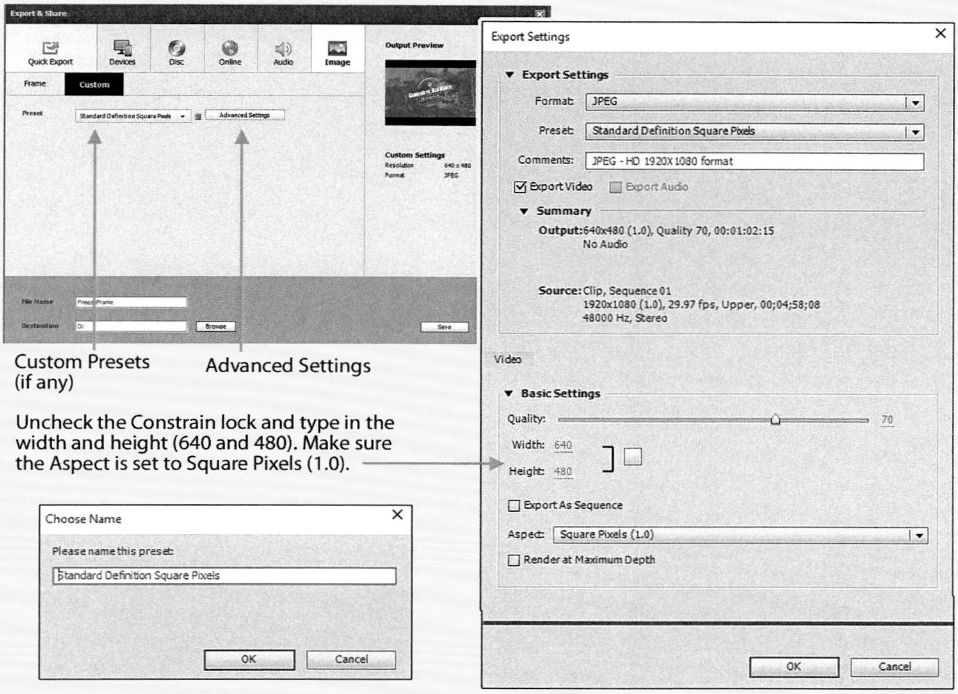

The **Image** output presets included with Premiere Elements are designed to produce a still photo that can be used in a video. Because of this, the standard definition options (**JPEG - NTSC SD** and **JPEG - PAL SD**) will produce a still that is composed of anamorphic – or *non-square* – video pixels. This means that, if you use one of these stills on a Website or in a print project, your photo will be oddly distorted.

For this reason, we recommend that, in addition to the pre-loaded presets, you create an additional, *square pixel* output preset for your general-purpose JPEG frame grabs.

1. Go to the **Export & Share** tab and select the **Image** destination option.

   Select the **Custom** tab.

2. Click the **Advanced Settings** button.

   The **Export Settings** panel will open.

3. On the **Export Settings** options panel, under the **Video** tab, set the **Aspect** drop-down to **Square Pixels (1.0)**.

   Click the chain link button to turn off **Constrain Proportions** and then set the **Width** to 640 and the **Height** to 480. (For widescreen video, use a **Width** of 854.)

   Click **OK**.

4. In the **Choose Name** screen, type the name "**Square Pixels**," then click **OK** to save it.

This **Square Pixels** option will now be available on the **Presets** drop-down menu whenever you use **Export & Share** to create a JPEG still of your current video frame.

Video output formats

The majority of video output formats available under **Export & Share** tab are either **AVI**s (Windows only), **MPEG**s, **WMV**s (Windows Media Video – available on Windows computers only) **MOV**s (QuickTime video – including **DV-MOV** files), **MP4**s and UltraHD **4K XAVC**s. You'll find at least one of these options offered under nearly each of the **Export & Share** output destinations.

Here is a brief discussion of each major format and its best use:

AVIs and DV-AVIs. At one time the ideal video format for editing on a personal computer, **DV-AVIs** – the format produced when standard definition video is captured from a miniDV camcorder – are still the easiest format to edit with both the Windows and Mac versions of Premiere Elements. Although affordable high-definition camcorders have pretty much made this format obsolete, it can still be found in many standard definition workflows, including DVD production. To output a **DV-AVI** from your project, select **Export & Share/Device/Computer/SD 480** (or **SD 576** for PAL video) with the **Format** set to **AVI-DV**. (This option is not available in the Macintosh version of Premiere Elements. However, the **DV-MOV**, discussed below, is virtually identical.)

Although the **DV-AVI** is the most common **AVI** video for digital video editing, the **AVI** format is actually just an envelope, a package through which video files are delivered. **AVIs** can be made up of any of *thousands* of codecs (video compression systems), not all of which are editable. In short, not all **AVIs** are the same, and some or more editable than others – and, at times, it may be necessary to find out what's *inside* the **AVI** in order to edit it.

MOVs and DV-MOVs are the Macintosh equivalent of **DV-AVIs**. It is the format that is created when miniDV footage is captured to a Macintosh computer. To output a **DV-MOV** from a Premiere Elements project, select **Export & Share/Device/Computer/SD 480** (or **SD 576** for PAL video) with the **Format** set to **MOV-DV**.

Like the **AVI** format, the **MOV** format is actually just an envelope through which video is delivered. And, like **AVIs**, **MOVs** can be composed of any of dozens of codecs. Like **AVIs**, not all **MOVs** are the same, and some are more challenging for Premiere Elements to edit than others.

MPEGs are a high quality video delivery format that can show up in a number of forms. A form of **MPEG**, called a VOB file, is the format used to store the video on DVDs. To output a DVD-quality MPEG from your project, select **Export & Share/Device/Computer/SD 480** (or **SD 576** for PAL video) with the **Format** set to **MPEG-PS**.

Most consumer high-definition camcorder video is saved as a form of high-def **MPEG** called an **M2T**.

M2T videos are high-quality, high-definition MPEG files. This is the format that is created when you capture video from an HDV camcorder or download video from an AVCHD camcorder, as discussed in **Chapter 5, Add Media to Your Project**.

To output an editable high-definition **M2T** video from Premiere Elements, select **Export & Share/Device/Computer/HD 1080 (1920x1080)** with the **Format** set to **MPEG-TS**.

To output an editable *AVCHD* **M2T** video from Premiere Elements (the current standard for editable high-def), select **Export & Share/Device/Computer/HD 1080 (1920x1080)** with the **Format** set to **M2T-H.264**.

AVCHD/H.264 is an advanced format for outputting your video. Its H.264 codec delivers high-quality video in a highly-compressed file. As noted under the **M2T** file description at the bottom of the previous page, at its highest quality **M2T** file, the AVC codec can produce good, editable

Export & Share Quick Reference

To Export & Share finished movies in a format that can be used as media in another Premiere Elements project.		
High-def video to be used as media in another high-def project	Devices/Computer/1920x1080	M2T-H.264
16:9 standard definition video to be used in another 16:9 standard def project	Device/Computer/720x480 (NTSC) Device/Computer/720x576 (PAL)	MOV-DV
4:3 standard definition video to be used in another 4:3 standard definition project	Device/Computer/720x480 (NTSC) Device/Computer/720x576 (PAL)	AVI-DV (PC only)
To Export & Share finished movies in a format that will load most efficiently into a third-party DVD or BluRay authoring program like Adobe Encore or DVD Architect.		
16:9 video for use in a third-party disc authoring program's BluRay project	Device/Computer/1920x1080	MPEG-TS M2T-H.264
16:9 video for use in a third-party disc authoring program's DVD project	Device/Computer/720x480 (NTSC) Device/Computer/720x576 (PAL)	MPEG-PS
To output video for manual uploading to a social media site or to create video to be played on a computer, projected from a computer or played on a modern HDTV.		
4K video to be uploaded to a social media site like YouTube	Device/Computer/3840x2160	MP4-XAVC-S
High-definition video to be uploaded to Vimeo, YouTube, Facebook, etc.	Device/Computer/1920x1080 Device/Computer/1280x720 (or Quick Export 1280x720)	MP4-H.264
16:9 standard definition video to be uploaded to Vimeo, YouTube, Facebook	Device/Computer/720x480 (NTSC) Device/Computer/720x576 (PAL)	MP4-H.264
4:3 standard definition video to be uploaded to Vimeo, YouTube, Facebook	Device/Custom/Advanced Settings/ Format: H.264 Basic Video Settings: Match Source	Custom MP4
Video can also be output as a sequence of still photos, each frame of your video represented as a separate photo. This is sometimes done in order to create a frame-by-frame special effect in a program like Photoshop Elements.		
Output your video frames as a sequence of still photos. (To create a movie from these individual photos, go to Premiere Elements' Preferences (under the Edit menu on a PC) and, on the General page, set Still Image Duration to 1 Frame. Once you've done that, import your photo sequence and add it to your timeline.)	Device/Custom/Advanced Settings/ BMP or JPEG Basic Settings: Check option to Export as Sequence	Custom BMP or JPEG

high-def video. At higher compressions, however, the **AVC/H.264** codec can also be used to create video for display on mobile device (see page 252-253) or to create a high-quality **MP4** file for upload to YouTube, Facebook or Vimeo.

In fact, if you are having problems uploading directly to a **YouTube** or **Facebook,** or if you're unhappy with the results using the **Export & Share/Online** tools in Premiere Elements, you can manually produce your own high-quality videos and then manually upload them using the To output an AVC file, select **Export & Share/Device/Computer/HD 1080 (1920x1080)** with the **Format** set to **MP4-H.264** or **MOV-H.264**. (Either preset will do. They each produce about the same quality video at approximately the same file size.)

Windows Media (WMVs) were once considered the Internet standard for web-based video. This was because Microsoft's ubiquitous presence meant that virtually every computer in the world had the necessary software to play them. However, in more recent years, **H.264/MP4** video, which produces a smaller file at a higher quality, has challenged its popularity.

WMVs can be created in the Windows version of Premiere Elements only by selecting a **Export & Share/Device/Computer/SD 480** option (or **SD 576** for PAL video) with the **Format** set to **WMV-VC1**.

QuickTime (MOVs) are the standard file type for video edited, stored and delivered by Macintosh computer programs. Since the **MOV** file is more of an envelope than a specific format, **MOVs** can be anything from highly compressed online video to video created for mobile devices to high-quality editable video to uncompressed video, depending on the codec, resolution and compression level of the file. You'll find a number of **MOV** output variations represented in **Export & Share/Device/Computer** (see page 249) as well as in **Export & Share/Device/Mobile** (see page 252).

XAVC/MP4 video is a Sony-created consumer version of **4K**, also known as **UltraHD** – a format with nearly four times the resolution of 1920x1080 high-definition. **XAVC** uses AVC/H264 compression to create an **MP4** which, though highly compressed, can be used to create some amazingly sharp and detailed videos (from 4K source video, of course). To output a 4K MP4 video from Premiere Elements, select **Export & Share/Device/Computer/4K UltraHD**.

Interlaced video vs. progressive scan

Back in the early days of television and video – back before TVs were essentially big screen computers – video was **interlaced**. This means that every frame of video was drawn in two passes, each pass drawing every other line of horizontal pixels on a 480 line screen. Each interlacing pass took one-sixtieth of a second, a process that created 30 frames of video per second. And that's fast enough to create the look of seamless motion.

But since the advent of HDTV, video frames are created in a single pass – a process called **progressive scan**. In progressive scan, a single pass generates 30 *complete* frames of video every second. (Video can be shot or displayed at 60 or more frames per second). The result can be much cleaner-looking video, especially when displaying a lot of motion or action.

Interlaced video is indicated with an "i", as in 1080i. Progressive video is indicated with a "p", and the frame rate is often listed after, as in 1080p30 or 1080p24 (1920x1080 pixel video at 30 or 24 progressive frames per second).

Traditionally, video that was to be shown on television – including DVDs and BluRay discs – has been interlaced (480i DVDs and 1080i BluRay discs).

Video created for viewing on a computer or online, on the other hand, is non-interlaced or progressive – which is why video generated for upload to YouTube or Vimeo is in a format like 1080p or 720p (1280x720 pixel video at 24 progressive frames per second).

Although, as televisions have become more advanced, even BluRay and DVD video is being delivered more often with progressive rather than interlaced frames.

Current versions of Premiere Elements output video for DVD or BluRay as interlaced video – though that may change at some point soon. And while a sharp eye can spot the difference between progressive and interlaced TV, for the most part it's indiscernible. Modern HDTVs do a great job of making interlaced video look virtually identical to progressive.

"Real World" System Requirements

Features not included in the Mac version

FTP Utilities

MiniDV and HDV Video Capture

Burn a Disc from a DVD or BluRay Image File

Premiere Elements Keyboard Shortcuts

A Premiere Elements Appendix

More things worth knowing

Recommended "Real World" computer specs

Most current off-the-shelf computers are capable of running Premiere Elements and editing standard consumer video (miniDV, AVCHD and video from smartphones and GoPro-type "action cams") with little or no modification.

The program does not use GPU acceleration, so there is little benefit to an advanced graphics card. (Even an onboard Intel graphics system will work fine.) Though, for best performance, we recommend a decent load of RAM (4-8 gigabytes minimum on a 64-bit operating system) and a current processor.

We've found the benchmark charts put together (and continually updated) by PassMark to be tremendously helpful in choosing and evaluating a processor. Any processor that rates a 5,000 or higher should be able to handle Premiere Elements and standard and high definition video formats with ease. For UHD 4k video, a processor rating 8,000 or higher is recommended.

PassMark's benchmarks can be found at http://www.cpubenchmark.net/high_end_cpus.html and its linked pages.

The addition of a second hard drive (either internal or external) – one dedicated to your video projects and source files – can give your workflow a tremendous boost.

Not only does it often make the process go more smoothly, since it keeps the video data flow and scratch disk files separate from your operating system's paging files, but it also reduces fragmentation of your video files.

If you install an internal second hard drive for video editing, make sure to set it up in your BIOS (the set-up that displays before the operating system launches, when you first start up your computer) as well as in your operating system.

And, if you're working in Windows, whether you use an internal or external drive, make sure that the drive is formatted NTFS rather than FAT32 (which all drives are factory formatted as by default) in order to avoid FAT32's file size limitations.

Converting a drive from FAT32 to NTFS is easy and you won't lose any data already on the drive in the process. The instructions for doing so are available all over the Web, including on the Microsoft site.

Features not included in the Mac version

Although the Mac and the Window versions of Premiere Elements function virtually identically, there are several features included in the PC version of the program that are not included in the Mac version.

The Windows version includes 87 video effects and 19 audio effects. The Mac version includes 72 video effects and 15 audio effects. The following **Video Effects** are not included in the Mac version:

Blur & Sharpen: Anti-Alias, Ghosting

Distort: Bend, Lens Distortion

Image Control: Color Pass, Color Replace

Keying: Blue Screen Key, Green Screen Key, Chroma Key, RGB Difference Key

Transform: Camera View, Clip, Horizontal Hold, Vertical Hold

The following **Audio Effects** are not included in the Mac version:

Denoiser, Dynamics, Pitch Shifter, Reverb

The Windows version of Premiere Elements includes 107 video transitions. The Mac version includes 50 video transitions.

The following **Video Transitions** are not included in the Mac version:

3D Motion: Curtain, Doors, Fold-Up, Spin, Spin Away, Swing In, Swing Out, Tumble Away

Dissolve: Dither Dissolve, Non-Additive Dissolve, Random Invert

Iris: Iris Points, Iris Shapes, Iris Star

Map: Channel Map, Luminance Map

Page Peel: Center Peel, Peel Back, Roll Away

Slide: Band Slide, Center Merge, MultiSpin, Slash Slide, Sliding Bands, Sliding Boxes, Swap, Swirl

Special Effect: Direct, Displace, Image Mask, Take, Texturize, Three-D

Stretch: Cross Stretch, Funnel, Stretch, Stretch In, Stretch Over

Wipe: Band Wipe, Checker Wipe, CheckerBoard, Clock Wipe, Paint Splatter, Pinwheel, Radial Wipe, Random Blocks, Random Wipe, Spiral Boxes, Venetian Blinds, Wedge Wipe, Zig Zag Blocks

Zoom: Cross Zoom, Zoom, Zoom Boxes, Zoom Trails

Valuable free or low cost tools and utilities for Windows

Audacity (audacity.sourceforge.net) is, hands down, the best *free* audio editing software you'll find anywhere. Easy to use, loaded with preset audio filters and yet extremely versatile.

Audacity can convert audio formats as well as adjust audio levels and "sweeten" your audio's sound. You can also record into it from a microphone or external audio device and edit audio with it. A real must-have freebie that you'll find yourself going to regularly!

FTP software

FTP software uploads files from your computer to a website and downloads files from a site to your computer. There are many great applications out there.

Here are a couple of personal favorites.

FileZilla Client is the current favorite FTP utility of a number of Muvipixers. Efficient, dependable and easy-to-use, sending files to a Website with **FileZilla** is as simple as dragging and dropping.

FileZilla Client is available free from filezilla-project.org.

Easy FTP (free from www.download.com and other sources) – Free and nearly as intuitive as **FileZilla**.

Disc burning software

Our favorite disc-burning software is, nicely enough, absolutely free!

ImgBurn is available at imgburn.com, and it's a great tool to use to burn your DVD or BluRay files to a disc as described in **Burn a disc from a DVD or BluRay image file** on page 277.

MiniDV and HDV video capture

Premiere Elements no longer includes a built-in tool for capturing video from a tape-based camcorder. The program still supports and edits miniDV and HDV footage. However, it no longer includes a video capture tool.

Here are our favorite third-party programs for capturing tape-based miniDV and HDV footage on a Windows PC. All are designed to work with camcorders that are connected to your computer via a FireWire or IEEE-1394 connection (also known as iLink).

Once captured with this software, your video should load and edit perfectly in Premiere Elements using the method described in **Import photos, video, music and other audio that is already on your computer's hard drive into your project** on page 55.

WinDV (free from windv.mourek.cz/) – A great DV capture utility with a simple interface.

HDVSplit (free from http://www.videohelp.com/software/HDVSplit – A great capture utility for HDV video. Though technically discontinued, the software still works great at capturing video from high-definition tape-based camcorders.

On a Mac, video captured from a tape-based camcorder via a FireWire connection using iMovie is perfectly compatible with Premiere Elements. An excellent third-party program for capturing miniDV video to a Mac is LifeFlix, available for $9.95 from the App Store.

Capture analog video through DV bridges and pass-throughs

There's a difference between a DV bridge and a plain old capture device or capture card. Capture devices merely digitize your video input to any of a number of video formats. DV bridges, on the other hand, are specifically designed to **convert any video and audio input into DV-AVI files**, the preferred standard definition video format for PC-based video editors. (Macs also prefer DV video, although they are saved as DV QuickTime files [MOVs] rather than AVIs. The video data content, however, is identical.)

DV bridges range from relatively inexpensive to high-end professional devices with time base correction and other video optimizers. The best value on the market in DV bridges and a Muvipix recommended "best buy" is the **Canopus/Grass Valley ADVC Converter**, a favorite of many videographers.

(Another great DV bridge device that, technically, has been discontinued but can still be found on the web is the **ADS Pyro AV Link**. Because this device is discontinued, it can be often found for as little as $100 on sites like eBay.)

The **Canopus/Grass Valley ADVC** will take any AV input (a VHS camcorder, a DVR, a VCR or virtually any other video source, including live video) and port it into your computer as a high-quality DV-AVI or, on a Mac, DV-MOV file. This great device can be had for a street price of under $200, a great value if you plan to edit a lot of video from non-DV sources.

Capturing video from a DV bridge is easy. Just plug your camcorder's, DVD player's or VCR's AV cables (RCA jacks) into the DV bridge's inputs and plug the bridge (connected by FireWire) into your computer.

Your computer will recognize the device just as it would a miniDV camcorder connection. You can then use a program like the excellent WinDV (discussed in **MiniDV and HDV video capture** on the facing page) to capture the video.

The capture process itself is essentially the same as capture from a miniDV camcorder. The only difference is, since there's no direct connection between your video source device and the computer, you won't be able to control the device with your capture software or break scenes by timecode.

But, once you've got the device cued up to the segment you want to capture, just click the **Capture** button and you're good to go!

By the way, the **Canopus ADVC** can also be used with DVD camcorders and hard drive camcorders, so it's a great way to make any non-miniDV video 100% Premiere Elements compatible.

An alternative to a DV bridge is a set-up called a **pass-through**, which essentially uses a miniDV camcorder as a makeshift DV bridge.

To set up a pass-through connection, attach your non-DV camcorder to your miniDV camcorder via its AV input cables, then link the miniDV to your computer via FireWire.

With the miniDV camcorder in play mode (but without a tape inside) the non-DV camcorder's video flows through the miniDV and into the computer, where it's captured as DV-AVIs.

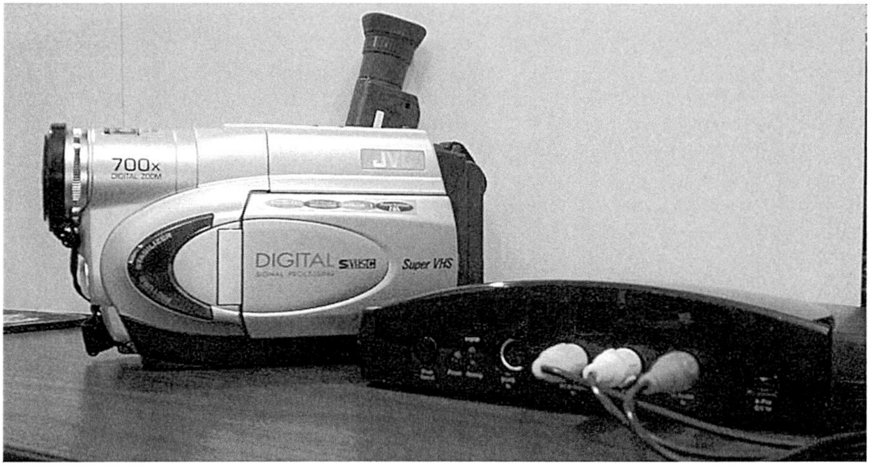

A DV bridge downloads DV video from a VHS camcorder over a FireWire connection.

The biggest challenge to using this method is that fewer and fewer new miniDV camcorders support a pass-through connection. And it's very difficult to glean, from most spec sheets, which camcorders do before you buy one.

But, if your miniDV camcorder is pass-through capable, this is a simple and effective method of digitizing almost any analog video input.

Burn a DVD or BluRay disc from an image file

For a number of reasons, you may want to save you finished DVD or BluRay disc as an ISO image file on your hard drive rather than burn them directly to a disc.

Sometimes it's out of necessity. Sometimes your computer operating system is configured in such a way that Premiere Elements isn't able to burn your DVDs or BluRays directly to a disc.

Other times it's by choice. I often *prefer* to "burn" my disc files to my hard drive for archiving, and then use a program like ImgBurn to burn copies from this ISO file to a disc as needed. That way I've always got a finished copy of my disc files available, and every "copy" I burn off is actually an original disc, based on the original Premiere Elements disc encoding.

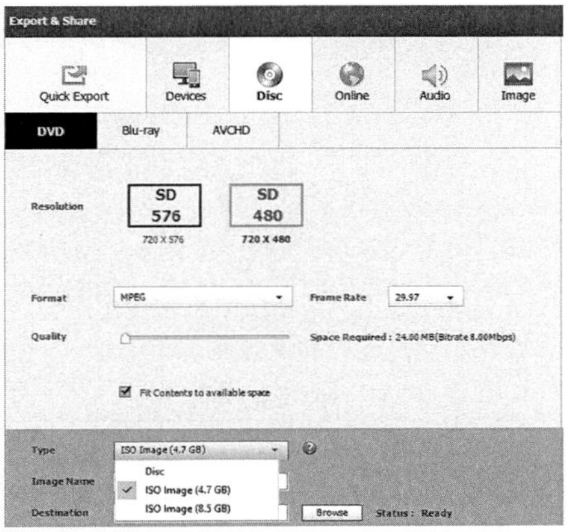

Whatever your reason, it's fairly easy to burn your disc files to your hard drive and then use a third-part program (like ImgBurn) to produce DVDs and BluRay discs from these files.

1. Go to **Export & Share/Disc,** select the **DVD, BluRay** or **AVCHD** option and set the **Type** to **ISO Image**, as discussed on page 265 of **Chapter 21**.

The program will go through the process of encoding and creating your disc files.

2 Once the disc files are created and saved to your hard drive, you can use your computer's burner software, third-party burner software like Nero or our recommended free disc burner utility **ImgBurn** (see **Disc Burning software** on page 275) to burn the image file as a DVD or BluRay disc.

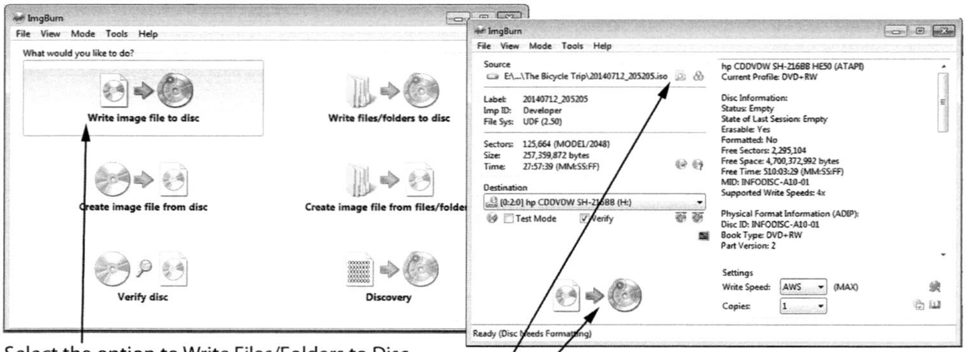

Select the option to Write Files/Folders to Disc from main ImgBurn page.

Browse to select your ISO file as your Source, then click Burn.

To burn a DVD, AVCHD disc or BluRay from an **ISO** file, select **Write Image File to Disc** from the ImgBurn main menu. When the software opens, click the **Source** button and browse to and select the **ISO** file, then click the **Burn** button.

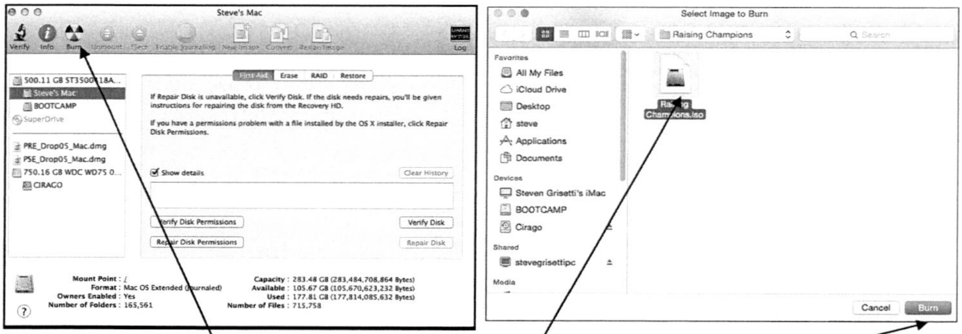

Click the Disk Utility's Burn button.

Browse to and select the VIDEO_TS folder or ISO image file, then click the Burn button.

On a Mac, the built-in **Disk Utility** tool can be used to burn your files to a disc.

To open the **Disk Utility**, go to the **Finder** menu and select **Go**, then **Utilities**. **Double-click** to open the **Disk Utility** tool.

1 Click the **Burn** button at the top of the tool.

A browse window will open.

2 Locate and select the ISO file created by Premiere Elements.

Click **Burn**.

Unpack your ISO

If you'd prefer to store your DVD or BluRay as a folder of individual files rather than an ISO image, you can unpack the image file using your computer's operating system.

On Windows:

1 **Right-click** on the ISO and select **Open with/Windows Explorer**. The browser window will reveal the disc's **OpenDVD** and **VIDEO_TS** folders.

2 Select the folders, **right-click** and select **Copy** and then **Paste** these folders to a new location on your hard drive.

On a Mac:

1 **Right-click** on the ISO and select **Open**. The browser window will reveal the disc's **OpenDVD** and **VIDEO_TS** folders.

2 Select the folders, right-click and select **Copy** and then **Paste** these folders to a new folder on your hard drive.

To use ImgBurn to burn a DVD or BluRay disc from these files, select **Write**

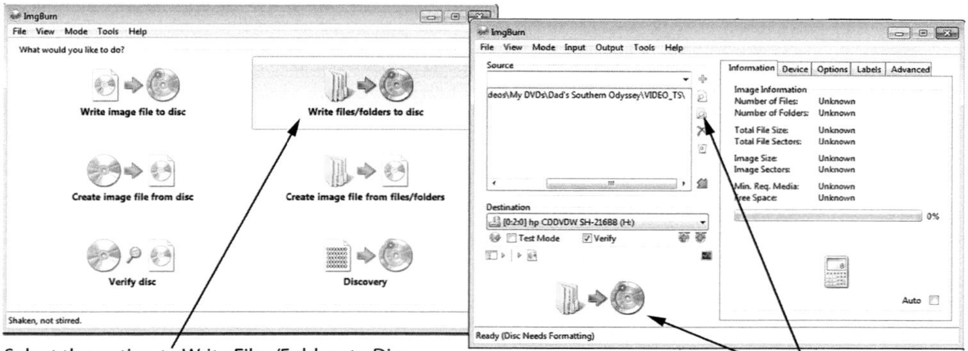

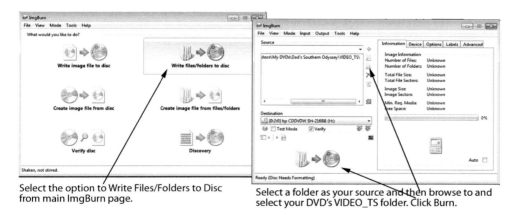

Select the option to Write Files/Folders to Disc from main ImgBurn page.

Select a folder as your source and then browse to and select your DVD's VIDEO_TS folder. Click Burn.

Files/Folders to Disc from the ImgBurn main menu. When the software opens, click the **Source/Folder** button and browse to and select the **VIDEO_TS** folder that was created when you burned your DVD or AVCHD files to a folder, then click the **Burn** button.

On a Mac, use the same process as you would for burning a disc from an ISO file to burn the **VIDEO_TS** folder to a disc, as described on the facing page.

Keyboard shortcuts for Premiere Elements

These key strokes and key combinations are great, quick ways to launch features or use the program's tools without having to poke around the interface.

In virtually every workspace the arrow keys (Down, Up, Left, Right) will move the selected object in that direction. Shift+Arrow will move it several steps in one nudge.

Many of these shortcuts are slightly different on a Macintosh computer. Usually the **Command**(⌘) key is used in place of the **Ctrl** key – although a number of keyboard shortcuts may not work at all.

Program Controls

Ctrl O	Open project	Ctrl X	Cut
Ctrl W	Close project	Ctrl C	Copy
Ctrl S	Save project	Ctrl V	Paste
Ctrl Shift S	Save project as...	Tab	Close floating windows
Ctrl Alt S	Save a copy	Ctrl Q	Quit program
Ctrl Z	Undo	F1	Help
Ctrl Shift Z	Redo		

Import/Export

F5	Capture	Ctrl Shift M	Export Frame
Ctrl I	Add Media	Ctrl Alt Shift M	Export Audio
Ctrl M	Export Movie	Ctrl Shift H	Get properties for selection

Media and Trimming

I	Set in point	Page Up	Go to previous edit point
O	Set out point	G	Clear all in/out points
Q	Go to in point	D	Clear selected in point
Page Down	Go to next edit point	F	Clear selected out point
W	Go to out point	Ctrl E	Edit original
		Ctrl H	Rename

Play/Scrub Controls

Space bar	Play/stop	Shift Right	Step forward five frames
J	Shuttle left	Home	Go to beginning of timeline
L	Shuttle right	End	Go to end of timeline
Shift J	Slow shuttle left	Q	Go to in point
Shift L	Slow shuttle right	W	Go to out point
K	Shuttle stop	Page Down	Go to next edit point
Arrow Left	One frame back	Page Up	Go to previous edit point
Arrow Right	One frame forward	Ctrl Alt Space	Play in point to out point with preroll/postroll
Shift Left	Step back five frames		

Timeline Controls

Enter	Render work area
Ctrl K	Razor cut at CTI
+	Zoom in
-	Zoom out
\	Zoom to work area
Ctrl A	Select all
Ctrl Shift A	Deselect all
, (comma)	Insert
. (period)	Overlay
Ctrl Shift V	Insert Clip
Alt [video clip]	Unlink audio/video
Ctrl G	Group
Ctrl Shift G	Ungroup
X	Time stretch
Del	Clear clip (non-ripple)
Backspace	Ripple delete (fill gap)
S	Toggle snap
C	Razor tool
V	Selection tool
Alt [	Set Work Area Bar In Point
Alt]	Set Work Area Bar Out Point
Ctrl Alt C	Copy attributes
Ctrl Alt V	Paste Effects and Adjustments
Ctrl Shift /	Duplicate
Shift * (Num pad)	Set next unnumbered marker
* (Num pad)	Set unnumbered marker
Ctrl Shift Right	Go to next clip marker
Ctrl Shift Left	Go to previous clip marker
Ctrl Shift 0	Clear current marker
Alt Shift 0	Clear all clip markers
Ctrl Right	Go to next timeline marker
Ctrl Left	Go to previous timeline marker
Ctrl 0	Clear current timeline marker
Alt 0	Clear all timeline markers

Title Window Controls

Ctrl Shift L	Title type align left
Ctrl Shift R	Title type align right
Ctrl Shift C	Title type align center
Ctrl Shift T	Set title type tab
Ctrl Shift D	Position object bottom safe margin
Ctrl Shift F	Position object left safe margin
Ctrl Shift O	Position object top safe margin
Ctrl Alt Shift C	Insert copyright symbol
Ctrl Alt Shift R	Insert registered symbol
Ctrl J	Open title templates
Ctrl Alt]	Select object above
Ctrl Alt [	Select object below
Ctrl Shift]	Bring object to front
Ctrl [	Bring object forward
Ctrl Shift [	Send object to back
Ctrl [	Send object backward
Alt Shift Left	Decrease kerning five units
Alt Shift Right	Increase kerning five units
Alt Left	Decrease kerning one unit
Alt Right	Increase kerning one unit
Alt Shift Up	Decrease leading five units
Alt Shift Down	Increase leading five units
Alt Up	Decrease leading one unit
Alt Down	Increase leading one unit
Ctrl Up	Decrease text size five points
Ctrl Down	Increase text size five points
Shift Up	Decrease text size one point
Shift Down	Increase text size one point

Media Window

Ctrl Delete	Delete selection with options	End	Move selection to last clip
Shift Down	Extend selection down	Page Down	Move selection page down
Shift Left	Extend selection left	Page Up	Move selection page up
Shift Up	Extend selection up	Right	Move selection right
Down	Move selection to next clip	Shift]	Thumbnail size next
Up	Move selection to previous clip	Shift [	Thumbnail size previous
Home	Move selection to first clip	Shift \	Toggle view

Capture Monitor Panel

F	Fast forward	Left	Step back
G	Get frame	Right	Step forward
R	Rewind	S	Stop

Properties Panel

Backspace	Delete selected effect

Narration Panel

Delete	Delete present narration clip	Space	Play present narration clip
		G	Start/Stop recording
Right Arrow	Go to next narration clip		
Left Arrow	Go to previous narration clip		

Note that Premiere Elements also allows you to modify any of these keyboard shortcuts and to create your own shortcuts for dozens of other tasks. You'll find the option to do so under the Edit drop-down menu.

Need some Basic Training?

Want some help with the basics of Premiere Elements?

Want some free hands-on training?

Check out my free tutorial series **Basic Training with Premiere Elements** at Muvipix.com.

This simple, eight-part series will show you how to set up a project, how to import media into it, basic editing moves, adding transitions and effects, how to create titles, how to add and customize your DVD and BluRay disc menu navigation markers and how to export your finished video.

And did I mention that it's free?

To see the series, just go to http://Muvipix.com and type "Premiere Elements Basic Training" in the product search box and then click the magnifying glass button.

And while you're there, why not drop by the Community forum and say hi! We'd love to have you become a part of our growing city. Happy moviemaking!

Steve, Chuck, Ron and the whole Muvipix team

Symbols

A

B

C

53678636R00169

Made in the USA
San Bernardino, CA
24 September 2017